LETTERS OF
LOVE *and* WAR

I Love You True with All My Heart.

By
GREGORY HUGH BROWN

Letters of Love and War
Copyright © 2021 by Gregory Hugh Brown

ISBN
978-1-956529-26-5 (Hardcover)
978-1-956529-25-8 (Paperback)
978-1-956529-24-1 (eBook)

TABLE OF CONTENTS

FORWARD

My story will be an account of my parents' lives given by a chronological listing of my mother's and father's letters that they wrote to each other almost daily during the later part of World War Two. My mother saved all these letters and I discovered where she had stored them within her secret places in her house when I was settling their estate. Their letters provide an incredible record of their amazing love for each other and of their triumph over the trials of war. My first chapter will be a long one as I transcribe their letters and the letters that they received from their close family and friends during that period of history. I think you will agree and understand upon reading and sharing their thoughts why their generation was referred to as the great generation.

PREFACE

This is the story of my parents' lives when they were young, and it took place about four years before my time. These were the parents that I was born to on August 9, 1948. This story will unfold as I record for you the cherished letters that my mother saved for seventy-five years. They wrote each other every day from late June 1944 to late October 1945. Of course there were no cell phones, emails or Facebook and their only means of communication were the handwritten letters that they wrote and mailed to each other every day. Sometimes the letters would take two or three days to reach one another by mail and sometimes, when sent to or from overseas, they would take three to four weeks or more to be delivered. These letters were their only connection over these long months of separation, and they were the prime source of keeping hope and love alive.

Their story begins with the first letters written just after my dad was drafted into the service on June 23 of 1944. My mother and dad married on February 25, 1941 after a short courtship. My dad met my mother at a dinner on the grounds picnic at a church in Hamilton, Alabama where he had been transferred by the C.C.C. (Civilian Conservation Corps) from Dadeville, Alabama. My dad was born and raised in Beauregard, Alabama, a small farming community just outside of Opelika, Alabama, my hometown. My dad's father, Gordon Brown, was a farmer and had a 200-acre cotton farm where he also raised food crops to support his family. His wife, and my grandmother, was Betty Owsley Brown and together they had and raised four children including by order of birth, Alma Brown Sanders, Robert Louis Brown, William Curtis Brown, and my father, James Gordon Brown.

My dad, James Gordon Brown, went looking for work when he turned twenty and found the trade he loved as a mess cook for the C.C.C. in nearby Dadeville, Alabama. It was not long before he was transferred to the Hamilton, Alabama C.C.C, Camp, where he would soon meet my mother at the church social that I mentioned.

My mother, Mary Elizabeth Palmer Brown was from a family of six children. Her father was Clover McKinley Palmer, a very talented songwriter, musician, artist and photographer who was tragically killed in an automobile accident in 1930 when he was 30 years old and my mother was only 8 years old. Her mother was Cora Lee Goodson Palmer, who married Clover on the side of the road in a ceremony performed by Clover's preacher uncle in 1920. Together they had six children, two girls and four boys. In the order of birth they were Harrison Roe Palmer, Mary Elizabeth Palmer, Iva Louise Palmer, Joseph Arthur Palmer, Herbert Hoover Palmer, and Horrice Edward Palmer.

My parents lived in Hamilton, Alabama for about two years after they married and lived in a little house across the street from her mother Cora Lee and her grandmother Dizenia Palmer, who all the kids called "Mammy". Dad continued his hitch in the C.C.C. in Hamilton and he was a fine cook and mess sergeant. They shared some good times there, and on December 10, 1941, just three days after Pearl Harbor was attacked, my mother gave birth to her first child, my older brother, James Roger Brown. Life in Hamilton, Alabama, with close family just across the street, went very well but soon the opportunity to earn more income drew my dad to accept a job in Childersburg, Alabama with the DuPont Munitions Factory. This turned out to be a happy move for both my mother and dad and their young son Roger. They made many new friends in Childersburg and it was not all that far away from Hamilton, where they could still visit their family. Dad made a good living there at DuPont and proved to be a very able worker that was well liked and respected by his fellow workers and supervisors as well. He was able to rent a small but cozy house for his family and also able to purchase a 1940 Ford automobile so that they could travel and see their families and friends.

Life was good for them, but the country was at war. Dad's brother Robert had already been drafted into the Army Infantry in 1941 and his other brother Curtis was drafted into the Army Air Corps. Dad had a marriage deferment that kept him out of the service for a while, but that was soon to end, and he too was drafted in June of 1944.

The letters of my parents do have a harmonious flow, as I was fortunate to have been able to access and organize them. They were all postmarked and most all were dated inside so that I was able to sort through them and place them chronologically. I am blessed that my mother saved all the letters that both she and dad wrote to each other, at least all that she was able have returned to her. I found these letters that both she and dad wrote to each other stored away in shoe boxes or large envelopes or tied together with string that had not been removed for 75 years. These letters give us slices of their everyday lives that otherwise would have been long forgotten. They also give an honest and straightforward insight into what life was like for a young couple very much in love but torn apart by the ravages of war. I am not sure that my parents would ever have approved of having their intimate letters exposed for public viewing, but after all, my mother did save them all her life and must have known that her son would discover them at some point. Her oldest son Roger, who is mentioned in so many of their letters, passed away on November 22, 1997 long before either of my parents passed so it was left to me to discover these letters after my dad's death in 2008. I found the letters hidden away in several locations in their house, in desk drawers, cabinets, and at the top closet shelves packed away in boxes and packets with various official documents and mementos carefully stacked on top of them. I waited for ten years before I started reading them and longer until I finally began organizing them for an eventual commemorative document.

Having said all of this, a written account is an undertaking that only the boldest will attempt. It takes much time and immense focus, and one must decide what to include and what not to include. One must decide whether to create a story from the letters or simply to create a narrative and let the letters speak for themselves. I decided to let the letters speak for themselves and in their simple and heartfelt manner, I think they powerfully do just that.

My mother graduated from high school and was very proficient in her use of grammar and correct spelling. She also wrote often to all her friends and family, sometimes four or five letters to each of them in a week's time. Dad only made it as far as the 8th grade, but he had a good command of the English language and wrote with passion and poetic sensibility. His command of grammar and spelling was imperfect at best but in keeping with the most forthright portrayal of his words, I have chosen to document his grammar and misspellings exactly as he wrote them. I believe this will make his words and his feelings impart their meaning to you in a much more personal way and you will get to know him the way he really was.

I also felt that as many photographs, drawings and memorabilia that I still possess should be included so that the reader also becomes the viewer, and the faces and memories will be put to the characters one reads about. The drawings I speak of are the "letters" or scribbles that my brother Roger "wrote" to my dad as a 3-year-old and were included inside the letters that my mother wrote to dad. These "letters" from Roger will be included with the letters as needed.

Chapter One

The Army Infantry, Camp Blanding, Florida

I begin this chapter by including my dad's first letters to mother after he arrives at Fort McPherson, Georgia. That was his first stop, and he would remain there a few days to be enlisted in the Army Infantry and then be sent to Camp Blanding, Florida where he would endure seventeen weeks of grueling training that would prepare him to face the enemy in Europe and possibly later in Japan. As stated in my Preface, I have transcribed dad's letters just as he wrote them and did not correct the grammar or spelling as I thought that would detract from the feeling and character of the content. As previously stated, my dad only had an eighth-grade education, but he used that education to the utmost of his ability throughout his life. Here is dad's first note to mother written from Fort McPherson, Georgia:

June 22 – 1944

Hello Eliz & Roger and all

I am at the Fort. And what a place. I dont think I will like the Army at all if it is like this place. I got here this afternoon about three oclock. They havent done anything to us yet, but they will tomorrow. I think they are putting everyone in the Infantry. My risen is still sore. I havent got a adress yet so be sweet and take care of Roger and I will send my adress as soon as I get one

Love James

That was dad's first postcard after he had been drafted into the service. The following is his first letter in which he includes his address:

Pvt James G Brown
Reception Center 34837097
Fort McPherson, Ga.
6-24-44

Just a few lines from a soldier, hope you and my boy are well and doing fine. For my self I am just taking orders. Well nobody dont know what the Army is till they git in. I don't know what part I will be in until I git stationed and started training. I do know I am in the Army I was sworn in today and got my clothing. I guss you will git my shirt and pants in a day or two, but I don't know when you will git me back – I hope it wont be long, right now would suit me sweet. You just be a good little girl and don't worry, I had to really fight to git you, now I am going to fight to keep you and little Roger boy. I sure would like to hear from you all, but you cant write till I git an adgress. If you need me for anything see the Red Cross If I am not at fort McPherson, Ga they will find me. I think I will be leaving Monday or Tuesday, where to I dont know till I git there/.

How is Herbert? OK I hope. Tell you mama and them all I said hello. Well sweet, I have been looking for this, so I am in it. I dident leave you because I wanted to, I had to. I want you to know all my love is for you, so be good and sweet. I will do the same sweet. Take good care of little Roger for me. I havent taken any shots yet. I guss I will Monday.

I will close. Don't have much to write now

Love and Sweet dreams James

So, as you can see, dad was not in the Army by choice, but was drafted and he definitely did not like the Army or to be away from his family. I believe that is how most men felt about going into the service. They did not want to be there, but they did their best to do their duty for God and their country once they were there. From the time my dad got in the service until he was finally discharged, he wanted nothing more than to be back home with his beloved wife and son. He and my mother prayed daily that the war would soon be over and that all the boys could come home to their loved ones. Of course, that was not to be though and many of those boys would never see their loved ones again.

Here is another of dad's letters from Fort McPherson, Georgia dated June 28, 1944:

Hey Sweet, Roger,

I am fine at this time, hope you and Roger are well and feeling fine. I am still at the fort working hard, been on guard duty for the last twenty four hours I mean it was hard all night and all day I guss I will have to pull K.P. tomorrow. I sure would like to see you sweet. I have some things to tell you. I hope to get a pass when I git stationed if I dont git sent to far from home. The Army is nothing like the C.C.C. I have tried to git cook but I dont think I will git nothing but the Infantry like all the rest. I dident think there was so many boys in Alabama. I saw Mr. Rinddles up here, he wasent laughing so much at everything like he was in good old Childersburg. Sweet, you dont know how much I do miss you and Roger. I will feel better when I can hear from you. We will git seventeen weeks training then we will git sea sick (in other words they will get shipped overseas). I have taken 2 shotes and a blood test. We have plenty to eat and a good place to sleep but the best they have are not like being at home with a sweet little girl like you. So when you write I want a letter every day, long and sweet and all the news. I havent written anybody but you yet. I havent had time to write they keep us moving from one barrack to another. I hope it wont be like this always. I guss money is getting short with you, If you need any before your check comes, write a check. All I got is yours! That's not much but maby you can git by on it till I git back which I hope wont be long. We will have to stay in the army six months after the war, that is if nothing dont happen to us. I have seen loots of things and learned plenty since I have been here. I know they gotten all the boys that are fit for any part of the army. If you could see them, you would think so to. It may be I havent got used to looking at them, they have all sizes and types.

Tell your mama and all I said Hello and Darling, sweet little girl, I dont have to tell you to be sweet and good because you have proven to me that you are the sweetest girl in all the world. Bye and may God bless you and little Roger, be sure and give him a big kiss for me every night. I will be thinking about you every night and day, you only sweet. I will never forget you no matter where they send me to. That's one thing the army cant git out of me. I will always be by your side in mind because you are mine and I am yours always.

True Love and Sweet kisses always, James

To Roger

P.S, Roger you be a sweet little boy for mother and dont worry her to much. I will send you something good when I git stationed, and your mother to, because you have a sweet mother.

Love Dad

You can see from the previous letter the deep love and devotion that dad had for mother. They were very much in love with each other and totally devoted to each other and were totally devoted to each other all their lives. Their letters will show this over and over and it was this undying love and devotion that got them through the trying times they lived in. I am blessed to have all their letters and I am amazed at the emotions exhibited by them. It was both revealing and surprising for me as I was born four years later, and I never experienced those kinds of emotions from them. I suppose this was because they were much younger then and because we were living in the much more conservative times of the 1950's when they had me. During my early years with them they kept their feelings for one another private and if they expressed them at all it was behind closed doors. So, it amazes me to learn from reading their letters how they truly felt and to learn how much they had to sacrifice to keep that love, affection, and passion alive. They were forcibly separated by war, but their hearts and souls were united throughout it all.

I will include many but not all their letters as I do believe they bring a unique enlightenment to us today about how the lives of that great generation triumphed over their trying times that were shattered by the horrors of war. So, I will now include my mother's first letter to dad which was written about the same time and addressed to Fort McPherson, Georgia on June 30, 1944 from Hamilton, Alabama. The letter was diverted to Camp Blanding, Florida where dad had been sent for his training.

Hello Sweetheart,

I don't know whether you will get this letter or not, but I'm going to take the chance anyhow. So, if you don't get it, I suppose it will come back to me.

I really was glad to get all your letters as I am so lonesome, I don't know what to do. It was so lonesome at your mother's when night began to come I just couldn't hardly stay there. Roger would talk about you all the time. He cried and asked where you were for a long time. He tells everyone now that his daddy is a soldier.

He told me yesterday, to go and bring his daddy back to him. He said tell you that he was still looking for that "something good" you had for him.

When do you think you will be stationed? I hope it won't be so far and you can come back to see us I would like to see you so much. I miss you more this time, than I ever have, because I know you can't come back until they get ready for you to.

Try to keep out of the Infantry if you can. I hope you won't have to go across.

Mamma got a letter from Harrison. He is in Asheville, North Carolina now. He is a Lieutenant. He sent her a very pretty purse. He says he may get leave before long.

Iva and Gerry are coming tomorrow. Mamma and I had our hair set today. Mine looks the best it ever looked. I haven't gone anywhere yet. I don't enjoy going without you.

I saw the Alabama Power man today and asked him about connecting our lights, so he came down this afternoon and stepped off how many feet it was to the post. I think he is going to hook the power on soon. I just hope so anyway.

Well, can you imagine what happened the day we came through Childersburg? Mr. Carrel was there to meet us at the bus. He brought us a thermos bottle full of water, which was very nice of him, as we were all very thirsty.

Herbert was a lot of help to me about taking Roger to the Rest Room, etc. Your daddy was afraid that I wouldn't ever come back to see them, but I will when I can.

I only had four dollars when I got to Hamilton, but luckily there was a check for me from DuPont for $8.00. It was what you had paid on another War Bond. So maybe I can make it until I get a check.

I don't want to draw any out of the bank if I can help it. I'm going to see about a job soon. I've been busy cleaning up the clothes. I have all your shirts etc. clean and had both pairs of your pants cleaned and put away in the wardrobe, so they will be ready for you when the war is over, which I hope won't be long off.

Roger wrote you a letter too. I'm putting it in with mine. He is well of his cold and is a rather good boy. He wants me to read your letters to him.

Mamma and all said to tell you "hello" and they would like to see you very much, and you just don't know how much I would like to see you. I'll stop now.

Good bye and best wishes. Write real soon. We love you always, Elizabeth and Roger

P.S. Mamma said she surely did wish you could be here the 4th and make some more of that good ice cream for us.

You got 2 letters from Robert, The last one was dated June 11th and one letter from Curtis, it wasn't dated. I'll send them to you later, as I'm afraid you might not get this letter and they would be lost.

I'm being a real good girl, but you knew that didn't you. I want you to be good too. Hear!

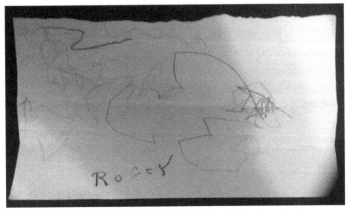

I am enclosing a scan of Roger's letter to dad
that mother included in her letter.

At first there were days that dad did not get letters from mother because of the different addresses he had from being moved from one post to another. Eventually though, her letters caught up with him. Not having those letters made him infinitely more lonesome than he already was, and the new regimentation of army life was extremely difficult for him to acclimate to. Without the letters that they each wrote to one another every day I doubt that dad could have held up to this military abuse as well as he did. They both looked forward to those letters each day and when they did not get them, they became extremely downcast and blue. Little Roger was affected deeply by the separation from his daddy too. He simply could not understand why the mean Army had taken his daddy away from him. Roger was mentioned in almost every letter and although he was only three years old, Roger "wrote" or scribbled letters of his own to his daddy that mother included in her letters that she sent to dad. I will include scans of these "letters" from Roger at various points throughout this book.

One can feel the anxiety and loneliness that manifests itself in all their letters. They often write of their memories of the good times they had together before the Army drafted dad and these memories are often recalled lovingly as they made promises to someday renew those experiences and to begin new and more meaningful lives together when dad returned home for good.

Here is a letter from dad during those first days at Camp Blanding, Florida that truly reflects the separation anxiety and loneliness that he was feeling. It was not dated inside, but postmarked July 3, 1944, 11:30 am:

Hy Sweet

Well this is old blue Sunday. No where to go – at least I cant go nowhere. If they would let me I would be with my sweet little wife. Darling, I miss you and Roger When I git out of this place things will be different with me and you. The Army will make anyone think of things in the past. We was having a swell time at Childersburg, just like you said when we was togather at Childersburg and how sweet you looked. Going to work and coming back in eight hours is heaven beside this place where I could see you all the time. You dident think I loved you when we would have some hard words but I dident mean anything I said. I will never be that way any more with me and you. When I git out of the Army and come back home to stay with you and little Roger we are going to have the best and sweetest home that there can be and where I go you will go to. You be sweet and take care of Roger. It wont be this way always and anything you want git it. I want you to have anything you want and Roger to. Anything you want to git will be alright with me. I want you to think of me and write me every day and be true to me, I will you I promise but dont worry about me, the Lord will take care of me. I pray that he will take care of you and Roger for me because I love you both You are the only thing I have to worry about. I dont worry about the car and furniture I can git more of them things, but I cant git another wife and little boy like you all, because I love you and I will prove it when I see you. You might think I am joking but what I am going through with will make you think what sweet times you had back home with your wife. After I git my training here I will git a ten day furlough and be transferred some place else. I guss you know where that will be. Maybe if I dont have to go across I will git stationed close by home where we can be togather more. I will git a GI hair cut. I wont be by myself – they have only 75,000 boys here – all kinds. I guss you will quit me when I git that wave cut off. Maybe it will grow back. You can make me one when I git back home.

I got my rifle and pack and all that stuff – you ought to see it. You would wonder how I carried it, but if you stick to me, I can do anything. I know you will, wont you Sweet? Write me every day. I will do the same if I can. Do you like this kind of letter? I could write you more but I guss you are getting tired of this stuff, so be good and take care of yourself and Roger. Tell your mother I said hello and stay healthy and all the rest. Your true love one, James

Write me all the news about everything sweet. P,S. My rison is just about well.

These letters that they wrote to each other tell the stories of their lives in a heartfelt manner that would have been lost if one were to try and retrace their lives from only recollections many years later. The letters have an immediacy about them that make one feel as if they are right there with them as one reads their words. For me, it is like an integral part of my parents' past has been returned to me and indeed to all of us that read them. For me it was exhilarating to discover and read all these letters and to experience just what my parents were like during that time of their lives. I was born four years later, and it was another three or four years and into the 1950's before I really have any memories of what my parents were like and by then they were older and more set in their ways. I never saw the raw emotion and passion that is revealed in these letters, so it was surprising to me to find that they had such strong feelings for each other. We were never very affectionate or loving in the way some families are. We never kissed or hugged or expressed our love for each other openly. The love was there but never outwardly expressed. My parents sacrificed for us and worked hard to make sure we had all we needed in life and that was their way of expressing their love. When they wrote these letters to each other in 1944 and 1945 they were young and showed their love for each other openly and affectionately with each letter. Dad was even open about his sexual needs and desires in some of his letters to mother. This was taboo when I was growing up. If they had sex, they were very discreet about it and my brother and I very seldom heard their bed springs rattle.

I will include a few more of dad's letters to mother and then include mother's second letter to him. These letters are important in that they give a feeling of what their relationship was all about. This letter from dad to mother was postmarked the same day on July 3, 1944, 11:30 am:

Hello Little Sweet girl,

I wonder what you are doing this afternoon – sitting around I guss thinking about me I hope. I been thinking about you and little Roger ever since I left. I wish I was there with you all, we would have a good time. This war sure do mess up everything. I wish I was in the CCC at Hamilton like I was once. We could be together <u>nearly</u> all the time then, but them good times are all over now. Sweet, did Arthur come home and Iva & Harrison? Did Iva get married? Have you got lights yet? I hope so. I want you to write me all the news about yourself and how Roger is. He was sick when I left. I sure hope he is OK now and stay that way and you to. I wish I could talk to you and hold you good and tight and kiss them sweet little lips. I am <u>really</u> home sick for you and Roger Sweet. I sure hope I can git a place here at the post where you can come and stay some <u>week-end</u>. I cant get a weekend pass until I stay here three weeks. When I find out more about it I will write you. I havent done much today so while I have time I thought I would write you another letter. I cant git you off my mind long anought to do anything els you little sweet darling. We was taking some training today on how to use our rifle, so one boy standing in front of me fell out

11

like someone dead. I dont like to see any one fall out – it will git you. Nobody dont know what the Army is till they git in it. I will never forget what Robert said about the Infantry. I can realize what he went through with and what he is catching now (Robert, dad's brother, was killed in action 27 days later on July 31, 1944 at St. Lo, France). I might haft to do the same he is doing. Just pray that I dont haft to cross Sweet, this is bad and that is to bad. I wrote mama and Alma (his sister) yesterday the first time I had to write, but I try to take time to write my sweet wife. I hope you feel the same way about me. Maby some day we wont haft to write, we will be togather to stay – wont that be sweet. Your love one forever, James

The next letter from dad was postmarked July 4, 1944, 1:30 am, and dated July 3rd on the letter:

Hello Sweet,

I will try to write you a few lines, hope you and Roger and all are well. Where are you planing on going tomorrow, the fourth of July? I dont remember what we done last fourth of July do you? Any way it was a loots different thin what this one is going to be. I have been out in the rain all day. I got sick one time at the stomach, but it was something I ate, I dident git to hot, I ate dinner and took a salt tablet, that is what got me sick but I was OK in a few minutes. It sure do rain a loot down here – we haft to go, rain or shine.

I am looking for a letter from you – it have been nearly two weeks since I heard from my sweet wife and boy. I couldent hardly hold the tears when I left you at the bus station. I thought I could leave about that but I couldent, it had to come out. It is hard to stay away from a sweet girl like you. I am going to try to write you every day, thin when I come home, you cant say why dident you write me more. I hope I dont haft to git on my sweet little girl. I wont let you down if you dont let me down – what you say Sweet? Be good and take care of yourself and my little boy.

P,S. Sweet, send me my soap case and tooth brush holder, and an old tooth brush to clean my rifle with, also buy me a little case to put my shaving outfit in. You can put them things in the case and send it all together. Tell Roger I will give him the soap case back when I come to stay, which I hope wont be long.

Bye sweet darling and Roger I haft to go now. This is the Army – when they say get out they mean it – they dont have no mercy on me.

Your true love always, James

Mother wrote dad every day, but as you learned from the previous letter from dad, he did not receive all of those letters, or if he did, I never found them in my mother's boxes or drawers where she kept all of their letters. One can only assume they were lost or were never forwarded to dad's new address at Camp Blanding, Florida,

Here is mother's second letter, or the second one that I was able to find, that was postmarked July 5, 4 pm, 1944 and dated inside July 5, 1944:

Hello Sweetheart,

Well, I got all three of your letters this morning. I really was glad to hear from you, but am sorry that you are in the Infantry and so far away, but it could have been worse I suppose.

So try your best to make the best of it and remember that Roger and I are with you in everything.

Don't worry too much, maybe when you have been in a little longer, we can come to see you. I will write to you every day and want you to do the same.

I would give anything in the world to see you. I just hope they won't send you across so soon as you think. Surely they won't do that.

We really were having a good time in Childersburg, but don't worry about the few unpleasant things that happened, as they were always soon over with. Neither of us meant to be that way.

So when this war is over, which I hope won't be long off, we will make up for lost time, and really have a good time together. Just remember that I will love you always and wouldn't do you wrong for anything in the world. You know that don't you Sweet? I'm sure that you won't do me wrong either.

I miss you more than anything in the world. Roger misses you too. He told me to go bring you back home. He is being a good boy. So just as soon as you can, get us a place to stay. Get it for us and we will be only too happy to come and stay with you.

Iva & Gerry came Saturday and stayed until Sunday. Harry & Margaret are here now. He is Lieutenant now. He is going to Atlanta Sunday and they will send him somewhere from there he thinks he may be stationed in Birmingham or Montgomery.

Arthur is coming Monday. He wrote that he would come through Atlanta, so that he could see you.

The Alabama Power man came down & signed us up for lights, so we hope to get them soon.

I'm going to see about my job this morning.

Did you get the letters I wrote you last week? (I never found these letters, so I presume they were lost.)

Well, we didn't have much of a fourth as we couldn't get any ice (They needed the ice to make home made ice cream.). I wouldn't have enjoyed it anyway without you.

I saw Opaleen (one of mother's close friends from high school) and her husband the other day. He is in Coast Guard Artillery but is going to be transferred to the Infantry.

If you can, I want you to send your Diploma etc. back to me. I'm sorry that they didn't do you any good. I know the Infantry is hard but try to endure it if you can, it can't last always anyway.

I'm sending you some letters from Robert & Curtis (These will be included later in the book.). I thought you would like to read them.

I wrote your Mother & Dad this morning too.

I'll stop now, hoping to get a long sweet letter from you every day.

There were two scraps of paper with Roger's
scribbles that he did for dad included in mother's
letter. I have attached scans of them here,

There can be no doubt that the war changed the way mother and dad
saw the world. It removed their innocence and moved them to make a pact
with God, that if dad survived and came home after the war, they would
dedicate themselves to God and live stalwart Christian lives and raise their
children as Christians as well. This would account for the obvious change
from the open, carefree attitudes that they had when they were young to
the stricter more Puritan attitudes they adopted later when raising my
brother and I. We all went to church three times a week and never missed
a tent revival meeting, or any other church function our entire childhood.
I think dad came so close to death that he vowed to God that he would
serve him faithfully all the rest of his life if only God would spare his life
and allow him to return to his wife. son, and loved ones. This is why,
I think, that I never experienced any of the open affection that they
once displayed and was never shown it during any of my childhood, The
fire and brimstone preachers they listened to, considered any display of
affection a sin and was not to be displayed to or shared with your children.
In any case, my family was like many of the World War Two families that
survived the ravages of combat, and by the grace of God, were allowed to
return to their loved ones. They were very rigid and strictly enforced their
religious beliefs which allowed little room for pleasures of the flesh.

I continue now with my dad's letters to mother. This letter from him
was in answer to the previous letter I included from mother that he received

from her dated July 5, 1944. Dad's letter was postmarked July 7, 1944, 11:30 am and dated inside July 6, 1944:

Hello Sweet,

I will try and answer your letter, sure was proud to hear from you and Roger and all. Glad you was well. I sure would like to see you all. I bet you do look good. I have never saw you look no other way. I have took three more shots today. I guss they will make me feel bad for the next day or two. We have got to go out and stay all night to night – that will be tough. I sure dont like the Army. Had to work K.P. this morning. I sure do wish I was back home with my sweet little girl. I will write more next time – got to go –

Bye Sweet and Roger

Dad included this note to Roger in the same letter:

Hello little Roger boy. I sure would like to see you and mother, and I hope to sometime soon. You be a good boy for your mother and take care of her for me.

Sweetheart I got your letter after so long a time. I hope to get one that was written sooner today – Bye Roger and my Darling wife, Love always

These letters literally carry one from one day to the next and that is their most endearing and enduring quality. There is a communication between my parents with their letters that has been captured as effectively as it would be in the emails of today. The downside for them was that it took so long to get a response by mail, usually anywhere from 2 or 3 days or 4 weeks if they were sent to or from overseas. So, it was to their credit that they kept at it. It is to my mother's credit and insight and yes, foresight, that she saved each letter written. Again, I am not sure that she or dad would approve of me revealing them for all to see, but I believe the larger good that will be achieved by doing so will more than eclipse any objections they might have had. They have indeed made an invaluable contribution to history with their letters, and I will endeavor to do my part to share them with you the reader.

There is much redundancy as one might expect and many times there was just not enough to write about. I believe that is a necessary flaw that should be endured to preserve the integrity of the whole. Keeping this in mind, I hope to create a flow that will navigate over the rippling waters of time.

I will include this letter from mother that was dated Hamilton, Alabama, July 6, 1944 and postmarked July 7, 1 pm,1944:

Dear James,

I got your letter this morning and was very sorry to hear that you were sick. I hope you are O.K. by now,

You said it rained all the time there, Well, it doesn't ever rain here. It really has been cold here yesterday & today, several people have been having fires in their chimneys.

I'm sending your soap dish, toothbrush holder, etc. I looked all over Hamilton for the case you asked for, but couldn't find one. So Harrison & Margaret are going to B'ham tomorrow and he is going to get one for you and mail it to you from there, so I suppose you will be getting it right away.

Roger hated to part with his soap dish but he said he would send it to his daddy and he would bring it back someday.

Sometime, when you have time, I want you to have some pictures made, as we would like to see how you look now. I know you won't look like yourself with that hair cut short, but that doesn't make any difference, I would like to have one anyway.

Well, be good and take care of yourself, and I will do the same, and remember that I'm thinking of you every day.

Love always, Your wife & Son,

Eliz & Roger

As you have probably observed by now my brother Roger was mentioned in many of the letters and one can deduce that the war affected him very deeply too. He was a very bright child of almost three years old and he was very aware of what was happening around him, and also very frightened by it. He prayed by his bedside every night for his daddy and always wanted mother to read dad's letters to him. When the content allowed her to do so she did. Roger also "wrote" letters to dad, which amounted to his childlike scribbles on scraps of paper. To Roger though, he was "writing" and he was very intent when doing them and wanted to 'write' about how he was doing so that his daddy would know. The following letter from mother had one of Roger's "letters" place inside within a small envelope, I will attach a scan of it at the end of the letter.

This letter from mother to dad was dated July7, 1944 and postmarked July 8, 4 pm, 1944. There was a note at the top as a kind of afterthought:

Mother & all said to tell you hello. Did you get your soap dish etc,? Iva & Gerry are getting married the 26th of this month. She is going to Okla, with him. She told me to write you about it.

Hello Sugar,

How are you after going through your day's training? I hope you are still making it O.K.

They really mean to make a tough one out of you don't they? You be sure to keep your head down when those machine guns start rolling over you, because I don't want anything bad to happen to you. I really will be proud

19

when you get over the worst part of your training and hope that you can be cook.

Tell them how good of a cook you are or just anything so they will let you cook.

I really do wish you were here to sleep with me tonight. I have to sleep in the whole bed by myself and it isn't very comfortable without you in it too.

Harrison and Margaret left this afternoon. They are going to B'ham from here. I gave him the money and he is going to get the shaving case for you and mail it to you, as I couldn't find one here.

I got the slip that you sent today, and I mailed it to Dupont with your address on it.

You said you guessed I was tired of of reading your letters. If I didn't get one every day I would be very disappointed.

I'll be so glad when we can be together again.

Roger said he wanted to get on the bus and go see his daddy. Every time anyone leaves he crys because he thinks they will do like you did. He thinks they won't come back.

Sweet, I want you to go ahead and do the best you can. You can make good in the Army for you always have everywhere else you have been.

I'll stop now & go to bed. So bye and be good. (write soon)

We love you, Eliz & Roger

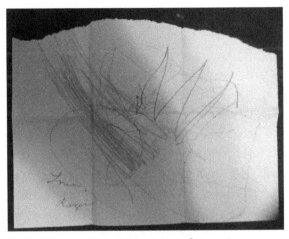

I am including a scan of Roger's
"letter" that was placed inside.

Dad wanted very much to get a place for mother and Roger to stay while he was at training at Camp Blanding, Florida. He could not get a pass for the first three weeks so it was a while before he could look for a place and places were hard to find as there were many other soldiers looking for them too. He did finally find a room for rent in a house behind the bus station in Starke, Florida, which was only a few miles from the camp. I will include a few letters from dad to mother in which he informs her of his progress in finding a place. This first letter is an earlier one which tells of the difficulties that he will face in finding a place for mother and Roger. This letter was postmarked July 9, 1944, 11:30 am, and probably written July 8, 1944:

Hello Sweetheart and Roger,

I am OK and feeling good at this time but I dont guss I will be that way long. I got wet all over and been that way all day. Sure hope you are well. How are you making out Sweet, by yourself and sleeping by yourself? I bet it is tuff, for myself, I mean it is tuff. I sure do miss your loving and kind words in the Army. All the kind words woulden be like one of yours, Sweet.

We havent had any more boys to fall out yet. I hope we dont. I sure hope I dont.

Sweet, write me about everything. I know what you are thinking – when will you get to come down here. When I get three weeks training I am going to try to get you a place to stay. The boys here says I cant get a place – every place is full up, but I will try. The place here at the post stays full up to and I cant stay with you at night unless I git special orders from the commanding officer. I haft to put in a week ahead to get you an apartment to stay in. This Army is something else – if I was in the ground air corps I could do more things, but this Infantry wont let you have any privileges. But dont worry Sweet just be thankful I am not in Conway's place (Carr Conway was the husband of mother's close friend, Johnnie Conway, and he was in a German P.O.W. camp for the remainder of the war,). I might be someday you cant ever tell, so just hope and pray that I dont ever haft to cross over.

I will be good and true to you Sweet. Dont worry darling, dont worry about that part. I dont worry about you doing things like that. I know you wouldent run (ruin) yourself like that. So you know I wont dont you Sweet?

By Darling and little Roger

Yours forever true Love James

Dad had been gone for almost two weeks before he got his first letter from mother although she had written him every day. She had gotten his letters, so it was hard to understand why he was not getting hers. They depended on these letters to get them through those lonely days, so it was rough on dad those first days that he didn't receive any mail.

This letter from dad is in answer to one of those first letters that he did get from mother and it was postmarked July 9, 5 pm, 1944. It was dated inside Saturday night, July 8th, 1944:

Hello Sweet & Roger,

I will try and answer you letter. Sure was proud to hear from you all. Glad you all are well. For myself I am doing pretty good, I was beginning to think that you had forgotten me, I have been looking for a letter the last two days. Everybody been getting mail but me, so I went to mail call this afternoon and still dident have any, so I came back to the barracks and just as I came in, the mail boy brought me a letter, happened it was from you. Said he looked over it. I was just fixing to write you and find out why I havent got some mail. I was beginning to worry about it. I wrote you last Saturday and I know that you had time to answer, but it came just in time, it sure did make me feel better. I know you havent forgot me now Sweet, so dont let me down. I havent let you down yet. I might not git to write every day later own, because we will haft to go out on the range and stay two weeks in tents, but I will write every chance that I git - that might be every day. We got a little brake this afternoon – havent had so much to do. I went to three shows this afternoon but they wasent like the shows we see at home. They wont let anyone see them – but soldiers that part of our training. Some of them are about venereal disease – shows what you catch when you run with sorry women, and how they work on a man are woman – it is awful – you wouldent ever want to do sorry if you saw one of these pictures. They dont hole nothing back, they show everything. The other pictures are war pictures shows all the action in a battle, I mean it is terrible – I can hardly look at them – shows how spies works. We sure do have a lot of training to do. (I am surprised the censors let this part of his letter get by.) I am in the heavy armed Infantry. We have M1 Rifle, thats for pretty close range and the big guns shoots a four pound shell and a forty five pistol thats for hand to hand fighting. We have several more guns they will

23

shoot about four or five miles and the machine gun, that one really shoots. We have plenty of things to fight with, dont let any one read this letter and dont say anything about this.

If I can I am going to make some pictures of myself for Herbert to put in his watermelon patch (I think dad meant his pictures would make good scarecrows.),

Sweet, I sure do miss you. I had to do my washing this afternoon and I havent any Ivory flakes, had to use GI soap. Sweet, I want you to git you a job but dont let it change you any way, Because you are a sweet girl and I dont want you any other way. If you do get a job, do your job the right way. I have one to do and I am going to try my best to do it right and be true to my darling wife and as you say when we do get back togather it will be sweet times and still true love. Thats what makes a happy home, husband not getting drunk and running around and leaving his wife at home all time. You dont haft to worry about me darling. I will never take up nothing but loving you more. You are the only girl I will every love. I think more of you thin anything in the world. I am going to show you some day if I live to see you again, which I hope and pray that God will take care of us all, and that some day very soon we will be back to gather again to stay and live happy and be sweet to each other and little Roger boy are never left out. Tell Roger I will send some thing just as soon as I can leave this place. They wont let us go anyplace within three weeks. I wont forget you Roger. You take care of my sweet little wife and keep being a good boy. I will close May God keep you and watch over you for a true soldier.

By Sweet & Roger, your true love one, James

P.S. Sweet I got the letters OK from Robert and Curtis, thanks (I will include the letters from his brothers, Robert and Curtis mentioned here a bit later with my chapter on relatives' and friends' letters.) Sure proud you got the check from Dupont (the powder and ammunition plant that dad worked at in Childersburg, Alabama before he was drafted). Write Robert and Curtis sometime, it will be OK. They would be proud to hear from you & Roger.

Dad mentions his brothers Robert and Curtis who were both in the service. Curtis was in the Army Air Force M.P. in England and Robert was in the Army Infantry like dad. Robert had been in the Army almost three years and was then fighting on the front lines in France. It was only three weeks later that Robert was killed in action at St. Lo, France on July 31, 1944. He was killed when a German artillery round exploded over his foxhole. Dad mentions Robert in this next letter to mother postmarked July 10, 11:30 am, 1944. It was dated inside Sunday morning July 9, 1944:

Hello Sweet little wife & son,

This is a blue Sunday again. I guss you are going to church. I dont know a better place you could go. I wish I was there to go with you – everything would be sweet and I wouldent be so blue this morning.

I sure wish you could drive the car. It would be so much better for you to go around where you wanted to and you could come to see me nely (nearly) every weekin and it wouldent cost so much, that is if you could get enough gas. Well we dont have much to do today, but next week we will go on a nine mile march. My legs are so stiff and hurt till I cant hardly walk. We must run half of the time which we will haft to do. They have a long rope hanging on frames over ditches we haft to run and grab them rops and swang across. Some of them fall in, its loots of fun

25

in a way but I miss my darling wife to much and boy you dont have any freedom in the Army.

I sure would be proud if this war was over today. I got a letter from Mama and Alma, they was all well. Mama got a letter from Robert (probably one of his last), he is in France. He said for us all to pray for him, if he got through it would be the Lord's will. He must be in battle, I hope and pray that he makes it OK. I will close. Write me a long sweet letter Sweetheart, and write Robert & Curtis.

Love always, James

Dad got letters from many of mother's family and friends as well as his own family and friends and I will include many of them as I believe it will add immeasurably to the story of my parents and to the stories of those who loved them. This next letter was from my mother's oldest brother, Harrison Roe Palmer, who was a Lieutenant in the Army Air Corp. He was stationed at Asheville, North Carolina at the time but this letter was sent from his new address in Atlanta, Georgia. His address was:

Lt. Harrison R. Palmer 0588 OBI
Section "N" 85ᵗʰ A.A,F. Base Unit
54 th A,A,C,'s Group, 7 N, Rhodes Center N.W.
Atlanta, Georgia

He writes on stationery from the Langram Hotel, Asheville, N.C. with a note:
"This is where I stayed while I was in Asheville, N.C.":

Dear James,

Well, well, you kind of pulled one on me, didn't you? You told me you were expecting to get in the Army soon – but somehow – I just wasn't expecting it so soon and when we got home the other day and Elizabeth told us you had already left, I was quite surprised. By this time I suppose you are becoming pretty well oriented into the raw and fascinating life of military discipline.

What do you think of the Army now that you have had a week or so of it? Elizabeth tells us that you have been assigned to the Infantry. I know you didn't like this very much, because it is indeed one of the most difficult branches of the service, nevertheless, once you get fully accustomed to the new kind of life, perhaps you won't find it nearly so bad as we have all heard. Here's hoping you will get to cook – I know that is what you'd be happiest doing.

I graduated from O.C.S. a week ago Saturday at Miami Beach, received my commission as a second lieutenant in the Air Forces and was transferred to Asheville, North Carolina, where headquarters for A.A,C,S, is located. However, I stayed there only 3 days and was again transferred to Atlanta, Georgia where the headquarters for the 54th group of A.A.C.S. is located. I was given a ten day delay in route and one day travel time from Asheville to Atlanta. We arrived here last Sunday afternoon. We were just sick when we learned that you had already left Atlanta because I am to report there the 10th (as soon as this leave is over). I don't think I'll be there but 3 or 4 days, but just the same, I would have been able, at least, to have seen you for a little while. It's too bad that things in the Army have to happen like they do. I'm going to miss getting to see Arthur too. His leave starts a day or so after I have to leave for Atlanta.

Well. I'm hoping to be transferred from Atlanta to Birmingham Air Base or some other place close around here. Here's hoping anyway that I'll be close to home for a change. If so, then when you get your furlough, maybe I'll get to see you. I would like to.

I believe they'll send me overseas in two or three months. Of course, I've not said much to Mama about it and won't until I know more about it. Anyway, it's my time. I've been on this side longer than most people now.

James, I do hope you won't find it too hard where you are and I hope with all my heart that you get to cook if that's what you want to do. I know you'll make them a good one if they'll only give you a chance. In fact, I know you'll make one of the very best soldiers at Blanding. I have the utmost confidence that you will succeed in whatever undertaking you pursue, you have the "guts" and courage that never fail a man. I've known this ever since I've known you. It is bad that they have to take married men, especially when they have children – but this is a bad war. We can only keep plugging – so keep your chin up, pal, and keep bucking. One of these fine days we'll all be back home and this whole mess will be over – until then – a lot of common country boys like you and me will have to suffer a few hardships here and there.

Write me soon as you have time and tell me all the news about yourself and your work.

Forgive me for waiting so long to write, I've been pretty busy the last 4 months and what writing I did was usually to Margaret. I had very little time to write anyone else.

Remember I'm for you 100% and I'm looking forward eagerly to seeing you.

Luck & Best Wishes – Harry

(This note was at the top of Uncle Harry's letter.)
Don't write me at Atlanta because I won't be there
long enough – I'll write you my new address.

That was certainly a long but inspiring letter from Uncle Harry to dad. Uncle Harry had wonderful insights and a gift for conversation and writing as you may have observed. His letters were some of the most informative and insightful of the relatives' letters that dad received while at Camp Blanding and I'm sure it was very uplifting to my dad to have felt my uncle's genuine concern for him.

Another brother of my mother's was my Uncle Herbert, Herbert Hoover Palmer. At the time he was too young to be drafted into the service and was still attending high school. He was quite helpful to my mother and Roger at the time and drove them places, cared for dad's car and did a lot of the manual labor around my grandmother's and great grandmother's houses. Both Uncle Harry and Uncle Arthur were in the service, so it was left to Uncle Herbert and the youngest brother, Uncle Horrice, or Horrice Edward Palmer, to fill in for their brothers and help support the family.

Here is a letter from Uncle Herbert to dad dated Hamilton, Alabama, July 6, 1944:

Hello James,

I wonder how this old Infantry boy is getting along. I bet it sure is tough. I sure enjoyed my trip to Opelika. It was pretty lonesome after you left and we went back home. Roger wanted to know where his daddy was. When anybody asked Roger where you are he says daddy gone army. He sure is a captain. I sure wish you could have been here for the 4th. Boy we made lot of ice cream. The hold family was at home except you and Arthur. Harry and Margaret are still here. Harry is an officer.

Arthur is coming home the 11th. I sure would like to see him. I bet he looks good in his suit. The Infantry is tough but I know you will make a good soldier. Well that is all I can write.

Good luck, Herbert

Uncle Herbert speaks of his trip to Opelika, Alabama, in this letter. He went with mother and Roger to see dad off from Opelika where dad was drafted into the service. Dad's family home was in Beauregard, Alabama, a small farming community outside of Opelika where his father, Gordon Brown, had a 200-acre cotton farm. After dad left, mother and Roger and Herbert stayed with my grandfather Gordon and grandmother, Betty Brown, a few days at their home. They returned to Hamilton, Alabama on a bus and Uncle Herbert came along to help mother with Roger on the trip back.

One can see the story of my parents unfold with the letters they wrote to each other every day, and also through the letters that their relatives and friends wrote to them and I will include many of these as we travel along the pathway of their challenging times.

I will include a few more of mother's letters to dad and his to her in response to keep the flow going between them and then include more letters from dad's mother and other relatives.

Here is a letter from mother to dad dated Hamilton, Alabama, July 11, 1944 and postmarked July 12, 9:30 am, 1944:

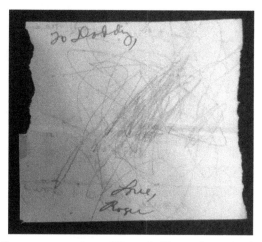

There was another of Roger's "letters" inside this next letter. I am attaching a scan of it here.

Dearest James,

I was very sorry to hear that you haven't been getting my letters very fast. I have been writing you every day since you sent your address. I suppose they must have lain over some place, but just hope that you have gotten them by now.

When I get your letters they are from 2 to 3 days old.

I haven't forgotten you at all. You know I couldn't do that. I love you too much to ever think of doing such a thing. I always answer your letters just as soon as I get them.

I would give anything on earth to see you again. I hope it won't be so long before I can.

Take care of yourself while you are out on the range those two weeks.

I know you didn't enjoy those shows. I wouldn't either. I suppose it was a lesson to some of the boys though. I know you wouldn't think of going out anyhow would you?

Don't worry about getting a job changing me. You know I wouldn't think of ever doing you wrong. When I start work, I'll just work and then go right back home.

I went to town this afternoon and had some pictures made for you. They aren't any good, but I'm sending them to you anyway. But please don't let anyone see them as they look so horrible.

Roger has a new haircut. He thinks his picture is the stuff.

He said he wanted to send his daddy one and his daddy would send him one of himself.

We will be very glad to get your picture & not for a watermelon patch either. I want one to keep to look at.

(I am including scans of two photos that
dad had made as I'm not sure which one
he was speaking of in the letter.)

I got me a little red & white flowered batiste (a fine, soft shear fabric of fine weave made of various fibers) dress this afternoon. It really is cool & and is so cute. I wish you could see it. It fit so good. I just gave $3.00 for it.

We got a letter from Harrison today. He said he had already mailed the case to you. Write and let me know if you get it and your soap dish & toothbrush holder.

Arthur is to be here tomorrow for awhile, but after he goes back, I think he will have to sail.

I just hope and pray that you won't have to go across. I hope you can get cook and stay over here so I can be with you.

Can you get your diploma, marriage license & etc. back? If you can send them to me.

I wish I could do your washing for you. How did you make out washing them yourself?

Well, I'll stop for now, so write me soon. Remember I love you more than anything in the world.

Your wife & son, Eliz & Roger

In this next letter dad was answering the letter he had received from mother. It was dated Tuesday night, July 11, 1944 and postmarked July 12, 11:30 am, 1944:

Hello Sweet & Roger,

I will try to answer your letter. Sure was proud to hear from you all, Hope you are well at this time, for myself I am OK just the Army life have got me down and I cant get on my feet again. I need you to give me a lift, you know how it is done dont you sweet darling? I sure do miss you every night and day Sweet, I try not to think about it so much, but I cant never forgit you no matter where I am are what I am doing you will be on my mind. Thinking of all the times we have had togather before we married and after. I sure do have the blues sometime. Sweet are you OK in your monthly hardship I sure hope you are because you have anought trouble as it is. Write me and let me know. I like to know you are OK just about as bad as you do.

Sweet you said you would like to see me coming – you dont know how much I would like to walk up and hole you good and tight one more time. I would feel good one more time to, been I havent for the last three weeks, just because I need you Sweet. You made me happy once and keep me that way till the Army got me, and if you could come and stay I would be happy again. You said your money was getting low. Sweet dont you know I dont want you to go around broke. Write a check, git as much as you want, I want you to Sweet. Your check should have come by now anyway, if it havent write me. I will see why it havent come, you ought to have two or three the way I haft to work at this place.

They sure are rough on some of the boys. I saw one boy crying today. He said something was rong with his leg, had been that way two or three years, but they make him go just like he was sound as a dollar. I felt sory for him but I couldent do anything for him because all I could do was keep up myself. That's the way you git treated in the army. They dont care for you. If I live to get back home I am going to stay with you six months and not do a thing but just what me and you want to do, and it all will be the sweet way, that the way we want it aint it sweet darling? You said you was going to work. Its OK with me, you need to do something to pass off the time. I know you get lonesome sitting around the house all time. I dont care what you do, just be sweet, then, when I see you again. Go ahead and enjoy yourself Sweet and have some fun. I dont mind, all I want you to do is be careful and dont git on the rong road, which I know you will never do. But if you do ever have a mind like that watch your step Sweet, you know what I mean dont you darling? How much will you make? I been getting a letter every day. I got two Sunday you sweet thing. You do love me dont you Sweet. I got your letter from Atlanta after I got here.

Sweet I love you with all my heart. I will be true to the end, then I am coming back to you and start a new life. I mean a sweet one to, you wait, I will show you darling.

By sugarfoot and be true, Love always, James

It is easy for me to understand now why my parents led such a Christian life all their lives and raised their two sons to live good respectable lives as well and to treat all people with respect and kindness. Being separated by the war made them appreciate the lives they had before, and they were determined to make life for themselves and their children as good if not better than that when the war was over. You probably took note while reading his letters how generous and unselfish my dad was with my mother. He was always that way with us and would literally have given the shirt off his back to help us all through life. We always knew how much he loved us by his generosity and devotion to mother and to us. we were not a family that showed outward displays of emotion, but we always knew we were loved by all the sacrifices that our parents made for us. They worked hard to provide a nice home for us and to give us the best education that money could buy. We never lacked for anything and we were always deeply loved even if they rarely expressed it in words. Their lives were seen as cherished gifts from God and that was the way they always saw it and they gave thanks to God all the days of their lives for sparing my dad and bringing him home from that horrible war.

I will include a letter from mother which was an answer to dad's previous letters that I have posted. Her letter was dated Hamilton, Alabama, July 12. 1944 and was postmarked July 13, 4 pm, 1944:

Hello Sweetheart,

I have just read the two letters I received from you today. I enjoyed reading them very much. I don't know what I would do if I couldn't hear from you every day. I miss you so much. I can't ever have any fun by myself. I hope you can find us a place to stay before long.

I hope you won't have to go across, Maybe something will turn up & the war will be over before you have to go.

I'll get the testament and send it to you tomorrow. The stores are closed this afternoon as it is Wednesday. I'm proud that you want to read the Bible instead of doing like the other boys. It doesn't help anyone to gamble. You will come out much better if you do the right thing.

I'm glad that you feel the way you do about me. I think you are the best boy in the world too. I feel that I can trust you anywhere & and I want you to feel the same way about me.

Roger said to tell you he was waiting for you to send him something. He looks at your pictures and talks about you lots. He is always so anxious to hear me read your letters to him.

Mr. Banks Carpenter said he thought you was a very nice guy and he thinks a lot of you. I told him I thought you were too.

I got my check O.K. and really was proud of it as I haven't started work yet. I think he wants me the last of the week.

I wrote your mother & dad & sent them the $5.00 you borrowed.

I hope Robert will go through O.K. Maybe he will. That is about all we can do, is to hope and pray that nothing will happen to any of the boys.

We are expecting Arthur tonight – he will get here O.K.

Iva will be here next Wednesday. She is quitting her job in the bank and going to Gerry as they are going to be married the 26th.

I suppose by now you have gone on the 5 mile march, I hope that you made out O.K. I hate to think of you having to do such things but I guess there isn't anything that we can do about it.

I'll go for now, so write me every time you can.

I love you. Elizabeth & Roger

P.S. Arthur got in tonight at 9:00 o'clock. He said to tell you hello, and wish you were here to. He looks nice in his suit.

To provide a wider perspective to mother and dad's story, I am providing in addition to mother and dad's letters to each other, also some of the letters written to dad by his mother and dad, his sister, his uncles and his friends from July 1944 and later.

Dad's parents had four children, three sons and a daughter. All the sons were in the service by June of 1944 and Robert, the oldest, had been in since 1941. Curtis was in the Army Air Corp and was stationed in an M.P. unit in England. Dad, of course, had just been drafted and was in training with the Infantry at Camp Blanding, Florida. The only communication my grandparents had with their sons were the letters that they wrote back and forth. The letters written overseas often took two weeks or longer to reach their destination. My grandparent's daughter was their oldest child and was named Alma. She married a man named Jeff Sanders, so I refer to her as Alma Sanders when including her letters to dad.

There were many letters written to dad from his parents and his sister Alma Sanders. I will include a few of them here. This first letter is from Betty Brown, dad's mother, and was dated July 5. 1944 with a postmark of July 6, 4 pm, 1944:

Dear James.

Will answer your letter I got today was glad to heare from you glad you was well for us we are well excep bad colds hope this letter finds you well & doing fine maby you will like better after you stay there a while I hope so hope you will stay well & go through all right soon come back home just trust in God he will take care of you anny where, we are having plenty rain now it rains about every day. Alma & them came yesterday & spent last night they was looking for a letter from you the kids all went home I havent got but one letter from Elizabeth & Roger sents thay went home I hope they are doing fine & will soon come back to see us I sure did miss them I got a letter from Curtis & Robert today thay was well Curtis was still in England when he wrote said he didn't know where Robert was but hope he was OK. Robert sais he was sum where in France but couldent tell where he was or what he was doing Said wasent but one thing we could do and that was to pray that the war would soon be over he said he know it would be only by Gods protecting if he come through O.K. I hope & pray that the Lord will take care of him keep him safe & all the rest & this war will soon bee over so you all can come home I will close wishing you the best of luck write soon

Love mother & dad

Continuing with my grandmother's letters, this is the second one dated July 12, 1944:

Dear James,

I will answer your letter was glad to heare from you sorry you are having a hard time I know it is bad Robert said the first 3 months was the worst I don't guess the is anny part good I hope you will stay well & go through OK for us we are doing well I guess hope you are well & doing fine It sure is hot weather up here I got a letter from Elizabeth & Robert today Eliz said she & Roger was well & doing fine Robert was allright when he wrote I hope he is now I will send you his letter I havent got a letter from Curtis this week yet hope I will get one Your grandpa (Fate Brown) is doing fine mene (mean) as ever I got a letter from Ola Piper (Fate Brown's youngest daughter) they was all well Pal (Palmer Brown, Fate Brown's youngest son and Ola and Gordon Brown's brother) is up there with them Ola got another baby it a boy 5 weeks old.

Elizabeth said she was coming soon as she found out what she was going to do I know she will go to you if she can I havent got a radio Battery yet hope I can soon get one I sure do miss my radio.

Your car sure do look lonesome I wish you was back home to drive it hope you will bee soon Well as I have got to write Elizabeth I will close write soon try to take care of your self the best you can.

With love & best wishes Mother & Dad

I will include one more letter from Betty Brown that was written about a month and a half later and dated October 2, 1944. It ws written over a month after Robert was killed in action on July 31, but she makes no mention of it. I must assume that she had not found out about it or perhaps it was just too painful for her to write about:

Dear James.

Will try and write you a few lines two let you heare from us we are doing very well excep bad colds hope you are well I got a letter from Eliz today thay was doing fine Elisabeth said Roger sure was proud to seen her (Mother had just returned from staying with dad at Camp Blanding, Florida during late August through September of 1944). I will be glad when they come I sure do wont to see Roger We got five little pigs & a little puppy he will have a time with the dog I know your daddy havent got out but one bale of cotton he wont get but 2 cant get it pick Roger said he wanted two pick cotton when he come I got a letter from Curtis he was well he wanted to know what was the matter with you said he hadent got a letter from you in a long time he wanted us two send him sum cigarettes your daddy couldent find anny in town cant get but a little pack at a time if this war dont stop I dont guess we can get anny thing much very long I sure do wish it would so you woulden have to go anny further be glad when you can come I know Roger will be glad to see you hope you can come back to stay with him Write to Curtis when you Can he wants to heare from you he said he sure was home sick I wish he could come Alma & Jeff was here Sunday They are doing all right I will close wishing you the best of luck may God bee with you all the way through write soon

Lots of love mama & dad

Occasionally dad would get letters from friends that he knew in Childersburg, Alabama while he was working at the DuPont Munitions Factory. I will include one now from a friend named Paul dated 7-15-1944. As I have mentioned before, mother and dad moved to Childersburg from Hamilton, Alabama when dad was offered a job at the powder factory:

Dear James

I received your letter and sure were glad to hear from you. I miss you lots and sure would like for you to be back with us We are all working hard at the plant. The nitrater has been down for the last 2 days. They have been putting in a new agatiter (agitator) We are using the tower in 907 now and are getting 12 reductions a day now so you see we are all working Webb has gone to (tyletrgl ?) and Dan has his place and Vic Carlson has his place Crowley has Vic's job and Rhodes is on E shift Now I am going to take Les

Coffman's place while he is on his vacations Well little boy take care of yourself and make the best of it you can. You always could do good on any job given you and I know you will on this one.

Best regards Paul P.O. Box 545, Postmarked Sylacauga, Ala. July 15, 1944

Dad's sister, Alma Brown Sanders, wrote him often while he was in the service and her letters provide much additional news and information about the time they all lived in. The letters I am including from her came from about the same time period of July 1944 and later. The first letter from Aunt Alma was dated Opelika, Alabama, July 6, 1944 and postmarked July 6, 7:30 pm. 1944:

Hello James

I will answer your letter I received yesterday Sure was pride to hear from you But sorrow dont like hoping you like better when you stay there awhile. That wheres Robert was wasant it (Robert had his Infantry training at Camp Blanding in 1941). He said it was an offil place. What did you do the forth. We dident do any thing we did go to the show & down to Mama Marvin & Harry (her two oldest sons) went to a big Barbecue at Pepperell, they siad they sure head a plenty to eat. Marvin got a big resining (sore) on is back. We got three days off for the 4. I got a letter from Elizabeth the other day I have just ansuder (answered) it she siad Roger was doing fine. I sure am pride he is, for he sure was sick before he lefe (left) down here. I got a letter from Curtis, he got thim pictures I sent him O.K. Siad the kids dident look like thimself. Well I sure hope this war will soon be over so you all can come back home.

Write soon Love Alma

Alma and Jeff Sanders had five children, three boys including Marvin, Harry and Jerry and two girls including Betty Jane and Marie. You noted Marvin and Harry were mentioned in the previous letter. Jerry was the youngest son and was born after this in 1946. Betty Jane and Marie were both young children during the time of this letter. Alma and Jeff worked in the Opelika Cotton Mill and Jeff was also a carpenter. They visited grandmother Betty and grandfather Gordon Brown a lot and often went to singings with Betty Brown at Providence Baptist Church and other local churches. Providence Baptist was my dad's church growing up in Beauregard, Alabama. Alma was the oldest child and dad was the youngest and Alma always thought of him as "her baby" and took care of him growing up. I will include more of Alma's letters to give a feel of her family's life and times living in Opelika, Alabama. This next letter from her mentions Robert and was from one of Robert's last letters to her. Aunt Alma's letter was dated July 10, 1944 and was postmarked July 11, 1:30 pm, 1944:

Dear Brother

Guess you wonder why I am writing again. Thought I would write as I know you cant git too many letters as you are lonesome & home sick. I am sorrow for you but theres nothing I can do about it. But just trust God that this offil war will soon be over. I got a letter from Robert Sat. dont know where you got one or not But any way I will write & tell you what he rote me. He some where in France Siad he cant tell whether he killed any Germans yet or not. But one thing he could say, thank God that they havent got me yet. I am trusting God they don't. God has taken care of him so far and I trust that he will take care of all my Brothers throu this war & send thim all back home safty.

I went to mama yesterday they was well as common. I know Elizabeth & Roger miss you. May be that you wont haft to stay away from thim long. I hope not any ways.

Well take care of your self. Write every time you can.
Love, your sister

There were always bits of information in Aunt Alma's letters about Robert and Curtis who were dad's brothers that were in the service. I just wish that they had written more about what was going on but I'm sure there wasn't the time or inclination for that and also the Army limited what they could write, and every soldier's letter home was censored. In this next letter Aunt Alma mentions that Hitler almost was killed and that she wishes he had been. Her letter was dated Opelika, Alabama, July 23. 1944. This was just 8 days before Robert was killed in action at St. Lo, France:

Hello James

I will try & ansur your letter. I read it the other day was glad to here from you glad you was well for us we all well at this writing. I have just got back from Mama & daddy they was doing very well. I left Harry down there to stay with mama this week Preaching started yesterday it run all this week. I went last night & mama went to. Griff & Mary (Mayberry) come to spend this week. Don't guess we git to go any more this week.

James, I got a letter from Robert the other day (This was no doubt the last letter she got from Robert.) it was rote the first of July — Siad he was well, mama got one rote July the 7. I sure hope he comes throu O.K. We didn't here from Curtis last week sure hope hes O.K.

James I sure wish I could git you out of that place. I sure do it — but no ways I can do you any good. Just hope & pray this war will soon be over so all the boys cab come home. Guess you herd Hittler likes to have got kill — wish he head. Maybe if he header the war would soon be over.

Well guess I better close & write Elizabeth When she coming to see you hope you can find her a room so she can stay with you, while you down their for you dont know where you go from there. write when you can.

Love & best wishes to you, your sister as ever

The letters from Aunt Alma always expand a bit on the family history of the Browns and also include information about close family relatives which is why I like to include as many of her letters as possible. There are mentions of Herman Owsley, her cousin, and Aunt Pearl Owsley, Betty Owsley Brown's sister in this next letter, and also there is a humorous reference to Fate Brown (my great grandfather) jumping off a moving pick-up truck. This letter from Aunt Alma was dated Opelika, Alabama, August 3, 1944 and postmarked August 4, 1944:

Dearest Brother

I will try ansur you letter I receaved yesterday Sure was proud to here from you, glad you was well, for us we all well at this writing. I got a letter from Curtis the other day, siad he was well & in good health Siad the sooner he left that place the better he would like, mama got a letter from Robert rote July 11th – siad he is still on the front lines & hope to go back for a rest I sure hope & pray he come throu O,K. & this war is soon over – so you & all can come back home & be happy once more (Aunt Alma has not found out yet that Robert was killed just four days before she wrote this letter.). They think this war will soon be end, I hope they think right – I sure hope & pray it ends before you haft to go across.

Ganther & them havent got but one letter from Herman (Owsley) sent he went across (These are Betty Brown's relatives.). Well, James I sure got a plenty to eat now, chickens peas & butterbeans – wish you were here to help me eat.

I sure would like to see you & your family when do you think you git to come. I sure hope with them just about all time. Aunt Pirl (Pearl Owsley was Betty Brown's sister.) is down there this week to. Pal (Palmer Brown. Gordon Brown's younger brother) come back again.

Guess mama rote you about Grand Pa (Fate Brown, Gordon Brown's father) jumping off Frank Hilyer truck & like to kill himself. Frank didn't stop to let him off and he thought he jump off. It didn't stop him from going tho, he up at Mama Sunday laughing about it.

Well it rain just about every day here. It raining today. Well guess that's all I know to write for this time So write soon.

Love & best wishes to you – your sister & family

P.S. Guess Elizabeth be there by time you git this letter. I know you was pride to see thim. I like to see Roger when he see you & I bet he wont know you. If you have any of your pictures send me one.

Before I return to my mother and dad's letters, I would like to include one written to dad from Mrs. Tom Owsley, wife of Betty Brown's brother. The letter was dated Opelika, Alabama, July 17, 1944:

Helo James

I try and ans you letter all got the other day. Sure was glad to here from you this leaves all well But me I am in bead I feel Better to day I sure was sick Sunday. Tom and Dorothy are at work. Bettie spent the night with Alma Saturday night Tom made 7 days last week if I can and eny Better I may go down to Bettie (Betty Brown, my grandmother). Sunday Eugenia and Rip was over here (her children I assume). Sunday when I git up it like I Been on a big drunk. Winfield give Bettie a puppy. One of Lee (Lee Owsley, another of Betty Brown's brothers) Boys was operation on last week. The Dr. told me Sunday that he was doing fine. Bud (Owsley) are at work to now. Tom will draw a good payday Friday and boy are I going to town with him and Dot will. As I got to lay down, I had better stop. Ans soon

From your Old Anty & Uncle Tom
Mrs Tom Owsley
Pepperell Branch
Opelika, Ala Box 1238

P.S. Dorothy got a letter from Robert the other day and boy was we glad to here from him.

(So, this would have been another of Robert's last letters.)

There was a definite flow to the letters written between mother and dad and it remained largely an unbroken one as they wrote each other every day. It was remarkable that dad managed to write every day even when he was on field maneuvers in the woods while in training. Sometimes the weather was brutally cold and there could be hurricane force winds and rain, but if he could, my dad still would find a way to write, if he had a pen or pencil and dry paper and envelopes. He would write to her unfailingly. My mother would always answer his letters when she received them and would write even if no letters had been received. There were periods, especially when dad was overseas, that the letters did not come, sometimes for two or three weeks, and that must truly have tested their resolve and their love. They knew it was the fault of the slow mail delivery and that eventually the letters would arrive, sometimes four, five or six letters at a time. I have tried as best as I could to sequence the letters so that a communication between them could be established so as to give the reader the feeling of being right there with them as they express their thoughts and feelings.

I realized for the reader's sake that their daily letters to one another can be repetitive and to prevent an abundance of redundancy I tried to include only the letters that would continue the flow between them without becoming bogged down with too much of the mundane that my parents, like all people, experienced in their everyday lives. So, with that in mind, I will continue with my mother's letters to dad.

This letter from mother to dad was dated July14, 1944 and was postmarked July 15, 4 pm, 1944:

Dearest James,

I got another one of your letters today. I'm always so proud when morning comes as I know I'm going to get a letter from you. They cheer me up so much. I just hope you enjoy my letters too, if they are business like.

Don't let the army get you down if you can help it. Just remember I am for you in everything.

Try to get by the best you can. I know it is hard, but there isn't any of it easy.

I'm sorry that you have to take such hard training. I think about it all the time, and hope you can soon be out of it.

This place looks so lonesome. I can look around and see the plants across the ditch, where we once had so much fun. Also under the plum tree, you remember that don't you sweet? The house where we lived in when we first married, we had the best time there didn't we?

Maybe when this whole thing is over we can have lots of fun again.

(I will interject my feelings about what my mother was writing here. She was almost poetic in the manner that she expressed her memories of their love making and their shared loving memories. This was a side of my mother that I never experienced. She was young then and more open to love and love making. It was very refreshing and exhilarating when I first read these words from her and to realize that she and dad had these feelings for each other. As I mentioned before, they never expressed any outward displays of affection afterwards, or at least during the time that I was growing up. It seems to me that the 1950's frowned upon any open display of love and affection, especially in front of one's children. Everything of a carnal nature was seen to be a sin and children needed to be protected from sin at all costs. The trouble with that kind of thinking is that it deprives children of affection and therefore deprives them of learning the ability to show affection. Also, it makes children want to see what they are missing and makes them want to sin even more. The 1960's Hippie Generation seemed to bear these observations out well, I think. I just wish the love that my parents shared for each other in the 1940's could have been more openly expressed with their children in the 1950's. It would certainly have improved my social skills and would have enhanced my relationships with all people immeasurably. I understand that my parents were only trying to protect us from evil. However, open displays of love and affection should not in any way be considered a sin. On the contrary, these displays should be welcomed and upheld as an example of having a healthy relationship. Well, now that I have that off my chest, I will return to mother's letter.)

I hope you can find a room or someplace for us. We could stay with you awhile anyway.

I got my check the other day so I'm O.K. financially now.

I sent the slip to Dupont that you sent me. Have you heard from it yet? I bet they get out of paying you that bonus though. It seems that would be to good to be true.

I was supposed to have started working today, but he hasn't sent for me yet. I'll make two dollars a day. That isn't much, but it will help out. Don't worry about my working changing me or causing me to do wrong in any way. You know it isn't in me to even think of such.

I love you too much to do you wrong and trust that you feel the same way about me.

Roger is fine, still mean as ever. He turns summersets all the time. He said "tell his Daddy hi" and to hurry back home.

I got a letter from Johnnie. She hasn't heard from Carr in five weeks. I hope that nothing has happened to him. I think it is due to the Invasion though. (Johnnie was my mother's best friend from Hamilton, Alabama. She was married to Carr Conway, an officer in the Army Air Corp. His plane was shot down over Germany and he and his crew were taken prisoner when they parachuted out of their plane, He and his crew remained in a German P.O.W. camp for the remainder of the war.)

You asked about my monthly periods. I have just gotten through with it. I really was proud as I would hate to have anything wrong with me & you gone.

I'll stop now, hoping to get a letter tomorrow.

I love you with all my heart, your wife & son Eliz & Roger.

(Mother adds more to this letter as a kind of P.S.)

I sent the 11th payment on the car today. There is only one more to make which will leave us owing $62. It's going down on our bank account but when I start work I'm going to save all I can and put it back in.

Mama said tell you "hello" & she wished we could get some of the rain you get down there. She said she hoped you could get cook so you wouldn't have to fight Japs.

The next letters from dad to mother find him answering her letters and thanking her for sending his shaving kit. He also mentions wanting to have her keep his car in Hamilton so that she can learn to drive it. Despite dad's persistence about having her learn to drive, she never really did and she never drove more than just a few practice runs all of her life. Dad did all the driving and took her every place she needed to go. So, I guess she just never felt the need to learn. Another thing was that her dad had been killed in an automobile accident when she was just eight years old, so I am sure that was a deciding factor as well.

The next two letters from dad were inside a single envelope, the content of which I will include here. The first letter was written about the same time as mother's previous letter and the envelope was postmarked July 14, 11;30 am, 1944:

Hello sweet,

I will try and answer your letter sure was proud to hear from you Sory you have a rison & I know it sure do hurt. I wont you to see a doctor it may be your blood. I know something is wrong are you woulden have them all times. I am doing pretty good I guss, we had a rain storm this afternoon. We was out in all of it. I never been so wet in all my life. Loots of trees blowed down and lightin struck all around. We was about three miles back in the woods had to wade water up to my knees. I may be sick from it I hope not. I will never like the army it gets worse every day. I have never saw a lake.

Sweet I would give anything to be back with you but I know I cant now. They got a letter here at the camp from General Macarthur. He said that he dident want any more boys from Camp Blanding he wanted some that wasent all ready dead. They are rough on the boys make them go till they cant we had one to fall out today. Sweet I sure hope your rison will be soon get well. Your letter was sweet. I like to get letters from you ever day. I want to know how you and Roger are and all the rest. I will close. Tell your mother I said hello and the boys to. By darling be a sweet girl and take care of Roger. I am hoping to be back home with you soon and have a sweet home again.

Your true love one always, James

Another part of a letter was enclosed in the same envelope. I believe it was a continuation of the previous letter as dad had mail call as he was writing it and decided to answer the latest letter from mother and place it in the same envelope. I will include it here:

…..Well sweet they just had mail call just as I was writing you so I will let you know how much I appricate the things you sent me the shaving kit was just what I wanted. Thanks for the soap you always have something extra dont you darling and it is the right thing every time. I bet you have me plenty something extra when I come home you sweet thing. I could squize your little heart out because I know what you have waiting on me. I sure wish I could sleep with you tonight. I know you are lonesome, I sure would like to finish that little space you have in the bed – just sleep clost to you one more time. I would be a proud soldier I would know how to apricate it darling you are my true and love one. I always be true to you sweet. When this war is over I will prove to you how much I love you so just wait and see – you will wont you Sweet? It wont be to long I hope dont you? Today woulden be to soon for me.

I want you to send me one of yours and Roger pictures. I want ones I can keep the one I have is old but they are sweet looking to me now. Dont you miss the car sweet I would give anything if you could drive. When

I come home I might let you keep it at Hamilton tell Herbert to git him some drivers licenc he can drive OK maby he can learn you how you know how to take care of it. Since I have some time to think things over it would be best for you to keep it something might happen as I am in this army up to my ears the car would do you no good sitting under the shid – if anything do happen to me I wont you to have every thing that I can give so it would be better for you to keep the car so thats the way it will be when I come home because I know what I am taking this training for I am not supose to tell anything it will be the Japs I will tell you when I can see you why. Dont worry sweet I feel like I will make it here and over there to. I know I have got to cross but god will take care of that part. When I come home I will fix every thing for you just like I wont you to have it. I will git one leave I might get it before 17 weeks is up if they need us before thin. I wish I could talk to you just a few minute it would be sweet. Darling dont worry about me I dont want you to, but I want you to know these things,

by sweet and Roger, I love you always true, James

Dad, by this time, had been away from mother over three weeks and his young libido was beginning to feel it. The next letter from him finds him, for not a better way to put it, pretty damned horny! The letter was dated July 14, 1944 and postmarked July 15, 11:30 am, 1944. This was not a letter that mother would have read to Roger, or at least not the risqué parts:

Hello Sweetheart and Roger,

I will try and answer your letter. Sure was proud to hear from you all. Glad you all are well for myself I am doing pretty good except my risin dont feel so good. The pictures was good Roger haircut look like mine they liked to have got it all, but it looked sweet to me darling you look so good. I wish I could see you I would like to hold you one more time good and tight. I would be a happy Soldier Sweet, that what it would take my sweet little wife to lay around on, and look at them big pretty legs, and thats not all sweet you know what pretty legs leads up to don't you?

Sweet I got my washing done OK but not like you have done it. I would give anything if you was doing it now I mean I would help you, I know it is hard to do a washing, maby some day I will be back to help you do things and do it the sweet way. I can think of a loot of thing now that will never happen any more when I git back with you sweet darling – when I git time I will try to have some pictures made and send you one. My hair cut not so bad when the barber made a whick at it I ducked so he left it about three inches long you ought to see some of the boys – Look like a pilled onion. Sweet I sure do miss you I cant do anything right staying away from you. you are so sweet and good looking if I live to be back with you I will never leave you sweet, you said you would give anything on earth to see me I would give I dont know what to see you anything. I bet you dress do look good and I want a date when I come home. I want you to have that dress on – I want it to fit tight and be short you know how I like them. I might take you for a ride, woulden it be sweet if we could take that ride tonight. Sweet you be good and I will. dont worry about me to much darling you know I woulden do you rong for nothing there not a girl in this hole world could make me do you rong, I love you and you only, I can git by till I see you thin we can have a good time and not have anything to worry about that we done rong, cant we sweet? I am going to show you a time when I come home, you sweet little thing, may god bless your little heart and keep you true and sweet for me only take care of little Roger sweet and your self. I have loots of things to tell you when I come. Just pray that I will git through this training OK it sure dangerous – you woulden relize how it was til you saw it.

By Sweet heart I love you only, you true love one, James

Dad mentioned his training and how rough it was in the previous letter. This next letter gives some details about the training he was receiving. It was dated July15, 1944 and postmarked July 16, 2;30pm, 1944:

Hello Sweet heart & Roger

I will try and answer your letter I recived this afternoon, sure was proud to get your letter as I am lonesome and dont feel so good, your letters are so sweet. I would give anything to be there while Arthur (mother's brother) is at home, tell him I said hello and I was sorry that I dident take the Navy (I was not aware that there was a choice but evidently the draftees could choose what branch of the service they wanted.). I sure did make a mistake one time in my life, boy I am having a time trying to make it, but I think I can take it if I dont have any bad luck. the last boys that took thire training here before we started, had some bad luck lost several lives and some hurt pretty bad going under that michine gun fire, we will haft to line up and let airplane shoot michine guns twenty feet in front of us I dont like that at all. they dont haft to make but one mistake thin your days are over, be sure and take care of your self and pray that this war will soon be over and we all can come back to our to our love ones and have some more fun like we use to have. I sure do miss living with you all, so take care of your self and have a good time while you are at home, I wish you all the luck in the world old boy (dad is referring to Arthur here.).

Sweet when I come home you be ready to have a good time (I think we all know what that meant at this point,) and you just as well forget that job while I am there, because I will have you plenty jobs to do, but sweet ones you know how sweet I wont them dont you little darling, I miss you so much darling, we dont have so much to do Sunday and that makes it worse knowing I could be with you and haft to lay around here all day and cant git a pass to go any where. I dont care for a pass unless you was here, then I woulden want to come back when it was up. I love you sweet heart. I will prove to you when I come home that I realy do love you sweet. this army have realy changed me in that way, when I git time to think about you like I wont to, I cant think nothing but some hard words I have said to you back in Childersburg. You know I said I wished I was in the army and something els which you have forgive me for saying havent you sweet?

I have changed my mind about this army and all the rest. I wished I was with my darling wife and boy. I woulden leave you for nothing sweet. If I live to get back I will be good to you and love you all time for ever more.

I got a letter from mother today (This was the one I previously included.) she sent me a letter from Robert. I will write in here the things he said.

"I am still in France and have been in combat or I should say fixing to go in to action. I have only had trouble with a few snipers and plenty of shells bursting around, one which burst over my head. I cant see but one thing that saved me from getting hurt or maby killed and that were God so I give God this credit for saving me that time (Sadly, Robert was killed in action almost identically the same way two weeks later.). So tell every one to pray for us Love Robert."

So dont forgit to pray for this war to soon be over. Robert is in a bad place. I just hope and pray that God will spare his life and that he will come back safe and sound, and all the rest of the boys.

Sweet I look at your picture every day tears come in my eyes thinking about all the good times we could be having but sweet we will do all we can to make up for lost time when I come home. I just cant hardly wait for that day to come when we can have us a home to ourselves again and let the springs rattle if they wont not. Wont it be sweet darling?

I am proud Mr. Banks thinks I am a pretty nice boy. I think he is OK. tell him I said not to flirt with my wife to much while I am gone. Well I dont worry that part sweet, the men know who to full with if they dont they will soon find out when they try you. That the way I like you to be sweet darling. I am proud that you think of me all time I do you to sweet. I love you always and will be true. Love James

(Dad answers Roger's letter here at the end of his letter to mother.)

Roger I got your letter it was sweet of you to write me. I think of you all time. I hope to be back with you some day and help your mother to bring you up to be a man some day, but not in the army I hope. You take care of mother for me, and keep being a good boy, By Roger

Be Sweet darling wife and be good

I love you only

The previous letter was a long letter from dad that covered a lot of bases from giving details about his training to updating news about his brother Robert to letting mother know that he expected her undivided sexual attention when he returned home. To cap it off he included a response to one of Roger's "scribble" letters added at the end.

The next letter was equally as long and dad was expressing suspicions that someone in Hamilton, Alabama was tampering with their mail – the mail was taking too long to get to them, and dad thought that someone was opening their mail and reading it and being nosy about what they were writing each other. I cannot help but surmise what my dad would think about me reading and copying all the letters they wrote to each other. Seventy-five years have passed but I doubt that his attitude about having someone reading their private letters would have changed. I defend my decision to publish their letters in this way. I believe the larger good of having their letters shared with us today will far outweigh any objections that he or my mother would have had. Besides, I have always made up my own mind about what directions I choose to take with my life. I have also to believe that my mother would not have saved all these letters for so many years if she had not expected her son to find them and save them for posterity. She would have destroyed them if she had wanted them kept secret. Having established my premise, I will continue with the recording of the rest of my parent's letters.

This letter was dated Sunday afternoon July 16. 1944 and postmarked July 17, 3 pm,1944:

Hy little sweet girl,

Just a few lines from your true love one. I had some of these watermelon pactch pictures made. I know I dont look that bad. I gave fifty cents for these three sory pictures, but dont take it to heart that I look harly that bad. Sweet I got the testermint (Bible testament) it sure is nice thinks a million but one thing I dident get was a letter maby I will get two tomorrow, but I had rather get one to day and one tomorrow. I cant understand if you write every day why I dont git a letter every day. Something rong somewhere that makes twice this week I havent got my mail, you wrote that you had wrote every day sinc I been down here.

I got two letters one day but that was before I missed a day getting one. Some one must be feeling (fooling) with your mail. I have wrote you every day and some time twice, and twice Sunday – have you been getting them if you havent write me. I would like to catch someone messing with my mail (Forgive me dad, but I am messing with your mail

57

big time!). I think some of them Hamilton people would like to read our mail, so if you havent got from one to two letters a day for the last two weeks somebody else have been getting our mail, you wrote me that you had wrote every day but if you have I dident get two of them, sweet dont think I am mad about the mail. I dont wont any one reading my mail but you (Sorry about that dad.). You know if you have wrote every day something is rong some where. You know how some of them people is they git your mail then say I am so sorry I broke your mail through a mistake. I will brake some body neck (Please don't break my neck dad!) through mistake to if they start something like that, because I like to git my mail when you write it.

Sweet I mean it is hot down here to day but we haft to sleep under a sheet and a blanket at night, it beats me such weather but one thing I cant figure out I am gaining in weight. I guss I will loose before it is all over with They feed us pretty good such as it is. The cooks not so good. I wish I was in the kitchen. I believe I could beat what they do. not but one thing that they have that I wont and that is a discharge. I sure would think (thank) them for one thing and that will be when they tell me you are free again. I would be a happy soldier because I would know That I would soon be back with my sweet darling and loving wife. Some times I think I would go over the hill, but that would never do. I am no better than any one else, but I think I have the best and sweetest darling wife that ever lived in this world, if there is a better girl in the world then you, I sure would like to see her. She would haft to be an angle (angel). So there not one on earth better thin you are sweet heart I woulden give you for them all sweet. I wont to see you so bad dealing, you little sweet lump of sugar.

I could write all day then coulden tell you what I wanted to. I like the real thing dont you sweet I would give any thing if I was in Hamilton with my darling wife. I havent ever saw a place I liked better then I do Hamilton thats the place I got you sweet. I will never forgit them good old days when we layed around on that grass and your sweet little head in my lap, you know we stay by our selves, dident like for anyone full (fool) around did we sweet? When I come back from this awful war we are going to have them sweet day over and keep them that way from then on. I mean that to sweet heart. Sweet dont laugh I will tell you something they have give me so much salt peter tell I will never be no more good, dont take that to heart sweet they give that to keep the bad boys down – they dont need to give me anything like that. I dont wont any dealing with any body but you sweet. I could never git enough dealing with you sweet darling. I love you and you only sweet heart.

I would give anything to be with you this afternoon – I would love you plenty. I feel just like having a good time with you darling, sweet dont laugh at my picture that the best I can do but later own I am going to have one made with my winter suit and buy me a cap.

I like their pictures like Conway had (Carr Conway was mother's friend's husband.). Sweet I have to go through the gas chamber Tuesday July 18th it all is bad but I think I can git through OK. I just hope and pray that I live to git back with you sweet I love you darling.

Tell your mother I havent forgot what I said about wishing I was in Toyko. I dident mean that. I thought I was having a bad time at Dupont but I had a good job. I would give anything to work shift wars for Dupont again.

Be a sweet girl and true. I will. Don't wory darling, tell Roger I said hello and be good to his mother.

By sweet I Love you James

Mother at this time was not getting letters every day from dad either and there was not an explanation other than they were being held up someplace. Her next letter though reports that she has received three letters from him in one day. She said when she got his letters, they were always three of four days old, so the postal service was holding them back for some reason I suppose.

The following letter from her was a long letter and was dated Hamilton, Alabama, July 17, 1944 and postmarked July 18, 4 pm, 1944.

Dearest James,

Well I'll try to answer your letters as I got three today. I had begun to think I wasn't going to get anymore for awhile. They must lay over in the post office or somewhere. because they are always from three to four days old when I get them. But I enjoy reading them anyway.

I'm sorry that you are having risins. I am too. I have been to the doctor, but he doesn't know anymore about to do about them Than I do. I hope you can have something done for yours.

I am so tired of this place I could die. I don't think I have ever wanted to get away from it so bad in my life.

I have tried and tried to get a job, but there isn't anything doing here at all. Mr. Carpenter said he wanted me to type, but he hasn't called for me yet.

I would give anything if we could be back in "Dear Old Childersburg" again. We did have fun there.

Where you are couldn't be any worse than it is here. It never rains to cool things off and it is so hot, that we could die.

I'll be glad to come to see you just as soon as you can get things arranged, only I wish I could stay when I get there. Isn't there a house anywhere near where you stay? I get so lonesome here. I'm sure that the Army will let you go hunt for one.

I wish this war would get over sometime, so you could get out of the Infantry and we could live where we want to.

You know I don't want to collect your insurance. I had much rather have you than anything in the world and you know that don't you dear?

Have you learned much in school? I'm sorry for you about taking so many shots because they aren't any fun, I'm sure.

I'm proud they didn't get all your hair. I really would like to see you. I bet I wouldn't know you with your hair cut short. Do you suppose? Yes I'm sure I would if I were to see you.

I'm glad you got the pictures O.K. & liked them. They weren't very good as they were just cheap pictures. I want one of yours just as soon as you can have some made.

I'll try to make you some candy sometime but I doubt if it would be fit to send after I made it ha! What kind do you want? I'll get my cook book out and look up a good recipe.

We made some ice cream today. It really was good. I just wish you could have been here to have helped us eat it.

If you can find any chewing gum send it to Roger as he talks about you sending him some all the time.

I got a letter from your mother today. She said she heard from Robert and he was doing alright. She says they are having plenty of rain there. She wrote Roger that the car certainly did look lonesome down there.

I wish we could get the power. I was afraid that they would drop it & not do anything about it. If I could use the iron, radio & refrigerator I would feel much better.

I'm going to be looking forward to seeing you soon. Get us a place to stay a few days anyway and maybe you can get us a room later.

I hope you don't get too worried about this letter. I just get so aggravated because I can't get a job. I had rather be with you anyhow. I'm looking forward to the good time you are going to show me when you come back.

I wish you could come back to stay & never have to leave us again.

I love you with all my heart.

I'll stop now, so write again soon.

Your own Elizabeth & Roger

Mamma said she wished you were here to get me up. That she thought that was the only thing that was wrong with me. I just miss you.

I love the letters from mother and dad that are longer and more detailed with more feeling expressed. Mother's letter that I just included really gets into her feelings of isolation and loneliness that she was experiencing because of dad's absence. I was surprised to read how she was tired of Hamilton and wanted so much to leave it because all of my life she had nothing but praise for Hamilton and always wanted to return to it. Times of war can certainly change a person's mindset as was evidenced by her letter. Dad's letters were often long and detailed as well. The Army would not allow him to write all about the details of his training and if he did the censors would cut those parts of his letters out. He did manage to get by them at times as is evidenced by his next letter to mother.

There were some good details about his army life in this letter dated July 17, 1944 and postmarked July 18, 11:30 am, 1944:

Dearest Darling Wife.

I will try and answer your two letters sure was proud to hear from you all. glad your rising are well, all of mine are well but one on my hip I mean it sure have hurt me to, I had to take another shoot (shot) today I mean it is killing my sol. we went on a hike today about six miles about stoping. I saw boy all along the road got to hot and fell out. we had one boy I tell you the truth I never saw nothing like it he had some kind of a fit, got to hot, it took five boys to hold him he was fighting jaking (shaking) all over and chewed his tung into a mush. I dont know where I can stand all of this or not, it gets me some of the boys around crying their legs – feet – and everything els heurting but still they wont do nothing for them. they go the doctor and you know what he tell them to git the hell out not anything rong with you. nobody knows what we are going through with but the boys that are in the Infantry. I never dreamed that they treated the boys so bad. I tell you I liked to have went down today. I get so hot I coulden see, you cant eaven rase your hand to wipe the swit out of your face you haft to walk straight. The swit even run down in my mouth and eyes and that salt burned my eyes so I coulden keep them open. you see if they catch you moving your hand any way you shoulden they make you work at night, and I mean work to. I sure did have a close place last Saturday one of the boys was throwing his bayonitt and it sliped out of his hand and just as he throwed I stuped over to fix some of my thing I guss, are something just told me to stup and that thing stuck up in the ground if I had been standing it would have been to bad for me the Sgt. Gave him a good talk, but the boy coulden help it.

Sweet I sure do hope I make it OK, and dont git sick and nothing happen to me. I wish some people had to go through what we do, then they would have more fillings (feelings) for the soldiers. tomorrow be a bad day we will go through the gas chamer I sure hope my gas mask dont let me down we been testing them all last week getting ready for tomorrow, so wish me good luck sweet, I will come through OK I think.

Darling you was asking about the plum tree and other things sweet I will never forgit all them good times we had. I am thinking about having some more good times to when I come home, what about you sweet heart? I love you with all my heart sweet darling, dont wory about the bank account it will be OK. spend what you wont to get anything you wont sweet heart, say did you get the Insurance paper and war bond paper I sent when I was at Fort McPherson I still have my papers, I think I will keep them for a while and see if I can do any thing. I know I wont git cook till I git my training over with, then I might not git it. All they wont is men for the Infantry now, I sure will be proud when this war is over sweet. I know you will be to and every body else. I think the war with Germany will be over this year, but the japs us boys training now will finish that part up, that's what we are training for, and if we live through the training we will know how it is done to, Sweet the testermint was OK just the size I wanted tell your mother I will keep it and remember who give it to me, and try to git some good out of it. Sweet you have a darling mother. I think the world of her, any thing me and you wanted to do it was OK with her Of course we dident ever do any thing rong and never will. Sweet I guss you have got my pictures by now dont git frighten and have a heart attack. Sweet I cant half write this – boys make so much noise I cant think about nothing maby you can make out what it is, I sure would like to see you sweet darling = those two letters was sweet, you said your letters was buisness letter they all are sweet I like them so dont wory about that be sweet and write all them buisness letters you want to I like them I know you love me. I know one thing I sure love my sweet little darling wife and boy. by sweet I love you with all my heart – your true love one, James

The letters have a nice flow to them, and I have tried to keep them organized so that the one answers the other. This letter from mother to dad is in answer to ones that he has written to her and I believe you will see that she was responding to his comments and inquiries. Her letter was dated Hamilton, Alabama, July 18, 1944, and postmarked July 19, 9:30 am, 1944:

Hello Sweetheart,

I was very glad to get your letter this morning. Sorry that you aren't feeling good. We are O.K. just lonesome as usual.

I would feel perfect if you were here with me. I really wish you could have been here while Arthur is with us. He really does like the Navy, he says they aren't hard on them at all.

I was sorry to hear that Robert is now in combat. I just hope that he can get through it without being hurt or killed.

I want you to be very cautious and take care of yourself while training. I couldn't stand it if anything were to happen to you. How much longer will you have to take such hard training? I hope you can get something easier soon.

If you will come home soon, I won't even think of working. Don't worry about that because I would be glad to see you.

Don't worry about the things you said to me in Childersburg, that has already been forgotten a long time ago. You weren't bad anyway.

We just had a few short words that didn't amount to anything at all. If we could be together now we wouldn't think of getting mad at each other now, would we sweet?

I will be so glad when we can be together again and even prouder when we can stay together always. It would be fun to have a house all to ourselves again wouldn't it? We could really have a time if we were together again.

Don't worry about me flirting with anyone you know I don't care anything about anyone except you.

I hope it won't be too long before you find a place for us. I get so tired of staying around here, when I would be much happier there with you.

Roger was so tickled over his letter. He will write you later, he is playing now.

Arthur will leave tomorrow, and we are really going to be lonesome. Iva will be here for a few days though.

I don't know when I'll get to work. I could pass the time off much better if I could work.

I got some pretty blue linen like material & some white poplin to make me some pleated skirts. I think they will be pretty. I am getting a few things to wear when I come to see you. so you just might as well be ready for me as I might show up at any time ha!

I am going to have Mammy to make them for me when she can. She is making Iva's wedding dress now. It really is pretty. Gerry already has an apartment ready furnished to go into. Iva can hardly wait to get there. I know she will enjoy being with him.

I'll sign off for now so write soon. Love always, Eliz & Roger

P.S. I hope you can read this. I'm trying to scratch with a pen stick and scratching is about all, as it is practically worn out.

Camp Blanding was about seven miles from Starke, Florida which was a town about the size of Hamilton, Alabama or maybe somewhat larger. Dad did his best when he got his first pass after three weeks training to go there and find a place for mother and Roger to stay. It was challenging because there was limited housing available and the soldiers at Blanding had already rented everything available for their wives. Dad was determined though, and he finally came up with a room in a house behind the bus station in Starke. The following letters will reveal how that story unfolded.

This letter from dad to mother was dated July 18, 1944 and postmarked July 19, 11:30 am, 1944:

Dear Sweetheart,

I will try and answer your letter sure was proud to hear from you all glad you are well for myself I am still able to go think (thank) god. they brought a truck load of boys in today fill (fall) out. sweet if I fall out they will haft to knock me out with a brick you know I am tuff but not in the army. Sweet I cant see why you dont git a letter every day I write from to three every day I wrote you three Sunday if you havent got them by the time you git this letter write me I will find out whats rong I have a good ida (idea). I went through the gas chamer today

67

my gas mask worked find, sweet you must be pulling for me, I hope so, I love you sweetheart, always be true and think of you all time darling. I hope you git my letters and I will write you every day where you git it are not, I got to go on guard duty tomorrow night and work all day tomorrow and the next day to. sweetheart I sure do miss being with you, darling I would give anything to be back with you again. we could have some good times togather if I was there now. I would be a month to late. I have been gone a month and it seems like two years to me sweet. I know you git lonesome staying around there and me not there, I could cheer you up if I was there and I would be a happy boy to if I was there with you we could have a sweet time coulden we sweetheart? Roger I got your letter it was sweet. I dont forgit to tell you goodnight if I am not there. I tell mother goodnigh and give her a big kiss every night because I love you both. dont worry I will be back with you both some day so you be good and dont forgit I am thinking of you all time.

Sweetheart be a good and true wife. I will make up for it all when I come home the camp is about seven miles from a little town they call Stark. I am going and see if I can git a place for you to stay if I can I dont have much hope getting a place. Some of the boys have been here a long time and they havent got a place yet. Sweet you know I will do all I can to get you a place dont you darling? I wont you down here just as bad as you wont to come, dont ever think I dont wont you with me darling. Sweet be good. I will.

Love to my darling wife and boy always – your true love only James

Kiss xxxxxxxxxxxxx--------------------

Dad's letters finally did get to mother but often they came three or four at a time. It seems the post office may have been holding them and sending them all at once. There does not seem to be any other explanation and I don't think mother's neighbors in Hamilton were getting them and opening them "by mistake".

This next letter from mother finds her having received three of dad's letters on the same day. It was dated Hamilton, Alabama, July 19, 1944, and postmarked July 20, 9:30 am. 1944:

Hello Sweet,

I received three letters from you today. I'm always so proud to get letters from you and I really am thrilled when I get several at once. It gives me more to read and think about.

You said you weren't getting my letters regularly. I suppose that is due to the fact they lay over someplace longer than they should. I don't know where it might be though. I write you every afternoon and I know you should get one every day, I don't know what I would do if I didn't.

I always want to know how you are making out in everything as you are my main interest. I hate to think of you having such a bad time. I would give anything if I could share your hardships with you, but I suppose I can't.

All I can do is to think about you and be true to you, as I will always be of course.

I love you more than anything on earth and I know you feel the same about me. I just hope & pray that you will get through the whole thing O.K. and soon be back with us to stay.

I know the Infantry is hard, but I want you to do the best you can in everything you do, and more than anything else I want you to be very careful. Because you have a wife & boy back here that wants you to be back with them.

I'm glad you got the testament O,K, and that you liked it.

It makes me feel good to think that your mind is on God instead of doing like some of boys. I knew you would be good anyway as you have never been any other way.

Thanks for the pictures. Roger just jumped up & down and said that's "my daddy", mother. He really was proud of his picture, he carried it around all day. I'm proud of mine too.

I think the one with your cap off looks the most like you it is the best. I'm glad they didn't get all your hair like they did most of the boys.

Arthur & Harrison's hair was real short. Mamma said she thought your pictures looked pleasing.

Say! I'm glad you're getting the salt petre ha! I won't have to worry about you doing anything bad will I sugar? No I never worry about you doing things like that. Just remember I am waiting for you and will be waiting for you only always.

I wish you were here to sleep with me tonight. I really would like to sleep close to you again. It would be lots of fun.

I hope you got through the gas chamber O.K.

I got a letter from Alma today – they were O.K.

Arthur went back to camp this afternoon & we really miss him.

Mammy made me a white pleated skirt, it really is pretty.

I hope I can come to see you soon.

Yours only, Eliz & Roger

P,S. Sweet, you know the Mr. Dyer that owned the house that Qwaits & Walls lived in don't you? Well, his boy was thought to have been missing in action in 1941. He was a prisoner of the Japs for awhile, then he got away and lived in the jungle the rest of the time. He came back home yesterday. They were so surprised and happy that they shouted & cut up. His daddy died last year thinking he was missing. I'm proud for his mother & all and for him too, I know he was happy to see Hamilton after what he had gone through with.

Mother's very next letter also comes in response to the letters dad had written to her as you will see. She is answering his questions and responding to his comments. This letter was dated Hamilton, Alabama, July 20, 1944, and postmarked July 21, 9:30 am, 1944:

Hello Sweetheart,

Well it finally rained this afternoon and everyone was proud to see it, as it has been so hot and dry.

How are you doing now? I hope you are still standing the training – I'm glad that you are strong enough to take it. I am sorry to think of you having to do such things, but I'm glad that you haven't fell out or gotten hurt anyway. I just hope you continue to go through everything O.K.

It really scares me to think of how close the bayonet got to you. I'm just thankful that it didn't hit you. Sweet, please be careful as I don't want anything to happen to you. I don't think I could even stand to think of such a thing happening to you.

Have you gone through the gas chamber yet? and how did you make out? I hope it didn't harm you in any way.

I wish you could be here this afternoon. we would really have a good time. I really would like to come and stay with you. I am getting mesome clothes to wear, so if I get to see you I will look pretty ha! Imagine me looking pretty. Mammy made me a white pleated skirt and Iva got me a pink sheer blouse in B'ham. It really looks pretty together/ I also have some blue material for a skirt.

You asked about the War Bond & Insurance papers. Yes, I have them, I'm keeping them for you. I just hope they won't ever have to be used.

Try real hard to get cook. It would be so much safer & easier on you too.

You are mistaken in who got the testament for you. It was Mammy instead of Momma. She already had this one and said I could send it to you.

I got your pictures and didn't have a heart attack. I think they are sweet.

Roger wrote you too, he said for you to come home & take him to the show in the car. He also said tell you his Aunt Iva is here and he is following her around afraid that she will go off & leave him.

Have you gotten the letter from me that said I was disgusted with this place? I was just going on. It would be O.K. if you were here with me, or if I was with you. It is so lonesome.

I'll stop for now, so be good & write me often. I love you only.

Your Wife & Son Eliz & Roger

I'll make the candy when I get a good recipe.

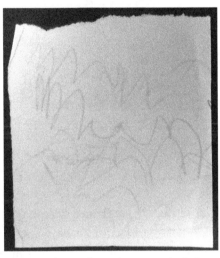

There was a letter from Roger included in this
letter. I have inserted a scan of it here.

At this point I will include another letter to dad from my Uncle Harrison Palmer, my mother's oldest brother. By this time, he and his wife, my Aunt Margaret, had been stationed at Maxwell Field, in Montgomery, Alabama where I live the present day. The letter was dated July 23, 1944, and postmarked July 24, 11 am, 1944:

Uncle Harry in his Army Air Corp uniform

Dear James,

We finally got settled. I'm stationed here in Montgomery now at Maxwell Field of course, we wanted to get to Birmingham Air Base but we can count ourselves fortunate, extremely so, to get even this near home.

After we left Hamilton, we went to Atlanta – stayed there a few hours and left the same day for Tampa, Florida where we spent one week before I was sent here. I'm hoping I'll get to spend quite a spell of time in Alabama now that I'm here.

My work is quite pleasant at Maxwell. I am assistant officer in charge of A,A.C.S. (Army Airways Communications System) facilities here on the field. It is much the same work I have done for the past 3 years. A.A.C.S. is the organization in the Air Forces which has charge of the radio communications such as the control tower, the teletype communications, telegraph communications, and radio range facilities.

We had an awfully hard time ever finding a place to live here. We hunted and hunted and finally the best we could do was to rent a room in a private home with a family here in the city. Of course it isn't like having your own place but it isn't too bad. The people are very nice and let us use their kitchen refrigerator, etc. We hope eventually to find us a furnished apartment.

James, I hope you like the kit I sent. Liz gave me some money when I left and I got the very best one I could find in Birmingham. I liked it very much myself.

Please let me know if you liked it or not. Also let us know how the Army is treating you now. Do you like it any better than you did? Do you think you are going to get cook?

Write us all about yourself because we are always very interested in knowing how you are getting along.

We hope everything works out for the best and shall be eagerly awaiting your letter.

Lots of Love Harry. Margaret & Coralie

There were hardly any families that were not touched by the war. The entire country was mobilized, and everyone was unified to work together to defeat Germany and Japan and to regain the lives they had before. No one realizes how good things are until they are taken away and that is how all the soldiers and their families felt. They did not want to be in this war, and they prayed every day for it to end but they all were willing to make the necessary sacrifices in order to win the war and make the country and the world a better place to live in for themselves, their families and their children. In my mother's family two of her brothers were in the service. Harrison was in the Army Air Corp and Joseph Arthur was in the Navy. In my dad's family there were three brothers in the service, including my dad. Robert was in the Army Infantry and was killed in action July 31, 1944.

Curtis was in the Army Air Corp and was stationed in England in an MP unit. My dad was in the Army Infantry and was almost killed in action December 30. 1944 in Bastogne, Belgium at the Battle of the Bulge. My mother's best friend, Johnnie Conway's husband Carr Conway, was in the Army Air Forces and was captured and put into a German P.O.W. camp during the war. Mother's sister's husband, Gerald Gamel, was in the Navy as well. Those too old to fight worked in the factories making weapons, aircraft and other military supplies to use in the war effort. Citizens had to live with rationing of food, gasoline and other necessities in order to supply the troops with what they needed to win.

I made mention of Johnnie Conway's husband, Carr Conway, who was captured and spent the war in a German P.O.W. camp. I will include this letter from mother's best friend Johnnie that was written July 28, 1944, Friday P.M. This letter reveals that Carr is alive and healthy and has been informed of the birth of his first child Carr Jr.:

Dear Eliz & Roger

How's tricks with you kids? We are sorta (I don't understand what she means there.) I enjoyed your letter so much. I can imagine from my own experience the time Iva is having. I'm glad for her. I'd like to have seen her wedding things. Remember Eliz when you and I married? It was heaps of fun. I suppose you gave Iva some pointers (on not) having a baby. She is so young.

Carr Jr. is fine. He is cutting his seventh tooth.

OK before I forget I've heard from Carr. Aprils the latest being 29th. In it he just heard about Jr. I mean he seemed to be almost jumping up & down. He said he imagined that he was the happiest man in the world. I'd liked for you to read the letter. It was so sweet and thoughtful. I don't guess I can hardly imagine how he felt those 4 months wondering if I lived and if baby did. Thank God he's heard finally.

Eliz don't worry about James just keep on hoping & praying for all. It's all tough – infantry – all of it – Air Corp, Navy, Marines – hope you can soon be with James again. Maybe it won't be long before the war'll be over. Can you imagine how glad we'll be when they come home. I've thought so much how it'd be – when Carr sees Jr. May God bless us all. Do write often.

Lots & Lots of Love yours, Johnnie Conway & Jr.

If my Uncle Harrison had questions about how my dad's opinion of the army had or had not changed, he should have read this letter from dad to mother. I think the way dad felt was shared by most of those boys that had been drafted into the service. This letter was dated July 20, 1944, and postmarked July 21, 3pm, 1944:

Hello sweetheart and Roger,

I will try and write you a few lines hope you all are well and having a good time. for myself I dont look for any good time in this place. Just work like a mule all day and night, we just come in for supper and got to go back out in a little while for the night. I mean I feel bad to be up all night last night and been on the go all day and got to go back out for the night, so I wont git any sleep till tomorrow night that is if we dont go out again, sweet they liked to have got me today hot and no rane (rain) sweet you are in a cool place I have been sweet (sweat) all day sweat run off in streams. I have never seen nothing like this. Sweet if I live through this training you can call me a man, and every one else that is in the Infantry. I sure would like to come home for a few days, but there not a chanch I know I sure will be glad when I get through training then I will get a ten day leave, Sweet I havent got a letter today but we will have another mail call in a little while. So I though I would write while I had time, they just had mail call. I got your letter it was sweet. I am sorry that you are having such a bad time. I wish I could be there with you sweet heart. you know we are in a war and we cant do every thing we want to. I would have done had you down here if I had my way about things but this is the army and they dont care for any body but you haft to look at it two ways if they had to build houses for all the married men they would have more women thin men, so there not a big town here close by, and all the rooms you know they only have 75,000 men here and they was here before I come so they have all the rooms, but if I can git a pass by all means I will do my best to git a room sweetheart. You know I want you to come darling. I would give any thing if you was here with me right now and I could squize you good and tight and git a big kiss which I sure have been missing. Sweetheart darling I hope everything works out OK and we can soon be togather again. Darling I could write more but I got to go, I will send Roger sum gum if I can git any. By darling

I love you with all my heart, James

Mother was keeping up with all dad's letters to her and answering them back just as soon as she received them. I am including as many of her letters as I think are necessary in order to keep the flow going between them. One must realize though that it was often two or three days or more until dad received her responses and that must have been a very trying time for him. I suppose it balanced out somewhat though when he finally did receive her letters and was reassured of her love and support.

This letter from mother was dated July 21, 1944 and postmarked July 22, 9:30 am, 1944:

Hello Sweet,

I got your letter today, and was very glad to hear you got through the gas chamber O.K. You said I must be pulling for you.

You know I am don't you sugar? I have really been thinking and worrying a lot over the things you have to go through with.

I'm just thankful that you have held out this far and hope & pray that you continue to do so. I don't want anything bad to ever happen to you, as I love you so much and simply couldn't live without you.

I hear from you every day now, sometimes three letters a day, and I really enjoy reading them as it makes me feel almost like seeing you. Although I had much rather see you if it were possible.

I hope you made it O.K. on Guard Duty.

Roger is really proud of his picture, he carries it around all the time. He tells me that he wants to go to the Army to see his daddy. He was tickled to hear that you tell him goodnight every night.

He never goes to sleep without saying his prayers and he has added to his prayer "Bless my daddy". He also tells you good night too.

I am glad you are not so far from town. I really hope you can find us a place to stay, as we would be thrilled to death to get to come.

I'm going with Iva to Birmingham tomorrow. She wants me to bring some things here for her, as she is going to Gerry Monday/

I got a letter from Johnnie today. She hasn't heard from Carr in seven or eight weeks. I hope he is still O.K.

Have you heard from Robert any more?

I'll stop now, so bye & be sweet.

I love you Eliz & Roger

This next letter from mother is practically a continuation of the previous one, so I will include it as well. It was written the next day and was dated Hamilton, Alabama, July 22, 1944 with a postmark of July 24, 9:30 am, 1944:

Hello Sweetheart,

Well, I have just gotten back from Birmingham. I made a round trip today, there and back. Iva wanted me to go back with her to get some of her things to ship to her later. Mrs, Gamel (Gerry's mother) is sending her a trunk here to pack them in. So I had to bring them back so that I could pack them in the trunk & send them to her.

She is leaving for Oklahoma City Monday afternoon at 1:00 pm.

I got Roger the cutest pair of pants, medium blue with gallouses (suspenders). Iva got him a small pair of sunglasses, he says he is going to wear them when he comes to see you. He really was tickled to see me come back tonight.

How did you make out, staying in the woods? I hope you won't catch cold from doing such things. I wish they would get through giving you so much of that awful training.

I think of you all the time. It worries me to know what you have to go through with. I'll be glad when the day comes that you can come back to me to stay, and I will be real good & sweet to you to make up for all the cruel things you have gone through with. I'll be true to you always & trust that you will too. I love you too much to do any other way.

I really would be proud if you were here to sleep with me tonight. The nights wouldn't seem so long for me, if I had you back to love, etc. ha!

We really have had some good times together, and I hope we can soon be together always.

I want to come to see you so bad. I'll be ready just any time you want me.

The War Dept. sent me some blanks to keep & fill out in case I change my address sometime.

I got a letter from Mrs, Carrel (a close friend from Childersburg, Alabama) also. They are O.K. She says practically everyone in Childersburg has mumps.

Have you heard from the slip I sent to Dupont for your bonus? I sent it to them just as soon as I got it from you.

Do you want me to send you some ink?

I suppose you think I have told you a story about making the candy for you. I'm going to just as soon as I can get more time. I want to have plenty of time so that it will turn out O.K.

You asked me about your letters. I hear from you every day. Do you get a letter from me every day? You should, as I write you every night.

I had better stop & go to bed as I am very tired & sleepy.

So bye & be good.

I love you only Liz & Roger

Dad had finally gotten his first pass and has gone into Starke, Florida, the small town not far from Camp Blanding, to look for a room for mother and Roger to stay in. He was determined to find something even though the other soldiers had told him the situation was bleak and that all the rooms had already been taken by other soldiers for their wives. However, dad was lucky, and he did manage to find a room for mother in a house, but the owners did not allow children to stay there. You will see what mother's reaction was to this news as you read the next few letters from her to dad.

This next letter is one from dad in which he informs mother that he thinks he has found a room for her. It was dated Saturday night, July 23, 1944, and postmarked July 24, 1944:

Hello Sweetheart Darling Wife,

I will try and write you a few lines, hope you are well and feeling fine, for myself I am OK but sure do git homesick sometime. I git a week in pass and went to Stark, the little town I was telling you about. It is a pretty nice little town. I looked everywhere for a room but dident have much luck. I think I have you a place. I dont know yet. The lady said she would drop me a card next week and let me know. it dont look good but you can make out with it I think. I found another place but they dont want any children and just have a place to sleep. I dont think I will git another place any where, so if I dont git that one, I will keep trying to git you some kind of place, you know the girl that you said was cute in the bus station the day I left, her husband is here with me, he went to Stark with me, if he dont find another place, his wife will come and stay in part of the house that is if we get it.

(I have a photo of this couple that
I have included a scan of here.)

I sure hope that we will git it. I would give any thing if you was here close by where I could see you ever once in a while. It would be sweet if you was down here we could have some fun. So I will keep trying to git a place. be sweet and good till I see you sweetheart.

By darling I will go to bed and try to git some rest.

Love always James

Dad was lucky and was able to get a room in another house and he is all set to have mother to come down but the catch is she will have to come soon and without Roger, as the people that have the house won't allow children. Here is another letter from dad dated Sunday afternoon, July 23, 1944:

Hello Sweetheart,

Just a few lines I am in the little town of Stark. I found you a room pretty nice, but one thing to bad they dont wont any kids, this is the only place I can git I mean it is plenty high but I will give anything to be with you a little while every week, all you haft to do is step out of the door and catch the bus to camp, you can come out to see me every evening that I dont haft to work at least. Write a check and cash it at Hamilton. Come on the bus leave where you will git here in the daytime. Come to Stark, Fla, Bus station which is in Stark, Florida. ask where it is, it is the bus station where you catch the bus to camp. The room I have is right behind the Florida Center bus station first house, Weller St. #205-71, phone # 56 J it is five or six blocks from the main bus station where you will git off the bus when you git here have some one to call 56 J and tell the girl where you are and she will come and meet you if you cant find it easy. I cant meet you as I would like to, so find this house and the girl will show you around and how to git out to camp and how to git me it will be a tuff trip but you can make it. When you git out of the bus here ask where Fla Center bus station is and the room is right behind the bus station. I sure would like for Roger to come but after you stay here a while you can find a room where they will let kids stay I hope, but if you dont wont to leave Roger to come write me right back and let me knownand be sure and bring that money outsid your bus fare, I will fix thing when you git here. have your mother to git a check for you and send it to you. I hop I have told you plain enough where you wont have any trouble. I would give any thing if little Roger could come. I think god will take care of him till we can git a place where he can stay.

by darling and good luck

be here by Thursday July 27 if you come

True love one James

Dad wrote still another letter to mother the same day after he returned from Starke to see about getting her a room. Everything was all set up. It all depended on mother now who had been telling dad all this time that she would do anything to see him. His letter was dated Sunday afternoon, July 23, 1944 and postmarked July 24, 11:30 am, 1944. Mother would barely have had enough time to get ready and pack and get there by July 27 on Thursday, as she would have only had a couple of days to spare, by the time she received dad's letters:

My Sweet and Roger

I will write you another letter I am back at Camp now maby I can write better. I think you will like the room OK. The girl that haves the house her husband is in camp here to, so she can show you around and the girl you said was cute (Mary Tucker) she is coming to stay in one of the rooms, I cant stand to think Roger cant come but maby we can git a place where he can stay you can look around when you git here I had to take what I could git, being I havent much time. I will haft to give $14.00 a week for the room and a place to cook you will haft to buy what you eat it is pretty nice have a bath good bed, you have a nice place to put your clothes bring you some hingers and I can git a pass next week in we will have a good time I hope. I wont to see some of the new dresses you have. Sweet I really like Starke, it is a bigger town than Hamilton, but the people sure will rob your pocket buck. we can git by I think by being close and not spend to much. I would give any thing for you to be down here. It costs 15 cents to ride the bus to Camp you can git a pass at the gate. you might not like at first but you will like better after you stay here a while. I sure hope you can come and I can git a pass next weekin. I will have a time once more. I know it will brake little Roger heart when you leave to, but if you dont want to leave him write me because I will haft to pay for the room this week to – bring at least $75.00 we sure dont want to git broke down here. you might git to stay two months. I dont know the last three weeks I stay here I will be out day and night – this might be our last time to be together any at all I might haft to go across when I leave here. I sure hope that I dont.

When you git off the bus at Stark, Fla, bus station come to the Center bus station cross town where the boys catch the bus and girls to, to come to camp the house where I got the room is right behind the station they have some white buses parked nily (nearly) in the yard at least ther was I guss it is the parking lot for the buses. You cant miss it the bus station dont have a sign up just ask someone you cant miss it and call the number I gave you in the other letter if you cant find it no other way, phone 56 J house # 205 N. Weller St (I checked this address on my GPS and it showed as 205 N. Keller St., so dad may have mistaken the name.) I will stop now darling hoping to see you Thursday afternoon if nothing happens which I hope dont.

By darling and good luck, hope to see you soon,

Kiss Roger for me your true Love one James

By now mother had received dad's letters about getting a room for her in Starke, Florida and she responded to him with the following letters. The first one was a real bombshell and after all her wishing and hoping that he would get her a room it must have come as quite a surprise to dad. The letter was dated Hamilton, Alabama, July 25, 1944, just two days before she was expected to arrive in Starke to be with dad:

Dearest James,

I got you letters today and I am very sorry that I can't come to see you. I would give anything on earth if I could, but it is impossible for me to come without Roger as he would cry his eyes out after me. He can't even stand for me to go to town without him now. He thinks I am gone not stay like you did, so he would probably go into histerics or something worse if I were to stay away from him that long.

Mother would be glad to keep him for us, but he wouldn't stay, I'm sure, because I couldn't hardly do anything with him after you left.

I wish it were possible for you to find a place for Roger & I both to stay.

I hate to think of letting the place you have for me go, but I suppose I will have to.

I didn't get your letter until today 25th. so it would be impossible for me to get ready and get there by the 27th.

I really would like to see you very much but I know Roger wants to see you too and he would never hear to my going without him.

You don't understand how Roger is now. He thinks that when anyone leaves they are gone for good. He cries every time anyone leaves.

So maybe when you have more time sometime you can find a place where Roger can stay too.

We heard from Arthur this morning and he is in a different Batt. now. He is so disgusted.

We also heard from Harrison. He is at Maxwell Field, Montgomery, Ala. Margaret & Coralie are with him. They are in an awful mess too. They had to pack up in one room with some people there.

Well, I'll stop now. I'm very sorry that I won't be able to come now, and appreciate your finding the place. I just wish I could come, but can't without Roger.

Write soon,

Love Always, Eliz & Roger

These next letters from mother to dad were written right after the previous one in which she told dad that she could not come and see him because she couldn't leave Roger behind. You will see the gradual changing of her attitude in the next group of letters. Mother never ceased to amaze me with her emotional highs and lows, and it was revealing for me to see that she was just as prone to having them when she was young as when she was older. This next letter was dated Hamilton, Alabama, July 26, 1944 and postmarked July 26, 9:30 am, 1944:

Hello Sweetheart,

I'll tell you again that I really do hate to not come to see you. It isn't because I don't want to, it is because I couldn't leave Roger. He just simply couldn't understand it (And yet mother had no such hesitation in leaving him alone later for a week when she went with her sister Iva to Illinois to visit her in-laws.) He would think that we had both just thrown him away.

He wants to see you too, and it would be wrong to leave him and go by myself. So you understand don't you sugar?

(Here she goes with the "I would give anything" again.) I would give anything if I could get on the bus and go right now. It would be perfect if we could be together again, but we would neither be satisfied without Roger, and I'm afraid he would cry his eyes out over us.

So, if you can possibly find a place where they will rent to anyone with children do so, that is when you can get time.

I understand that you have a lot to do and don't have very much time for anything.

I would love being with you again, it would be lots of fun. So please don't get sore at me as I can't come under the circumstances.

Remember I love you if we are apart, and always will.

I'll stop now, bye & be good your own Eliz & Roger

This next letter finds mother still insisting that she cannot come to see dad and desperately trying to come up with excuses to explain why. It was dated Hamilton, Alabama, July 26, 1944 and postmarked July 27, 4 pm, 1944 about the time she should have arrived in Starke, Florida had she gone:

Hi Sugar,

I wish I could be with you tomorrow. I got your letter asking for the money to pay down on the rent on the room today. I got it after the one telling me to come to see you.

It was written before the one I got yesterday. I don't see how that they got all messed up that way.

I suppose you have gotten my letter telling you why I can't come. But we have Roger and he has to be looked after.

Of course, mother would be glad to to keep him, but he would never stay without giving her trouble worrying about us.

The first thing he asks every morning is "where is mother"?

So, if he were to wake up some morning and find me gone, he might get started crying and they couldn't do anything with him.

He worried over you being gone for the first two weeks, and he still asks about you.

I have always been with him and never left him at all. He just wouldn't know what to think if I left him now.

I'm sure there must be some place you can rent where children are allowed, other people take their children, besides we only have Roger and he won't be any trouble.

I can make the trip O.K. with him. I'm not worried about that. He is a big boy now.

Isn't $14.00 a week more than we could ever dream of paying for rent. That would be $56.00 per month, besides groceries, etc. and I only get $80.00.

The next time you get off, look again for a place. I'm sure there must be places where children can stay too.

I really do want to come and be with you all I can, but we have to consider Roger's feelings too. He wants to see you too.

Thanks a lot for the cushion cover. It is very pretty. I made me a cushion for it this afternoon. It looks very pretty on the couch.

(I have included a photo of the pillow here.)

Does the girl who is going to get one of the rooms have any children? I bet she doesn't though as they look so young to have been married very long, I was afraid that things would turn out this way as we have a child. People told me all the time that you couldn't get a place if you had a child.

I really do hate to disappoint you by not being there tomorrow afternoon the 27th. But it seems that it is going to be that way.

I didn't get your letter until yesterday if I could have gone it would have been impossible to have gotten there Thursday, as I wouldn't have had time to get my things together and get the bus there by that time.

I'm still looking forward to getting to come later anyway. I'm sending you $10.00, so that you can pay down on a room in case you find one.

Mamma said tell you she was losing her last daughter about now. Iva is getting married right now if nothing has happened.

I got a letter from your mother they were O.K. She said she heard from Robert last week & he was O.K. (Robert was killed in action five days from the date of this letter.).

Well, sweet please don't be mad at me, for I still love you hear!

I'll be glad when we can be together again.

We love you, Eliz & Roger

With this fourth letter we find that mother has reversed direction 180 degrees from her previous responses to dad's request for her to come to Florida. I know a woman has the prerogative to change her mind, but mother seemed to turn on a dime in this case. I believe her mother and grandmother (Mammy) must have given her " good talking to". This letter was dated Hamilton, Alabama, July 28, 1944 and postmarked July 28, 9:30 am, 1944:

Hello Sweet,

I suppose you will think I am crazy after reading this letter and the others I have written to you. I have decided to come and leave Roger if you can still get the room for me.

Mamma & Mammy both say that they think they can manage him O.K.I guess he will do all right.

I couldn't have possibly been there this afternoon as you had planned, because I didn't get your letter soon enough to get ready for the trip.

So write me if it is still O.K. for me to come.

If it is I can get my things together and the money.

Maybe my check will come by the first of the month, if not I can get some money out of the bank, and mamma can send my check to me.

I hope you won't be sore at me for not coming on. I just didn't know what to do about leaving Roger, but they seem to think he will be O.K. (Mother should've remembered that her grandmother and mother raised six kids including her all by themselves,)

School starts Monday and the boys will be in school (her brothers Herbert and Horrice), so Mamma will be here by herself anyway.

Let me know if you can still get the room.

If you can, I will get information from Mr. Price at the bus station on where to and where the bus stops, changes, etc. I'm sure I can find the place O.K.

When I get there and learn my way around I suppose I can find a place for Roger and come back and get him. I hope I can, for it would break his heart for us to stay away from him very long.

It'll be lots of fun to be together again. I just hope I haven't waited too late about making my decision. I haven't have I sugar?

If you can't get the room you wrote me about try to get another one, and I'll be sure to come this time.

I sent you the money to pay down on a room this morning.
I hope you got it O.K.

Well, we got a telegram from Iva & Gerry this morning,
They were married last night. It was signed: Mr. and Mrs.
Gerald W. Gamel.

I really would like to see them now wouldn't you sweet?
I bet they are having a time up there by themselves ha!

It really is raining here now. Mother and Roger are in the
storm house as usual ha! He seems to enjoy it very much.

He told me to go and see his daddy but to come back.

I'll be so glad when I can come to see you. It would be so
nice to be together again.

I love you so much, I just didn't realize how much I would
miss you until you were gone. I just can't stay here or
anywhere else without you.

I'll stop, hoping to hear from you soon.

Love Always, Eliz & Roger

By this time dad had received mother's letter telling him that she
had decided not to come to see him. He was not at all pleased as you will
discern after reading this next letter to her. Unlike most all of his other
letters to her, this letter was hand printed as if he were truly focused on
the impact that his words would have on mother. The letter was dated July
27, 1944, the day mother was supposed to have arrived in Florida, and
postmarked July 28, 11:30 am, 1944:

Hello Sweet heart & Roger,

I will try and answer your letter was proud to hear from you but sory you coulden come. I had Everything Fixed up For a good time this afternoon but just as I was getting ready for you to come out to camp I got your letter. I sure was dispointed but I know little Roger wants to come to so I will do my best to git a place where he can stay to. I would do any thing to see you both if I can git a pass this weekin I will try again to git a place where Roger can stay to. We cant leave him out I know he wonts to come I would give anything to see him to. Sweet you know what you been douting me about. My pay from Dupont well I got a big gift yesterday $410.00. I think that was nice of them as we need some extra change dont we sweet? I will send it to you and you can have a big time this weekin if you want to I know you will. I sure was looking forward to a big time this week in with you in my arms but you fixed that up sweet by not coming. I dont know how many whippeths I will owe you when I do see you darling, I would have give any thing if you would have come and stayed this weekin I mean I would have showed you a good time but I will try to git a place by next weekin if I can but I dont think I will have any Luck. Robert and Curtis is still OK at least they was last week (Robert will be killed in action 4 days later on July 31, 1944 at St. Lo, France,). They was last week I sure hope they make it and all the rest of the boys. The news is good on the German Front. I sure hope they soon make peace are do something and git this thing over with. Sweet I havent wrote you for the last day are two because I was looking for you to come but I will make up for lost time when I have time I owe so many letters I dont know where to start. I havent answered Hubert (Herbert) letter but I will tell him I havent forgot him and to write me again if I havent answered. I owe eight letters and dont have time to write my darling wife but try to take time to do that. Did you git the little present I sent you (the Camp Blanding pillow cover) wasent much but I feel just that way Sweetheart darling (These are the words embroidered on the pillow that I attached the previous photo of: "To my Wife A Darling Little Wife Has Made My Dreams Come True She Blesses All My Life Her Name Is Only You You Are My Partner Sweet You Share In All I Do And Make My Joy Complete By Simply Being You!"). Never felt no other way. Sweet they have just about got me down here in this hot weather – but I can stand up and walk by being Real Careful. I sure will be glad when I get out of this place cant tell I might git a worse place than this when I leave, I dont see how it could be unless I go across which I will do when I leave here. You can look for that sweet, darling dont worry about me just take care of yourself and Roger. Maby I will make it some how, If I live through this training you can bet on me being a good tuff soldier. Maby I can git me a job on the WPA if I git tuff boy wont that be something?

Sweet what do you do theis long lonesome days they git longer every day dont they darling I bet you dont git lonesome do you sweet? How many boy friends do you have, you must have plenty of them you coulden eaven come to see me this weekin. Darling be careful and dont git snowed by none of them guys. I might be back some day you cant every tell I might wont you back to, so be a good little girl, hope to see you in about 15 weeks if nothing dont happen so dont worry.

Be sweet, your true love James

Tell Roger hello I will see him before long I hope

There were a few more letters written back and forth between them but dad did not receive mother's letter in which she had changed her mind and decided to come and see him until just before she actually came and then she ended up staying in the house behind the bus station for two months. The last letter I have from either of them during this time period until September 27, 1944 was this one from dad postmarked July 29, 9 pm, 1944. Dad was able to get the room he had wanted, and mother came to stay with him. Of course, there were no letters during this two-month period. Here is dad's letter from July 29, 1944:

Hello sweet

I am in Stark at this time trying to find a place but no luck at all so far. I will try again but I think we just as well call it off. Sweet I sure wish you was here this afternoon we could have some fun I know. I got a weekin pass OK. I came up here and stay a while then go back to camp. A pass dont do me any good much but if you was here I would make use of a pass. If I could see you now a weekin pass woulden be longer anough. I come up here to send you the check but the post office had closed when I got here. I will send it later.

By sweet and Roger

Your true love one James

So, we have only to assume that mother did get through to dad and he was still able to get the room that he had told her about earlier in the house behind the bus station. In fact, that is exactly what did happen. The next letter I have from dad to mother was written September 27, 1944 just after mother had returned to Hamilton, Alabama after staying with dad in Starke, Florida for about two months:

Hello Sweet heart,

I am hoping and praying that you made your trip OK and your cold are better, you find every one well and doing fine – for myself I am doing OK, except I miss you sweet to night. I know you are on your way some where while I am writing theas few lines. I hope where ever you are god will take care of you for me sweet. I love you with all my heart, and I do hope you enjoyed yourself while you was down here with me. I sure enjoyed you staying, I had a very nice time, and I hope some day I can be with you in a sweet home again where we can do like we want to and dont haft to do everything so easy. Well be sweet and tell Roger I said he is a good boy, and maby I will git to see him some day, tell your mother and them all I said hello and take care of there self, by sweetheart darling – write soon.

Love always James

Mother was responding to or perhaps was just writing to dad as she arrived back in Hamilton, Alabama with this letter. It was dated Wed. Nite Sept 27, 1944 and written on U.S.O. stationery:

Hello Sweetheart,

I got here today at Noon. I really was surprised to get here so soon. I didn't have to wait over anywhere over thirty minutes, so I suppose I was very lucky.

I had a nice trip and no trouble at all, as I sat by a girl all the way. That was quite a relief from what I sat by before.

Roger was really glad to see me. He asked me the first thing, why I didn't bring you. He said he would just have to make you get out of the Army. You ought to hear him talk. He told me today that he wanted a tomato. So I handed him one. He said I want salt on it though and handed it back to me.

He really won't let me out of his sight a minute. He says he will tie me to a tree and I can't leave him anymore.

He talks about you lots. He says he will just have to go back and find him a place so that he can see you. He is sleeping with me tonight.

I bought him a cute pair of winter shoes. Brown and two sweaters, also a pr. of corduroy overalls.

Mamma said she was glad to have me back but would like it better if you could be here too. I really would like it better too,

I miss you so much sweet. I hope you aren't too lonesome. Did you get your socks and the note?

I'll be so glad when we can be together to stay.

I wrote the girls a card. Mrs. Norris' daughter met me in Quincy. She brought me a cheese & meat sandwich. Also a bar of Hershey candy.

It really was nice of her don't you think?

How is your training? Just about like it was though I suppose. Let me know when you get ready for something to eat.

I'll stop so take care of yourself and remember I love you. Be careful,

Love Eliz & Roger

The following letters give some idea of what mother and dad did during her time at Camp Blanding with dad and also give some information about the people they met and became friends with like dad's friend Wilmark Tucker and his wife Mary who stayed in the same house as mother did behind the bus station. I rely on these letters written after mother returned home to Hamilton to fill in the gaps and give some notion of what their lives were like during those two months that mother visited dad.

The next letter from dad to mother seemed to answer mother's previous letter as he mentioned that he had received the socks she sent him and also received the note she enclosed. The letter was postmarked September 28, 11:30 am, 1944:

My Darling Wife,

Just a few lines hoping you got there OK. I sure do miss you sweet heart more than ever this is a lonesome place now. I can make it OK when you are around, where I can see you ever once in a while.

I got the socks and note OK, it was sweet of you to send the socks and note. Tucker brought the socks Tuesday night when he come in – said he sure did miss me and you beeing up at the service club. I miss going up there to see you to, sweet be sure and do something for that cold and take care of your self and Roger.

I got six bars of soap when I git six more I will send it to you. I havent been able to git any candy yet, I hope to git it by the time I send the soap. My training gits harder every day sweet I might haft to send after you to help me finish this training the way I feel tonight, darling be sweet and write me. I love you darling dont forget, I will be true to my darling wife.

By sweet I love you, James

This letter is another mother wrote just shortly after she returned from Starke, Florida. It was dated Thursday, September 28, 1944 and postmarked September 30, 9:30 am, 1944:

Hello Sugar,

Well, I'm kinda rested up over my trip now. My cold seems to be much better. I put Vicks in my nose & take some too.

Roger is thrilled to have me back. He just stays with me all the time. He really is a sweet kid. He talks so proper. I just wish you could hear him talk some. They don't have him very spoiled. He minds me good thus far. He talks about you all the time. He says he will be glad when you get out of the Army. I put his soldier cap, shirt & kaki overalls on yesterday. He really was a cute kid in them.

(I have a similar photo of Roger with that
outfit on that I will include here.)

I sent four War Bonds in this morning. I ought to get the money soon.

I had seventeen dollars left when I got home.

I got Roger some new clothes yesterday afternoon. I wish you could see them. I got him a pair of brown shoes size 8 ½ they are too large, but will be O.K. by winter. I got him two wool sweaters, one pink and one blue, also a blue pair of juvenile corduroy overalls. He has a supply for a while. I got all that for ten dollars.

Have you seen Mary since I left? (This was mother's friend who was married to Tucker. They were the couple that rented the other room in the house mother stayed in.) Did you get your socks O,K. I hope they fit.

I really do miss being with you I know you are lonesome too, but you can write me every night when you come in. And think of me too, because I think of you all the time. I would give anything if you were here with us.

We had chicken today. I wish you could have had some of it too. It really was good.

I went to get a gas ration book today.

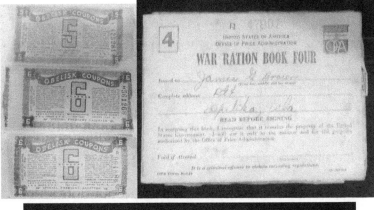

(Here are scans of a gas ration book and
food and gas ration coupons.)

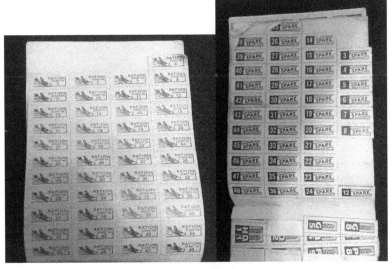

(I am including scans of some
pages of the ration books.)

She filled everything out for me except the mileage on the speedometer. I didn't know that so I'm sending for your mother to see what it is on the car and send it to me. They will give me the book then.

Roger is writing to you now. He is telling you about how proud he was to see me.

It really is raining here now.

I polished the furniture today. It really is shining now. It seemed funny to be working again after 8 weeks of rest ha!

I put my watch in the shop today to have it fixed. I hope it won't take him very long.

Take care of yourself and be good.

Go to town on weekends and don't forget to have a picture made for me.

I wish you could see Roger folding his letter he is sending to you.

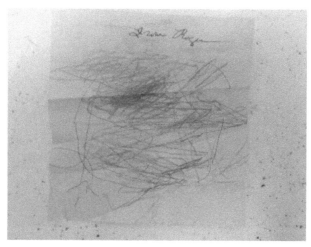

(I am including a scan of Roger's letter here.)

He took so much pains to fold it right, then he put it to his tongue like he was sealing it. When he got through, he said now that is to daddy.

I'll stop, so write me real soon,

We love you, Eliz & Roger

Dad wrote mother several letters after she went back to Hamilton, in fact he wrote every day, but it was about a week before he got a letter from her in answer. It was not because mother didn't write but because the mail delivery was slow for some reason. I will include some of dad's letters to mother. He was showing signs of fatigue and frustration because of the brutal training and loneliness from having to face it all without mother being there. Not getting any letters from her was taking a toll on him as well.

This letter from dad was dated September 29, 1944 and postmarked September 30, 11;30 am, 1944:

Hello Sweet dear Darling,

How are you today fine I hope, for myself I am OK at this time only a little tired been on another parade this afternoon the man was here this time, maby we wont haft to go on another one. I havent got a letter from anyone since you left. I hope to get one from you in a day are two. I will be worried about you till I hear from you sweet. I sure hope you made it OK, I dont like to go any where about you with me. I like your company Sweet, I dont feel right when you are not with me darling. I love you with all my heart. I would give anything to be back home with you sweet heart darling dont forgit I will love you always no matter what happen sweet.

I sure do miss you sweet so much I dont know what to do. Sweet forgive me for all the hard words I said to you

I dident mean it, sweet you know I was always tired and dident feel so good, they dont give any body any rest around this place, on the go all time, I got a letter from Mary Mayberry she dident write much. she said she had to have a operation she dident say what the trouble was. I guss they have to many children I dont think it pays to have to many children in the long run. I have always notice the women that have loots of kids always have trouble when they git older. I think Mary have about twelve so I guss that her trouble. I havent herd from home yet. be good sweet and take care of your self and Roger.

I love you sweet, by darling, Love James

Most of dad's letters concerned his training and how it was getting harder every day. As he hasn't heard from mother yet, there was a lapse in their communication back and forth.

This letter from dad was dated Sunday morning, October 1, 1944 and postmarked October 2, 3 pm, 1944:

Just a few lines hope you feel good today for myself I am OK except I am so sore I cant hardly walk and all the boys are, they liked to have killed us last week, and next week will be just as bad, this place sure is lonesome with you gone I feel so blue no one to love and have fun with sweet. I miss you so much. I went to church this morning. I cant enjoy anything when you are not with me you little sweet heart darling. Wont it be sweet when we can be back togarher to stay I cant wait for that day to come when they give me a discharge to come back to my sweet little darling wife and boy. I will be happy once more, this war seems to git worse instead of getting over with Icant figure it out, the whole world against two little nations and still cant do any thing with them, sweet I got to work K.P. this afternoon for Tucker. I dont feel like working but if I dident he woulden have got a pass I know he wanted to see his wife just as bad as I did but mine is far off, but I hope she wont be long you little sweet heart, I guss I will git a pass next weekin and go to Stark and try to git your little gift. I wish I had plenty monet where I could really git you something nice like other men git there sweet heart and love ones, but maby some day I can git you what I want you to have sweet. Sweet I love you true love and I want you to love me and think of me a loot, and write me every day, because I like to know how you and Roger are every day sweet heart.

by sweetheart be true and remember I love you with all my heart, Love James

The next letter from dad is dated the very next day and was a continuation of of the previous letter where he mentions pulling K.P. for Tucker. It has some interesting details and comments though. It was postmarked October 2, 11:30 am, 1944:

Hello Sweetheart,

How are you making it this blue afternoon, for myself I am OK, working K.P. but havent done much, cut some pork chops and diced some bacon and made hot cakes, made me think of the CC (C.C.C. Civilian Conservation Corp) wish it was like it use to be, we had a good time back in them old days, no war to take you love one away. we dident relize what a good time we was having me and you. Car and Johnny had some good times, but time changes everything, thats a true song dont you think? I was just thinking if the war was over today what a proud soldier I would be, to think I would soon be back with my wife you sweet darling. I wont you to git anything you wont and cash as many war bonds as you wont to and be good and take care of your self and Roger, dont worry about me sweet I think I will be OK as long as I stay on this side, if they do train us hard I think I can take it allright if I dont they can send me home and that would suit me just fine to be back with a sweet darling wife like you I would give my right arm to be with you right now darling, no body knows how much I miss you. I believe I could go through anything if I had you by my side then I would know I had the best and sweetest girl in the world with me.

Sweet you can make more friends thin any body in the world just think a girl meeting you at the bus station with every thing good to eat if a girl would do that no telling what a man would have for you if you would let him. You are a sweet girl. You know what Tucker said, he said if I got killed he was going to quit his wife and marry you So I guss I had better try to live through this war, if I dont you might git another husband. Dont write Mary any thing about that she might not like it and I dont wont to git any thing started, of corse tucker was joking I hope Well stay out of devilment and be sweet darling.

I love you always

James Love

At this point dad has finally received mother's first letter to him after returning to Hamilton and was answering it with this next letter. She had written every day, but it was taking 3 or more days for dad to get her letters. I have already included those letters that she wrote to him previously. This letter from dad was dated Saturday night, October 2, 1944 and postmarked October 2, 11:30 am, 1944:

Hello Sweet heart,

I will try and answer your letter sure was proud to hear from you, glad you made the trip good and dident have any trouble, I guss god answered my prayer, my darling wife made it OK anyway, sweet I love you more thin you think I sure was proud not git your letter this after noon I was thinking I wasent going to git one, I havent herd from home yet I dont know why they dont write I know I wrote last (It could have been they were trying to deal with Robert's death at St. Lo, France on July 31, 1944 and just haven't had the heart to write to anyone.).Sweet I crawled under the mechine gun fire today made it OK, but I have the dangerous thing yet the village fighting I dont care anything about going through that. I will haft to crawl under the mechine gun fire again Monday night, and we have our village fighting Monday to. I have never been so darty (dirty) in all my life, sand all over me and down my back you ought to have saw my hair and face full. dynimait blowing up all around me and all that sand would come right down on me, and thim bullits singing a song over your head it makes you have some funny feelings, what makes it so bad we got to go through it again Monday night. I mean they are really putting us through now all most the real thing. I mean those bullits dont sound so good sanging around your head, sweet take care of Roger and tell him I will come home some day and be his daddy again at home I hope, be good sweet and take care of your self, tell your mother and all I said hello I hope to see them before long.

by darling, your true love one J.G.B.

kiss,,,,,,,,,,, James, Love

I will include two more of dad's letters to mother and then return to more of her letters to him. This letter was dated Tuesday morning, October 3, 1944 and postmarked October 3, 11;30 am, 1944:

Hy Sweetheart Darling,

Just a few lines hoping you all are well and feeling fine for my self I am OK, got in this morning and went to bed about one oclock so you can amagin how I feel I got through the mechine gun fire OK. I havent went through the village fighting yet got to do that today. one boy got hurt going through yesterday he jumped off a building and made a bad landing. I mean it is dangerous mechine gun bullits flying everywhere, sweet try to get a gas book if you can, and tell hurbert to git him some drivers licenes I want him to take care of my car when I leave it I think it will be better running than standing then he can teach you to drive. I know you can learn if you try I wish you could drive now you could come down when I git through with my training sweet (I think mother never wanted to learn how to drive because her father was killed in a car wreck when she was eight years old. In any case, despite all my dad's encouragement, she never did learn and she never drove a car more than a mile or two.). Tucker said he sure did miss you being down said he sure did like you ha, I bet he do any body would like you sweet but not as much as I do. I think you are a swell little kid and sweet as you can be. I love you with all my heart and I hope to be back with you very soon if it is gods will. so pray that this war will soon be over and we will have us a sweet home again like we once had. I think of it a loot what a full (fool) I was having a sweet time with a swell darling wife like you and not thinking much about it. be sweet and may god bless you and keep you sweet for me.

by Sweet heart, your true love one always, James

Here is another letter from dad in which he writes more about his training and tells mother he will be sending her some bars of soap. Soap, like most household items, was hard to get during wartime as everything was rationed so that the troops would have the supplies they needed. The letter was postmarked October 4, 11:30 am, 1944:

Hello little Darling wife,

How is my little sweet girl today fine I hope for my self I am just about give out we marched ten miles this afternoon I mean I am tired to. I guss it was a good thing you went home I havent had much time off and since you left dont think any body will git a pas this weekin any way the captain said no one would – I was in hopes I would git one and git you that little present you wanted.

I just mailed you eighteen bars of soap I dident think I would git it through, it was so heavy they asked me if it was amination (ammunition). I told them they shot all that over my head last night I dident think they had any more, so they laughed and took it, I hope you git it OK and I hope it dont turn into amination (ammunition) before it gits there Sweet your two letters was sweet I recived this afternoon tell Roger I will send him some candy when I can git some they havent had any I dont think since you left. I havent been able to git away any way.

by sweet I will stop now and go to bed. love and best wishes your true love James

My Sweet darling Wife

The next letters will be those written by mother in answer to dad's letters that I have previously included. There is indeed a pretty good flow as I have organized their letters in an attempt to keep them as communicative as possible. This letter from mother to dad was dated Saturday afternoon, September 30, 1944 and postmarked October 2, 9:30 am, 1944:

Hi Sugar,

Well this a lonesome Saturday afternoon for me.

It is different from what I have been doing on the past eight Saturdays.

I have been so lonesome today just thinking of how I was always so glad for the past Saturdays to come so you could come to see me.

I'm more lonesome tonight because you were usually with me over the weekend.

I got your letter today. I'm glad you got the socks O.K. I hope they fit. I didn't know what size to get.

I'm sorry your training is so hard. I just hope you get by O.K.

Don't worry about me. My cold is well and Roger is fine.

He plays and is a very good boy. He minds me fine. I haven't had to whip him yet.

He has a few mosquito bites on his legs. He said he would just have to tell his daddy that he had a whole lots of sores on his legs. He really does say some funny things sometimes.

We got a letter from Iva & Gerry today. She said his mother & Daddy Aunt and Uncle visited them over the weekend. She said she made biscuits, and they all liked them.

We will be glad to get the soap and candy.

I miss that good P.X. candy, but most of all I miss being with you.

I know you miss going to the Service Club & into town on weekends.

I want you to go to town when you can and not stay around Camp all time.

Mamma is going to Birmingham tomorrow to get her permanent. She will be back by Monday night (Her sister Rowena owned a beauty school and shop in Birmingham.).

I washed my hair and Louisa rolled it. It really looks nice now I think.

I'll stop now, so be good and take care of yourself. Remember I love you.

Love, Elizabeth & Roger

Continuing with mother's letters to dad I am being selective and not including them all but just the ones that continue the flow between them. This letter was written a couple of days later and dated October 2, 1944, It was postmarked Hamilton, Alabama, October 3, 4 pm, 1944:

Hello Sweetheart,

How are you today? I'm rather tired myself. I have strung a bushel of string beans today all by myself. Mamma is going to can them tomorrow.

I got your two letters today. I suppose you have gotten mine by now.

I got my check from the War Bonds today. It was $75.49 for four Bonds.

I got it just in time as I was broke. I left Fla with $17.00 but I spent it on clothes for Roger, etc.

This is your fourteenth week isn't it? Is it any harder than the others were? I hope not. Let me know when you want me to send you something to eat. You will go on Bivovac next week, won't you? Be real careful hear!

I'll be so glad when you can come home to stay too. Don't worry about anything you said to me. I have already forgotten it anyhow. I love you sweet and know you do me too.

I wish you could see Roger now. I bet you wouldn't know him. He is so much larger and he doesn't cry now when he is bathed or when I put him to bed. He still says he loves his Mother & Daddy when anyone asks him who he loves.

He says his lips are for your sugar.

I'm glad you went to the show. I bet it was good. They always have good shows there at camp.

I haven't been to one yet. I've been catching up with my sleep that I lost while traveling.

I really do miss being with you and going places too.

I'll stop now so be good and take care of yourself. I will too.

All our love to you – Elizabeth & Roger

(There was one of Roger's "letters" included inside mother's letter "To Daddy From Roger". I will attach a scan of it here.)

Continuing with my mother's letters to dad I felt it noteworthy to include as many of her letters that served as direct responses to the letters that dad sent to her. This is one of those letters dated Hamilton, Alabama, October 3, 1944 and postmarked Hamilton, Alabama, October 4, 4:00 pm, 1944:

Hi Sugar,

How are you? We are fine, except for being rather warm. It really has been hot for the last two days but it is cold at night and early every morning.

How has your training been this week? I hope it won't be so hard on you.

I got a letter from Mary today. She says that her & Tucker really misses having us with them. I miss being there too.

She says you were pulling K.P. for Tucker one day. Don't work too hard. I bet he was glad for you to do that for him so that he could go to see her.

She wrote me a very sweet letter. I also got a letter from Eloise (Robert Brown's fiancé) and Mrs. Carell (a close friend from Childersburg, Alabama).

We have been canning beans today. We got twenty-four qts.

Mamma has a pretty permanent. It is machine less.

Mamma said tell you she wished you were here to help us eat beans. We are getting another bushel tomorrow. I wish you were here to help string them. It would be fun wouldn't it? No. I wouldn't make you string beans. I would let you rest, because I know you get enough of that to do while on K.P.

I didn't get a letter from you today. I suppose it was because I got two from you yesterday.

I hope to get two or three tomorrow though.

Roger is fine. He plays outside a good bit. I'll stop now, so be good.

I love you, Elizabeth & Roger

Often a day or so would pass with no letters and that left both mother and dad feeling lonesome and blue. Usually, the letters would come all at once a day or so later, as with what mother relates in the next letter to dad. It was dated Hamilton, Alabama, October 4, 1944 and postmarked October 6, 9:30 am, 1944:

Hello Sweet,

I got your three sweet letters today and was really proud to get them.

I'm so glad you went under the machine gun fire O.K. I have been thinking and worrying about that lots. I just hope you will make the next one O.K. too.

I'm glad you went to church. Roger & I did too. He wore his Soldier's Cap, in fact he wants to wear it everywhere he goes.

He is outside playing with the cats & chickens now. I'll be so glad when you get to come home. Roger wants to see you so bad, that is all he can talk about. I want to see you too. I miss being with you so much. I really enjoyed being with you the eight weeks.

I got my check today, I put it away and am not going to use any of it if I can get by without it.

I sent you a box of candy today. I didn't make it though. I bought it at the market. I got some for us this morning and it was so good that I decided to get some more to send to you.

Let me know when to send the other things.

Sweet do you remember how many miles is on the car? If you do let me know as I have to know before I can get a gas ration book. I wrote your mother to see how many miles the speedometer registers and write back and tell me. She hasn't yet. I suppose she hasn't had time. I got a letter from her today though. They are O.K. They said they didn't have their cotton picked yet.

I think Roger & I will go down there about Thursday of next week.

Sugar it was very sweet of you to pull K.P. for Tucker so that he could see Mary.

Don't think anything about what he said you know he was just kidding.

You know that if anything were to happen to you that I would never marry anyone, I love only you sweet. I just hope & trust that nothing ever happens to you. I think about you all the time.

Sweet don't worry about the gift for me, anything that you get will be good enough for me. I do want you to have a picture made for me though.

The best gift you could give me is to come back home and stay. I really will be glad when that day comes too.

Mr. Brassfield who works for Furniture Company passed by here yesterday. He told me to give you his best regards.

Take care of yourself and be sweet, I love you with all my heart. Eliz & Roger

With this next letter mother is informing dad that his mother has sent the mileage on his car and that now she was able to get the gas ration book. Her letter was dated Hamilton, Alabama, October 6, 1944 and postmarked October 7, 9:30 am, 1944:

Dearest James,

I was glad to get your letter today. How are you? I suppose you are just about rested up over the ten-mile hike by now aren't you? I'm rather tired too. We travel today.

I hope you get your pass this weekend, but don't worry about it, if you can't get a gift for me. I understand how it is about getting a pass.

I'll be glad to get all that soap as we need it now.

I suppose I will get it tomorrow.

I got a card from your mother, she also sent me the mileage on our car so I got the A book today without any trouble at all. So when you come home everything will be handy.

I'll be so glad when you do come home. I can hardly wait to see you again.

Roger wrote you a letter too. He is out playing with a little girl now.

(I will include a scan of Roger's "letter: here.)

Mamma & boys said to tell you "hello". Be careful while on Bivovac and watch for spiders, snakes, etc.

Roger & I have decided to go to Opelika Friday morning at 6:00 o'clock.

Alma says she will meet us at the station.

Be good and take care of yourself.

We love you, Eliz & Roger

Mother sent dad a lot of food items through the mail and considering how long the mail took to arrive in those days it was amazing that they arrived safely, undamaged and unspoiled. This letter from her dated Hamilton, Alabama, October 7, 1944 mentions some of the food items that she often sent. At the upper left corner of the letter mother had inserted a note, probably after finishing the letter as a kind of P.S," I got a new blue sweater & a red one too. They are very pretty.":

Hi Sweetheart,

How is my hubby tonight? We are all fine, but could feel much better if you could be here with us. I'm glad you feel lucky to have me, I'm also lucky to have you for a husband. I miss being with you so much. I'll be so glad when you can come home, only I wish it would be to stay.

Roger is O.K. He has been having a big time playing today.

Well, I'm just about through menstruating. I was early this time. I started the 4th. I'm safe now ha!

I suppose you go on Bivovac tomorrow night, don't you?

I sent you a package today. I hope you can get it and will like what I sent. It was a jar of jelly, peanut butter, crackers, two cakes, an apple & orange and a tomato also. Mother sent it. She said not to bless her out about it if it was rotten ha! Did you get the candy?

Roger & I are going to Opelika Friday, Alma will meet us at the station.

I got a letter from Mary. She says she is going home Monday.

I got one from Gladys also (Gladys and her husband Carl were another couple that mother and dad made friends with at Camp Blanding,), She sent the picture of you & I that they made and also one of her & Carl. I really am proud of them, Mary said she let Tucker have hers to show to you.

I am enclosing a scan of the picture
of Gladys and Carl here.

I hope you the best of luck while you are in the woods. Be careful & write often.

Love always Eliz & Roger

Mother's letter dated Hamilton, Alabama, October 9. 1944 and postmarked October 10, 9:30 am, 1944 mentioned that she had received the soap that dad sent to her:

Dear Sweetheart,

Well, I suppose you have sampled part of your two weeks Bivovac today.

How did it come out? Write and let me know how you are doing, as often as you can, as I'll be thinking and worrying about you all the time.

I just hope it won't be too hard on you, and that you will go through without any trouble. I love you sweet, and don't want anything to happen to you.

I'll be so glad when you're all through and you can come home, but I hope you won't have to go overseas.

I got two letters from you today, they were very sweet, I can hardly wait from one morning until the next to get your letters.

Roger was so tickled to get your letter this morning.

We got the soap this morning just in time to, as we washed today. Thanks so much for it. It will be lots of help as it is so hard to get here.

Mamma is proud of it too. Roger made choo-choo trains with it. I think he enjoyed playing with it just because it was from you. He is writing you too.

I suppose you have received the package I sent to you. I'll send you another one Wed or Thursday but will send something different from what I sent before as you might get tired of eating the same things. I hope it wasn't all torn up and spilling out.

Let me know when you want your money and I'll have it ready for you.

After Friday write me to Opelika as I'll be there until you come.

Mamma & all said they wished you best of luck.

We love you, Eliz & Roger

(There was another of Roger's "letters"
inside this letter. I will include a scan here.)

These next letters are from dad to mother and the first one was the letter in which dad mentioned how lucky he was to have her as his wife. As you will recall, mother mentioned that earlier in her response to this letter. I have tried to keep these properly sequenced, but one slips through the cracks now and then. This letter was dated Wednesday night, October 4, 1944 and postmarked October 5, 11:30 am, 1944:

Hello Sweetheart Darling,

How is my darling wife tonight well and feeling fine I hope, for myself I am OK. Darling I been thinking of you a loot today how sweet you are and what a lucky man I was to git a sweet girl like you. I love you with all my heart sweet heart. I sure miss you, no where to go at night just lay around and think of you wishing I was with you, I know I could have a good time. I have never fail having one with you darling.

I got a letter from Mama & Alma & Curtis today they was all OK. Said they was looking for you to come down there in a week or so. I wont you to go and stay with Mama and daddy when you get ready to go down there, they need some one to cheer them up. I know they git lonesome down there with us all gone and cant come very often and one that will never come again, that what make it so bad (this was the first mention by dad of Robert's being killed). I sure will be proud when this war is over. I git so tired staying away from you all – darling you dont know how much I miss you and Roger and all the rest. I hope it wont be so much long before we can be back to gather to stay. I will never forget Camp Blanding fla. and when I leave here I dont never want to see this place again not to take any training any way. tell Roger I havent got any candy yet but maby I will.

by sweet Love always James

Dad is about to go on Bivouac and is beginning the last two weeks of his training at Camp Blanding. After his training was completed, he would get a ten day furlough and get to spend some time with mother and Roger and her folks and his before being sent overseas. I will include a few of his letters to mother that lead up to his final days at Camp Blanding.

This letter from dad was dated Friday night, October 6, 1944 and postmarked October 7, 11:30 am, 1944:

Hello Sweetheart,

I will try and answer your letter hope you are well and feeling good, for myself I am OK I guss, only tired and worried out. I sure wish I could see you. this weekin I know I could have a good time dont you? We always have a good time dont we sweet I miss you so much darling I dont know what to do. I am going to Stark Saturday night if they give any passes and git some things I need and something for you. I wont git to Jackersonvill (Jacksonville) until I git back off Biviac which will be two weeks from now, we will go out Monday morning at three oclock. I know I wont like sleeping out on the ground we will be on night problems nely (nearly) all time we are out I know I will loose some weight – one boy got his neck broke in another company out on Biviac last week. Sweet dont worry about me, I will be real careful for you only darling you wont me to dont you sweet?

I got your letter this afternoon you said you dident git one from me one day I have wrote one to two a day. I guss the mail just gits missed up sometimes like everything else. The Captain said we would leave from here the eighteen week which will soon be here, if the time flys by like it have been doing, sweet send me about two boxes a week while I am out small boxes they wont let us have large ones, we haft to eat the stuff up when we git it they wont let us keep it around camp. Sweet dont think any thing about it if you dont git a letter every day while I am out, it might rain and git all my paper wet we dont have any place to keep any thing dry, the old tents not any good. be sweet darling and take care of Roger and you self I love you both.

your true love one, James

There was a postcard of a cowgirl on a horse with the caption "Headed for the Last Roundup" from Roger written to dad by mother of course. It was postmarked October 7, 11:30 am, 1944:

I am including a scan of the cowgirl postcard here with
note on back.

Hi Daddy

How are you. I'm fine. I have lots of fun playing with
Nora Ann.

Write me soon,

bye bye Roger

This next letter from dad was particularly touching as he was reflecting
on the thoughts of not ever seeing his beloved wife and son again if he went
overseas. It was postmarked October 7, 11:30 am, 1944:

Hello Sweetheart,

I will try and answer your letter I just recived I was thinking I wasent going to git one today. I dident git one yesterday but I got two the day before that but I did git one this afternoon and was proud to hear from you all glad you are well for myself I am very tired they are really putting us through now, I will write you when to send me some money I dont need it yet and I dont know how much I need I am glad you got your money for the Bonds if you need any more send some Bonds and git them cashed.

Sweet I sure do miss you I sure hope I dont haft to go across and leave you and Roger thin I know it would be a long time before I could git to see you all thin if ever any more, it gits closer by every day, and I think about it more to. I know I am no better thin any one else but I do wont to be with my darling wife and boy some more. I guss a loot of the boys felt that way but they wont ever see thim any more, that what I think about, never to git to see my darling wife and boy any more. I love you both with all my heart darling, so be good and dont strang to many beans. I love you darling, your true one forever.

My darling wife I love you sweet and Roger Love James

Dad often wrote to Roger and enclosed his notes to Roger inside his letters to mother. One letter he wrote was written on U.S. Army stationery and had pictures of army artillery, guns, canons, Jeeps, tanks, machine guns and a U.S. Seal at the top. Dad knew Roger would love seeing pictures of all those. The letter was not dated but probably was written around the first week or so of October 1944.

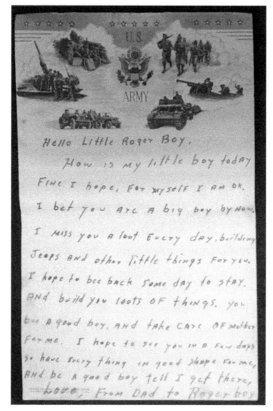

(I will include a scan of the Army stationery here.)
Here is the letter that dad wrote to mother:

Hello Sweetheart,

I dont have much to write about just thought I would write while I was waiting to go out on a night problem. I am sending Roger's letter to you with some pictures on it (the army guns, canons, jeeps, etc.) you said you was going to the sanging, I wish I was there to go with you. I hope you have a good time sweet, well I got to go to the woods and stay till twelve oclock so bee sweet. I love you darling Love Always James

Here is the letter that dad wrote to Roger that was enclosed. It was printed rather than handwritten:

Hello Little Roger Boy

How is my little boy today Fine I hope, For myself I am OK. I bet you are a big boy by now. I miss you a loot Every day, building Jeeps and other things for you. I hope to bee back some day to stay and build you things. You bee a good boy till I git there.

Love, From Dad to Roger Boy

(I am including here a scan of Roger in his Jeep.)

This next letter was nice because it gave more information about Tucker and Mary, the couple that mother and dad shared the house with, in Starke, Florida while he was in training. This letter was dated Saturday night which would've been October 6, 1944 and postmarked October 8, 2:30 pm, 1944:

Hello Sweetheart,

I will try and answer your two sweet letters I recived to night. I went to Stark this afternoon with Tucker and went to the show with him and Mary, they sure was sweet to me. I went down to the house and we ate a pie. I enjoyed being with them very much. Mary sent me some cookies last week to it was nice of her Tucker brought them to me. I like them very much. I also got your little present for you. Mary will mail it to you Monday. I wont have time. I had some pictures made I will bring them when I come. I carreyed my coat and got a O.D. garson cap, they ought to be good. I had three enlarged and two small ones for $5.95.

(I will include a scan of dad in his uniform here,)

I wont git them until two weeks if they are any good I will bring them to you, Sweet I sure did miss you in Stark I went by the house where you stayed but dident go in. I would have give anything if you had been down here. I mean we would have had a good time sweet. Sweet I havent got the candy yet I guss I will git it tomorrow I hope so. I bet it is good, darling you are the sweetest girl ever lived I will always think of you that way, sweet I love you with all my heart I always have wanted you to have the best of every thing if I havent got it for you darling, I can never tell you sweetheart – I will never forgit the sweet times we have had to gather. I hope some day we will have some more good times. I hope it wont be so much longer to, sweet the car have about 29,265 miles that closer enought anyway you can send me the money the last week I am out on Bivovac (Bivouac) I will let you know how much to send in a day or two. Sweet go to the show and any where you want to, and enjoy yourself.

I guss I had better close and go to bed it is about twelve oclock now, by darling and take care of Roger and yourself, your true love always,

Love James Kiss ==============

The following letter from dad found him having finally received the candy that mother had sent to him, so we are moving right along with what seems to be a proper sequence of events. The letter was dated Sunday afternoon which would have been October 7, 1944 and postmarked October 8, 11:30 am, 1944:

Hello sweet heart

I though I would try and write you a few lines before I went out on Biviouc (Bivouac). we been busy all the afternoon getting ready for the next two weeks which I dread. I hope it dont rain all the time we are out if it do – I guss I will be sick when I git my leave I sure hope it will be dry out there all time, sweet I dident git to go to church today did you and Roger go? you said you was going down home be sure and let me know when you are going there I will know where to write thin you wont miss a day gitting a letter if I git to write every day. well it have started raining all ready, gitting a good start I guss. I wrote your mother a letter this morning at least I answered the one she wrote me about a month ago. I got another letter from Marry Mayberry the other day.

Sweet when you git down home open the car shed doors and roll the glasses down and let the car air out some, be sure and have the tires pumped up and some gasoline put in by the time I come I dont wont to waste my time doing all of that. I wont to be with you all time and show you a good time and have a good time myself.

Sweet I got the candy today it sure is good whats left of it, those boys like candy to I told thim you made it and they tried to eat it all, they dident think so much of it till I told thim you made it, say where did you buy that much candy at a time anyway? I cant git candy down here at all havent got any since you left. I sure will be a proud soldier whin this war is over. I git so tired staying around here, I think it will be a long time yet before this war will be finished up.

Sweet be good and take care of yourself and Roger – remember I love you my Darling wife I will always be true to you sweetheart,

Love always, James

Now it is time to return to including more of mother's letters to dad. As before, you will see that she was responding to the letters that dad wrote to her as when she commented on Mary and Tucker taking dad to the show. This letter from her was dated Hamilton, Alabama, October 10, 1944 and postmarked Hamilton, Alabama, October 11, 4 pm. 1944:

Dearest James,

I was so glad to get your letter today. I'm glad you had a nice week-end. It really was nice of Mary and Tucker to show you a good time. I know you enjoyed going with them to the show & to their room too.

I think Mary was very sweet to send you the cookies too. She is a sweet kid anyway.

I hope you have gotten the candy I sent you now.

I'm sending you another package tomorrow.

I sent fruit in the other. But I won't in this one, as I'm afraid they might get me about it. I've heard it is a violation of the law to send fruit from one State to another.

I'll be very glad to get the present you got for me. In fact I can hardly wait to see it. It was very sweet of you to get it for me.

I'm so glad you had the pictures made. I know they are good. They would have to be good if they look like you though. I can't wait to see them. Most of all though I want to see you.

I got the A-Ration book for you. I think that I'll have to get a tag for the car too. I'm going to see about it tomorrow and if I do I'll get it soon.

How are you making out in the woods? I think of you every minute. I just hope you have pretty weather while you're out.

It really is cold here now. We have the heater up & a good fire now.

I made eight pillow cases for Mamma today and we are going to can another bushel of beans tomorrow.

Be sure to write me in Opelika after Friday. I went to the bus station to find out what time we will get there and it will be 3:00 Friday afternoon.

By the way, we have a new bus station built here. It is across from Greens Market. It is a very nice one too. Our new mayor has finally decided to clean the town up. It looks much better too.

I had better stop and wrap your package so that I can mail it tomorrow.

I love you sweet with all my heart, so be careful. I don't want you to get hurt in any way. I think of you all the time.

Roger is now crying. I had to whip him as he was misbehaving ha!

We love you, Eliz & Roger

(There was another of Roger's "letters"
inside so I will include a scan of it here.)

Dad wrote every day to mother and sometimes he only had time to write a few lines or a short note, but this next letter was longer and included more detail and personal observations. There was no date inside, but it was postmarked October 11, 11:30 am, 1944:

Dear Darling wife,

I received your sweet letter and Roger's card, and the box also it sure was nice, as I was hungry and worried out, I havent got any sleep worth nothing yet. I liked to have froze last night, dont ever say it dont git cold in fla. I had to be on Pig Guard last night from two oclock till four. We dident git to lay down till about ten oclock last night and I couldent sleep for thinking about the bugs and things crawling on me and the ground is so hard, you havent ever tryed sleeping on the ground have you sweet are in a fox hole which we will sleep in friday night. darling I would give my right arm to be out of this place and back home with you where I could sleep close to the sweetest girl in the world, no body knows what a Soldier have to put up with I wish they did, thin they might think more of the Soldiers, loots of people never feels the effect of war, if some of those big shots had to go through what a soldier had to go through with this war would be over in a day or two.

I sure will be proud when these two weeks are over I have a cold all ready – I dont know what I will have before the end of two week, sleeping on the ground and eating anything not fixed right. I dont like it at all but I cant do any thing but make the best of it, but dont worry sweet I will make it OK. I think loots of them have went through it and I can to. Sweet send me $40.00 next week I dont know how much I will need and I dont think any bod knows any way they wont tell us. Send it in a registered letter no money order are check. Sweet I sure will be proud to git to see you and Roger and all the rest. I git some lonesome staying away from you darling think of you all time sweet heart. if I could only be back with you to stay I would give any thing sweet. When I do come my stay wont be long – thin I will haft to go for a long time, I hope not but thats the way it looks now, but dont worry sweet I feel like I will make it any where I go. god will take care of me for my darling wife who I love better thin any one on earth, I will always love you so be sweet and take care of your sweet little self, I will write the rest of your letters down home, unless you change your mind about going down there, I dont guss you will. So I guss you will have some mail when you git there if nothing happens. if you cant git any thing to send me down there I will understand. I know you cant go as much down there to the store and places.

by darling,

I love you always James, kiss----------------

The next letter found dad describing the ordeals of staying in the wilderness during his two-week bivouac. He was still trying to get mother to learn how to drive and had even drawn a diagram of how to shift the gears on his car. It was all for naught though as mother never did completely learn to drive a car and preferred to let dad drive the whole time they were married. The letter was not dated but was postmarked October 12, 11:30 am. 1944:

Hello Sweetheart,

Just a few lines hope you and Roger are OK down home – for myself I am still out here in the wilderness with the wild animals, it havent rained since we got out here but I have been looking for it any time now, you know how it does, rain most any time. I mean it is cold down here at night, and hot in the daytime, we all went in swimming today, and at night I sleep under two Blankits and all my clothes on thin just about freeze. I dont understand this weather. sweet I sure do miss seeing you every once in a while, that was better thin never. I dont see any body but soldiers out here and wild hogs. I guss we will be wild when we leave here. Sweet, write me all the news and let me know how mama and dady are gitting along, if you wont to git some one to drive the car and tak you any where you want to go but you keep the key in your purse when the car is parked dont let it go without you in it no mater who it is. you know how I took care of it. I know you can see that it is drove right and not to fast and reckless. I wish you could drive I will do my best to lern you when I come. I know you cand drive if any body else can, no reason in the world for you not to, so you can start learning the gears that all you dont know you can sit in the car and learn which is the right one low gear you push up and pull back then to second you push from low. Sweet try to learn where the gears are and you wont have any trouble at all you know you start off in low thin to second thin back to high and push your clutch in every time you go from one gear to the other. Sweet try doing that the car dont haft to be running for you to learn the gears. by Sweet and good luck,

by darling Love always James

The next letters were from mother and as before were generally her responses to dad's letters to her. She was still mentioning going to Opelika to be with dad's folks until he arrived there on his furlough in about two weeks or so. The letter was dated Hamilton, Alabama, October 11, 1944 and postmarked October 12, 9:30 am, 1944:

Hello Sweetheart,

How is my husband now? How are you getting along in the woods? I hope it isn't hard on you and that you will get through O.K.

I was so very proud of your two letters that I received today. They were very sweet.

I read the one you wrote to mama too. I'm glad you feel the way you do about me. I feel the same about you. I think you are the sweetest & best boy in the world.

I'm also glad you got your candy and liked it.

I'll get you some more and send and send it with your other things.

Did you get the package I sent? I hope you like the things I got for you.

I'm going to Opelika Friday morning. I'll have the car filled with gas etc. so that it will be ready for you when you come. I'm going to get a car tag tomorrow as we have to have one before the 14th of next month, and I don't want you to have to bother about getting one while you are here.

Roger is writing you too. I had to stop and draw a bird, a boy and a girl for him.

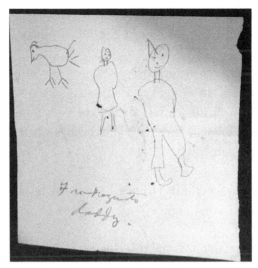

(I will include a scan of mother's
drawing of a bird, boy and girl here.)

I got a letter from Mary today. She sent me a picture of her & Tucker.
I really am proud of it.

(I had included this photo before but will include
a scan of mother's photo of Mary and Tucker again here.)

She is home by now I suppose, but I can't write her as I don't have her address. Maybe she will write me again.

She said she sent the present you got for me. So I suppose I'll get it tomorrow anyway. I'll be so glad too when you are back in civilian life too. We had such a good time didn't we. We will have more good times when this war is over though.

I'll be glad when the day comes that you can be home with Roger and I every night.

We miss you so much and think of you all the time. I hope & pray that nothing will ever happen to you so that you can be back with us.

I love you with all my heart & know that you love me too. I wouldn't do you wrong for anything. I could never do a thing like that.

You are too good to me for me to do wrong.

Roger just can't wait for you to come home. He talks about it all the time.

Everything he does he says that he is going to tell "daddy about it when he comes".

It really is cold here now. I hope it isn't there as you are out in the woods. Be careful not to take cold and take care of yourself. Write me as often as you can. I'll be waiting for every letter.

I love you sweet,

Love & Kisses Eliz. & Roger

Here is another letter from mother saying that she had arrived in Opelika to stay with dad's mother and dad. It was dated Opelika, Alabama, October 13, 1944 and postmarked October 16, 1944:

Hello Sweetheart,

Well here I am in Opelika! I got here O.K. this afternoon about 6 o'clock. I missed the 6 o'clock bus this morning and had to get the 8:50 bus, but made it O.K.

I'm at Alma's now, and will go to your mothers tomorrow.

They are all fine, I got your two letters before I left Hamilton this morning. I'm sorry that they are putting you through so much. Be careful with the cold.

I just hope that you won't be sick or get hurt in any way.

I love you sweet and don't want anything to happen to you.

I'm so glad you got your package and liked it. I sent you another one the other day. I suppose you have it by now.

I'll try to send you another one tomorrow and the $40.00 too.

I hope you get it O.K. and that it will be enough.

If it isn't let me know and I'll send you more later.

I hope it is warmer there now so that it won't be so bad on you. If it is as cold there as it has been here it is bad, because we have almost frozen for the last few days.

Sweet do the best you can, remember I'm thinking of you all the time.

I'll stop so write soon. We love you, Eliz & Roger

P.S. I'm sending you the money in this letter.

With this letter mother had spent the night with Alma, dad's sister, and was now at dad's mother and dad's home. It was written the next day after the previous letter and dated Opelika, Alabama, October 14. 1944 and postmarked October 16, 4:30 pm, 1944:

Hello Sweetheart,

I'm now with your mother and Daddy. They are both doing O.K. We are too. I got to Alma's last night at six. They are all fine. She said to tell you that she still lives at the same place.

I went with her to the mill last night and went through it. I was almost deaf from the roaring noises they carry on in there ha!

I sent your $40.00 dollars to you today. I registered it so it ought to reach you safe and sound I hope. If it isn't enough let me know and I'll send more.

I went in the car house and looked the car over this afternoon.

It seems to be in perfect condition, but looks rather lonesome.

Roger said he was going to drive it.

I'm going to learn to drive if possible.

I'll study your drawing of the gear, and also sit in the car and see if I can learn it. Your mother said not to go wild like those hogs if you could help it ha,

I'll be so glad when you get out of the wilderness too. I know it is bad, but be careful and do the best you can.

I'd be so proud if you could come home to stay.

Maybe this war won't last always, I hope not anyway.

I have another package all wrapped but can't send it until Monday as it is Saturday afternoon now, and the mailman won't be by tomorrow.

I'm sending pineapple preserves, peanut butter, crackers, cookies & candy.

Alma sent the cookies to you. They ought to be good as they are fresh from the bakery.

Sweet if you can get some Lucky Strike Cigarettes get them and I'll send some more money if you need it.

Curtis wrote for some and your mother & Daddy can't get them here. It is too late to send him a Christmas present now, but we can send cigarettes anyway. You haven't sent him anything yet have you?

Sweet your letter was here when I got to your mother's, I really was proud to get it too.

The present you were talking about hadn't come when I left, I suppose Mamma has it by now. She will send it as soon as she gets it though.

I'll stop now, so be sweet. I love you with all my heart.

Love & Kisses Elizabeth & Roger

As we learned from the previous letter, mother was at dad's parent's home in Opelika. Alabama, or more specifically, in the Beauregard community. Gordon Brown, dad's father, had a cotton farm and it was harvest time. It had been hard on Gordon because his sons were all in the service and one of them, Robert, had been killed in action. It was hard for him to find able bodied men to pick the cotton and Gordon simply could not handle the task all by himself. Mother had offered to help as she was raised in Hamilton where she had picked cotton frrequently as did all her family. This letter tells of her cotton picking and also of dad's mother sending some chicken and biscuits in a package for dad to eat. The letter was written from Opelika, Alabama on October 16, 1944 and postmarked October 17, 4:30 pm, 1944:

Hi Sweet,

I received your two letters today, and was so glad to get them.

Sugar, I'm sorry they are so tough on you. Maybe it won't be that way always. I wish there was something I could do to help you, but I suppose all I can do is to send you something to eat and write you every day.

I'll be so glad when we can be together again.

I love you sweet, so take care of yourself and be good.

I will too. I;m always good, you know that don't you sweet?

I sent your packages this morning. We will send the chicken and biscuits by Thursday anyway.

We will try to go to town by then and get some more things too.

Roger and I picked some cotton for your Dad this afternoon. He didn't like to pick very much. He said he got tired.

I picked three sacks full.

I'm going to pick some more tomorrow. It helps pass the time off anyway.

Your Grandpa (Fate Brown) got back this afternoon. He spent last week with Ola Piper (his daughter and Gordon Brown's youngest sister). He seems to be feeling fine.

I got a letter from Johnnie today too.

I'll stop now so be sweet. I love you with all my heart.

Love & Kisses Eliz & Roger

This next letter was pretty much a continuation of the events mentioned in mother's preceding letters, but I believe it helps to present a more complete view of her experience there in Opelika at that time. It was dated the following day on October 18, 1944:

Hello Sweetheart,

I was very glad to get your letter today. I have been picking cotton again today. I didn't pick very much though as we went to town this afternoon.

We went in our car. Wash (Mayberry) drove it for us. He took it off the jacks, put air nin the tires and 4 gallons of gas, also a quart of oil. It rides as easy as ever. The new battery works fine.

It seems so strange to be riding in it without you. Wash is a good driver though.

I'll leave it out and air it tomorrow. I'll try to shine it too.

We will send your chicken tomorrow or Thursday. We haven't caught it yet. I got you a coconut cake in town today.

I made an appointment with the dentist to have my teeth filled Monday afternoon. I hope I can go then.

My watch is still in the shop at Hamilton. I hope he will soon get it fixed.

Sweet I'll be glad when you can come home.

I love you so much sugar, so take care of yourself & be good.

Roger is fine, still mean as ever.

The car cranked fine today without any trouble. I'm going to try to learn to drive ha!

I'll stop, so be sweet we love you, Eliz. & Roger

The following letters from dad were written at the same time as mother's letters to him were written, so they probably crossed paths in the mail as dad was asking about how his car was cranking just as mother was writing to tell him it had cranked fine. This was probably the letter mother was referring to as just having been received on October 18, 1944. This letter from dad was dated Saturday morning, October 15, 1944 and postmarked October 15, 2:30 pm, 1944:

Hy little darling wife

Sweet I have been thinking of you all time, wishing I was with you and never had to leave you again darling you are a sweet little wife I love you and think of you all

146

time sweet. I dont guss you can read this writing at all I do the best I can no where to write and no time of corse. I cant do much good at the best sweet. I guss you think I am trying to make a man out of you having the car all ready when I git there write me and let me know if the car will crank, if it wont, dont let any body full with it but someone that knows what they are doing. Jap know what to do if anything is rong if he cant fix it you butter wait till I come just any body dont fix a ford. They can fix it where it will cost me a forthen to have it fixed, Sweet I have one more week out here in the wilderness. I hope to git back tame by the time I come home. Sweet I sure will be proud when I can git to sleep with you again and hold you just as tight as I can close to me darling you dont know how much you mean to me. I know I have some one waiting for me when I leave this place to love and have a good time with with a good looking and sweet darling wife thats what I always wanted so I have one and I am proud of you sweetheart darling I love you with all my heart. till Roger to draw me more picture.

by darling wife, Love James

Dad did not often give details of what his training exercises involved. The Army did not allow the soldiers to write about what went on because of the danger of spies getting the information from stolen mail or in other ways. From time to time though, dad did give some hints about what he was going through as in this letter written Sunday afternoon, October 15, 1944 and postmarked October 16, 11:30 am, 1944:

Dearest Darling wife,

How do you feel sweetheart fine I hope, for myself I am OK, except I have a bad cold and a sore throat which makes me feel bad. I hope to stay well while I am out here, it is bad anough for a well man, the weather makes you sick, cold at night and hot in the day time. I guss my cold will be worser they made us all go in the lake this afternoon. we have a hard week coming up we will be out nely (nearly) every night, then next friday night we will leave here at nine oclock on our 25 mile hike. We will march from nine till five the next morning – we are supose to be in camp at five saturday morning – that will be the end of our two weeks think God I sure will be proud when it is over with to.

Sweet what have you been doing today! did you go to church? I havent been but one time since you left, havent had time to go anywhere much, Sweet I might not get to write every day next week. We will be out from tuesday morning until wednesday afternoon on a problem which will be the dangerous one we will have during the seventeen weeks. I cant tell what it all is. I dont know myself, but I do know we will be advancing on the enmany (enemy) and all the big guns and canons will be shooting over our heads and the shells bursting in front of us. I sure will be proud when it is over with to. that will be the last real dangerous problem we will have. Sweet dont worry about me you know a man dont haft to be in the army to git killed he can git killed most any where I think. I try not to worry about it, sweet you can send me the money where I can git it by Saturday. I think $40.00 will be enough if you need any more money write a check if you dont have time to cash any war bonds. I bet you are getting lonesome down there have you picked any cotton yet! I bet Roger have havent he, I havent got a letter today and the box havent come yet. I guss I will git it tomorrow. I dont see how we can even git anything out here in this place, an air plane cant hardly fly over it, ha. by sweet and be a sweet little girl Love James

This letter from dad just about wraps up what details he could give about his two weeks training in the woods, He acknowledged that he received the $40.00 mother sent but had not received the box with the chicken and biscuits. One must wonder how that chicken could have survived so many days in the mail anyway, but is was common practice to send food by mail in those days. The letter was not dated but was postmarked October 17, 11:30 am, 1944:

Dear sweet heart,

I just recived your letter and the money but I havent got the box you sent yet, I guss it got lost. I got one box from you last Monday, maby I will git it. some of the boys git them in ten day after they are sent from home, I dont know why it takes so long to get a package, dont wory about it sweet, I been gitting plenty to eat such as it is. you done your part darling if it dont ever git here I think I have plenty money, if I need more I let you know sweet where I will have time to git it. I dont know where I will be sent yet so I dont know how much it will take, so I sent for anought to take mw where I think I am going – R.O.C. fort mig – that's where they sent all the other boys that left the other day, I hope I git to stay on this side, but you cant ever tell, just hope and pray that it all will be over with before I haft to go, it is bad anought over here. I can git to see you ever once in a while, but I cant over there. Darling I am proud you made the trip OK. hope you enjoy your stay down home sweet you go any where you wont to dont haft to stay around there all time, if you can git any body to drive go in the car. well it have got to dark to write – by darling – I love you Love and Kisses, James

Dad makes some meaningful observations about life and how the Army has affected the boys that have been drafted into service with this next letter that was dated Monday afternoon and postmarked October 17, 11:30 am, 1944:

How is my little darling wife fine I hope, I feel pretty good for the treatment I have had. We made it pretty easy today, only it rained all the morning and we was out in it but we havent done any hard work, we had rifle inspection this afternoon and a few other little things, taking it easy for the rest of the week, starting tomorrow they wont have any mercy on us till we git in camp Saturday they will give all of us passes thats able to go any where and the rest will go to the hospital to git their feet treated that twenty five mile hike will ruin your feet if your shoes and socks dont fit just right. When you make these two weeks and that hike they call you a Soldier. if that what it takes I dont care anything about being one but it looks like I cant help my self. Sweet I guss you git tired reading the same old thing every day, but I dont see any thing but trees and wild hogs to write about and I am sure you dont want to hear about them, How is Iva making it, write me when you hear from them write all the news you know just anything. I like to hear about any thing just to keep my mind off staying out here in the woods. when I was growing up I wanted to do something like this, camping out, but now since I have a sweet little wife, I like to stay with her, you know out where you can have some freedom dont haft to take orders from just any thing they stick a strip (stripe) on. Sweet I would like to take orders from you. I would do any thing to be back with you darling. I wish I could see you it would be sweet time again. I never dreamed a soldier had to go through with all this stuff. You know I said I wanted to go to the army, well I have learned my lesson, if God will forgive me, I will never say that again, not in the Infantry. I just think about what Robert went through (This is one of the first times dad mentions his brother Robert who was killed in action.) then had to get killed not only Robert but millions of others this place is alright for a boy that drinks gambles and dont care for any thing. loots of the eighteen year old boys being ruined in the army taking up all kinds of habits, that they woulden never done back home they know better but the army dont teach any better thats the way they want you. They can have my part. I dont want it that way.

Sweet be good and take care of your self, I love you with all my heart darling.

your true love one James many kisses

These next letters from mother show her concern about dad being in the woods and having to go through all the hardships that he had told her about in his letters to her. This first letter was dated Opelika, Alabama, October 18, 1944 and postmarked October 19, 4:30 pm, 1944:

Hello Sweetheart,

I was so glad to get your three very sweet letters today. I just look forward from one morning to the next for your letters.

It won't be long now until you go back to camp will it? I'll be so glad for you.

I know all the training is hard and dangerous. I hope you won't get hurt.

I would be so glad if you could be stationed and not have to go across though.

How is your cold? I hope it won't get bad like it did last winter.

Your mother said to tell you she would be glad when you get out of the wilderness so that you won't have to eat any more sand.

She is dressing the chicken to send now. We are sending it tomorrow along with the letter.

I'll be glad when you can come home and drive this car, It looks lonesome here without you.

I'm going to wash it off some tomorrow. It is rather dusty now.

I picked up two sacks of cotton today. Your daddy is almost through as the Negroes came to help today.

Sweet it really has been cold here. I wish I had you to sleep with me. I almost freeze every night ha!

Write and let me know if you got your $40.00 O.K. I sent it Saturday.

Your grandpa (James Thomas Lafayette Brown or "Fate") is here now. He said to tell you to "make haste and come on" ha! I don't know what kind of perfume he has on. It really smells loud though.

I'll stop now, so be good and take care of yourself.

Yours only Eliz. & Roger

Mother mentions the hurricane that was occurring in Florida in this next letter. She did not realize that dad's company was out in the woods and being nearly drowned by the torrential rains and winds from it. They all had to be rescued and brought back to camp and of course there was a period of several days that dad could not write to her. She became worried about not getting any letters but eventually dad wrote and explained everything when he returned to camp. Her letter was written the following day after the previous one and was dated Opelika, Alabama, October 19, 1944. The postmark was October 20, 4:30 pm, 1944:

Dearest James,

Well, I suppose you wonder why you didn't hear from me. I missed the postman yesterday and today, but am going to meet him and make sure this one goes.

I'm sending the other the other two on. I'm so sorry I didn't get to mail them earlier, but I just can't get accustomed to the mail box. We are sending your package of chicken, biscuits, cake and preserves. I suppose you will be in camp by the time you get it though.

I'm so sorry you have such a cold, sweet do be careful. It would be so dangerous about getting pneumonia with such a fever.

I hope you will be in camp and doing fine Saturday morning.

Have you gotten your packages I sent? I sent two more that you ought to have by now.

Sweet, I haven't gotten the present you sent. Mary wrote me that she was going to mail it, but I haven't heard from her since she came home.

When you see Tucker ask him if she has sent it yet. I hope it didn't get lost in the mail.

I'm glad you got the money. It didn't take long to go did it? I mailed it at the post office in Opelika though.

I hope you can come home soon now.

I hope you won't have to go to a P.O.E. station.

Maybe you will get to stay in the states. I hope so.

I can't bear to think of you going over seas. I'd be so glad if you could come home to stay.

Sweet don't worry about me being lonesome here. It is lonesome for me as you know but I can put up with being lonesome if you can go through with what you do.

I'm looking forward to when you come home anyway.

I have one new skirt and two new sweaters. I'm keeping them to wear while you're here.

I want to look as good as I can for you although I know I can't look very good.

It really is cold here today. The wind is blowing so hard. I suppose it is off the hurricane they are having there in Fla.

I hope it isn't anywhere near you.

Write and let me know about it soon.

I love you with all my heart

Love & Kisses Elizabeth & Roger

This next letter finds mother having received her present from dad at long last. She had not received a letter from dad though and was concerned. As I mentioned before the weather was very threatening because of the hurricane in Florida and dad was not able to write. This letter from mother was written the following day on October 20, 1944. I was unable to read the postmark:

Hello Sweetheart,

Well, I didn't get a letter from you today. Nor I don't suppose you did from me as I missed the postman a couple of mornings.

I got the little Rifle pen today. Thanks so much. I'm so proud of it. It really took a long time to come. I suppose it was like everything else in the mail now though.

I hope your cold isn't any worse. Sweet be careful with it. I wish you were here so that I could rub you like I did last winter.

Roger and I are fine. We washed the car today. It really looks nice too. I aired it out and swept it also.

Your Dad & mother are doing fine. He just about has his cotton out now.

We are going to town tomorrow to get some things to take to the singing here Sunday.

I'm going to get my teeth filled Monday afternoon.

I got a letter from Mamma today. She says Arthur is on a ship now. She hasn't heard from him in over a week though. Harrison has to go overseas soon. They think he may come home first though.

I got a letter from Iva & Gerry also. She says he thinks he will be there until Christmas and they will get a furlough then.

Is Mary back in Starke now? I haven't heard from her since she came home. I don't know why. I wrote to her & sent it to Tucker's address.

I have a roll of film so we will take some pictures when you come.

I hope it is soon. I want to see you so bad sweet.

I'll stop now so take care of yourself & be good.

I'll do the same.

All my love Elizabeth & Roger

(There was a drawing from Roger enclosed in this letter,)

(I will include a scan of Roger's "letter" here.)

Mother had really started to worry by this time because she had not gotten any letters from dad in several days and several of her letters voiced this concern, As I've mentioned she did not realize that he had been caught in a terrible storm out in the wilderness and was unable to write for awhile until the storm cleared and they were rescued and led back to camp.

This letter from mother was dated Opelika, Alabama, October 23, 1944 and had an illegible postmark:

Hello Sugar,

How are you today? How is your cold? I hope it is much better now. We are all fine.

We all went to town today. Wash (Mayberry) drove the car. I don't suppose we will go any more till you come as we will have to save gas as we will have plenty then. I think the car needed to be driven some though.

It seems to be in good condition.

We are planning to go to church tomorrow, they have a singing tomorrow afternoon.

Sweet, I have been kinda worried. I haven't heard from you in two days. I hope there is nothing wrong. I won't get a letter tomorrow as it is Sunday.

Write and let me know if you got your package O.K.

Mamma says Arthur is on a ship now. I suppose he is going across. His address is New York now.

I hope it won't be too long before you can come home now.

Did you get your pass this weekend?

Don't forget my pictures. I can hardly wait to see them.

Roger wants you to hurry and come on. He says his daddy can drive that car and take him to town. He got in it this afternoon when I was sweeping it out and said "I better get out because I might get Daddy's car dirty," I'll stop now, so be good and take care of yourself.

Love always, Eliz & Roger

Mother was continuing to worry about not receiving any letters from dad as indicated by this next letter which stated she hadn't gotten a letter from him in four days, The letter was dated Opelika, Alabama, October 23, 1944 and postmarked October 24, 4:30 pm, 1944:

Dearest James,

How are you today? We are all O.K. It is still cool here, is it there?

I still haven't gotten a letter from you this is the fourth day. I just can't understand why I don't hear from you.

I suppose it is because you haven't had time to write.

The last two days I got letters from you I got three each day.

I really do miss your letters too. It makes me so lonesome not to hear from you.

I hope your cold is better now.

You are back in Camp now aren't you?

I hope you won't have anything else that will be so hard on you.

I'll be glad when you get home.

The car is just ready for you.

I have been sitting in it trying to learn the gears. I think I know all of them now. Maybe I will learn to drive day (Mother lived to be 84 years old and never learned how to drive.).

Have you been getting my letters? I write you every day.

I'm just hoping to get one from you tomorrow. If I don't, I think I will go crazy.

Your mother wrote you too, so I'll send hers along with mine.

Roger is fine. He and I have been cracking hickory nuts this afternoon.

Be good and take care of yourself.

All our Love Eliz. & Roger

Here is the letter that dad's mother wrote to him that was included inside mother's letter. It was dated Opelika, Alabama, October 23, 1944:

Dear James

Just a few lines two let you hear from us all we are doing all write I guess.

hope you are well and doing fine we haven't got a letter from you in 4 days hope two get one soon I dident heare from Curtis last week hope he is O.K.

Roger has a time with the puppy & cats we went to the singing Sunday wish you could seen Roger singing.

hope you have got your box by now. your daddy got through picking cotton two day I sure am glad wish you could of bin here two went to two the singing we will be looking for you soon hope you will get to come guess you are back at camp now hope so. I will be glad when this war is over I hope it will be soon. I will stop as I dont know anything new to write hope to see you soon write soon

with lots of love mama, dad Elizabeth & Roger

This was most likely the last letter dad wrote before he went out again to the woods on bivouac and got caught in the hurricane force winds and rain. He related the grueling experiences that he had the night before with his training, but he had no idea what was in store for him the next few days and nights. This letter was dated Wednesday afternoon before the storms came on Thursday and it was postmarked October 23, 1944:

Dearest Darling,

I just come in I mean I am tired and sleepy. I got your two sweet letters this afternoon when I come in I dident git to write you yesterday, but I will make up for lost time. We sure did have a bad night last night, tryed to sleep in foxholes, but I coulden eaven close my eyes. dident have any cover, nothing but a raincoat and jacket we all like to have froze. I got out of my hole and walked around all night thinking about you sweet wishing I was in the bed with you insted walking around in the woods freezing. we had to go about seven miles from our little old tents, which are not much better, you can lay down in the tents but you cant in a fox hole. my cold stays about the same, I have some feaver and a headache now, but I will be OK I hope, maby I can finish this week out where I wont haft to go through it again I wont git any sleep this week to amount to any thing that will make it hard on my cold. Sweet I guss we will haft to give up that box it havent come yet, so I will start looking for that one you sent Monday maby I will git it. I got the money OK. I cant see how some of the boys wives live they git all of her check from home and gamble and loose it, then borrow all they can from the boys in Camp they dont know I have any so they dont ask me for any – it woulden do any good anyway. Our Sargent wont let wife come down and stay with him, so he goes out and spends the week ends with some other woman. I saw a letter on his bed the weekin before we came out from his wife, it layed there from Saturday to

Monday he was out having a big time, so when he come in he throwed the letter in the waste basket with some other junk. I happen to be looking at him when he did it so when he went to look for his letter and coulden find it, so I told him to look in the waste basket and he would find it. I mean that sure did git him, thats the way some men do there wife, mostly the boys from the north that does that – they like these southern girls better than the northern girls. I guss thats the reason they go out so much on there wife, sweet how would you like for me to do you that way it woulden work. I can answer that. Sweet thats one thing you wont ever haft to worry about. I will never do my darling wife rong – no matter where I am or what I do, I will be true to the end sweet. I love you and you only darling. I will never love no one else but you sweetheart. I know you will be waiting for me no mater where I am are how long I am gone. You will always be my true love one wont you sweet heart? I dont even think of living with any body but you sweet. I could stay with you all time, and if this army ever turns me a loose, I will show you how much I like to stay with you darling, if I ever git a good place to stay again and a sweet little girl to sleep with and be with, you are so sweet and good. I think of it a loot sleeping out here on the ground and have the sweetest darling wife in the world, I could be with, but when this war is over and if I am still living, I will show you how sweet three can live together darling. Sweet I hope you can learn the gears by the time I come home, I wont you to learn to drive, I dident know how much better it would be till now. I can see you need to know how to drive, you might have a job some day and need to drive the car to work. you can git you a job when I come and leave this time, good looking sweetheart, pretty built and sweet little bubbies, ha, I sure would like to play with them sweet. I bet they are big ones now aint they sweet. I think you are built sweet, and I think some body else think the same thing to, the way they fulled (fooled) with you down here, ha, sweet I cant blame any body from wanting to full (fool) with you. I think you are the best looking kid I ever saw. You are kind and have a sweet smile, you dont ever frownd like some girls do when a boy looks at them, thats the reason you make so many friends you sweet thing you. I never did like a girl that frownd up ever time some body looked at her, the boys ask me about you all time, wanting to know if you have gone home, and wanting to know how I got sucher good looking wife. I tell them it takes a good looking man to git a good looking wife. sweet, you take care of you sweet self and when I come I wont you to have the tightest sweater on that you have where those little bubbies will really show up for me ha ha – you know how I like it dont you sweet by sweet heart and take care of Roger. I hope to see you all in about two weeks and really have a big time once more wont we sweetheart.

your true Love one James

With this letter, the first one that he had a chance to write after returning to camp, dad had endured a harrowing day and night in the woods in which he and his fellow soldiers had nearly drowned in the rainstorm that came off the hurricane. This was the first of several letters that he wrote to mother relating that experience. Mother finally did receive the letters and I am sure she was relieved to find out what had happened, and that dad was not injured during the storm. So, this is the first letter that he wrote explaining what had happened during the storm. It was dated Friday night after the Thursday that the storm had occurred. It was postmarked October 23, 11:30 am, 1944:

Dear Sweetheart,

just a few lines, hope you all are well, for myself I am OK at this time. I am in Camp, we had to come in Thursday night. I guss you have herd about the storm well we liked to have had one this time. I mean it rained and the wind blowed all night and day. I stayed wet all that time and all the rest. I never caught so much hell in my life, if you dont mind me saying that word no body knows what we went through with – just the lord will we living. Sweet I am sorry I havent wrote you but I coulden my paper was all wet. we had mail call this afternoon for the first time in three days. I got the box and a letter from you and mama, thinks a loots. I guss I will go to Stark tomorrow and git the pictures. I will send them to you if they are any good. Sweet I love you darling and I hope to see you in a few days, by sweet – I will write more later I got to go to bed

Love James

I will include these next letters from dad to mother as they are the ones mother referred to after having not gotten any letters from him in four days. This is a nice long letter. It was dated Saturday night and postmarked October 23, 11:30 am, 1944:

Hello Sweet heart,

I will try to write you a few lines if it is late. I just come in from Stark went to the show with Tucker and his wife (Mary), had a nice time. She said write her in Stark as she would be down here till Tucker left. I will send the pictures they are not much good but you cant expect to look any to good. Sweet I got your sweet letter to night when I come in, so I had to answer them if I dont git any sleep. Sweet I wish you was here with me tonight I was so lonesome for you, sweet you said you coulden look good. I think you look better than any girl I have ever saw. Sweet I relly love you and no one else, I will be so proud whin I can see you and keep you warm at night. I bet you git cold, but for love that's what you git cold for just like I do, you little sweet darling wife of mine, darling I think

163

of you all time, I never forgit you no mater what happen, sweet if I cant write sometime, just rember I am thinking of you with all my mind and heart to I am proud you got someone to drive the car it is good for it to be drove and wash (Mayberry) is a good driver to I forgit to tell you to git him he will take you any where you wont to go and have you teeth fixed and any thing that you wont to do just be careful and take care of yourself because you mean the hold world to me darling, I coulden live without you sweet heart, I love you so much. sweet I sure have had a bad time this last week, the lord was just with me because I was already sick and that storm come and we stayed wet from one afternoon until the next night at tin oclock just standing and laying out on the ground and in fox holes but I am OK just have a little cold, but it might stark showing up in me in a day or two, I hope not, mary said she sent the present I am sorry you havent got it, was just these little rifles – if you dont git them I will send you another set. sweet dont pick to much cotton, say could that you picked be wayed? I bet if it did you had a rock in the sack ha. I saw one of my boy friends in Stark today that was in Hamilton (C.C.C.) Camp with me – Eagerton you know Jean Smith went with him he is in the parshoots troops fixing to git discharged. He been over seas two years got wounded twice if you know where Jean is write her and send this adgress and till her he said hello and write him.

Pvt. Haywood Eagerton Overseas Reassign Station Complement on Camp Blanding fla

Sweet I got to go git some sleep

By Darling sweetheart Love always James

Dad would write longer more detailed letters to mother when he had more time, as on Sunday afternoon. Sometimes, if he was really intent and focused, he would hand print his letters rather than hand write them. This was the case with this next letter dated Sunday afternoon and postmarked October 23, 11:30 am, 1944:

Dear Sweetheart

I will try and write you a few lines, hope you are well and feeling fine, for myself I am doing fine. Just a little homesick for you darling sweetheart. I would give anything to see you darling. I got me a garson (garrison) hat today and a belt For my coat. I think it looks good. I got the pictures but they are no good, but I will send them any way, the studio man are making them over, they are good pictures but they don't show up, to dim, he said he could Fix them OK and it woulden cost me anything. I will send you three and you cand do anything you wont to with them I will get the others thursday and send them are bring them when I come, I want good one for you. Sweet I got the two packages today thinks a loot, I think I can make it now I will have nely (nearly) all of it, but when the boys come in they will finish it up for me. A box dont last long here but is good long as it last. Sweet it wont be long now before I git to see you I hope, one week and a half. we are supose to ship out some where, we git ten day, and four day traveling time, you know thats not long, but I will be proud to git that long. I just hope they dont send me across, but hoping dont do any good, you just haft to take what comes and make the best of it. Sweet I will do my best. Then if I fell (fail) I cant help it. I wont to do my part, but I would like to come back to my darling wife and boy. I love you sweet I would give anything to be back with you and Roger and all the rest.

Thinks for the chewing gum you sent yesterday in the letter, Sweet send me fifteen dollars I dont know where I will need it are not but I would hate to be left down here because I havent anought money to buy my ticket. I am pretty sure I have anought but I had rather have to much. Send it pretty soon I dont know when we will buy our tickets, send it the same way you sent the other, - just a few days there thin haft to leave.

The chicken and stuff sure was good. I hope Mama have some more of them when I come, say you and Grandpa butter take it easy ha ha till I git there. I wont to have a good time to, tell him I said hello and that I will be there in a few days I hope, and not to be traveling around to much he might git in trouble with them good looking girls that travels to.

Sweet the days getting where they seem like weeks now, waiting for the time to come when I can be with you a few days, Sweet be good and take care of your self and Roger. I love you both, I bet Roger have growed a loot, I can see him Running around after the cats and things.

by Little darling sweetheart your true love one James many kisses sweet

I believe the next letter was the last of at least four letters that mother got from dad all at once. She had not gotten any letters four days running because of the storm in Florida. This letter was written Tuesday afternoon and postmarked October 25. 11:30 am, 1944:

Dearest Darling Wife,

Just a few lines, hope you are well and feeling fine, for myself I am OK. I got your letter and the picture it looks OK, your part do, you always look good sweet darling. I sure will be proud when this week is over I wont to see you so bad. I wont git to stay for long, but that will be sweet to stay just a little while with you darling. I havent had time to send the pictures we have a night problem every night this week they cant hurt me now sweet unless they dont let me come to see you, then I will be hurt.

Saturday will be the last day to trane any here, we will graudate saturday and git our diploma.

Tucker is in the Hospital I think he haves the flue maby he will be back in a day are two I hope so, he got your letter said it sure was sweet ha, said he would answer in a day are so.

Sweet be good and take care of your self, I will see you soon I hope.

by Darling, your true Love One Always, James

many kisses to you sweetheart

By this time mother has at long last heard from dad as she relates in this letter. She had received four letters, the ones I included previously, all in one day. Her letter in response was dated Opelika, Alabama, October 24, 1944:

Hello Sweetheart,

I was so thrilled today, when I went to the mail box and got your four letters. I had really begun to worry, because I hadn't heard from you in so long.

I'm sorry you got so wet during the storm but I am thankful that you weren't harmed any other way.

We read in the paper that $29,000.00 damage was done to the fruit in Miami, Fla and eleven Soldiers were drowned somewhere in Fla.

I'm so glad you are back in camp now. I hope your getting wet won't make your cold any worse. I'm glad you had a good time over the week - end. Wish I was down there with you now, we really would have a good time couldn't we sweet?

I'll be so glad to get the pictures, I know they are good, if they are anything like you. I suppose I will get them tomorrow.

I'm glad you got your packages we sent. I hope you enjoyed them. I'm sorry they were so late that you didn't get them while you were out in the woods.

I'm sending your $15.00 along in this letter. I'm going to Alma's tomorrow, so I'll have it registered in town. Before I mail it.

I'll only stay with her one night, so just write me here as usual.

I didn't get my teeth fixed, as I couldn't get anyone to take me to town yesterday afternoon.

Everyone is busy now, picking cotton or pulling corn. I'll be so glad when you get here, then we can go to town occasionally.

I haven't even seen Jap or Emma since I've been here. I think Jap got tired of fooling with the car. Your mother said he just wouldn't come and crank it.

Jeff put gas in it and cranked it once or twice before I came.

I think Jap did it at first, but no one has seen him since.

Sweet, I can't wait to see you. I'll be so glad. This week and a half will seem more like a month to me.

I got a letter from Harrison & Margaret. He wrote to you too. He thought you were here on furlough.

He is back at Maxwell Field Montgomery now, and wants us to come by to see them if we can. He doesn't think that he will be there long.

I bet you were surprised to see Eagerton. I'm glad he got back alive. He was lucky I suppose.

I'll write mamma to give Jean his address when she sees her,

She is in Birmingham now, and I don't know her address. I know she will be glad to hear about his being back.

Roger really was tickled when he heard you had gotten the chicken.

He said "Mother that postman did take Daddy his chicken," He worried a lot about it. He was afraid that you wouldn't get it.

Sweet, I got the Rifle pen a day after I wrote you that I didn't get it. I really am proud of it.

I wrote Mary and addressed it to Tucker as I didn't know whether she was down there by the time the letter got there. I wonder if she got it. I'll be looking forward to you coming home soon.

So be good, and write me soon, all our Love & Kisses
Eliz & Roger

Mother's letters to dad give an informative sequence of events, time and places and establish somewhat of a daily routine while she and Roger were in Opelika, Alabama waiting with dad's parents for him to come to see them on his furlough. It must have been boring for her to stay there with nothing to do but pick cotton and wish and hope that she could find someone to take her to town where things were at least somewhat more entertaining. She, as always, was very considerate of everyone's feelings and tried not to let on how truly bored she might have been. This letter finds mother staying at dad's sister's place in Opelika, so at least, that offered new surroundings and different family members to pass the time with. The letter was dated Opelika, Alabama, October 25, 1944 and postmarked October 27, 2:30 pm, 1944:

Hi Sweet,

How are you today? We are all O.K. We are now at Alma's. I didn't get a letter from you today. I really did miss it too.

I sent your fifteen dollars today. Write and let me know when you get it.

What do you do now Sugar? You don't have very much to do now do you?

Roger and Marie (Alma's youngest daughter) are having lots of fun playing together.

I wish you were here with us now. We get so lonesome. It won't be long now though until you come I hope.

I got a letter from Mamma today. She says Arthur has gone overseas. He went on the U.S.S. Randolph Ship. Said it really was a beauty.

I just hope he can go over there and come back safe.

Harrison is back at Maxwell Field. Mamma says he will get his ten day leave soon. It may be the same time you get yours.

Alma said she would be looking for you to come to her house when you get to Opelika.

If you know what time you will get here write and let me know so I can get someone to meet you.

I'll stop, so be good. We love you Eliz. & Roger

Mother's letters indicated how lonesome she and Roger were and how she wished dad could be there to share time with them and take them places. Even though dad's car was at his parent's place mother could not drive it or find anyone to drive it for her. Staying at Alma's place was at least a diversion and Jeff, Alma's husband, could drive them to town and back to Gordon and Betty Brown's farm.

This letter was dated Opelika, Alabama, October 26, 1944 and postmarked October 28, 7:30 pm, 1944:

Hi Sweet,

How are you today? We are O.K. but it really has turned cool again.

We are going back to your mother's tomorrow afternoon. I just can't wait to get back to see my letters from you.

I really do miss them. It makes me lonesome to not have any of your letters to read.

Alma & Jeff have gone to work again.

It isn't quite as lonesome for me here as it is in the country.

There are plenty children to keep me company ha.

I don't have very much trouble with them though, They mind pretty good.

Did you get your money O.K.? Write and let me know.

I hope you will have plenty to get your ticket, because I surely don't want you to be left down there.

I can hardly wait till you come. I want to see you so bad. I wish I could be down there with you now, We could have lots of fun.

I'm going to write to Mary to see if she will write me. I might have a letter from her at your mother's though.

I love you with all my heart sweet, bye & be good,

Love & Kisses Eliz & Roger

Here is one more of mother's letters to dad before I return to his in answer to hers. It was dated Opelika, Alabama, October 29, 1944 and postmarked October 30, 4:30 pm, 1944:

Hello Sugar,

I will try to write you if Roger will let me. He is writing you too and is asking me more questions than I can answer him!

He asked me to look his letter over & see if it was good.

He is just waiting for me to get through so that I can draw him some birds.

Today is another lonesome Sunday for us. We didn't go to church today as they didn't have any.

I hope you will be here to go with me next Sunday, I wish you could be with me every day from then on too.

I miss you so much.

Let me know the day you are coming, because if I were to write you many more letters, you would be here and the letters would be in Fla.

I'll stop now so write me soon, All my Love Eliz

There is a letter/drawing from Roger that has the caption "From Roger ", he said he drew a bird for you to catch,

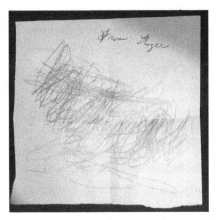

(I will include a scan of Roger's drawing here.)

Here are the letters that dad wrote to mother during his last days of training at Camp Blanding. His focus was on enduring the harsh training and making it back to his beloved wife and son. He didn't know what the future held for him or even if he would live to have a future, but his ten-day furlough was what kept his hopes alive for at least the next few days. This letter was dated Wednesday afternoon and postmarked October 26, 3 pm, 1944:

Hello Sweetheart,

I will try and answer your letter sure was proud to hear from you all. I dident git a letter yesterday from you, but I got two today. you should have got one nely (nearly) every day. I havent missed but one day writting, maby two days. Anyway I am back in Camp where I can write now. you said you was going to have some teeth filled. I had one filled today, got five more to have filled some time this week. I think he got the worse one the way it felt. I stayed up ther, from seven oclock this morning until five this afternoon and got only one tooth filled, it ought to stay in ther forever. I am proud you got your rifles, glad you like them, sweet I won't be there this weekin but I will next weekin if nothing dont happen. I would give anything to be there now darling we would have a good time sweetheart I sure do want to see you, it wont be so much longer now before I git to see you I hope sweet. I am proud you had a nice time at the sanging. I would have give any thing to been there with you darling. I know we could have had a dandy time togather, we always do dont we sweetheart? Sweet go out where you want to I think I can git plenty gas to go where I want to, tell Roger I am proud of him not letting you dirty the car up. so you better be careful he will git you in high the first thing you know. Sweet be careful and take care of you little sweet self. tell Roger I sure do want to see him and he better show me he is a man and not a baby when I come.

by sweet your true Love one James

many sweet kisses darling

This next letter from dad had him giving some details about his night training with gas masks and he also related details of some strange dreams he had been having. There was no date written inside, but it was postmarked October 28, 3 pm, 1944:

Hello Darling wife

I will try and answer your letter I recived yesterday afternoon, sure was proud to git your sweet letter. I am working day and night . I had my shoes off none time since last Sunday night. I mean they dont have any mercy on us. I would give any thing if this war was over, we haft to take some hard training and plenty dangerous to. I dont like to do some things they have for us to do. I am making it OK, havent had any trouble yet, had to sleep with my gas mask on last night they throwed tear gas all around our tents, I mean it burn your eyes out if you dont git your gas mask on.

I dont sleep at all. I have dreamed more this week thin I have all the rest of my life. I doze off and cant rest on this hard ground, when I do git a chanch to lay down, I dreamed about Robert all last night and you night before but it was bad about you. I dreamed you was dead but yet I was with you and the law was after me for killing someone so you cand see I rest good by the way I dream. I dreamed I was fighting in Germany and the bullets was falling all around me. Lord do help I will be proud when these two weeks are over. tell mama and them I will write just as soon as I can, I dont have time to write much, we dont have any lights at night, we haft to feel our selves around and git to out tents when we come in off those night problems. So you see we cant write at night. Sweet how are you making out down there, try to enjoy your self and have a good time if you can. I know you git lonesome down there, but I could stay there the rest of my life with you and never git lonesome after staying down here at this place. I would stay any where to git out of the army.

Sweet take care of your self and Roger. I hope to see you soon, send me any thing you can git to eat a hungry man cant be choice about eating. by sweet and be good.

I love you darlin, Love James

Dad had just about finished his training by this time and had found out when he would be shipping out with this next letter. Actually, there were two letters placed inside in the same envelope and I will include both of them here. This first one had Saturday night written at the top and the envelope was postmarked October 30, 3:30 pm, 1944:

Dearest Sweetheart

I will write you a few lines hope you well and feeling fine for myself I am OK, sure have been having a tuff day. I bet you havent thought of me a time today have you sweet? I didn't git a letter anyway but I got three yesterday which was very sweet, darling I am on guard duty tonight trying to write and the boys are making so much nose I cant do nothing. Sweet I havent had time to send the pictures I might just wait till I come and bring them. Well my time is gitting short around this place, I am proud my training is over in a way but you know what that means so I dont know which is the best. I try not to think it no more than I can help. Sweet be careful and dont worry about me. I will be OK. I hope to see you next week tell Mother & Dad I wont write I will wait and come, by darling Love and sweet dreams

I love you sweet, I got to go Love James

This is the other letter that was enclosed in the envelope:

Dearest Sweetheart

Sweet I been thinking of you all day wishing I was with you thinking of next Saturday hoping I will be there with you darling. I got the pictures, they are pretty good. I wont send them, they might beat me there, and when I git there you might be gone, so I will bring them, and you can see them while I am with you. I dont wont you to quit me, so I am playing safe ha. Sweet I got my shipping orders to go to the poe fort magChealin (Fort McClellan) so I guss I will bee going places pretty soon. I sure hope not, but thats the way they want it looks like now, I was afraid of that all time if nothing happen I will bee there sometime next week, about Thursday I hope, so bee ready for a big hug and kisses, tell all the family, I said hello and not look for a letter from me, I hope to come, by darling and bee sweet

I love you sweetheart tell Roger I said bee good, Love and Kisses James

This letter from dad was written the next day as it had Sunday afternoon written inside. It was postmarked the same as the previous letters on October 30, 3:30 pm. 1944:

Hello Sweetheart.

Just a few lines, hope you are well and feeling fine, for myself I am OK. havent been anywhere this weekin, been washing some clothes and things. I think we will ship out on Wednesday so I will git there some time Thursday if nothing happens. I dont know what time I will git to Opelika thats the reason I dident have you to meet me. the army wont let any body know what time a troop train will go from one place to another on the count of spies, might rack (wreck) it, so I dont know when I will git there. all I know we will leave sometime next week. So dont be surprise to see me any time after Thursday are maybe before then it wont take long to git to you after I git to Opelika. I will be on my own then I wish they would let me go from here on my own. I would git there quicker and fell better when I git there.

Sweet I dont think Tucker will git to leave he have been in the hospital a week. I think he is leaving from there tomorrow and come back to camp, he have lost a week training so they might hold him over a week are so to make up for that, they might let him go I dont know yet. I dont know where Mary is still down here or not.

by sweetheart abd be sweet, Love and kisses

I forgit and took the ring off today for the first time sweet Love James

This next letter was dad's last letter written before he went on furlough and this will end this first long chapter on Camp Blanding, Florida. The letter was dated Monday night and postmarked October 31, 5 pm. 1944, so I am assuming he shipped out on Tuesday, not on Wednesday as he had expected.

Dear Sweetheart,

Just a few lines, hope you are feeling fine and dandy – wish I was on my way to see you darling, but it wont be long now, just one more day and I will be coming that way I think. I have turned in all my things but what I will cary with me, I will have plenty left to cary to more thin I want to full (fool) with. I sure hope you will be well and feeling good while I am there I feel like having a good time dont you sweet? I know you are having a time with all thim kids, I know you to well, well be sweet. I will see you in a day are two I hope.

Love and Sweet dreams, yours true for ever

many sweet kisses

Chapter Two

Letters from Friends and Relatives

This chapter will include letters from close friends of mother and dad that they made while at Camp Blanding, Florida and from close relatives and friends that lived in Hamilton, Alabama, Opelika, Alabama, Childersburg, Alabama and other places that these friends and relatives may have lived in at that time. I believe these letters to be of great importance in expanding the knowledge of my parent's background and for giving a broader scope of the times and places they lived in. One must keep in mind that people in these days may have had limited education due to being raised on farms and having to work the fields of their family's farms in their childhood. There was little opportunity for schooling so many of them only had limited writing and grammar skills at best. I have kept letters from friends and relatives just as they were written and have not corrected any of the grammar or spelling, just as I did not correct the grammar or spelling of my dad's letters. I feel to alter the letters in any way would be to take away from the colorful personalities of the people that wrote them. So do not accuse me of not using spellcheck. I am not using it by design.

The first letter is from Mattie Owsley. dad's aunt, who was married to Lee Owsley, my grandmother Betty Owsley Brown's oldest brother.

Hello James,

I will ans your welcome letter which I recived a few days passed. Sure was glad to here from You And to here you Was Well. This leaves All Very Well at present except Jasper he was orpatedid on Friday for Appenendictis.

He is doing fine I have just been to see him. Aunt Pearl (Betty Brown's sister) went with me she is at my house now (Aunt Pearl never had a house of her own but would stay with relatives. She would move from one relative's place to another all her life. They all loved her and were proud to have her stay with them as she took care of their children and helped out with all the household tasks, It worked out very well for all of them. Things were different in those days and I'm not so sure that they weren't better in those days.). She sayed she is going down to Bettie just as soon as Jack gets better And stay a While With him.

Lucille & her baby is doing fine. he was a mo. Old the 15 of this Mo. I sure would like to here form (from) your wife & Baby. Aurther & Dugger got a letter from Hurman (Herman Owsley) Saturday he has landed in Ing (England).

I sure do hope and Pray that this War Wont last much longer so all the boys can come back home. Well as it is getting late guess I better close by saying Good by Ans soon and take care of your self and be good.

May God take care of you and all the other boys in servise.

There was a letter from Lee Owsley, Mattie Owsley's husband and Betty Owsley's oldest brother, included inside the envelope of Mattie's letter and I am adding it here:

Opelika, Ala RFD 3

Mr. James Brown

(This is Lee Owsley's photo taken in the early 1940's.)

Dear Nefue

glad to here from you we are all well but Jasper. He was operated on Friday is doing fine Hope you will get to come home soon would be glad to see you. hermmon Owsley landed safe in england.

soon to you write

lee Owsley RL #3 Opelika, Ala

The next letter was written to dad from Aunt Rhoda Boyett, my mother's aunt and her mother Cora Lee Palmer's half sister. It was a birthday greeting to dad, who had just turned 24 years old on September 11, 1944. The letter was dated September 18, 1944 and postmarked September 18, 4:30 pm, 1944:

Dear James: I was at Cora Lee's and she told me about your Birthday. Also about your brother's death. Please except our sincere Sympathy. I was very sorry to learn about his death. I seen a letter he wrote. it was so good I had Elisabeth copy it off for me. And as much as we hate to give him up from the letter I seen I am sure there is peace where he is and we ought to be content for him to be there instead of in the war. While I feel like I know something about how hard it would be for you know I am likely to hear the same news about mine any time. Harlan was at Pearl Harbor at the Bombing then he went to the Marshal Is, then to Saipan and help that place and now we think he is gone on somewhere else. Stanley is likely to cross any time. I will send you Harland's address and know he would be glad where he is to have a line from anyone and he sure thought a lot of you. Well I had better close, May the Lord watch over you is my prayer from Rhoda and Boys.

P.F.C. Harland H. Boyette 341077071

Co. A. 1341st Engrs. A.P.O. # 244 %

Post Master San Francisco, Calif. I made a mess of San Francisco. I will write again.

Aunt Rhoda included a letter to mother that was enclosed in this envelope:

Dear Elisabeth,

how are you. I saw your boy and mother they was fine, Roger said Aunt Rhoda has come he sure is sweet he was wanting to go somewhere and pick cotton him and Chloe's boy too are wanting a Job ha, I know you would like to see him (Mother was with dad at Camp Blanding when

183

Rhoda wrote this letter.) but you will have more time to stay with him than do James and I don't blame you to stay a long as you can. I guess James will be surprised to get this letter but I felt so sorry for them all I wanted to write. I haven't Harland yet about it. I don't remember it if I have I hate to write him anything that way where he is. I am afraid it will just make him feel worse but of course he has to see such as that every day, So anything you want to write him I don't guess could make it worse.

bye and Lots of Love from Aunt Rhoda

In a similar vein, I will include this letter from mother to her mother, Cora Lee Palmer, as it related to what other relatives were writing to dad and mother at the time. This was about the time that dad was preparing to leave on his ten-day furlough from Camp Blanding, Florida. The letter was dated Opelika, Alabama, October 25, 1944 and postmarked October 27, 12:30 pm, 1944:

Dearest Mother & all.

We were so sorry to hear that Arthur has gone overseas.

I just hope that he won't have any trouble or get sick.

Don 't worry too much about him. He will just go over there and come back when his mission is over.

I know it is bad but I'm afraid all our boys will have to go over before the war is over. Maybe it won't last much longer, and they can all come back.

I got a letter from James and he says he will get his leave next Wed, or Thursday. He gets ten days and four days traveling time.

Then he goes overseas after that of course. I hate to think of it, but it is something we can't do anything about.

I got a letter from Harrison yesterday. He thought James was already home and wanted us to come by and see them.

Maybe he & James will get their leaves at the same time.

I suppose I will get the skirt tomorrow. Thanks for sending it.

I'm at Alma's house now. We came up here this morning & will stay a day or two. She said to tell you hello & she would like to see you.

Continue to write me to Rt, 4 though as I'll be back with Mrs. Brown by the time you get this.

I'll write later and let you know when James & I will be there.

Mamma I'm sending you some money. So get Arthur something for Xmas for me. I'd like to be there to help you send it. Have you asked at the post office how to send it? I think you have to send it in a syrup bucket. That is the way they send them from here.

I'll stop now so take care of yourself and don't worry too much about Arthur.

He will take care of himself the best he can. Lots of Love
Eliz. & Roger

Keeping with mother's side of the family, this next letter was from my Aunt Iva Gamel, mother's sister and was written to mother, October 17, 1944 and postmarked October 18, 1944:

(I am including a scan of Aunt Iva and
one of Uncle Gerry and Aunt Iva here.)

Dearest Elizabeth,

We surely were glad to get your letter. I suppose by now
you & Roger are in Opelika.

I surely would love to see you. Sorry I won't be able to see
James when he comes home. Tell him hello & give him
our regards. I can't wait to see Roger. Bet he is cute in his
new clothes. Tell him his Aunt Iva says Hi & I'm sending
him some gum in this letter.

Mammy says Harrison will get to come home. I surely
hate to miss him, but I can't leave my husband and we
never know when he might be shipped out. We hope to
be here at least till Dec. If we do, we will get a furlough
& go home. Will you be home then. I hope I get to see
you. I get so excited when I think of going home. We've

been out here almost 3 months now. It's been wonderful, but I'd love to see home just the same.

I called Gerry before I left the bank & he is working the night shift tonight. Will be in at 12:00. So I'm catching up on my letter writing.

Please write us real soon and let us know how everything is with you.

Glad you liked the joke. I thought it would be a good souvenir as well as a joke. There's lots of things like that in the stores out here.

All our love,

Iva & Gerry

This letter from my Uncle Arthur Palmer, who was in the Navy at this time, fits well within the writings of mother to dad and of other letters written by relatives that were writing about his being shipped overseas. It was dated November 24, 1944 from the U.S.S. Randolph:

(I am including a scan of my Uncle Arthur's photo here.)

My Dearest Sister,

Got your letter today thanks a lot sure happy to hear from you again.

I know it must have hurt you something terrible to see James go back (Dad's ten day furlough had ended and he was to be shipped overseas,). I know his leave must have seemed short. I know they always do. I hope he makes cook soon. I know it would be so much better for him.

Thanks for the cakes and candies. It was good. I enjoyed it very much.

I hope Iva gets her same old job back again because you all will be close together (Her old job, before going with Gerry to his post, was working at a bank in Birmingham, Alabama.).

Thanks to Roger for his letter it was very interesting. Tell him to write again.

Well I must close as time is short. Hoping to hear from you soon.

Love Joseph A. Palmer – Joe

There were many letters from friends that mother and dad made while mother stayed in Starke, Florida for two months while visiting dad at Camp Blanding, Florida where he took his training. Dad had rented a room for mother in a house there that he shared with her at nights and on weekend passes. They became close friends with a couple that also rented a room in that house. Dad's friend that he trained with, Tucker, and his wife Mary stayed there and Mary became instant friends with my mother. Mary and mother wrote each other often after mother returned home to Hamilton and I will include those letters here. The first letter from

Mary Tucker was in answer to a letter mother sent her which I included in Chapter One.

Mary's letter was dated Starke, Florida, October 4, 1944 and was postmarked October 4, 7:30 pm, 1944:

Dear Liz,

I got your letter a few days ago was so glad to hear from you. I took your letter over to Gladys (another friend of theirs at Starke). With me yesterday & let her read it. She hadn't heard from you but she knew you had written her – see Carl didn't come in as he was on guard duty I think. Guess Carl brought your letter to her today. She gave me a picture of you & James they made one Sun. She's going to send you one just like it. I'm so proud of it. It's real good of you both. I'll send you one of us soon as I can.

Sure am glad you had a nice trip home. I remember the girl you was sitting next to.

I hope I'm as lucky as you about making good connections. I know I'll have to wait two hours in Macon, Ga. tho. Gee I sure do dread going home by buss. I'll be glad to see Mama tho.

Yes, it was nice of Mrs. Norris daughter to meet you. I bet you enjoyed the sandwiches & candy. Mary wrote Mrs. Norris about it.

Mozell & Juanita (two other friends of Mary and mother's) goes to breakfast with me most every morning. It's not like having you here although I like them lots I think they are nice. I still miss you like everything.

(I am including a scan of the Starke
Diner where they had breakfast.)

I go out to camp most every nite – can't go Thurs Nite tho,
Jr got a weekend pass Sat. but was around 9 o'clock getting
here. James pulled K.P. for him. I really do appreciate it
& you know Jr, does to, I got 40 cents worth of cookies
& took them out last nite & told Jr. to give James half of
them. I wanted to let him know I thought it was real nice
of him to work on Sun for Jr. but I couldn't find a thing
I thought he'd like – you know what's in Starke, Jr. said
he wanted to treat him to a show & ice cream one nite
so maybe he'll come up to Service Club with Jr. tonite,
I haven't seen him since you left. I gave Jr. the picture of
you & him & told him to show it to James but to bring
it back to me as I wanted to keep it & Gladys is sending
you one like it.

Yes, Juanita come in Tue – the day Mary left. Shes sweet
as she can be – She isn't like Holmes said she was at all.
I think they was just kidding me. I sure do like her &
Mozell. The girl whos supposed to take your room hasn't
come in yet. Don't know why tho. I wish you was back
in it myself. I sure do miss you Liz. Seems as tho some

ones dead or something. Jr. misses James coming up there with him at nites & on the weekend almost as bad as I miss you.

I'll be leaving here Mon. P.M. sure do hate to leave Jr. but if I stayed, I couldn't see him. I got Gladys' suit-case yesterday & I've packed a few of my things.

It makes me hungry to think of cornbread, biscuits & chicken – you shouldn't write me things like that till I go home & can have some to (Ha Ha). Yes, I know it was good you don't have to tell me that honey. Hope Mama has lots of (cornbread) cooked when I get there & and on the table. It'll be so nice to get home & eat what you want for a change – huh?

Maybe we'll all be in Opelika at the same time when they get furloughs or at least I hope so. I sure do want to see you.

It hasn't rained down here for two whole days – can you beat that – Ha,

Boy it was cold last nite – we had to sit inside most of the time. Started to go the show but decided not to as it was kinda late & I was afraid we wouldn't get to see all the picture so we didn't go but Tucker ate ice cream right on as cold as it was – Ha.

It seems when I get started writing you I can't stop. I guess you can see that – Ha.

Take care of yourself & write me every chance you get.

Bye Bye for now – Lots of Love Mary

Mary Tucker must have written many more letters to mother and there was a Christmas card I found, but I only found one more letter from her that was dated Phenix City, Alabama, November 26, 1944, and postmarked November 26, 6 pm, 1944:

Dearest Liz,

I got your letter a few days ago, Sure was glad to hear from you.

Yes, I know you've been mighty lonesome & I guess you are still as for that matter. I've gotten kinda use to Jr. being away almost. I sure did feel blue yesterday tho. I got a letter from Jr. & he couldn't tell me much but said he was still in the states. I know he'll be leaving for across soon tho. I hate to think of the day he'll leave tho. Its like you say Its one of those <u>many</u> <u>things</u> we have to put up with & make the best of it. It'll be the happiest day of my life when this war is over, I only hope Jr. & the other boys will return safe but you know theres some that wont come back to my sorrow. In Jr.'s letter he said he saw James for a few minutes & that he seemed to be just fine. I wish they could be in the same co. don't you? Jr. hasn't seen but two or three of the boys from Blanding either. I know they are so lonesome. I was hoping to see Jr. again before he left but thats out of the question now.

By all means send me a picture of you & James if you can. I'd love to have one. Wish I could send you one but I can't as we couldn't find any films at all here. I sure did want to make some of Jr. anyway.

Its real cold up here too & its been raining off & on nearly all week. Gee I hate rainy weather you can't do a thing. Maybe it'll fair off soon I hope.

Jr. hasn't got a one of the packages I sent him yet. I sure hope they'll catch up with him soon but doubt it as he's had 3 different addresses. I'm dying to go to the post office & see if I've heard from him today.

I went to two shows yesterday. I was so blue & thought if I'd go to one it would get my mind off things & it helped some.

I haven't heard from any of the girls since I left them in Starke except Mozell. She said Mae & the other girls had gone home. When have you heard from Gladys? I hope shes getting along fine. I'd like to see all of them again.

I've got to hurry & bathe this PM as I want to go to the post office & I think mama & them wants to go to another show Ha. Take care of yourself Liz & I hope to see you again sometimes.

Write me & every time you can & send me that picture if you can. I'll close for now.

Lots of Love Mary

P.S. hope you can read this Bye Bye Mary

Mary mentioned Gladys in her letter to mother. Gladys Braungard was another close friend of mother's and Mary Tucker's while they were with their husbands at Starke, Florida during their training ar Camp Blanding. I have several of Gladys' letters to mother and I will include them here in the order that they were written. The first letter from Gladys was dated Starke. Florida, October 3, 1944 and postmarked October 5. 3:30 pm, 1944:

Dear Elizabeth,

I received your card Tuesday saying you arrived home OK. I'm so glad. I thought it was swell of Mary (This is another Mary, not Mary Tucker,) to meet you and give you the lunch.

She seemed so nice when she was at Norris.

It just the same as ever here in Fla only I think we've had cookie (kooky) weather. Mary was over yesterday and spent the afternoon with me. She took my suit case to pack some of her clothes. She says she can hardly imagine shell be home next week.

I guess Im really stay till Jan, I had decide after you went to go home the first of Nov But my sweet husband changed my mind ha ha.

I guess you gave me home fever.

I have to laugh at Roger. I'll bet he sticks close.

I am feeling lots better my medicine help me and I don't have to go back unless I'm worse again.

I am sending you the snap shot we took that Sunday. I thought they turned out real good.

I had 3 made one for us and Mary and one for you. The ones of Carl and I were good and I'm having more made like those too.

As soon as there finish, I'll send you one.

When Mary was over yesterday she let me read your letter. I see in here you were enjoying the corn Bread and chicken – ha ha.

I could stand the chicken myself But of course the corn Bread never have us hearing of it.

I couldn't say But if it like grits, you can keep it all.

Well Eliz here comes my hubby and Im not even dress. Im in my house coat. Its only 230 Surprise Monday nite I was alone all nite he pulled guard.

Sure seemed funny But I lived. Yesterday we got a nice big box from Carl's mother. It had everything in fruitcake, cheese, crackers, cookies, cigars, ha ha – lots other thing, you can just see us opening it, scramble, scramble, Guess I close.

Write soon. We miss you.

Know you glad to be home.

Love Gladys & Carl

The next letter from Gladys Braungard was dated Starke, Florida, October 26, 1944 and postmarked October 28, 3 pm, 1944:

Dear Elizabeth,

Guess I get busy and ans your letter before you think I've forgotten.

I really didn't do that But we had quite a bit of electricity last week with the hurricane & all, Suppose by now James has told you. Carl was one of the boys they sent out to get James and the boys and bring them back to camp. He was restricted for two nite. Don't think I wasn't lonesome and scared, This time it really came and the first one I was ever in.

It didn't do much damage in Starke as other places. But it was plenty to suit me.

Well Carl was restricted Wed. & Thursday nite, came home Friday and didn't see him again until Monday nite. He pulled guard duty over the weekend wasn't that nice – 4 nite in one week. It sure was a long weekend. So I slept till noon Sunday. Got up and dressed and went to the show by myself in the after noon. I sure wish you or Mary were here, Pin up Girl (the name of the movie), It was real good.

When I got back here Sat a note on my vanity from Mary. She & Tucker had been here and got the suit case. I sure was disappointed I miss her. But she came back again Monday and see me. She's now out at the Guest house for 3 day. She looked real good said she had a nice time home.

Well Elizabeth I must tell you my Surprise. I guess I will be going home with 3 of us instead of two can you imagine.

I have miss twice now. I guess Dr, Adams don't know everything. You know when I went to him. I miss a peoid and he said it was cause from my infection. I was so swollen I couldn't. I sure don't have infection now. I regained a lot of weight all in one spot. I feel small. Feel much better than I did before. I haven't had a bit or morning sickness (yet). As near as we can figure I'll be 3 months the 18 of Nov. I'm going to a Dr. out at Camp it doesn't cost me anything and if we are here when the baby comes I can go there to the hospital for nothing. I have company you know cause the one girl down stair always goes. She's 6 mos. Just imagine nearly 5 years and here I am. Good old Florida ha ha. I really don't care or feel bad Carl's tickled to death about it if everythings OK. We both hope it's a boy. We're not telling any of our folk.

They sure will die when they see us hear ha ha. Really tickles me. Well Eliz I guess Iva told you all the new. Hope Florida did give you a pleasant souvenir ha ha. I'll never forget it now. The news sound pretty good. I hope the old (war) is soon over we can all go back home Live again. I don't know if I told you I've been out and see the whole of Camp Blanding Sure is some place. Well guess I better get busy do some work. I hope James soon get home you can have a good time.

I'll can't just imagine how lonesome it is there for you and Roger. I will love to have a couple snap shots if there good.

I don't know if I told you yet my hubby got a promotion to corporal. We are both real glad and please. It will sure help us. We'll get $12.00 more a month you know how far that will go here.

Hope this fines you all well & happy.

Write Soon, Love Gladys & Carl

This next letter from Gladys Braungard was misdated Starke, Florida, October 9, 1944. I know this date had to have been wrong because Gladys wrote about the re-election of Franklin Roosevelt which took place on November 3, 1944. So, the correct date must have been November 9, 1944:

Dearest Elizabeth.

Guess I answer yo letter to nite. Carl sit here writing his mother of course, he's using the pin. So you'll have to excuse my pencil.

I suppose by now James has been home (He would've gotten there around the first week of November,) his furghlow eather over or nearly. I hope you both had a sweet time (This is also a reference that proves Gladys misdated her letter.).

I'll bet Roger sure was glad to see his daddy, what did he say when he saw him.

It's raining hard here to nite. Carl and I started up town for a walk, But had to hurry back so we wouldn't get wet.

I'm just getting over a bad cold didn't want to catch more.

Yes I see Mary the day before she and Tucker left for home. She was quite worried about him being in the hospital. Yes Elizabeth I guess I'll get to walk in home with a baby all right. Little did I think when I told you girls about that It would ever happen. One never knows. I'm feeling fine so far. Haven't had any morning sickness. I'm 3 mos, maybe I'll escape that. I'm glad you hope it will be a boy – that what we want too.

Was sorry to hear about your young brother (Arthur was shipped overseas.). Hope he has lots of good luck. It a same (shame) being so young. My sister Husband both have been sent over seas since you were here. One is in France and the other in England.

Maybe the one in France only went in the army last April, got shipped that soon. Sure beats all. How did you like the election (This proves the date could not have been October 9. 1944 but must've been November 9, 1944.). I'm glad Roosevelt got it. This is no time to change I don't think. Guess you were glad to seen the returns Alabama was for him.

Guess I better close.

Write soon. Love Gladys & Carl

This next letter from Gladys Braungard was the last one I found other than Christmas cards. I can only surmise that it was the last time mother heard from either her or Mary Tucker, although there could be other letters from them written much later that I have not yet discovered. The letters that I am using for this book are from 1944 and 1945, so there may be others from 1946 and later that I have not found yet. This letter was dated December 10. 1944 (which incidentally was my brother Roger's third birthday) and postmarked December 12, 5 pm, 1944:

Dearest Elizabeth.

Well guess I'll get busy answered your lovely letter I received some time ago,

I am sorry I've been so slow answer But I have been doing quite a lot of crocheting and making Christmas presents it took up a lot of my time.

Im way behind on my writing today late I decide we make a day at it and get caught up.

It is 9 o'clock and have just finished writing to Mary. She wrote me right after she went home.

I took a snap shot of her just before she left and I'm sending you one. I think it was pretty good for the day we had.

(I am including a scan of this photo of Mary.)

It was late in the day and starting to rain.

How did you and James enjoy his furlough, good I know, except they go much too fast. Where is he now?

Elizabeth Im still feeling fine I have to go to the Dr, again next week. I am expecting the baby about the 15th of May. I sure hope we are here. I am going out to Camp to the Dr. and will be there to the hospital if Carl is here.

It doesn't cost a cent and they give you swell care. They have just a special place for women to go.

We haven't told any of our folks. Carl is almost busting to tell it.

I'm waiting to see there eyes pop if we should get home in Jan, I'd be about 5 mos. I'm having plenty beginning to tell already.

Carl bought me one of my Christmas presents of dresses 1 cotton and 2 good dresses – guess I'll make them do me. I'm not having to wear pest (I'm not sure what this term means – probably a form of corset.) yet soon will. One is the new color cherry rose its real pretty color.

How is the weather there are you having plenty of snow, Mother wrote me from back home. There having a lot. I often thought of you kids. Its real cool here nite and morning but no snow.

I ask Mary if she had her fill of corn Bread yet. Carl nor I have gotten to eat any of that yet. But we just can't miss it before we leave the south.

The couple that lives next door are from Tenn. They talk of it all the time too.

So maybe we'll get some yet. Sure love to taste. Hope it isn't like Grits.

I was sorry to hear about your young brother. Sure hope he's all right (She is referring to Arthur being shipped overseas.).

My sisters husband has been wounded quite bad in the right shoulder and I guess getting shipped back to the states.

I feel sorry for her. He's only been in the service since last April. They sure can go a long ways in a short time. This was in Metz in Germany.

I've never seen Mr, Norris since the day you left. I met Mr. Uptown one day.

Well guess I close running out of news. Hope this leaves you and Roger feeling fine, Happy and with Good news from James, Have a nice Christmas – Write

Love Always Gladys & Carl

These were all the letters that I was able to find from the time that mother was in Starke, Florida and that dad was in training at Camp Blanding. There were other letters that I will include in other following chapters that were written to him overseas and after he returned to the states.

Chapter Three

Dad Goes Overseas

The next letters are from when dad returned from his ten-day furlough that he had from the end of October to around November 14, 1944. He had been issued a ten-day furlough with four days travel time. The first correspondence was a postcard from dad from Washington D.C. that was postmarked November 14, 5 pm, 1944.

(This was a nice souvenir postcard and
I have included s scan of it here.)

Hello Sweet.

I am in Washington at this time, got here at ten this morning – I am fixing to go out to camp now, will write more when I get there.

Love James

The next letter is the first letter from dad to mother written from H.G.F. Replacement Depot No. 1 Fort G. Meade, Maryland. It was dated November 14, Tuesday night and postmarked November 15, 11 am, 1944. Dad had returned from his furlough in Alabama with mother and Roger and was writing his first letter to her after arriving at his new destination:

Hello Sweetheart,

I am at Camp now, just like all the rest of the army camps lonesome without you sweet. Well I have hurd loots about Washington but they can have my part of it. One thing you can get plenty pretty clothes and cheap to, most anything you want. I dont know what they are going to do with me yet. maby I will know more when I write again. I am going to try git cook if I can. I hope I git it to, havent done anything since I got here but they will start on us tomorrow. Sweet I sure did hate to leave Monday Morning but dont wory darling just pray that some day we will be back together someday real soon because I dont like to stay from you sweet. I coulden tell you any thing much while I was there for thinking about leaving you again. I would have gave my right hand to stayed with you sweet. I guss you are thinking its cold up here but its not, warmer up here thin it was down there, but I guss it will be cold. I had good luck when I got to Atlanta caught the streamline to Washington me and one more boy from Opelika they had two seats vacon – So we got in Washington five hours before the other boys did and dident git so dirty Sweet you can write me to this adgress, but watch when it is changed I might not be here but a few days by darling and take care of your self and doctor that cold. Love always James

Pvt ASM 34837097 A.G.F. replacement Depot No.1 fort George G. Meade. Maryland

I am not sure what happened to mother's letters in response to dad's letters during this time period. There was a four-week span that I know she wrote him each and every day but those letters were not saved with all the others. I doubt that mother misplaced them, but I suspect that for some reason dad never received them. Dad was being moved from one camp to another so that might account for some of it. I did manage to find a few of her letters from this time period though, so I will include them here.

This letter from mother to dad was dated November 22, 1944, Hamilton, Alabama. There was no envelope:

Dearest Sweetheart,

I got the Christmas present today. I hope you won't get mad when I tell you that I opened it just as soon as I got it. I didn't notice that you said "do not open till Christmas" until I had already starting cutting the string. Anyway sugar you know I couldn't wait until Christmas to see it. I'm so proud of both of them the musical powder box and the bracelet

(I still have the musical powder box
and am including a scan here.)

You couldn't have gotten anything that I would have liked better.

The powder box started playing before I got it unwrapped. It really had a pretty tune, but makes me wish I could see you. I'll just be so happy when we can be together again.

Sweet, do be careful and Remember Roger and I are looking forward to the day that you will come home.

Roger enjoys hearing my box play. He says you will send him something too. If you can find anything and have time, get him something because he will be so much prouder of anything that you get him.

I'm going to get you something for him too, if I can find anything. I just don't know what you would like.

We killed the hog today and have plenty good meat, I wish you were here to help us eat it.

I didn't get a letter from you today. I hope you aren't on your way across. I just can't bear to think of your having to go over there, but maybe this war will end soon, and you can come back.

I got a letter from Mary yesterday, she is O.K.

I also got a letter from your mother & Dad They both have colds. I write them often.

Did you get the candy I sent you? I hope you like it.

Be sweet and take care of yourself, I'll always love you only.

Love & Kisses Elizabeth

Here is a letter from mother to dad that I found later in another file that I had overlooked. As it fits in well here, I will include it. It was dated by mother Hamilton, Alabama, November 20, 1944 and postmarked November 21, 4:30 pm, 1944, Hamilton Alabama:

Hello Sweet,

I was very glad to get your two sweet letters today.

Sugar, I'm sorry you can't get to stay on as cook, I know you did all you could though. I just wish you were thirty now so that you wouldn't have to go across.

I hope and pray that nothing will happen to you. Be good and take care of yourself and God will take you through.

I'm glad the cooks wanted to keep you. Anyone would want to keep you though. I had rather have you here myself if I had my way about it.

Well get ready for a shock. I went to Windfield this afternoon and actually got my teeth filled. I had my front teeth fixed, and they really look nice.

Someone else had an appointment at the time I got mine fixed, but didn't come so I was just lucky. It cost me $14.00 but I was glad to get them fixed.

Our pictures came today so I'm sending them to you. I sent back for more for myself. They are good pictures I think.

Well be sweet, and be careful.

I love you with all my heart.

Your own, Eliz. & Roger

I don't have all the letters that mother wrote to dad and don't know what happened to them. This next letter was dated about 1 ½ week later, December 4, 1944, Hamilton, Alabama:

Dearest Sweetheart,

How are you today? We are O.K. except that we miss you so much. I'll be glad when I can hear that you have arrived there O.K. (Evidently mother had received a letter, telling her that dad was going across.).

I've been rather busy today, as I typed just about all day. I've been working some for Mr. Carpenter lately.

We went to Winfield this afternoon to see the Alabama Power Man.

He said they would have some transformers by the first of the year, and that he would see that our house was connected, I just hope he will too. I would be glad if I could listen to the radio. I listen to my musical powder box now. It is a lot of help.

Roger is calling you up with the little telephone that Iva & Gerry gave him.

We got a letter from Arthur yesterday. He was O.K.

Sweet, I don't think I told you that I'm O.K. now. I mean about minustrating. I started the twenty eighth. I'm glad I'm O.K. as I have to be here by myself.

Sugar, do be careful and remember we'll love you always.

Be sweet Love & Kisses, Elizabeth & Roger

Since I do not have all of mother's letters to dad, my only option is to continue with dad's letters to her which were all accounted for. I will include some of them here.

This letter from dad offered an explanation why he might not have received her letters from that period of time. It was dated November 15, 1944 and postmarked November 16, 11 am, 1944 and was sent from yet another address: He was still at Fort Meade but had a new address:

Hello Sweetheart,

I am still in meade but want be here long they are shipping us out just as fast as they can. I have tryed to git cook but havent had any luck to many D. class men, and wacs in the army to cook. dont wory darling just pray that God will take care of me till we meet again. I dont know where I will go, all I can do is waite till I git there, the way it looks now I will git there quicker then I want to. my adgress have been changed again (This may explain why some of mother's letters were missing as they may never have been delivered to him,) probly will be changed again tomorrow you never know here. so watch for a change any time till I git settled down somewhere, which I hope will be in the states, but I dont have much hopes of that, they are sending every thing over from here, darling take care of yourself and Roger.

Love always your true love one, James

Pvt-----ASN 34837097 Co. C 12th Bn. 3rd Regt. A.G.F. Rd. #1 Fort George G. Meade, Md

This next letter from dad gives some information about his progress on trying to make cook and also mentions that he had only seen a few of the boys so far that he had trained with at Camp Blanding, Florida. The letter was dated November 17, 1944 and postmarked November 18, 11 am, 1944:

Dear Sweetheart,

Just a few lines, hope you are well, for myself I am OK. I am still here at meade waiting to be shipped out someplace. I am cooking while I am here, but they can't hold me here – cant hole any body under thirty years old. I havent saw but a few of the boys I was trained with, they are scattered all over this place, havent saw tucker yet, I saw bolt and Ingram, they are in another company, they are on shipping orders all ready. sweet when you write mama and them till them I am OK. I dont have time to write much, the cooks here want me to stay but they cant do any thing to keep me, the Captain said he would like to keep me but he coulden I was to yong – they need two cooks here where I am. I have done my best so I will take what ever I git and make the best of it and think of my darling wife every day, wherever I go, so be true to a true Soldier till we meet again which I hope wont be very long.

Your true love one, James

May God keep you and watch over you and little Roger ever day and night and all my prayers be answered. I will do my part in the best way I know how so just pray for me, thats all you can do and the best thing, dont wory I will be OK

Love James

This next letter was interesting from dad as he wrote about a surprise weekend trip to Washington, D.C. and gave some bright and uplifting observations with good details about his trip. Evidently the army thought it would be a good idea to treat the soldiers to a tour of Washington before they got sent overseas to fight for the ideals it stood for.

The letter was written on U.S.O. stationery on a Sunday afternoon while he was visiting Washington D.C. with his company for the weekend. Apparently, this was a surprise trip as he had made no mention of it coming up in his previous letters to mother. This letter provided interesting information about his trip and the places he saw there. It was dated Sunday afternoon, November 19, 1944 and postmarked November 19, 9 pm, 1944:

Dear Sweetheart,

I have been having a nice time in Washington this weekend wish I had knowed I was going to be here for the weekin I would have had you to come up for the weekin I know you would have enjoyed it. this is a nice place (This was quite a change of tune from his first letter in which he said everyone could have his part of Washington.) everything you want to see, me and my boy Friend which is married and is a very nice boy – just my type, dont run around with wemon and drink. they have taxes (taxis) to cary soldiers around all over the place and show you around we went to the white house and the captial and to all the big building and saw all the status (statues) and the history of the United States, saw all the old things that I always wanted to see. I would have give anything if you could have been with me we could have had a lovely time. Sweet I was thinking of you all the time, some day when this war is over I want us to come and go through all of it we can it would take to weeks to go through it all. I will promise when this war is over and I come home to stay we will go to loots of places take a long honey moon which I always wanted to do. I promise I will if its Gods wild (will) for me to live through this thing and come back to my darling wife and son which I hope he will spare me to do, some sweet day soon. I am at the Depo in Washington fixing to go back to camp. Sweet I sent you a Christmas present I hope you like it. I coulden git what I wanted to but I will some day if I live. I havent got Roger any thing yet I hope to but if I dont you git him something and your mother and them, do that for me sweet, I will let you know if I cant git Roger anything or not, I wanted to try to git him a trice sickle (tricycle) if I could. Sweet I am on shipping orders now we ship out next week I am a mechine gunner so you see if I go I will be in a tough part, so if God dont take care of me and bring me through I will be in a bad place. I feel like if I do my part he will bring me through, but if I dont just remember I done it all for you and my country. For you to live in and bring Roger up in. If it takes my life I am willing to give it any day for you and all darling.

So be sweet and Rember me as a true love one and I will never forgit you Darling.

Love Always James

This letter found dad being close to being shipped overseas but to what country he did not yet know. He wrote that there might be a period of two weeks that he would be unable to write, so this would explain the gaps I have wondered about in their letter writing. This letter was postmarked November 21, 1944 but was not dated inside:

Dear Sweetheart,

Just a few lines before I leave hear, I am OK at this time hope you are well and feeling fine. havent got a letter from you yet – dont guss I will git one in along time as I am leaving tomorrow at 7:00 am, so my mail wont catch up with me for sometime. Sure would like to hear from you before I left here. I just hope and pray that you are well and all the rest, so sweet dont worry I will do my best to take care of myself – out of Ink – I sent my bag home you will git it in a day are two, sweet I dont guss I will git to come Christmas, but sweet I will be thinking of you, so dont forgit me sweet, if I dont git to write any more in a couple of weeks dont worry sweet, I dont know where

I will go – but I think England – they give me all new clothes and equipment.

Sweet bee good and true I will, I will be looking forward to the day when we can be togather again then we will make up for all of this time – I wish I could see you before I left, but I cant, may God bless you till we meet again.

Many sweet kisses, Love always James

This letter from dad has yet another change of address so it was little wonder that mother's letters never got to him. He had been shipped to a new location on the east coast. His address changed to: Pvt James G. Brown 34837097 Company E APO #15605%Postmaster New York New York. The letter was postmarked November 23, 4 pm, 1944 and unlike most of his other letters it was hand printed:

Dear Sweetheart,

Just a few lines hope you are well and doing fine. For myself I am OK. I am somewhere on the East Coast. Cant tell you much but I can tell you I still love you sweet. I hope to see you sometime real soon if it is God's wild (will), so bee good and take care of your self. I saw tucker he is OK. I havent saw Curtis yet but I will if I git time (Dad is speaking of his friend Curtis, not his brother Curtis who was stationed in England,). I will close for this time take care of Roger and your self. Love and best wishes, James

The next letter was hand printed as well and was dad's response to the first letter that he had received from mother since he returned from his furlough. I did not find her letter or I would have included it here. It was misplaced as were several others during this period. This letter from dad was dated November 24, 1944 but not postmarked until December 1, 1944:

Dearest Darling,

I got your letter today was I proud to hear from you, that was the first letter I have got since I come back. glad you and Roger are OK. I am doing fine at this time. I am still somewhere on the East Coast. Sure did have a nice thinksgiving dinner. Every thing that any body would wont to eat. I havent saw Curtis (This is not his brother Curtis, but a friend named Curtis that he had in training,) yet he is over in another company somewhere. if they will let me I am going to look him up tomorrow. Tucker and Ingram, I havent saw them any more have you heard from tuckers wife lately. Sweet you said for me not worry about you and Roger, well I dont worry about you all but I think of you every day and pray that God will take care of me and you all and someday real Soon we will be back togather For the rest of our lives in a peaciful world that all good Americans love. Hitler Run his bluff own loots of countries but he went to Far when he tryed Uncle Sam. We have to many good soldiers that dont mind fighting it out and I think Hitler have found that out to. He was doing Fine tell he stured up the rong man Uncle Sam. he stured up a peaciful Fighting Nation. the Reason they Dont mind Fighting they have something to fight For good old America and there love ones sweet hearts and darling wives like mine which I love with all my heart I hope and pray that God will see my way through this war and bring me back to you darling So just pray for me and bee sweet. I will be coming back when it is over with.

Tell your mother and all I said hello. I will stop, answer soon.

All my love to you and a Mery Christmas Love James

That letter from dad was certainly inspirational and I think reflected much of the way most fighting men felt about defending their country and their loved ones. It was truly an expression of love that came from his heart, This letter from dad to mother was postmarked December 9, 1944. There was about a two-week gap where no letters were to be found. I know that dad was sailing across at this time so that could explain the two-week gap. He had said in an earlier letter that he might not be able to write at sea. I suppose the missing letters from mother were just lost. I will never know but I just feel extremely lucky to have found all their letters that I did. Here is the letter from December 9, 1944. This letter is also powerful and filled with dad's observations about he and mother's situation and how they really are helpless to do anything about improving their lot in life but to just hope and pray that things will be better soon:

Dear Sweetheart,

I am well and feeling fine at this time hope you and Roger are well.

All I can say is I am still sailing. I guss you will git tired of this stuff but this is all I know. All I can see is water. I cant mail any letters till I git where I am going (This explains the two week gap in letters.) my adgress will be changed some when I git there (This may explain why no letters from mother were received during this period.) so be sure and watch for that becaus my mail wont git to me as quick if you dont. I sure would like to hear from you all – it makes things worse when you cant hear from home special when have some one back home you relly care for as much as I do you, things dont go right whin you cant go home and cant hear from home but there not any thing that can be done about it just wait hope and pray that we will have a better world some day soon, I have tryed to git cook but havent done any good yet. I hope to later own. I have some good officers so far. I think they will help me git cook if they can, so dont wory I will do my best at what

215

ever I git with the lords help. So be good and take care of
your self and pray for us all.

Love always, James

I know that dad wrote mother every day when he was at sea but had
to hold onto them until he could send them. I believe this was because the
army held mail back and shipped them all at once for reasons of efficiency
being that they were at sea and mailing every day would have created
technical problems especially during war time. This next letter was also
heartfelt and almost poetic in its expressions of my dad's feelings. Even
though it was postmarked December 9, 1944 it may well have been written
several days before:

Dearest Darling Wife,

Just a few lines hope you are well and feeling fine to night.
for myself I am feeling pretty good. Except I wish I was at
home with you darling. I went up on Deck this afternoon
Everything looked so good and calm the sun was shining
so bright and the sky was clear as a christal All day – the
waves wasent rocking the ship much, So that diden't make
my head swim. I stayed out as long as they would let me
looking Every thing over and thinking of you Sweetheart,
wondering if you was thinking of me at that time. We
had Church service up there and most all the boys was
there, they all looked pleased, but you could see that home
look in there eyes. All the boys seem to be peaciful. We
havent had a Fight since we left as I know of. I like for it
to bee that way because we all are over here for the same
thing – to git the war over and come back home to our
love ones. So quicker we git it over with quicker the ones
left will git back.

Darling Christmas will soon be here and Every body will
bee having fun thats not in the war yet. I am proud some

can have fun if I cant, it makes me feel good to know some body is having Fun, it sure would be A messed up world if nobody dident have some Fun. I wish they would have there Fun the Right way, if they would all go to church and pray for the boys over here and live right, did Christmas instead of going out and getting drunk and Running Around, go to Church and spend Christmas Night praying we all would git some good out of it, but God knows they wont do that, they are to mean.

Sweet I wont you to Enjoy yourself and dont wory about me. I will be OK. And will do my best to take care of myself. God will be with me through out my troubles and hardship and some day he will bring me safely home to my darling wife and son which I love with all my heart, have you got your Christmas present, I hope so I sent it before I left. bee sure to git Roger something, git him something he can play with something large if you can, dont mind the price, I wont him to have something where he will know it is Christmas, he is getting large enough to rellize things like that now. Sweet I havent spent but a few Christmas with you, and I want you to know that they was the sweetest ones I have ever spent. So I hope and pray that next Christmas I will be with you in a peaciful world Good Old America, Darling bee good and Remember I will always love you and Roger.

Sweet Dreams and best of Luck, Many Sweet Kisses, Love James

This letter from dad to mother was written on December 11, 1944, apparently after he had landed in southern France and had been shipped to his first camp there.

My Dear Darling Wife,

This is another blue sunday with me no where to go and nothing to do but think of you, and wishing I was at home with you & Roger. I got my pistol and trench knife today, I guss that my Christmas present from Uncle Sam. I just hope I dont haft to use it. I hope this war will be over with by the time I haft to go up.

I saw Tucker today, he is here pretty close to me in M. Company he is unhappy to so I am not by myself. I am cooking now but for all I know I might be fighting by the morrow. Sweet write mama and them and let them know I am OK every time you write. I cant write much – it take all my time trying to think of something to write you. I havent wrote Curtis yet but I am tomorrow. I dont guss he knows where I am unless mama wrote him. I got my letter back from Robert I wrote him in July. It said he was killed in action I guess I will go crazy yet every time I git kindly settled down I git something else to remind me, are make me think of it more, how are you making out with the car have you learned to drive yet, I would give any thing to see you drive by your self, be sure and let me know when you learn how. Sweet be careful and dont worry about me. Worrying wont do any good any way. I will stop for this time.

love and sweet dreames and many sweet kisses, Yours true, James

The following letters are the earliest dated letters that I was able to find from the time dad left for overseas somewhere around November 18, 1944. I know mother wrote him every day but because of the many different addresses he had during that time the letters may never have been delivered to him. At least I was able to find these letters though and here is the first one dated Tuesday, December 12, 1944 and postmarked Hamilton, Alabama, December 13, 1944:

Dearest Sweetheart,

How are you today? We are fine, but the weather is freezing. It is cold where you are?

I got a letter from Eloise (This was Robert Brown's fiancé.) today. She has been having trouble with her wisdom teeth.

I told you about getting the lumber for the car house didn't I? Loranzie Nichols said that he will build it for me next week. I'll be so glad when it is finished.

The boys are still in school (These were her brothers Herbert and Horrice.), will get out next Friday for the Christmas Holidays.

I hope that I will start getting your letters soon (Mother had not been getting any of dad's letters either.).

I hardly know what to write you, as I can't hear from you, and there isn't any news here.

I forgot to put Roger's letters in yesterday, so I'll send it right on to you now (I don't have the "letters" of Roger's that she is writing about.),

I don't go anywhere very often, except to a show occasionally, and I miss you so much then that I don't enjoy them.

I may go to your mothers after Christmas, they want me to come back to see them.

Sugar, I hope you are O.K. and will soon be back home.

I'll love you always, so be sweet, and write as often as you can.

All our Love, Eliz & Roger

As I do not have all the letters that mother wrote to dad during this time, I feel it is important to include the ones that I did find. This first one was dated Hamilton, Alabama, December 14, 1944. The envelope was missing so there was no postmark. To my surprise there was no salutation at the beginning of the letter:

Well, I must tell you that I finally got my enlarged pictures today. The one of you, Roger & I while you were on furlough.

(I am including a scan of a similar photo here.)

I got three enlargements of it. One for your mother, one for Alma and one for me. They really are nice ones too. The pictures were already in frame and were just 90 cents each. I wish you could see them. Did you get the pictures I sent you? I hope you will get them, if you haven't already.

Sugar, I think of you so much, and I wish you were here with us. We just miss you so much. I hate to think of you being way over there & in so much danger.

I hope & pray that nothing will happen to you, and that it won't be long before you will be back home.

Roger has gone to bed. He tells you good night before he goes to sleep.

Be sweet and write me when you can.

Yours only, Elizabeth

Here is one more letter that I found from mother to dad dated Sunday afternoon, December 17, 1944 and postmarked December 18, 1944:

Hi Sweet,

We went to church today and have just gotten back and settled down to writing.

I don't suppose you can go to church now can you?

I dreamed last night that you were back with us, and we were having so much fun, I only wish it were true.

I got a letter from your mother today, she says your Grandpa is going back to Ola's again. He has been in Opelika for the last week I think.

She said she had received the present I sent, and liked them.

I also have to write Johnnie as I haven't answered her last letter. She still hears from Carr regularly.

(I am including a scan of Johnnie and Carr Jr.
in the first photo. The second photo is of her
and Carr and family about five years later.)

I'm hoping to get a letter from you this week, as it has been three weeks since you left, and I haven't heard from you in that length of time (The reason that she had not received any letters is that the military held back all soldiers' letters and mailed them all out the same day. Many of dad's letters to mother were postmarked December 10 or December 16, 1944, no matter what day they were written.).

I'll be so happy when I can get your letters again.

I hope you will have as nice a Christmas as can be expected, for you to be over there & away from home.

My Christmas won't be a very happy one and you gone, of course I just hope and trust that you will be with us before another Christmas comes, and believe you will, as I'm hoping this war will be ended before then.

I'm always thinking of you.

Be sweet and remember we love you.

Love & Kisses Eliz & Roger

I found a large number of dad's letters that were postmarked December 10, December 16 and 17, and December 24. This indicates that the soldiers' mail was held up and sent out once a week. This would explain why it took over three weeks for mother to receive any letters from dad. I believe this letter from dad was dated December 10. 1944 but the postmark was unclear. There was no salutation at the beginning whereas he usually wrote Hello Sweetheart or similar:

> How are you fine I hope for myself I am still living. I sure would like to see you and Roger. I git pretty lonesome sometime. All I can do is think of you all way out here in the middle of the ocean. I got two letters from you before I left. I sure was proud to git them to as I havent herd from you since I come back. I am still pretty sea sick hope I will soon git use to it. I dont have much I can write about. I dont like my trip very much I guss it would be allright if I dident git sea sick and this war wasent going down and I had you along with me. When I git back home I dont think I wont to go any where for at least six months I think I will be fed up on going places.
>
> Sweet dont wory about me git you a job and try to forgit it all, some day I will be back with you darling if its Gods wild (will). I feel like every thing will be O.K. I havent felt bad over it. I have my part to do – so what ever that part is I will make the best of it. Sweet I love you and hated to leave you but some day we will be back to gather and make up for it all. I sure would like to be back where we could go to church togather and other places like we use to. We have church here but its not like being at home, going places togather is what I like, sweet dont worry I will do my best to take care of myself. God knows best and he will do his part if I do my part, so I will do my part the best I know how in ever way.
>
> Sweet take care of your self and Roger
>
> Love and best wishes James

There were several V-Mails (These were photo-stated postcard size copies that the military made of letters that soldiers wrote to their families or that their families wrote to them,) that dad wrote to mother that were postmarked December 16, 1944 but were written several days before. Evidently the military held back the soldiers' letters home and mailed them all at once in bulk as they were being sent from overseas and in such large quantities. This V-Mail of dad's, like many of the others was postmarked 10 am, December 16, 1944:

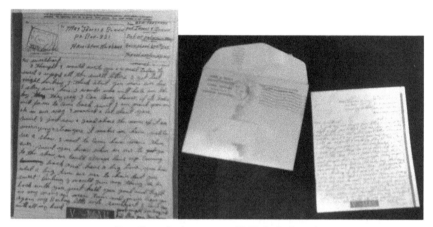

(I will include scans of V-Mails here.)

Hello darling wife

How are you fine I hope for myself I am OK at this time, I bet you are at the show to night. I wish I could be with you but I know I cant. I am still sailing, getting maty (mighty) tired of it to, if I had you to pass the time off with it would be OK. We have shows and things to go to but its not like being at home where we could go places to gather. I guss you miss getting my letters dont you? I sure do miss yours to, but they will start coming again pretty soon. I hope then they dont stop till I come home to stay which I hope will be sometime soon. Take care of your self and Roger. I will be thinking of you all and looking to the day when I come back to you all for always, James

The next V-Mail was postmarked the same time, 10 am, December 16, 1944, but had to have been written several days before as I know dad landed in Southern France December 9, 1944:

Hello my Dear Wife.

Here I come with the same old line nothing to talk about. I am still on the ship. Sweet I think of you all time wondering if you are OK. I hope so and pray that you stay well and in good health while I'm away and Roger to. bee sure and take care of him and make him mind you, and do Right. do he have much to say about me this time. I Rember what he said while I was there, he said Daddy was going to kill them old Japs with his big gun. I pray to god when we git through with all, this time they wont come back in twenty more years and start another war which our kids will haft to fight and die for no cause. I think they will have enough fight to last them a while this time, tell Roger I will do my best to git them old Japs and Germans to and I pray some day to come back and tell him about it. tell him I havent forgot his birthday which will bee the tenth of this month (Roger would turn 3 years old December 10, 1944.), but I cant bee there as much as I would like to. So give him all my love and kisses and I hope and pray that he will have many more and I will be there with him. I will never forget how he looked when he was talking about them Japs. So may it be God's wild (will) that we win,

Give kisses to him for me, Love always James

Several of dad's V-Mails were written while he was at sea being shipped to Southern France. These were very brief letters as V-Mails were limited in size and many were postmarked, as those included before at 10 am, December 16, 1944 even though they were written more than a week before. I will include a few more of his V-Mails. Here is another one that was written while he was at sea:

Hello Dear Little Wife,

Here I am lying on my back in the middle of the ocean trying to write you and let you know I am O.K. hope you are well and feeling fine. I guss this better thin beeing in a fox hole some place. we have pretty good eats on the ship. I havent went hungry yet you cant do any thing much, not much you need to do but keep the place cleaned up. I guss we will have plenty to do when we git where we are going, have you herd from Gary (Gerry Gamel, Iva Palmer Gamel's husband) since he left. let me know where he is when you find out where he is, you said Harrison was coming home Christmas I sure hope he gits to come. I sure would like to bee there to, but you cant have every thing like you want it. If we could this war would be over by Christmas, So all we can do is hope and pray that we will bee living in a peaciful world by next Christmas, tell your mother and all I said hello

Yours true always, Love James

Here is another of dad's V-Mails postmarked 10 am, December 16, 1944. It must have been very hard on him to write his letters every day but not be able to have any response from mother. There was a period of three weeks or so that he received no letters because of the slow delivery of mail to soldiers at sea or overseas:

Hello Sweetheart Darling,

I have been thinking of you all day wondering if you are OK. I got two letters before I left they are getting old now, you said that Geneva husband got a medical discharge. I wonder what was wrong with him. I hope some day pretty soon we all can git a discharge but not a medical. I hope this war will be over with, we have loots of married men with children it sure will be bad if they dont come back to them and the single boy have love one and sweet hearts so its bad on them all, so all we can do is stay in here and git this war over with, if every body would live right and pray God will help us git this war over with, so think (thank) God that he is with us, be sweet and dont wory about me darling. God will be with me from now own through my life

Love for ever James

There were several more V-Mails from dad to mother that were postmarked a bit later in the day at 2 pm. December 16, 1944. Again, these all had to be written before December 9, 1944 because dad landed in Southern France on that date. It was hard for me to properly sequence these V-Mails as most of them were not dated inside:

My Dear Darling wife.

How are you to night! Fine I hope for myself I am OK at this time, Just got off K.P. dont mind working K.P. makes me think of old days when I use to cook in camp (C.C.C.) at Hamilton and work like everything to git through cleaning up after supper, where I could go to see you. I dont think I was ever late was I Sweet, Well I am going to work hard now, and try to do my job well and not be late coming back to you when this war is over. I dont see why I cant git back I like cooking better than any thing I have ever done. Maby they will need a cook somewhere, they haft to have cooks over here to, So I still stand a chance, So dont wory sweet whatever my Job is I will make the best of it with God on my side because I am doing my best to live Right. I know there wasent a better boy in the army than Robert, but he dident git a break the three years he was in the army, but God took him to a better world where he will rest in peace. Maby God will find a way for me. I pray that he does. So be good and pray for me Sweet.

Yours Forever James

Here are two more V-Mails that dad wrote while he was on the ship going overseas. This first one as the previous ones was postmarked 2 pm, December 16, 1944:

Dear Sweetheart,

I am OK and doing fine at this time hope you and Roger ar well. I guss you are at church now, I went to service this morning was OK but not like at home it was different but you can git some good out of any service if you try and want it. Some of the boys go to church then go right back gambling. We have some good boys just like every where els, they are very few good ones. Well I am still sailing and dont have many things to write about but the ocean and that's not much. I dont think I would like the navy if it is like this git so sick cant go any place but on the ship. Of corse the ship is going but where I dont know all you can do is waite. I think this war will soon be over where we all can come back home and start a new life all over and I hope every one lives better then they did before this and try to keep a peaciful world to.

So be good, loots of Love James

Here is one more V-Mail written by dad to mother while he was on board ship. Being at sea for so long with no communication from home and family had to be hard on all those soldiers. They were facing an uncertain future and they all knew that where they were headed may well have been their last journey, It had the same postmark of 2 pm, December 16, 1944:

Dear Elizabeth (It was odd that he used Elizabeth here as he would always use Sweet, Sweetheart; Darling or Sugar.)

Well I am still out here in the ocean somewhere. I am OK at this time. Just about to git over being sea sick. I hope so any way its no good Feeling, I have Just about Run out of any thing to write beeing I cant git any letters from you till I git where I am going. How is every body around Hamilton still the same old thing I guss. I guss Roger likes better now after I left the car where he can ride sometime. Tell Herbert to have the car greased and the oil changed pretty soon I guss it needs it – be sure to keep the tires checked all time. When Harrison comes you can go to Birmingham are any place you want to. Just be careful all I ask. If Herbert can drive in Birmingham he can cary you all I care Just dont have a Reck and git hurt. Well I had better stop. I will always be true to you darling wife. So Sweet dreams James

This next letter, and it was a letter, not a V-Mail, found dad had landed someplace in Southern France. He could not say but we know now it was Marseille. This letter was written December 9, 1944 and postmarked December 10, 1944:

Dear Sweetheart Darling wife,

Just a few lines hope you all are well and doing well for myself I am doing pretty good I guss. I landed safely somewhere in Southern France. You know I dont like over here I had rather be back any where in the USA but its not what you like its what you git. So Darling dont wory to much about me I will be back some day if its God's Wild (Will). I know now what Robert wanted to write me. I havent had to dig any fox holes as yet. If I live to git back home I will appriciate a good home to live in and good meals cooked by a sweet wife like you. You can look at France and tell our boys have done a good job over here,

Tell your mother I said to take care of her self and that I will do my best to sweet tomorrow (December 10) is Roger's Birthday. I hope he is well and doing good and have a happy Birthday. I see loots of little frence children over here, we give them some of our food the people in america dont know how they have been blessed, and still they are not thinkful (thankful) – they dont know what hard time is they git more to eat in one day then these people git in one week over here.

I cant write but one letter now but I will write more later own, so you write mother and them and tell thim I got here OK and that I am well, and I will be back before long, the war will soon be over I hope and for them to not worry about me, you all just pray for me. Sweet I would like to say loots but I will be coming back in a short while and I hope to stay when I git back to,

So be sweet darling.

Love always many sweet kisses James

The next correspondence from dad to mother was also a letter and not a V-Mail. In it he states that he has finally gotten a letter from mother with some pictures inside. It was dated inside December 14, 1944 and postmarked December 16, 1944:

My Dear Darling Wife,

I recived your sweet letter and the pictures they sure are good. I woulden take anything for them, special the one you wrote on the back of, I will bring them back home some day when this war is over which I hope will be real soon.

Sweet I am doing pretty good I git pretty Cold sometime. I havent sleep in tents for the last night or two, but I dont know how long it will be before I will haft to go back in them. I havent been to the front yet. I hope and pray I never haft to go up but if I do I will make the best of it and pray that God will take care of me and some day come home to my darling wife and son and with the boys that's left. I wish we could all come back but we cant do nothing about that part of it just pray and live right, sweet I dont like France to much the people are not to friendly I can see that if I cant understand them. I havent been to town but I've been through loots of them Darling dont worry about me I feel like I will be OK. just go ahead and enjoy yourself and have a good Christmas. I am proud you got your teeth fixed after having so much trouble trying to git thim fixed while I was there I told you not to be so worried about it that you could git them fixed.

I havent saw Tucker since we got off the ship. I dont know where he is if I dont git to see him, you write Mary and find out where he is and let me know are send me his adgress.

Tell your mother I still have the testament and I woulden take nothing for it. I have something to read no mater where I go. Something that will do me some good and I am doing my best to live up to it. So you all just pray for me and some day God will bring me Safely back to my sweet darling wife. May God bless you and keep you for a true Soldier.

Love and sweet dreams, your true love always, James

These letters from dad to mother were quite informative and I will include most of them. The next letter was written about a week after he landed in France and dated December 16, 1944 with a postmark of December 17, 1944. Dad had used some stationery that had a cartoon of soldiers in Army trucks admiring the French girl's "bombers" as they passed them on the road. I am including a scan of soldier's admiring girl's bombers which was at the top of the first page of dad's stationery and a scan of two soldiers flirting with a French girl which was at the top of the second page of his stationery.

Dear Darling Wife,

How are you today? fine I hope, for myself I am OK at this time Except I have a cold which I have had all my life I think. I will never git read (rid) of it I dont think, how is Roger? have he had any colds yet? I hope he dont have any this time.

I am still at the same place in france dont know how long I will be here I will start cooking today while I stay here but you never know one day what you will be doing the next, so I dont know how long I will be cooking. I hope from now own. We are getting plenty to eat now. we will git every thing fixed up in a few days where it wont be bad at all, if they let us stay here it will be OK to be in France.

Sweet the girls are just like you herd they was. I havent saw but a few and if they havent got any that looks any better then thim, france havent got any thing to brag on. I guss they been treated so bad they cant look good. you would be surprised to know all about how they do in france. Its not like the good old U.S.A. I would give anything to be back at Camp Blanding where I could have you with me. it is just like you said, we was having a good time down there. but maby it wont be so long before we can be back to gather again, I hope and pray that this war will soon be over.

I am sending you some france money to keep if you want to. this is 24 cents in American money. Well Christmas is only nine days off. I hope you have a merry Christmas and a happy new year, enjoy your self and have a sweet time for me and you both.

Love and Sweet Kisses, Yours true forever James

There were two letters dated December 17, 1944 that dad wrote to mother. The first one was dated inside December 17, 1944 and postmarked December 19, 1944. The letter after this one was postmarked December 17, 1944. It seems that I am wrong if one goes by the postmark. If one goes by the content, it seems that I am right and this one should come first. So, I will include the one postmarked December 19, first:

Dear little Darling Wife,

I recived your sweet letter to night (The next letter states that he has received two letters so that is why I think I have them ordered correctly.) was proud to git it as I havent got one in several days, the letter was wrote the 24ᵗʰ of Nov (In the next letter mother's letter was written November 28, so this also seems to confirm I have the ordering correct.) so you can see all the mail we git here have been following us for quit a while. I dont guss you have been getting any till here lately, but dont stop writing when you dont git any mail from me becaus I will write every chanch I git and I like to git mail from you if it is old, it is still sweet and I know you are thinking of me anyway. Sweet I think of you all time and I will do my best to take care of myself and come back real soon as you wanted me to – dont forgit I wont to come back to my darling wife and son because I love just as much as you said you loved me, but if something do happen just remember I love you more thin any one on earth, but I think God will take care of me, for a sweet and good wife like you. Sweet I will always be true dont wory about that, I dont wory because I know I have a Sweet wife waiting for me, all I want is to live and git back some sweet day real soon. Tell your mother I have got where I like sausage so she can save some for me when I come back. We have plenty to eat Now I dont know how long that will last. I would give any thing to be there and help you all eat that fresh meat, sure would be good, I know. Sweet dont wory, May God keep you and bring me back safely sometime real soon. I love you with all my heart.

So have a nice Christmas Love for ever James

This next letter from dad to mother was probably written the next day and postmarked December 17, 1944. There was no date written inside:

Dear Sweetheart,

I recived your letter last night which was wrote the 28th of Nov, but I was proud to git it, that makes two I got since I landed. I wasent expecting to git any mail in at least two more weeks. I am proud you liked your Christmas present. I will git you what I wanted to when I come back you can depend on that, but if I happen to any bad luck you git it. Sweet I havent had mine off since you put it on the last time (I believe he was talking about his wedding ring.). I hope I will be with you next Christmas where we can enjoy it, I cant have any fun only when I am with you.

I think we will be out of this war by next Christmas any way. Thin we can have a big time once more so be sweet and dont worry about me sweetheart. you said you saw Opaleen Husbon have he gone overseas yet? I hope not I wish they dident haft to send another Soldier over here in this place. We have a pretty good place where we are now for the shape it was in when we come here but I dont know how long we will be here. I hope we dont ever haft to move from here but we coulden be that lucky. It is cold and muddy but I dont mind that. As long as I dont haft to dodge bulletts. Sweet take care of yourself and Roger, True Love, and sweet Dreams, Love James

Continuing with dad's letters to mother I am proceeding as much as possible in chronological order, but an exact ordering has been made difficult as some are dated and some are not, Postmarks are not very helpful either, as sometimes the letters were held back and sent several days later than they were written. This letter was dated inside December 18, 1944 and postmarked December 21, 1944:

Dear Darling Wife,

I got your letter tonight sure was proud to hear from you. I got the wash cloth you sent to, tell your Grandy I said thinks (thanks) a loots (lots) for it. Sweet I hope you are well, for myself I am OK except I have a cold. You said you sent me a box I havent got it yet I hope I do if it haves what you said it did in it. I am still in the same place cooking but I wont be cooking long I dont think they need a cook but they cant keep me same old thing every where I go. I sure will be glad when I can git out of this place and come home that's what I wont more than any thing els, but some times I dont think this war will ever be over with it just keep dragging along. I think about what you said down at Blanding about the war, but we will git Germany pretty soon I think. I sure will be a happy Soldier whin we all

Can Come home, we have loots of good boys. I sure would like to see them all come back, because that's all they talk about is home sweet home there's no place like home I have found that out loots of times since I have been in the Army. I got a letter from Harrison and Curtis today, Harry said he was coming Christmas I wish I could be there with you all. I hope you all have a nice time – dont forgit I will be thinking of you sweet. I hope I will be back with you sometime soon, so dont wory. I love you with all my heart darling, just pray for me and take care of yourself and Roger.

Love and sweet kisses, James

The next letter was a V-Mail It was dated inside by dad December 18, 1944:

Hello Sweet heart Darling,

I will try and answer your letter I recived this morning. Sure was sweet to git it as I got one last night. I Relly Enjoy getting letters as we dont hear much news the people over there know more about the war then the Soldiers do over here. Sweet I havent got the box yet that you sent me maby I will some day, I am proud you liked the presents I sent you. I wish I could have been with you this Christmas but it had to be this way for some reason so I just hope and pray that we all will be back home Real soon. last year I was wondering where I will be this time this year. Now I am wondering where I will be this time next year. I hope at home with my darling wife and son if its Gods wild (will). Sweet I would give anything to be back with you I know I could be having a good time because I always did when I was with you I dont have the least ida (idea) what I will be doing Christmas. I hope not Fighting.

by darling and be sweet – I will be true always Love James
"Sweet Kisses"

Dad's next letter included a scathing review of the life and culture of
the people of France. He did not like their behavior or customs. The letter
was dated inside December 19, 1944 and postmarked December 21, 1944:

Dear Darling Wife,

How are you tonight fine I hope for myself I am OK at
this time, I git so lonesome around this place. I dont know
what to do, so I just try to write letters and forgit it all
but that is a hard thing to do to forgit this place over here
when you know you got to stay here no telling how long.

I guss every body fixing for a big Christmas around
Hamilton. I wish we was togather this Christmas like we
was the Christmas after Roger was Borned, we had a sweet
time had a nice Christmas tree and got plenty things to go
on it, I hope some day we can have good times like that
again, Sweet git your mother and grandy and the boys
some thing for Christmas for me. I cant git anything at
all over here, I wanted to git you something els but I Cant
git it now but I will when I Come home if I live to git back
which I think I will if it's Gods will.

Sweet you know what you was worried about when I left,
did you make out OK? I hope so, you write me all the
news when you write again about every thing you think
I care about knowing. I guss Harrison will be there when
you git this letter if he is tell him he had better stay out
from over here if he can. I have found it very differeyce
from what I thought it would be. its not like the good old
U.S.A. you cant go places and do thing like you can over
there no where to go, any single boy that thought any
thing of his self woulden go with theas girls, much less a

married man, this is a awful place if I ever saw one theas people dont care for nothing – they do some funny things but I cant tell you in a letter, it woulden sound good to the stenciter (censorer) sweet dont worry about me I have more respect for you thin to do like some of the boys do over here. I will stop for this time.

Love and Sweet kisses, Yours true for ever James

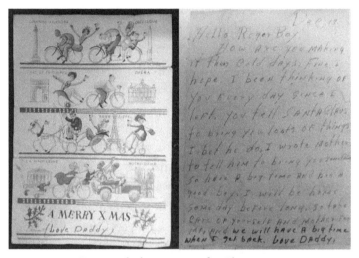

I am including scans of a Christmas
card that dad sent to Roger.

It shows scenes of Paris, France on the front and on the back dad wrote to Roger. It was dated December 19, 1944:

Hello Roger Boy,

How are you making it theas Cold days, Fine I hope. I have been thinking of you every day since I left. You tell Santa Claus to bring you loots of things I bet he do. I wrote mother to tell him to bring you something so have a big time and bee A good boy. I will be home some day before too long So take care of yourself and mother for me and we will have a big time when I get back. Love Daddy

Here is a letter from dad that was dated the same day, December 19, 1944, as the Christmas card he sent to Roger. It was postmarked December 21, 1944:

Dear Darling little wife,

How are you today fine I hope for myself I am doing pretty good at this time, I just come of (off) shift – seem like old times all except I cant see you when I get off from work. I wish I could stay here and cook. I like all the Cooks. they seem like boys I use to cook with at Hamilton. I will never forgit thim good old days. Sweet I dont know how far I am from where Robert got killed. I wish I knew – if I could I would go and see his grave, but I dont guss I will git to.

We havent had any air raids around here . I sure hope it stays quite to and I Can stay here. When you have time git you a life magazine for the next month are two and you will enjoy looking at it, you might see the outfit I am in, at least some of it. they took loots of pictures anyway so I think they will be in the life magazine, in a month are so, have you been going to the show any. I havent been since I been over here. I dont think they have any around here anyway, unless they are france shows and I coulden understand them anyway, Sweet did you ever git any lumber to build a shed for your car. I wish I was there to build it for you. I bet Roger is having a time since you all killed the hog. he dident like it when they killed it did he? I know when I use to kill a chicken he would cry and say porre chicken is he still tender hearted about things like that? I will stop answer soon with a long letter. Darling I will always love you and be true.

Many sweet kisses, Love and sweet dreams, James

I feel it is important to include all the letters from dad from the period just before he was sent to fight in Belgium in relief of the American troops at the Battle of the Bulge. General Patton called up all available troops, including the company dad was in, and marched them with his 3rd Army across the frozen, wintry landscape of France to relieve those American troops in Bastogne, Belgium that were being overwhelmed by Germany's final desperate offensive drive to retake France. There were no letters from dad during that time as I am sure General Patton's 3rd Army kept him hopping and there was no time to write. Besides, I am sure dad was more focused on dodging German bullets and artillery shells than he was looking for pen and paper to write letters on. Dad did tell me in his later years about his near-death experiences in battle and some chilling life-threatening enemy confrontations that he managed to survive. When I conclude these letters from Chapter Three, I will relate the stories that he told me from that time in the following chapter: Chapter Four: Dad's Stories from the War. I know that dad was wounded in Belgium on December 30, 1944 and I will relate what he told me about that as well as other close calls in Chapter Four. The last letter that dad wrote to mother before those events was on December 27, 1944.

Here is a letter from dad to mother written a week before that on December 20, 1944:

Dear Darling Sweetheart,

How are you today sweetheart fine I hope, for myself I am doing pretty good except a cold. Sweet I sure would like to see you and Roger. I git pretty lonesome over here no body to have any fun with, just stay around Camp and pass the time off the best I can. Sure would be nice if I could be with you and Roger this Christmas I know we would have some fun. We always do when we are togather. I sure do miss it to. I wish this war would be over this Christmas it would be a big Christmas present for us all. I know I would be proud and all the rest of the soldiers they all are getting fed up on this war. I have talked to some of the boys that been over here three years, they think the war will soon be over but no body knows all you can do is to hope and pray that it will soon be over with. I havent got a letter from home since I been over here. I have wrote every week I dont know where they have got them are not. I have got several letters from you, so write me and let me know how they are ever time you git a little from thim, tell your mother I am still looking for that letter from her. I like to git loots of mail over here as I cant git any news any other way. We dont Have any Raidoes. We git a little paper about once a week – thats good around this place I dont see how we Can git one that often. I am still at the same place hope I dont haft to move, but that day will rock around pretty soon I guss, I will haft to go when my time comes so I am doing like the rest waiting. I will stop for this time so dont wory sweet.

I love you my darling wife – Love and sweet dreams, James

Here is another letter that dad wrote to Roger that was postmarked December 21, 1944. This letter may have been written before the previous one. It was not dated inside:

Hello Roger How do my big boy feel today I sure would like to see you, I bet I woulden hardly know you and I bet you woulden know me neather. Well I got to go out on a night problem so be good and dont wory your mother to much. Well I got to go catch a hue owl, I will be back at twelve oclock and git in bed about one I hope, by and be good love Dad

I can be more certain of the dates on these next letters to mother from dad as they were dated on the inside. This letter finds dad having been moved from camp toward a new destination which I assume was toward the front at Bastogne, Belgium with General Patton's 3rd Army. Dad was able to give some details about the outfit he was in but some of the lines of his letter were cut out by Army censors. This one was dated Sunday December 24,1944;

Dear Sweetheart Darling wife

just a few lines hope you all are well and feeling fine for myself I am doing pretty good I guss. I have moved since I wrote you last, I mean it is cold up here snow is everywhere. I nely (nearly) freeze me feet froze the other night I never had any thing to hurt as bad in all my life. it is plenty tuff up here, loots of people thought I woulden haft to Bee in this part, but I am ready to take my part and my part is tuff going. I am in a rifle company – same thing Robert was in, dont wory darling I will be OK God will take care of any one if he sees fit, This is Christmas Eave, but it dont seem that way to me, I would give anything to be home with you and Roger. Sweet you all pray for me if I ever needed it I will need it from now own. I will probly be up on the front before you git this letter. I have joined my outfit they have---------------------(There is a section two lines long that had been cut out of the letter here by the censors. Probably this was done to prevent dad's outfit's position from being revealed to spies.)----------------------------to give us a little training and they are plenty tuff to. the Germans dont like that part. I sure will be proud when this war is over, where we can come back to the good old USA. I havent saw tucker since I left the other place. I hope he is OK. some of the boys came ahead had some trouble I dont know where tucker was with them are not. I havent got my box you sent me dont guss it will ever catch up with me. I move to fast, maby I will git it when I git back to the states, sweet take care of yourself and Roger. I will do my best to tell your mother and the boys I said hello.

Love and sweet dreams, Yours true, James

Dad somehow was able to write mother even as his outfit advanced toward the front as with this next letter. He would soon be in the thick of battle though and his letter writing would have to be put on hold. This letter was dated December 24, 1944, France:

Dear Sweetheart,

I have been thinking of you all day sweet wondering what you are doing Darling. I would give any thing to be there with you and Roger, but I am not by my self we have thousand of boys that feels the same way. darling my love is all for you. No one knows how much I love you. I just hope and pray that God will take care of me and bring me back home safe to you. Sweet I know you love me I dont wory about that because you have proved that long ago, we havent spent mant Christmas to gather but them we have spent togather was the sweetest ones I have ever spent, because I was with the girl I loved with all my heart and I pray that God will see a way for us to spend loots Moore togather. if we Are Far Apart this Christmas, I dream about you nely (nearly) every Night sweet. I wish some of them was true, I dreamed I was back home with you, was that sweet tell I woke – then I dident feel good at all lying up in a hay loft somewhere in France dont git the Ida (Idea) I sleep in a hay loft all the time. We just happened to good luck that night. I havent got a letter from home yet I hope to soon. Sweet write me all the News About what you have done this Christmas and what good things you had to Eat. we had C rations today. I dont know what we will git tomorrow. I will write you all I can but I wont git to write Much From now on, we get off tomorrow. Sweet my Adgress have been changed I dont think I said anything about it in the other letter. Sweet heart bee good and dont wory About me Just pray that God will take care of me. Sweet I love you with all my heart if any thing happens Remember I love you darling

True Love And best wishes, James
Pvt. James G. Brown
Co. F 134th Inf. A.P.O. #35
% Post Master New York N.Y.

Dad was certainly the victim of ill fate and bad timing as were many thousands of other American soldiers as they spent their Christmas away from home and their loved ones on December 25, 1944. Many of them were just days away from being critically wounded or killed on the front and my dad was one of them as he was about to march through the frozen countryside of France with General Patton's 3rd Army Infantry. They would meet a horrible fate at the hands of the Germans in Bastogne, Belgium who were giving their final desperate push for victory at the Battle of the Bulge. Had it not been for the farm boys like my dad who defeated the Germans my story may well have been written in German today.

This letter to mother from dad was written on Christmas day and was dated December 25, 1944 Monday afternoon:

My Darling Wife and son,

just a few lines wishing you all a Merry Christmas and a happy New Year, today is a lovely day, the sun is shining so pretty it makes me home sick. I been washing some socks and things out, we have today off no training, as my company is back for a rest. Darling I hope you are having a nice Christmas. I would give any thing in the world to be with you all, but I have been thinking of you all day sweet about the sweet times we have spent togather, hoping someday we can spend them all over again in a peaciful world. I pray every day for this war to end where we all can come back to our love ones. I know I have a darling wife waiting for me and I am going to do everything in my power to come back if its Gods wild (will). Darling this is the only Christmas we havent spent togather since we have been knowing each other, but if it was Gods wild (will) I would be with you sweet. I had rather be with you thin any one on earth. I love you with all my heart and some day I will be back. I hope that day will be real soon, sweet go ahead and enjoy yourself dont worry to much about me. I feel like I will make it OK, go ahead and learn how to drive the car where I wont haft to drive when I git back. I will be coming back dont give up hopes, I know I am in the worse part of the army, but that dont mean I cant make it OK with God on my side I will be coming back I got to come back to my darling wife and son. I know they are waiting on me, so sweet dont worry just pray for me that all can do. Love and sweet dreams, yours true for ever, James, many sweet kisses to my darling wife, this is Germany money you can keep it if you want to.

Dad was spending Christmas night at Camp as the Army gave them at least Christmas day off. They all would soon be off and marching through the frozen landscape of Northern France toward Belgium though. For many of those soldiers it would be their last march and their last Christmas. Dad wrote this letter to mother on Christmas night, December 25, 1944:

Dear Darling Little Wife,

Just a few lines hope you and Roger are well and having a good Christmas. For Myself I Am OK but not having any Fun Much, Just staying around Camp thinking about you and all the good times we used to have. I hope we can have some more pretty soon maby before next Christmas I hope. Well someone knocked the ink of and spilled it every where I guss you can tell that by the looks of my letter. Did Harrison come. I hope he did git his leave I hope they dont do him like they did me give him a leave, then dont stop moving him tell he gits to the front lines.

I hope Not. I dont wont Anybody to come over that can git out of it. I know I would like to be back where I could see you and Roger ever once and a while but I know I cant tell the war is over Now. If I ever do git back I will make the U.S.A. My home the rest of my Life. I dont like over here – darling be good and dont wory I will be back some sweet day. I Love you darling, I will always be true to my darling wife. Love And Sweet kisses by darling Love James

The following letter was a V-Mail written to mother from dad just after the previous letters. This V-Mail was dated December 27, 1944. This was the last correspondence that I found from him before he was wounded in Belgium December 30, 1944:

Dear Darling Wife,

Just a few lines hope you and all are well, for myself I am OK at this time. I stay on the move I dont know one day where I will be the next. I am some where in------------ ------------------(This part was censored) now I guss you been keeping up with the news, we dont git much news over here, but we can see and hear what's going own, that's anought for me and to much to. I mean it is Cold here, the snow is pretty and white every where, but the weather have been pretty good for the last few days. I havent got a letter in about two weeks. I sure would like to git one. I havent got the box yet. Darling dont wory just pray for me. I Love you sweet your true, James

I will now include the only letters I was able to find from mother to dad during this same time period of around December 10, 1944 to late December 1944 and early January 1945. There are two possible explanations as to why dad did not receive all her letters. One explanation could be that all the letters that she wrote to him every day never caught up with him as he had so many different addresses and, therefore, he never received them, I cannot imagine that mother would not have included these letters with the others if she had them in her possession. Another explanation could be that dad lost these letters. Dad mentioned in a later V-Mail to mother in January 1945, that he lost everything but his pocket book, pictures, and Testament when he was wounded, so he could have lost these letters then.

Here is a letter from mother dated Hamilton, Alabama, December 21, 1944:

Hi Sweetheart,

Well, it is raining again as usual. I do hope it will soon stop.

I didn't get a letter from you yesterday or today. I really do miss them too.

I hope you have landed safely by now.

Roger is playing inside with his toys today. He talks a lot about Santa Claus. He wants him to bring him a toy blackboard, and some candy, nuts etc.

(I have the blackboard still and will include a photo here.)

I got him a bag of raisins one day and he wanted to send them to you, so I sent them along with some candy & nuts, while you were at Ft. Meade.

Roger is writing you too.

(I am including a scan of his letter here.)

Well it won't be long now until Christmas. I wish you could be here with us.

Iva is coming Saturday, and Harry, Margaret & Coralie will be here too.

Sweet, I suppose I will go to your mothers after Christmas, as I get too lonesome staying here all the time. I miss you so much anywhere I am.

I hope this war will soon end, so that you can come back to us.

Be good & be careful. I'll love you always.

All My Love, Elizabeth

The next letter I found from mother to dad was written on Christmas Day. I was dated Hamilton, Alabama, December 25, 1944:

Dearest Sweetheart.

Today is Christmas. We have all enjoyed it fine.

Roger & Coralie really were excited over their presents & candies, fruits, nuts etc. this morning.

Roger got a blackboard from mother & me, a pair of house slippers from Iva. A car & bar of soap from Margaret and Harry.

Alma gave him a color outfit.

It has been a messy time for Christmas though as it has rained for the last week & is still raining.

I hope it will stop sometime.

I had a letter from your mother today. She said she had three letters from you.

Iva went back this afternoon. Harry & Margaret will stay until Wednesday.

I surely hope that I will get some more of your letters soon.

I hope and trust that you are O.K. and are having to eat etc.

I will be so happy when you can be back home with us. Maybe it won't be so long.

I'll love you forever.

Love & Kisses Always

Eliz & Roger

This was a letter from the very next day from mother that I managed to find. It was dated Hamilton, Alabama, December 26, 1944:

Hi Sweet,

Well I've just gotten back from a show. I enjoyed it very much. Every time I see good shows, I think of the good times we used to have, Especially when we got home ha!

I hope we will have more good times someday soon.

Roger enjoyed the show too. It was a horse race show. "Home In Indiana" was the name. He has gone to bed. He told you good night & asked God to bless you before he went to sleep.

He talks about you lots.

Herbert washed and simonized the car today. It really looks nice too. I'm hoping to get the car house built this week while Herbert is out of school.

It finally stopped raining & is rather cold today. I really was glad that it wasn't raining for a change.

Sugar I'll stop & get dressed for bed. So be sweet & take care of yourself.

I love you always, Eliz. & Roger

I was lucky to find almost all the letters that mother wrote during the week of Christmas. Of course, mother had no idea that dad was marching across the frozen landscape of northern France with General Patton's Third Army when she wrote this letter. This one was dated the next day, Hamilton, Alabama, December 27, 1944:

Dearest Sweetheart,

It started raining again last night, and is still pouring. This is Hamilton for you ha! We can't even get outside it is so muddy.

Harry & Margaret are going back to Birmingham this afternoon. They have one of those Gov't houses like Clara has.

Roger is out to Mammy's playing with Coralie. They really have lots of fun playing. He is gonna miss her when she goes home.

Sweet do you remember getting any bananas at Mr. William Sullins store here about eight months ago? He says that you got them and forgot to pay him. I think he is mistaken about it, but I'll pay him anyway. It's just

50 cents he says. Anyhow it doesn't make any difference people around here are half – cracked anyhow.

I would give the world if you could come home and we could move to some nice place and have fun again.

I'm going to your mothers as soon as the car house is finished. I'll write you when, so that you can write me there.

Bye Sugar & be sweet. I love you, Elizabeth

This next letter that mother wrote was sent back to her stamped" Hospitalized". Dad had been wounded by the time it arrived and they had no mailing address for him. It was dated December 28, 1944 and mother was worried because she had not heard from dad in so long. It would be about two weeks before she would hear what had happened to him. I have included a scan of the envelope her letter was enclosed in:

Hi Sweet,

How are you today? We are fine. We can't get outside as it is raining, so I suppose we won't know what to do if the sun shines again.

I haven't heard from you in so long. I just hope I'll get a letter soon though. I hope you had a good Dinner for Christmas Did you?

Harry & Margaret went back to B'ham yesterday.

I've been cleaning house today, as usual ha! There is nothing else to do except that though.

Mother and I may go to the show tonight to see +The White Cliffs of Dover". We get so lonesome sitting here. Roger is anxious for me to get him ready to go to the show.

Sweet, I think of you so much & wonder if you are O.K. or where you are. I hope you will be safe & will soon be back home with us.

I just miss you so much. I know you miss us & would like to be back too. It won't last always though I hope.

Be sweet & take care of yourself.

Love always. Eliz. & Roger

Since this letter from Alma Sanders, dad's sister, was written about the same time, I decided to include it here and I will return to mother's letters afterward. She wrote her address as Opelika, Alabama. Rt 4 Box 109 with the date of Wednesday morning, Opelika, Alabama, January 3, 1945:

Hello James

I will try & answer your letters I recieved yesterday James I sure was proude to here from you & that you was well. I just pray to God that ever letter I git that your well & in good hilthe (health) for us we all well at this writing I was at Daddy & mother Sun. they was doing very well. been

253

sick with cold But was better. James I just pray to God that you git throu O.K. & nothing bad Happy (happens) to you & I pray that God will take car of your Family & all your foeks (folks) till you can come back. have you herd from Curtis sent you been over there, the last letter I got he was well & in the best of hilthe.

You wanted to no if we was working in the mills agin, I rote you that we have moved I will write in Jan & try to tell you where. On the old columbus rod (road), 6 miles from town. We have a farm. Jeff bought a mule the other day. Marvin & Harry sure are proude of him. they going to be plow boys this year if nothing happy (happens). I not going to work in the mill because I going to git me a cow & some chickens & I cant work in the mill thin. The kids are going to Beauregard school now. I sure want thim to go ever day. James Joe (Sanders) is thinking about marrying he bought his Girl a ring for Christmas Mrs Sanders sure dont want him to married.

Well I guss I rote all I know to write for this time so you write ever time you can Pleas dont worred about mother & Daddy Just pray. I will close wishin you the best of luck. I guess you can read this this old pin wont write nothing & you know I can write no way with the best of pins.

Lots of Love your sister

This letter from mother to dad was dated Hamilton, Alabama, December 29, 1944 and postmarked December 30, 1944. Mother had no idea that dad would be wounded in battle the very next day:

Hello Sugar,

Well, here I go again with another letter. I don't know very much to write about, so there is no news here except that it is still raining. I don't think I have ever seen it rain so long before, without stopping a minute.

We haven't seen the sun since Dec, 20th.

Herbert Simonized the Car the other day, So I think it is O.K. He had it greased and air put in the tires yesterday. We had the oil changed about two or three weeks ago.

We are taking care of it so that it will still be in good condition for you when you get home.

Lorenzie says he will build the car house as soon as it stops raining. I hope that will be soon too. I want to go to Opelika as soon as it is finished & the car can be put in & locked up.

We don't have our lights yet. The man promised to fix them the first of the year, but he will have to hurry now to do it by that time.

You write to him if you want to (I don't think dad had time to write him as he was he was dodging bullets.) and see what the trouble is that he can't get to it. Just write to the Alabama Power Company, Winfield, Alabama.

I wish we could get it fixed. We could hear the radio & that would be so much company to us. Your mother said she finally got a radio battery. I know she is glad.

Have you been getting my letters? I'll be so glad when I can start hearing from you again.

Sweet, I miss you so much. Be careful & remember I'll always love you.

Love & Kisses Eliz & Roger

In this letter from mother to dad she stated that she had finally gotten a letter from him. This would have been the first one in about a month. Her letter to dad was dated inside Sunday afternoon, December 31, 1944 and postmarked January 2, 9;30 am, 1945:

Dearest Sweetheart,

I was so glad to get your letter today, and was also proud to hear that you have been getting some of my letters too.

I hope you didn't have to fight Christmas and also hope you didn't now. Today is the last day of 1944. I just hope that we will have peace in 45, and that you will be back with us before another year is gone.

We went to Church today. Can you imagine who was there? Corbett Bishop. You know the boy from H'ton (Hamilton) who fasted for forty days because he had to leave his business in Chicago and go to the Army.

He now has a discharge. I don't know what kind though. I think he claims to be crazy, or least he appears that way, as he has a long beard like Santa Claus and is just about 35 years old.

He must not have been very crazy to get out of the army though, he must have been rather clever some way, don't you think ha!

Well, here comes the same old H'ton news. It is still raining here. It started last Friday and rained without stopping all last week and looks as if it might rain all this one too. I hope not though.

I got a letter from Mary. She says she had some V Mail letters from Tucker and that he was with you.

I also had one from Johnnie. She had a letter from Conway recently.

I dreamed last night that you were here with me, I only wish it were true.

I'll love you always.

So be careful & write when you can.

All my Love, Elizabeth

I believe this letter that mother wrote to dad was returned undelivered to her as it was later stamped Air Mail and postmarked Army Postal Service Feb 15, 1945, which meant it could not be delivered as dad had been wounded in Belgium. Mother had dated the letter inside Hamilton, Alabama, January 3, 1945 and its original postmark was January 4, 1945, Hamilton, Alabama. So, this letter circulated for a month and a half before it was finally returned to mother:

Mother wrote a note in the upper left-hand corner of this letter:

P.S. I still have the corner of the $20 bill that you gave me the morning you left. I pasted it in my scrapbook (That scrapbook is now in the collection of The Roger Brown Study Collection of The School of the Art Institute of Chicago and the $20 bill corner is still inside it.).

Hello Sweetheart,

I'm just wondering what you are doing today (He was laying wounded in a hospital in Bristol, England.). I hope you aren't fighting (He was fighting for his life,).

I hate to think of you being over there and having to bear all these hardships. I believe though that you can go through without being harmed if anyone can (That was unfortunately not the case,). You've always been lucky before and I trust that you will this time too (He was lucky to be alive.).

I just wish that I could be there with you.

The happiest day of my life will be when I see you coming home again.

I wish you could have seen Roger today while he was eating his dinner. He really did stuff the rutabaga turnip & cabbage. He said he was trying to get big like his daddy.

When he finished he asked "Mother am I nearly as big as daddy now?"

He tells you good – night every night before he goes to sleep, just like he used to do.

Arthur has a new address now. It is San Francisco, California. I suppose he is going to the South Pacific.

Harrison is at Shepherd Field, Texas now. He is going overseas too, and Gerry is still in Utah, waiting for overseas shipment.

I hope you are getting more of my letters now. Mother & the boys said to tell you "hello" and the best of luck to you.

I got a letter from Eloise today. She says she is going back to work now. She has been sick again.

Sweet I'll stop now wishing you the best of luck.

I'll be thinking of you every minute.

I love you with all my heart.

Yours only, Elizabeth

This next correspondence is another letter that may have been returned to mother while dad was in the hospital in Bristol, England. The envelope was stamped "HOSPITALIZED". At the point that mother wrote this letter she still did not know that dad had been wounded. Mother dated the letter inside January 4, 1945, Hamilton, Alabama. It was postmarked Hamilton, Alabama, January 5, 1;30 pm 1945;

Dearest Sweetheart,

I just received two more letters from you today, you can imagine how happy I was to get them. I'm so glad you got my letter too, even though it was old.

Sweet, you told me not to stop writing if I didn't hear from you every day. You know I wouldn't do that. I have been writing you every day, except about twice since your address has been N.Y. So when you do start getting them you ought to get several every day.

I'm always thinking of you and hoping that you are O.K. I know it is bad what you are going through with, but do the best you can and remember that we all love you and want you to come home as soon as possible.

I'm glad you are having plenty to eat and hope you will continue to get plenty.

I hope and pray that the lord will take care of you wherever you go.

Don't worry about Roger and I. I'll take care of him and myself too. I'll always be true to you.

I finally got a man to start building the car house for me. I hope he will soon get it finished before it rains or snows again. The car still looks nice. I'm trying to keep it that way for you when you get back to drive it.

Don't worry about me having a wreck. I haven't tried to drive anymore. I may sometime though. Sweet, you don't really mind if I don't try to drive very much do you?

I'm glad you are cooking. I just wish you could do that instead of having to fight.

I know you are glad that Tucker is near you.

Mamma said to tell you that she canned some sausage to have for you, when you & the other boys come back, and she will have some fryers too.

We thought of you while we were eating the fresh meat & chicken.

Sugar, I'll stop now, hoping that you will always be safe.

All my love,

Eliz. & Roger

(Roger had a drawing inside on the back of the page,)

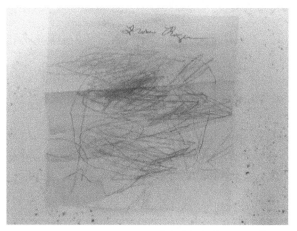

Here is a scan a scan of Roger's drawing.

I am assuming that the next letters that mother wrote to dad were indeed delivered to him as they were not stamped returned. This letter was dated by mother, Hamilton, Alabama, January 5, 1945. It was postmarked January 5, 4 pm, 1945;

Hello Sweet,

I was so happy to get your two letters today, and hear that you are cooking and aren't in such a bad place. I do hope you get to stay there and don't have to go into battle.

Thanks for the France money I'll put it with my other collection of souvenirs.

I'm also glad that you got another of my letters.

I'm writing your mother too. I'll tell her about you.

Yes, I was so very proud of my Christmas presents. I have the bracelet on now. Everyone says it is the prettiest one they have ever seen. It would have to be though as the best looking man on earth sent it to me.

I do hope you will be rid of that cold. Take care of yourself.

About those French girls, I hope you won't find any good looking ones ha!

You asked about Opaleen. I got a letter from her the other day. She is in Little Rock, Arkansas with her husband. He is a Lt. in the Infantry and expects to be shipped overseas soon.

Roger is out helping build the car house ha!

Mother said to tell you that we had some more of those good ole Eatwell Sardines, like she used to have right after we married. Remember them? Boy! Would it be nice if we lived over across the road from her now.

I'll be so glad when you get back & we can be somewhere together again.

I'll always love you

Love & Kisses Elizabeth & Roger

The next letter that I found from mother to dad was dated Hamilton, Alabama, January 6, 1944. Mother was telling dad what a brave little boy Roger was at the dentist and how the dentist bragged on him for being such a great patient, especially considering that he was only three years old:

Hello Sweetheart,

Well, this is news! Today is Saturday and it is raining down again, as it never fails over the week-ends.

Roger wants to go to the show tonight, but I suppose it will be too bad.

I took him up here to the Court house, yesterday and had the Dentist to fill two of his back jaw teeth.

I know you think he is mighty young to have had his teeth filled. He has been crying with them for quite a while. I didn't think of him having any bad teeth.

The dentist wouldn't pull them, as he said that he should keep those teeth until he is twelve years old.

Roger really has the nerve too, as he hardly moved while he was filling them. He didn't even cry at all. The Dentist told Roger to write you that he had never done any work for a better boy. He also said he had never seen a little boy that was any more of a man than Roger.

I wish you could have heard Roger asking him to pull his teeth for him.

Roger is so proud that they are fixed, he says he can eat now and it doesn't hurt his teeth.

I wonder what you are doing now, sugar (Mother had no idea the dad was in an English hospital recovering from serious battle wounds.). I hope you are still cooking and are O.K.

I just hope you aren't in bad weather over there, like it is over here,

I think of you all the time, and hope you can soon be back home.

Sweet be careful and remember we love you.

All our Love, Eliz & Roger

(This is a scan of a photo of Roger
when he was 3 years old.)

This letter from mother to dad found her caught up with dad from the letter he wrote to her December 24, 1944. Her letter was dated inside Hamilton, Alabama, January 8, 1945 and postmarked January 8, 4;30 pm, 1945:

Dearest Sweetheart,

I got your letter this morning which was written Dec 24. There was a line cut out of it, just wish I knew what it was. I suppose you will know though.

You said you had joined your outfit and they had--------
---------that was the part that was cut out. I really hated to hear that you are going on the front. Do the best you can to take care of yourself and I believe God will take care of you.

Sweet, I love you so much and I hope & pray that nothing will happen to you. I had much rather it would happen to me. Sweet, I'm so sorry that you got so cold and the weather is as awful there. I think of you when I'm here in a warm room and a good bed to sleep on.

I hope you will be back to share it with me someday.

I got a letter from your mother too. She says she has had two letters from you and one from Curtis. Says he is really wanting to come home too,

I do hope I can hear from you regularly so that I'll know how you are etc.

Remember we are praying for you I'll always love you.

Bye & Kisses Elizabeth & Roger

I managed to find one more letter from mother to dad written during this time period. It was dated three days later, on January 11, 1945. This probably was her last letter in which she still did not know that dad had been wounded. It was dated Hamilton, Alabama, January 11, 1945:

Hello Sugar,

How are you doing today? I hope you are O.K. I haven't heard from you in the last three days.

I hope and pray that you are safe.

I think of you so much. I hate to think of your being so cold over there. I just hope the weather will soon be better, also the war, so that you won't have to go through so much.

I got a letter from Mary today. She said that she had several letters from Tucker lately, and that he was in the

35th Division of the third army and he was probably already fighting.

Can you tell me what Army you are in?

I do hope you are getting all my letters. I hope I'll get one from you tomorrow, as I worry when I don't hear.

I got a letter from your mother. She says pearl (Pearl Owsley, her sister) is with her now.

I got one from Alma too. They are all O.K.

I'll be so happy if this war would end and you could come home.

Be careful, sweet, and remember we're always thinking of you.

I love you, Elizabeth & Roger

P.S. Roger is fine.

With this letter from mother. the letters from her this time period concluded or at least I could not find any others. There would be no more letters until January 1945, and they were from dad while he was in the Army Hospital in Bristol, England recovering from his wounds. I will include those letters from him and those from mother in response in Chapter Six: Dad's Hospital Stay in England. Before that though I will have Chapter Four: Dad's Stories from the War, and Chapter Five: More Letters from Family and Friends.

Chapter Four

Dad's Stories from the War

Unlike the previous four chapters, Chapter Four will not include letters from mother, dad, relatives and friends but instead will include stories that my dad told me about his experiences in battle. Like most World War Two soldiers my dad never wanted to talk about the war. The war was too horrible, and he wanted to put it out of his consciousness forever. When he finally returned home to stay, he was ready to start a new life with his beloved wife and son. He spent his life devoting himself to his family and making a life for them that he could be proud of. Later in life when he was in his eighties though he did become introspective about it and decided that he should share his memories of those experiences with me. He thought that I should know what his experiences were and the sacrifices that he and his fellow soldiers had to make to fight for and defend their country, their loved ones and their way of life.

I can only recall those stories that he told from my own memory and I will do my best to tell them as accurately as he related them to me. There were many stories, and I grew to admire and respect my dad more and more with each one that he told me. I also gained a much greater appreciation of the value of human life as I realized how close my dad came to death and how close I came to never having been born at all. So, I will try and tell the stories in the order that they must have occurred in my dad's own personal history and not necessarily in the order that they were told to me. I will start with the earliest days of his being called to the front around December 28, 1944 and work my way through the days that followed up to and including the days that he spent in the hospital in Bristol, England beginning around January 1, 1945.

Dad and his company had been stationed somewhere in France and were waiting to find out where they would be called to serve next. Dad along with thousands of other infantry soldiers had been shipped overseas and arrived in Marseilles, France December 9, 1944. From there the soldiers were separated and sent off in different outfits for destinations unknown to them. Strategies and troop locations were carefully guarded by the Army lest spies get hold of the information and relate it to the enemy. So, my dad and all the others really had no idea what part of France they were deployed in and even less about what their future mission would be,

On about December 28, 1944 dad and his company were joined up with General Patton's 3rd Army Infantry and marched through the frozen, snow covered landscape of Northern France toward Bastogne, Belgium where they were to relieve the American troops being devastated by the German Offensive at the Battle of the Bulge. Dad and his fellow soldiers had no idea what they were up against or whether they would ever live to see their homes and loved ones again.

One of my dad's letters to mother was written from a hay loft somewhere in France along the itinerary of that bold march to Bastogne. He wrote to mother that he was lucky to have found the barn with hay loft and was able to get at least some shelter and warmth away from the freezing winter temperatures, He said normally, they would sleep on the cold ground if they slept at all and their feet would freeze and become frost bitten. He said his feet were so frostbitten that they hurt worse than any pain that he had ever had in his life.

Dad related a story to me about that march and what they found in the frozen landscape along the way. His company was slowly advancing being careful to watch for German snipers as they marched through a forested area and came upon a clearing. They could see a group of German soldiers up ahead that had gathered and encircled a campfire that was no longer burning. The German soldiers were just sitting there and not talking or showing any signs of being aware of dad's company, in the 134th Infantry. approaching them. With rifles aimed and ready dad's company slowly drew closer to the German soldiers who were still seated around the now dead campfire. Even as dad's lieutenant announced in German that they were surrounded and not to resist, the German soldiers remained motionless as they sat encircling the once warm fire. Suspecting a trick and a possible ambush dad's company held back and a small team of soldiers was sent in advance to see what the Germans were up to. It wasn't long before the sergeant in charge of the team yelled out "They're all dead! They're all frozen stiff and have been for some time!" So, this gives one an idea of just how cold it was in Northern France in late December of 1944.

Dad's company continued to march and advance toward the front. They were uncertain of what was going on because they were given little if any information about what their destination was, Dad and the other soldiers did know where they were going was going to be rough though because they could hear the artillery shells exploding and gunfire from all directions. They knew that they were not far away from what we now know was the last desperate German Offensive of World War Two. Many American soldiers had already died and many more, including many in dad's company would be killed in action as well.

By this time dad's company was meeting with stiff resistance from German artillery rounds and German soldiers charging toward them with German tanks in their lead. The weather had been overcast so it was hard for American Army Air Corp to give dad's company air cover, Dad was now learning what all that tough Infantry training had been about during his seventeen weeks at Camp Blanding, Florida. He would need to draw on that training to save himself and to save his buddies who were beginning to get shot down all around him. Many of dad's fellow soldiers were killed that day as the Germans advanced toward them, The American troops were situated on a high ridge and had fixed their location so they could fire down on the approaching German soldiers. The Germans had tanks that were leading the charge and firing round after round at the resisting American troops. My dad was laying down covering himself behind rocks on the top of the ridge and he could see a German tank advancing directly toward him. Dad thought this might be the end for them all but suddenly the gray skies began to clear, and the clouds began to part. Dad looked up in the sky overhead and saw a squadron of American Army Air Corp planes fly over his head tipping their wings to him as they approached. Just as the German tank was about to reach the top of the ridge where dad was laying, the American planes fired on the German tank and it exploded into flames as dad watched in amazement. It was then that dad knew God had listened to all his prayers.

After this close call, dad was wondering what could possibly happen next. What was left of the soldiers in his company were still fighting off

269

the remaining Germans who had been thoroughly disoriented by the American Army Air Corp planes and the severe shelling given by them had scattered them in all directions. One might well understand that the Germans were now so confused that they could not decide which way to run. Dad had used almost all his ammunition firing at the onslaught of German soldiers and had it not been for the American planes neither he nor I would have lived to tell his story. Dad fired at the few remaining Germans that were either too brave or too stupid and he had now used up the bullets in his pistol. One German came running up the hill and dad pointed his pistol at him and signaled to him to throw up his hands and surrender. Dad must have been convincing because the German threw up his hands and surrendered. Dad marched him behind the lines to a position where he was taken prisoner. Dad truly had God and Lady Luck on his side that day because there were no bullets in that pistol he had pointed at that German soldier.

If dad thought the worst of it was over, he was proven wrong by what was to follow. It was next to the last day of the year on January 30, 1944 and it would be a day that my dad would never forget, Although the Germans had been scattered there was plenty of fight left in those that continued to resist. Dad's friend had been ordered to replace the machine gunner that had been killed by enemy fire at the top of the hill. Dad was a machine gunner too, but his number had not yet been called. Dad was positioned behind a few feet away in his fox hole where he was standing in about a foot of water that had collected in it from all the recent rainfall. Dad's sergeant noticed that he was standing in water and yelled to him "Brown get out of that fox hole! You'll catch Pneumonia!" Dad had placed his rolled up sleeping bag next to the fox hole and had been resting his head on it. The sergeant told him to come back some and get behind a small hill that the other soldiers were using for cover. On his way a German artillery shell exploded in the tree directly over my dad's fox hole and sent shell fragments flying everywhere. Dad was hit in the left ankle and right hip with many of those fragments and fell instantly to the ground, At the same time, dad's friend who had replaced the machine gunner, was struck in the head by a German bullet. The bullet passed through his left cheek, through his open mouth without breaking a single tooth, and out through the right cheek. He was bleeding like crazy but not fatally injured. Dad told me that the artillery round blew a hole in the sleeping bag where his head would have been twenty seconds earlier. What happened here was very ironic because Robert Brown, dad's brother, had been killed in his fox hole by an exploding German artillery round on July 31, 1944 at St. Lo, France. Dad's friend, bleeding and severely injured as he was, ran over to dad and picked him up and took him to an Army Medic Jeep and they both were taken to an Army Field Hospital, where their wounds were treated. I do not know if you would call what happened to dad and his friend luck or not but they both survived and lived long and happy lives.

What happened next was that dad had to be taken to an Army Hospital located across the English Channel, in Bristol, England. He would remain there recovering from his wounds for about four months. Before he got there though he had more unneeded excitement coming his way, As was often the case the weather was stormy over the channel and the B-29 flying my dad had a very rough time of it. Dad said after surviving the Germans he was almost killed in an airplane crash crossing the channel. The B-29 dropped a thousand feet or more at least twice on the way across and dad thought he was surely a goner this time. He must have had a good pilot though because they made it and dad was on his way to more adventures in Bristol, England. Dad swore that he would never fly in an airplane again and he never did!

Thank goodness that the Army had the best hospitals and the best doctors and nurses, or my dad may never have survived his injuries, His left ankle was severely broken in several places and had to be carefully placed back together causing him great pain and the inability to walk until it totally healed which took many months. His hip healed eventually but they were never able to get all the shrapnel out and he lived with it there all his life. He also developed pneumonia which almost killed him. He lost around fifty pounds and had high fever. He told me that he had an excellent nurse that stayed with him and watched him day and night. His fever was so high that they had to place him in a tub of ice to get it to eventually come down. Even while all of this was going on my dad wrote to my mother but never told her about the medical problems he was having. He only told me about this as he did his other stories many years later and I have now revealed them to you.

Above is a scan of a photo from the Army Hospital in Bristol. England where my dad was treated for his wounds from January to April of 1945. Dad is at center front in the wheelchair. Below is a scan of a photo of the doctor, nurse and other patients.

Chapter Five

More Letters from Family and Friends

Chapter Six will be my second chapter in which I include letters that dad got from family and friends. The letters will include letters from Curtis Brown, his brother, Betty Brown, his mother, Herbert Palmer, mother's brother, Alma Sanders, dad's sister, Mary Mayberry, a cousin of dad's, and Gerald Gamel, my mother's sister Aunt Iva's husband. There are letters from Robert Brown, my dad's brother who was killed in action, and from his fiancé Eloise Green, as well as from other friends and family.

The first letter was from Curtis Brown, dad's brother. It was a very heartfelt letter in which Curtis expressed his feelings about the death of their brother Robert who was killed in action in France. It was dated England, September 22, 1944 and postmarked September 23. 1944:

I am including a scan of a photo of Curtis Brown here,

Hello James,

I will answer your letter that I recived today sure was proud to hear from you and I hope this letter finds you still well and in good health.

I am still in england doing fine and in the best of health but am I getting home sick. I sure would like to see this war over where I could get back home I hope it will be over soon so we all can go back home to our love ones.

I recived a letter from home and one from Robert out fit the same day that said he was killed in action. I have never had anything to hurt me like that did. I try not to worry but giving up someone like Robert is hard to do. I got to see him last May he were in good health We talked about what we were going to do when the war were over – he had a girlfriend (Eloise Greene) back home he was very much in love with and some good plans on what we were going to do, but it all over with him and it is up to me and you to take up his part and carry on the best we can with the help of God we can carry on but without God we can not do anything so pray to God for help and he will help.

I will close wishing you the best luck in the world – write soon love Curtis

Uncle Curtis mentions Robert's girlfriend Eloise in the previous letter. Thanks to my cousin Dianna Ennis, Uncle Curtis' daughter, I have been able to find out more information about Eloise who Robert loved very much and was his fiancé whom he would have married had he not been killed in the war. Dianna was able to get the information for me from Eloise's niece who wrote to her this response: "My Aunt Eloise maiden name was Elois Green. After the loss of her fiancé (Robert Brown), she met and married another soldier, Henry Lewis. He was an amputee from a war injury. She was the mother of seven children (two sets of twins). One of the twins died at birth. Her only Son served in Vietnam and died from Agent Orange several years after he was discharged. This son was the twin of the twin boy that died at birth. Aunt Eloise died last year at the age of 99 on Christmas Eve after spending all day with her children and Grandchildren. She came home – told her Daughter she was going to bed and dropped dead on the way. She was raised with three brothers and three sisters. She loved your family and continued to visit for years."

I really appreciate that Dianna was able to get this information from Eloise's niece as it fills in many gaps about her importance to Robert Brown and to the Brown family who always considered her one of their own. Eloise kept in touch with the Browns the rest of her life.

I am including a scan of a photo of Eloise here.

I felt that this would be a great time to include a letter that I found from Eloise Greene that was postmarked March 8, 1944 several months before any of my parent's letters. Her letter expressed so well her feelings toward Robert and helps give a better understanding of their relationship. Eloise was going through what so many wives and sweethearts were going through during these trying times of World War Two. People do not seem to learn how horrible wars are until they have to endure the consequences of them for themselves.This letter was written over 4 months before Robert was killed in action. She dated the letter March 7. 1944, Tuesday Night, 8528 Den Air, So. B'ham 6, Ala.:

Dear Elizibith,

How are you all to Night. Guess you thought that I wasn't going to answer your letter but honey I worry so much these days it a wonder I write any at all.

I tell you the last month sure have been bad for me. I've lost eight lb. weight and everybody talks like I show it two. but I've had a time with my hand.

than at night I go to bed and cry for a spell. I can't eat like I should. People will tell me not to worry. but how can I help it. Sometimes I wonder how some people have Children and Sweet heart in this war and never worry one bit. they must not love them Very much.

I love Robert better than my self. and I tell you I cry every thime I talk or even write about him. I haven't heard from him in over a month now and will I be glad when we won't have to wait on letters and write each outher.

Hows James & Rogers. Wish I could see them. Tell them I said hello. I'm coming to see you all as soon as I get to looking better. and when the weather gets pretty. What have you all been doing these days. the same old thing I guess.

Well don't you all work to hard. write me when you get a chance. tell Alma & her Children hello for me. I'll write and let you no as soon as I hear from Robert. Will have to close. Can't write for crying. So good night and Sweet Dreams.

Lots of love Eloise

I cannot even begin to imagine how Eloise reacted when she found out that Robert had been killed in action July 31, 1944. This kind of grief was multiplied by the millions in that horrible war. I have always wondered what Robert and Eloise's lives might have been like had he lived. Eloise had to survive without him and she did eventually find someone else to love and to love her but I know the void left in her life by Robert's death must never have been filled.

The next letter was from dad's mother, Betty Owsley Brown. One can hardly imagine the emotions she suffered through having had all three of her sons drafted into the service and having one killed in action and another that would soon almost be killed in the same manner. Families across the country and indeed all across the world were experiencing the anguish of having their loved ones taken from them and placed on the fronts and battlefields of war that they possibly would never return from. Whether volunteers or draftees the ones that served all faced an enemy without a face or name that was trained to kill them just as they had been trained themselves. My dad said in his letters that only the soldiers knew what war is like because they were the ones that had to fight them. If the big shots that declared them had to fight the wars, then the wars would be over in a week!

This letter from Grandmother Brown was dated October 9, 1944.

Betty L. Owsley Brown & Robert Louis Brown

I am including a scan of Betty Brown here as a young woman holding her infant son Robert Louis Brown. The drawing of her was done by my brother Roger when he was a teenager.

Dear James

will try and answer your letter I got two day glad you was O.K. I aint well I dont never feel well hope you are well, it is cold up here two day it dont look like your daddy will get through picking cotton by Christmas he wont get but two bales I had a letter from Elizabeth today & also Curtis & Elois. Curtis said he was well & had goten a letter from you Elois is still working I sure am glad Elizabeth & Roger is coming friday your Grandpa (James Thomas Lafayette Brown or "Fate") is gon up to Ola (his daughter) I guss he will come back saturday sure will be glad when you come & hate for you to have to go back maby this war will soon be over I hope so I havent heard any more from Robert I wish I knew how he was killed (Robert was killed when a German artillery round blew up over his foxhole at St. Lo, France, July 31, 1944) but I dont reckon I will ever know. I have got back three letters I wrote him I hope you wont have to go across, it bad a nuf on this side. Mark Hilyer is gon across they say he is we sent Curtis a box of candy I dont know what Alma sent him I hope he will get it I hope this war will be over Christmas it would be a happy Christmas if it was to be over I will close hoping to soon see you – write soon

Lots of love & best wishes Mama dad

The next letter was from Alma Sanders, dad's sister, who wrote him often. As with all the letters, I have transcribed them the way they were written without corrections except for sometimes placing the corrected word in parenthesis next to a questionable word in order to better understand the meaning. Alma, like my dad, had limited education but both had unlimited love for their families and their words needed not to be grammatically correct to get the meaning across. It was dated Sunday night, October 1, 1944 and postmarked October 3, 1:30 pm, 1944:

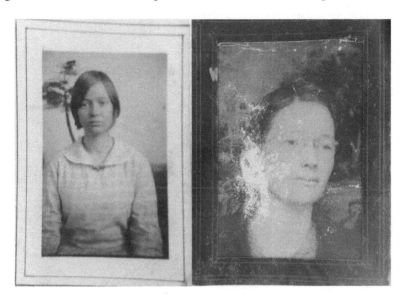

Here are scans of Alma Sander's photos. The one on the left is of her as a teenager and the one on the right is of her in the 1940's after marrying Jeff Sanders.

Dear Brother,

I will try to answer your letter I recived yesterday sure was glad to hear from you & was glade that you was well & hope & pray when this reaces you it find you well and in health for us we all well at this writing I have just got back from down at mama & Daddy they was doing very well. I wish that they was closte to me I dont like for them to be way down there by themselves Mama sure do want to leave that place she siad she cant hadly stand to stay there they dont need to be way down there Daddy is not able to wash. I dont know why he want to try to run a farm I just wish that this war would end the way thing going now it not going to end soon. I know you miss Elizabeth. Mama got a card from her siad Roger sure was prode to see her (Mother had just returned from 2 months with dad at Camp Blanding, Florida.) Siad he wanted to know why she dident bring you poor little fellow I sure would like to see him you & Elizabeth to. Guss Elizabeth & Roger will be down in a week are two. I hope so. I know Mama & Daddy will be prode for thim to come & stay with thim for you know it lonesome for thim dont never go away just stay there & worry but that hard to do. Jeff red in the papper to day where one of his uncle just died a few weeks ago. Mr. Sanders last Brother thay tryed to get the boy here But could not.

Well, I guess I rote all I can for. I cant see how.

Love your sister write soon

This letter was one of two from Mary Mayberry, a cousin of dad's and was dated Bristol, Florida, Thursday am September 28, 1944 and postmarked September 28, 3 pm, 1944:

Dear James & Elizabeth

will ans your letter recd some time ago sure was glad to hear from you all and that you all were well.

I would have done ans your letter but I have been sick now for about two weeks the Dr. says I must have a opieation to ever be well again. I sure do dread it I cant make up my mind to have it done of course I dont mind dying for I am ready to go but if I should not live I would hate to leave my children but the lord no best I hope this war will soon be over where all the boys can come back to there homes it is alful all this war because of sin. I hope Elizabeth is still with you (at Camp Blanding) I'm sure she misses the baby (Roger) but her mother will take care of him and its so much better for her to be with you. We went up in Ala. Last week. went one day and came back the next didn't get to go see Aunt Betty & Gordon. I went with my brother and didn't have time to go see them. I saw Alma in town, James I wont you to trust in the lord he is our only hope we no Robert was a Christian and if we are Christians we will meet him some day. I feel so sorry for Aunt Betty & Gordon. We havent heard from my brother that is in France but once in over a month, we had a letter from Roy, he is OK. guess have written all the news ans. Soon

With lots of love Mary & Family

The second letter from Mary Mayberry was dated Bristol, Florida, October 5, 1944 and postmarked October 5, 3 pm, 1944:

Dear James

Will ans. Your letter ric'd a day or so ago sure was glad to hear from you and that you were well. We are all well as usual, Griff says he feels better now thin he has in a long time. I hope he stays that way. I no you miss Elizabeth but I no the baby (Roger) was glad to see her (back from Camp Blanding). I no it was lots of pleasure and comfort for you when Elisabeth was with you for I no how bad it is to be apart, for Griff worked away from home over a year and it was tough going. I do hope and pray this war will soon be over. I had a letter from Aunt Betty Monday she said they were about sick with colds. We may go up there next week and carry mother she is going and stay a while with Eunice & Mable, if we go we will go see Aunt Betty and Gordon. We are having some cooler weather now and I am glad, it has been so hot. Yes it hurt us all about Robert we all loved him but he is in a much better place thin we are we can go meet him but we cant Bring him back, We are praying for you all I always think of you all in my prayers. All our hope comes from the lord. I dont no any news to write so I'll close.

ans. Soon with lots of love from Mary & all

Here is an earlier letter from my Uncle Herbert Palmer, my mother's next to youngest brother. At the time he was in High School and too young to be drafted into the service. It was dated Hamilton, Alabama, August 2, 1944 and postmarked August 3, 9:30 am, 1944:

I am including an early photo of Uncle Herbert here.

Dear James,

I will answer your letter – hope they are not treating you too bad. But the Infantry has no mercy on no one. I sure wished you had joined the Navy. Arthur (Uncle Joseph Arthur Palmer, my mother's next to oldest brother) say it is not hard I will take your advice if I have to go. I will dodge the Infantry.

I have started to school now. I am taking Sr.1. My subjects are English, History, Biology, and Agri. I sure do like school. I played some football the other day and I am pretty sore now you have to be a mean to do that.

Tell Elizabeth that mama has been working me since she left (Mother was with dad in Florida at the time Uncle Herbert wrote this letter.). I had to peal peaches this evening till in the Night and tell her also that her shoes has come and mama will send them when she finds out where to send them (This was just after mother arrived at Starke, Florida, where dad was stationed at Camp Blanding,). Roger is getting along just fine. Roger says goodnight to daddy and mother every night. He went to town with momma today. He sure likes to go to town. Roger said that Mother had gone to the bad Army too, to get his daddy. He sure is a captain. Well that is all I can thing of. Love Herbert

P.S. Mother said to tell you Hello, Eliz. too. She said that she hoped your leg was better and hoped that Eliz. got there OK.

There are other letters and V-Mails that I will include at this point as well that are from family and friends. The first ones to be included are four V-Mails from Robert Brown to dad that he wrote beginning in May of 1944. After those I will include correspondence from a variety of friends and relatives.

This first V-Mail from Robert Brown was dated May 29, 1944:

Here are two scans of Robert Brown photos. Robert is to the right of my dad in the first photo. He is in the middle of the second photo and is holding Alma's oldest daughter Betty Jane. Robert's sister Alma is on the left and holding her youngest daughter Marie and my mother is on the right.

Dear James & Family

I will answer your letter which I received last Friday sure were glad to hear from you. I am doing fine hope you are the same.

I am sorry to hear that they are still trying to get you in the Army and hope above all things that you can stay out but if they do get you try to make the best of it and I hope and pray that you wont have to stay in long not as long as I have been in anyway.

I got a letter from Curtis a few days ago he was doing fine he said he were coming to see me again the first of next month. I went to London a few days ago. I wanted to go see Curtis but dident have time. I will close for this time – answer soon.

With love Robert

These letters from Robert are quite special to me as he was killed in action and I was never able to meet him. Little did anyone know at the time that these would be his last letters.

The second V-Mail from Robert was dated June 11, 1944. I have included photos of Robert from when he was in high school and later when he was in the service. Robert was drafted into the service in 1941 and served until he was killed in action in his foxhole by a German artillery shell at St. Lo, France July 31, 1944.

Dear Brother & Family

I will write you and let you know that I am doing fine hope you are the same

I guess they have you in the Army by now but I hope not. If they get you try and make the best of it.

I havent heard from Curtis in about three weeks. I was looking for him to come see me the first of this month but he dident get to come. I will close for this time hoping and praying that this war will soon be over and we will all get back home safe.

With love, Robert

Here is a third V-Mail from Robert that was written to his mother and dad. It was dated June 27, 1944:

Dear Mother & Daddy

I will answer your letter which I received the other day. Sure was glad to hear from you these few lines leaves me doing fine hope you are the same.

I am still in France and have been in combat or I should say fixing to go into action. I have only had trouble with a few snipers and plenty of shells bursting around, one which burst over my head. I cant see but one thing that saved me from getting hurt or maby killed and that were God so I give God the credit for saving me that time. I guess James is in the Army by now. When you hear from him send me his address. I will close for this time so tell everyone to pray for me.

With love, Robert

This was Robert's last V-Mail to dad and was written just about a week before he was killed in action on July 31, 1944 at St. Lo, France. It was dated July 23, 1944:

Dear Brother,

I will answer your letter which I received a few days ago. I wrote one the next day after I got your letter – but it were turned down. I guess I tried to tell the truth about this place over here and they dident like it so they sent the letter back – but it were for the best I guess because I don't want to tell something that will help the enemy.

I have been in plenty bad places over here and through God's protecting I have come through all of it so I owe my life and everything I have to God and I have faith in him to carry me through anything that might yet be ahead.

I will close hoping and praying you will make good in the Army and don't remain a part like I have for about three years.

With love, Robert

Thanks again to my cousin Dianna Ennis I was also able to see the letter that Robert Brown wrote to her dad, Curtis Brown which was written the same day, July 23, 1944 as the letter Robert wrote to my dad. It struck me how remarkably similar the two letters were. I will include Dianna's letter here:

A.S.N. 14183051	CO. "C" 117 INF. A.P.D. 30
1251 M,P. CO. AVN	%PM. New York, NY
A.P.D. # 639	July 23, 1944
U,S, ARMY	

(The address on the left is Uncle Curtis Brown's.
The one on the right is Uncle Robert Brown's)

Hello Curtis,

I will answer your letter which I received a few days ago sure were glad to hear from you. I wrote you about two days ago but I put something in it I should have left out and they sent the letter back so I wont try to tell everything I know this time.

I got a letter from James the other day he is in the army and he is stationed at Camp Blanding Fla. I don't guess they will draft any more from our family they have all three of us now.

I have been in plenty close places since I have been here it have only through God's protecting that I came through O.K. and I have faith in him to take me safely through anything that might yet be ahead so I owe my life and everything I have to God. I will close now so be sure and pray for us.

With love, Robert

The next V-Mails are from my Uncle Curtis Brown to my dad beginning in June of 1944. Some of them were not dated so I've sequenced them chronologically as best as I could. The first V-Mail was dated 6/12/44:

Dear James,

I will write you a few lines to let you hear from me, this finds me well and Doing fine, hope you and your family are well and in good health and I hope you are still at home and not in the Army. I havent got a letter from Robert in four or five weeks. I dont know where he is now I hope he is OK. till All the folks I said hello. I will close now write soon

Love Curtis

This next V-Mail from Uncle Curtis was not dated but related closely to the previous one:

Dear James

I will answer your letter. Sure was glad to hear from you this fines me well and doing fine. hope you and your family are well and in good health. I'm sorry you are having to go to the army and live your family and job but all I can say is good luck and dont let the army get you down. I haven got a letter from Robert in six weeks (So this places the date on this letter sometime near the end of June 1944.) I dont know where he is, I will close write soon

Love, Curtis

This V-Mail from Uncle Curtis was not dated either, but I can tell from the content that it was written a couple of weeks after the previous one:

Dear James,

I will answer your letter which I recived a few days ago Sure was glad to hear from you and I'm sorry you are having to go to the army but it look like they are getting all the men, this few lines fine me well and doing fine hope you and your family are well and in good health.

I haven got to see Robert but one time but I hope to see him again soon if I can get a pass I got the pictures from Alma today. Roger is still fat like he always was.

I will close write soon love Curtis

This fourth V-Mail from Uncle Curtis was dated 7/14/1944 and was postmarked July 22, 1 am, 1944:

Dear James,

I will answer your letter I recived today sure was glad to hear from you. this fines me well and doing fine. hope you are well and in good health. I am still station in England and sure would like to see this war over so I could come home I got a letter from Robert last week he is in France Now he was well and in good health I hope he stays in good health and gets back home OK. I will close wishing you all the luck in the world write soon, love Curtis

Although this V-Mail and one letter from Uncle Curtis were from almost a year later, I will go ahead and include them here just to keep his correspondence to dad unified and in one place.

This V-Mail from Uncle Curtis was written much later after dad had been wounded and placed in a hospital in Bristol, England. The V-Mail was dated July 2, 1945 and by this time dad had been in hospitals for several months, so that gives some idea of the serious nature of his wounds. Dad had been released from the English hospital sometime around mid April 1945 according to the content of Uncle Curtis' V-Mail.

I did not have any V-Mails from Uncle Curtis during the first six months of 1945, although I'm certain he must have written several. One must assume they were lost or never received by dad when he was recovering in the hospital.

There is also a letter that Uncle Curtis wrote in August of 1945 in which he discusses the death of Robert that I will include after this V-Mail dated July 2, 1945:

Dear James,

I will answer your letter I recived a few days ago sure was proud to hear from you glade you got back home OK (So dad had been released mid April, 1945.) hope you can soon get outer the hospital (This would've been the hospital in Mississippi.) and outside the Army for good, I dont know what they're going to do with me. I'm still

290

station at Huntingdon England with the Eight Air Forces but in anoughter outfit I dont do much work. Nowe I'm getting in good shape for the Pacific. I'm taking a seven day furlough in two weeks I gest I'll go to Bristol that where you were in the hospital over here. I'm goning to try and have a good time because it will be the last Furlough I'll get in England. I gest I'll be home sometime in Sept If they dont change it again. Say hello to all the US, girls for me. Wishing you all the best of Luck.

Love Curtis

This last correspondence from Uncle Curtis was a letter rather than a V-Mail and was dated England August 18 and postmarked August 21, 1945. At this point the U.S. had dropped the two Atomic Bombs on Hiroshima on August 6, 1945 and on Nagasaki on August 9, 1945 that ended World War Two. Uncle Curtis was fortunate that he now did not have to be shipped to fight in the war against Japan:

Dear James

I will try and answer your letter I recived a few weeks ago. Sorry I diden write sooner but thought I would be home by the time you got the letter but I'm not. I'm still in dear old england in the eight air forces at Huntingdon where I were when you wer over here, but hope to be home some tim in Sept if they dont change the date agan, like they have the last three months.

I have been on a seven day furlough this month I went to Bristol and London. Bristol is the town where you was in the hospital. I diden stay there long. I spent most of my time in London. I had a very good time the weather was good and the lights are on agan you can see what the girls look like nowe at night – before she takes you home are to a danc.

I got a letter from home this week. Moma and dady said they were well and doing fine. I hope they stay well and in good health – the rest of ther time which I know is not many years, for they are getting old and have had a lot of trouble the last few years. I'm guning to do every thing I can to make them happy and in Joy the rest of ther time. I know we will never get over losing Robert but we can make the best of things he died fighting for. I know that way he would wont us to do.

Nowe that the war is over (The war in Germany ended with Germany surrendering to the Allies on May 7, 1945 and in Japan after the August 9, 1945 bombing of Nagasaki and eventual official war ending ceremony on September 2, 1945.) and we have peace agan. I gest you will be getting outer the army soon and back home with your family.

I gest I will try to get a discharge when I get home if I can. I think I am needed at home more then in the army because I have moma a dady to see after and a job waiting for me when I get back and that not all Im getting old and got to get me a wife soon are I will be to old to make love.

I will close wishing you and youre family good health and good luck write soon –

Love Curtis Im sending this to your wifes address

This ends my chapter on letters from relatives and friends, but I will have more of them as I continue with my parents' story in letters. The next chapter will cover the time period from early January of 1945 to mid April of 1945. These were the four months that my dad was in the hospital in Bristol, England recovering from the wounds he received on December 30, 1944 in Bastogne, Belgium.

Chapter Six

Dad's Stay at the Hospital in Bristol, England

Dad wrote to mother as soon as he was able to after he had arrived at the Army hospital in Bristol. England for treatment. I am not sure when mother was notified by the War Department that dad had been wounded but I know her first letters to dad from early January 1945 made no mention of it. Dad never really revealed the extent of his injuries and his bout with pneumonia which almost killed him in his early letters to mother either. He did not want to worry her, but he was really in bad condition when he first arrived at the hospital. The fact that he stayed there four months gives some idea as to the seriousness of his injuries.

I will begin with mother's letters to dad beginning around the first of January 1945. At that time, she did not know that dad had been wounded and was in the hospital in England. I will concentrate on just the letters from mother before I include dad's early letters to her. This letter from mother to dad was dated January 1. 1945, Hamilton, Alabama and was postmarked January 2, 1 pm, 1945:

Hello Sugar,

How are you today? We feel a little better as the sun is shining again. It is rather cold though.

Mother and I washed today.

I got a letter from your mother & Alma too. They said they had gotten the pictures (the enlarged one of you, Roger & I) that I sent them.

I hope you have gotten the snapshots I sent by now.

Your mother said that your dad had some new teeth. I would like to see him now wouldn't you?

She said that he didn't wear them much as he couldn't get used to them.

Herbert & Horrice started back to school today again.

That makes things much quieter around here ha!

I may work for Mr. Carpenter again tomorrow as he said he had a good bit of work for this week.

I only made two dollars a day but I suppose it beats sitting around the house. It is also good practice too.

I would give the world if you were here with me. This place & everywhere else is so dull without you.

I'll be so happy when this war is over & you can come home.

I'll always love you only.

Be sweet & write Eliz & Roger

As I have related before, I do not have all the letters mother wrote, and this next one was written over a week later and dated Hamilton, Alabama, January 9, 1945. There was no envelope:

Dearest Sweetheart,

I got the V-Mail with your change of address. I hope and pray that wherever you are that you are safe. I do hope that the weather will soon be better there.

I think of you so much, when I start to bed of how you have to sleep out in the cold. I hope & pray that you won't have to go through with that much longer that you can soon be back home.

I have been washing today. Wrote up some law cases for Mr. Carpenter also typed some.

The car house is all finished now & the car is in it. It really is a nice one too. I'm so proud of it as it will protect the car from bad weather.

I think I will go to your mothers next week. I suppose I'll go to see Johnnie first & from there on to Opelika. Just keep writing me here though as I'll probably be back before you would have time to write me to Opelika. Mamma can forward your letters on to me. I just live from one of your letters to the next.

Roger is asleep now. He says at the end of his prayer "Bless Daddy". He also tells you good night every night. Last night Mamma said "Sweet Dreams" to him, and told him to dream something good. He said "I'll dream that daddy will come home". He talks about you all the time and wants you to come home.

We got a letter from Arthur yesterday. He is now in San Francisco, California. Says he enjoyed his trip to the South Sea Islands and saw several of those girls.

He is going back foe 18 months now.

I'll be so glad if this war is ever over so that all of you can come back home.

Be careful and remember we love you.

Love & Kisses Elizabeth & Roger

In this next letter mother mentions the letter she received from dad that had been censored and some lines had been cut out of it. This was from dad's earlier letter that I have previously included where he mentions that he has been moved toward the front lines. The army censors cut out the part that told his location. Mother's letter was dated January 12, 1945, Hamilton, Alabama. There was also no envelope for this letter (There was a P.S. written at the top,):

P.S, Johnnie says she has had two letters from Carr (Carr was in a German P.O.W. camp.)

Dear Sweetheart,

I was so happy to get your letter this morning. You told me where you were but it was cut marked out. The best I could make out though it must have been Belgium. If it is when you write again let me know by saying right or wrong. I keep up with the War News as I take the News paper now.

You said you haven't had a letter from me in two weeks. Sweet, I write you every night.

I do hope that you will soon start getting them more often.

Sweet, I know that you are in a dangerous place, and have some awful things to go through with. I hope and pray that God will take care of you though and you can come back home when this thing is over.

Sugar, you tell me not to worry. Of course, I can't help worrying about you, but I try to look forward to the day when you'll be back with us to stay.

I've been working for Mr. Carpenter this week. I like the work fine.

Roger is O.K. He has to stay in the house today, as it is raining again.

I'm so glad the car house is finished & the car is out of the rain.

I'm going to Johnnie's Tuesday and on to your mother's. Continue to write me here though as I'll be back soon.

Mamma will forward them to me. Be careful and remember we love you.

All our Love Eliz & Roger

This next letter from mother to dad was written two days later, on January 14, 1945. She was responding to two letters written to her by dad on Christmas Day 1944. This was five days before dad was wounded in Belgium on December 30, 1944:

Dear Sweetheart,

I was so happy to hear from you today. I got two letters and the German money. Thanks a lot. They were written on Christmas Day. I had a V-Mail from you Thursday that was written later though it was the 27th.

Sweet, it helps me so much to know that you feel like you'll be back soon. I believe you will too. I want that more than anything in the world. Tomorrow wouldn't be too soon for me.

I pray that God is taking Care of you & will continue to wherever you go & whatever you have to do.

Remember we're always thinking of you. I dream about you every night. I waked Iva last night talking about you.

I thought you were fighting and I was over there too. I wish I could be over there with you.

Iva came this weekend. It has been such pretty warm weather, that she & I took a walk down to the School house & around. It was lonesome for me though, as I thought of the times we used to walk down that way.

Roger is asleep now. He told you Good night and asked the Lord to bless you.

Arthur is in California. He says he has seen several movie Stars. That is what he likes. He'll probably be dancing with those girls ha!

Sugar, I'm sending you another picture. I'm afraid you won't get the others I sent.

I'll always love you only, Love & Kisses Eliz & Roger

I will continue with mother's letters to dad but will point out that it was around two months before dad got any of these letters. He was moved from place to place and had several address changes plus the mail normally took two weeks in those days anyway during war time. So, there was not a communication back and forth with them as neither mother nor dad were getting many letters from around January to March of 1945. This letter from mother to dad was a V-Mail and was dated January 19, 1945. There was no envelope:

Dearest James,

We arrived in Opelika yesterday. Iva came too. We are now at Alma's. Had a very nice time at Johnnie's.

Roger has been having lots of fun riding Marvin and Harry's mule this morning,

We are going to your mothers now. I surely hope mother has sent my mail on to me and that I have some from you.

I do hope you are O.K. (Mother has still not been notified that dad has been wounded and is in an English Hospital and has been for 20 days.).

Love Always Elizabeth & Roger

To establish more clearly a storyline of events I am enclosing two letters from Mary Tucker, mother and dad's good friend whose husband and she roomed with mother and dad while dad and Mary's husband were being trained at Camp Blanding, Florida. She wrote about dad's being wounded and provided useful information, so evidently mother had finally been notified of dad's being wounded.

Here are the letters that Mary wrote to dad. The first letter from Mary was dated Columbus, Georgia, January 28, 1945:

Dear James,

Guess you will be surprised to hear from me but I thought I'd try & write you a time or two. Liz wrote me about you getting wounded in your left hip & leg. I was really shocked too as I didn't think you boys had time to get to the Front line but I see I was wrong. I'm really sorry you got hurt & I sincerely hope you will soon be alright. Maybe they will send you back to the states when you get well or I hope they will any – way.

I got a letter from Tucker the other day & it was written Jan 6th & he was in Belgium then. I sure wish I could see him. I'll be so terribly glad when this war ends but who wont.

We've been having some rotten weather over here, We'll be glad when the sun comes out again. Tucker said the weather over there was awful too & that he stayed cold all the time. Wish you boys was back at Camp Blanding. Guess that place would seem like heaven to all of you now or would it?

I'm hoping this war will soon end & that all you boys can come home again to stay.

Liz sent me some pictures of you three while you were on furlough you've got a mighty cute boy. I wish I could see him & Liz. I write her every week & I hope to see her soon.

You take care of your self & heres hoping you'll soon be able to walk again.

I don't know any news to write you so guess I'll close for this time – You write me how you are getting along if you can.

Your friend Mary

The second letter from Mary to dad came about one month later and was dated Columbus, Georgia, February 27, 1945:

Dear James,

I got your letter the other day & was more than glad to hear from you. I sure was surprised to learn you had had Pneumonia as Liz hadn't written me about it. I'm so glad you are well of it tho. Here hoping your leg is well enough for you to walk on it by now any – way.

As for my-self I'm fine only missing Tucker something awful.

I got seven letters from him last week. He is in Germany now & had been sick from eating some frost bitten apples. The last letter he wrote he was OK & is now in a mortar squad instead of a rifle outfit. He says he was lucky to get into that. I sent him a box of stationery Sat. as he was out and couldn't find any place to buy any – I hope he'll get it soon as I want to hear from him real often. He has asked about you in nearly every letter I get from him. He thinks a lots of you too James & I know you two had fun picking at one another in Camp Blanding. I sure wish I could see Liz too.

We are having some pretty weather here for a change & Gee, its good to see the sun out again. What kind of weather are you having there?

I've got to stop now & iron my weeks wash. You take real good care of your self & write me if you ever feel like it. I hope & pray you'll soon be out of the hospital & that they will send you back to the states. I'll say So long for now.

A Friend Mary (Mary includes Tucker's address)
Pvt. Wilmark Tucker Jr.
34837696 Co H, 137 Inf,
A.P.C. 35 % P.M. New York, N.Y.

I will now return to mother's letters written to dad. By this time mother must have known about dad's being wounded and must have been writing to him at the English hospital. This letter was written about ten days after the previous one that I included. I know that there were more letters written to dad in that ten-day period, but I was not able to find them. This letter was dated Opelika, Alabama, January 29, 1945. There was no envelope:

Hi Sugar,

How are you today? I hope you are doing fine.

I'm here with Alma's kids now. Alma & Jeff are working. I don't have very much trouble with them though and know how to manage them.

I hope your mother will forward my mail on to me as I'm almost sure I got some mail from you today.

I can hardly wait from one day until the next to hear from you (It seems here that mother is now getting mail from dad on a regular basis,). I wish you could come back to the states (This indicates that mother knows he is in the hospital and wishes that they would send him to a hospital in the states.) – then I could see you when I wanted too or it would suit me even better if you could come home to stay. Then I could take care of you.

I hope you are getting my letters now. I know it is aggravating not to even be able to hear from me. I don't know why you can't get them. I keep writing, so maybe when you do start getting them you will have plenty to read.

Sweet, I'm going to send you some candy right away.

That is when I get a chance to get it. The postmaster said he would let it go through for me.

Roger is fine. He and Marie are having lots of fun playing.

It really has been cold here today. I'll be so glad when Summer comes.

Sugar, be careful, and remember I'll love you always.

Love & kisses Elizabeth & Roger

The next letter I found from mother to dad came three days later, on February 1, 1945. In it, mother mentions dad has been having chest problems (probably from pneumonia) and she also mentions that she has received his purple heart in the mail, so although she does not give many details, we know that she is fully aware of dad's condition and the nature of his injuries. Here is the letter:

Hello Sugar,

I got another letter from you today, Sorry to hear that you have been having trouble with your chest. Sweet, be careful for I want you to get well soon. I worry about you so much.

We are fine, except Roger has a cold. He is better now. I gave him some Castoria last night.

I had letters from Mary, mother, Iva & Mrs. Carell too.

Mary says Tucker is in Belgium now. She says she is writing you too.

Iva says Gerry is on his way over seas. I suppose he is going to a bad place too according to his address. I don't think there are any good places over there though.

His address is Sgt. Gerald W. Gamel, 16081290, Sq, A=3 APO, 16993 – A% P.M. San Francisco, California.

Mamma and all are O.K. Say they miss Roger and I a lot. Your Purple Heart came. I'll take good care of it for you until you get home.

I am including a scan of the Purple Heart here.

Mrs. Carell says they are really hiring new hands at Childersburg now. I wish we were there or somewhere together don't you sugar? Maybe it won't be long though.

I love you only – Love & Kisses Eliz and Roger

Here is a letter mother wrote to dad from a few days later dated February 7. 1945. In it she acknowledges that she is aware of dad's having pneumonia and was relieved to hear that he was improving:

Hello Sweet,

I'll try to write you another letter, although I don't know very much to write about, as nothing of importance ever happens here.

I've been with your mother almost four weeks and am going back to Hamilton Tuesday February 13th, so write me to Hamilton.

I do hope your pneumonia is well by now & that you are feeling good.

Your mother said to tell you that she was glad to hear you were improving.

I'm just praying that you will soon be back with us, That will be the happiest day of my life. I only hope it won't be very long off.

Roger is fine. He is out with his Grand Daddy.

Today is a rather pretty day. I just hope it will stay that way.

Sweet, I sent you a box of Valentine chocolates yesterday. I do hope you will get them, if not for Valentine's Day, maybe you'll get it by the 25th which is our Wedding Anniversary.

It doesn't seem that we have been married 4 years, does it? I hope you will be with me before we have a fifth anniversary.

Remember the cake I baked last year? Ha! You said it was ragged but right.

Maybe I'll learn how to cook good Someday.

Be sweet & take care of yourself.

I love you Love & Kisses Elizabeth & Roger

In this next letter mother has found that dad has finally received some of the letters that she had sent him. It had been about a month and a half and I can imagine how happy dad was to at last have some news from home. Mother had received notices from the Army on dad's condition and was informed that he was continuing to improve. This was no doubt reassuring and comforting to her.

This letter from mother was written one week later than the previous one and was dated February 14, 1945. There was no envelope:

Hi Sugar,

Well, I suppose I was just about as happy to hear that you had received some of my letters as you were to get them.

I know it made you feel so much better to hear that Roger and I are doing fine.

I wrote your mother that you had gotten a letter from her too. I know she'll be so glad.

I stayed with them four weeks. They seemed so glad that I was with them. I know they get lonesome by themselves so much. I tried to get them to come back with me but they wouldn't.

Your grandpa (Fate Brown) lives with Ola Piper (his daughter) now. He has moved. I certainly did miss him around the places Dancing etc. ha!

I spent two days with Johnnie (her best girlfriend). I had a rather nice time. She really has a cute boy. He walks now. She has had about eleven or twelve letters from Carr in the last two weeks. He seems to be doing fine.

Iva is coming home this week and we'll be glad to see her too. I haven't seen her since we were in Opelika together.

Sweet it won't be long now until we'll be married four years and the first time we've been apart on our anniversary.

Gee! I'll be so happy when you're back with us to stay.

Today is Valentine's Day. I hope you get the box of chocolate I sent you. I know you couldn't get it today but maybe you'll get it later & it'll be just as good.

Sweet, write me and let me know if you want anything else, for I can't send anything without a request.

I suppose you wonder how I sent the candy. Well it is a long story. On one of the V-Mails you wrote which wasn't taken a picture of your mother wrote a request for me. I was afraid that I couldn't write enough like you so I had her write it for me. We got by with it. I just hope you get it.

I got a card from Washington D.C. telling me that you were improving normally Feb 3. I got one in Jan, too. It made me feel good to hear that you were still improving.

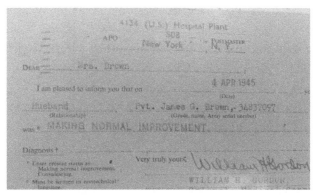

(I have these cards from January, February and April,1945 and am including a scan of one here.)

I'm praying that you'll soon be home again, and this awful war will end. I believe it will now before long.

Sugar, I love you. Write often as you can.

Love & Kisses Eliz & Roger

This letter came as a surprise to me because mother states in it that she has learned to drive and had driven their car a couple of miles. I have never known mother to drive at all and dad always drove her anyplace she wanted to go. This had to have been a very brief inspiration for her though as she never made a habit of it then or in the future. This letter was written two days past the previous one and was dated February 16, 1945:

Hi Sweet,

I feel rather blue today as I didn't get a letter from you today. I hope you are getting mine.

I've been working some for Mr. Carpenter today. I do his typing & bookkeeping for him when he needs any done.

Well I can drive now. I drove about two miles out in the country today and back. Herbert says I do fine,

I'm going to drive some every day until I learn to drive good.

I'll be so happy when you can drive it again. I hope it won't be long before you can be home again.

It really has been pretty here for the last few days.

Sweet, I hope you get your candy soon. Write me if there is anything you want me to send you.

I suppose Iva will come tomorrow night.

Roger really will be glad to see her. He says she will bring him candy.

Sugar take care of yourself & don't try to walk and stand on your leg too soon, for I want you back home soon.

I love you only – Eliz & Roger

The next letter I found was dated ten days later, on February 26, 1945. Mother was responding to a letter that dad wrote her on February 4, 1945. I have that letter and will include it after this one in order to establish a communication between the two of them:

Dear Sweetheart,

I'll write you an air mail for a change and have some newspaper clippings that I thought might be of interest to you.

(I have the clipping of casualties and
am including a scan of it here,)

One of them gives the names of all the Alabama boys who were wounded in Europe when you were. Your name is on it too. You may know some of the others.

The other is a picture of a well matched couple don't you think? ha! (It was a clipping of a 50 year-old man who had just married a 15 year old girl. I was not able to find this clipping.)

I got an airmail from you today too. It was written Feb 4. I try to write you V-Mails mostly as they are much faster, although I like to write you a long letter sometimes.

I got a letter from your mother today. They are both O.K.

I've been getting plenty typing to do lately. I typed some for Mr. Middleton, The Judge. It helps out. I made two dollars for working about three or four hours and the work is easy.

I work for Mr. Carpenter three or four days a week. I don't want a regular job anyway. I'm too lazy.

Sweet, the car still looks just like it did when you left it. I had a nice car house built for it. I can drive some now, but it is hard for me to back. You know how dumb I am.

Roger is fine. He wore his little suit to Church yesterday and he really looked cute. He went to the card Class. He said the teacher asked him what his name was and he told her "Oger Burow". He said they sang too, but he didn't that he would try to the next time.

Sugar that was the cutest Valentine you sent me on the V-Mail. I'm so proud of it. The verse was so sweet. I hope you get the Valentine Candy I sent you & the Valentine too.

You said you hoped you won't have to go back into battle. Surely they won't put you back again. It wouldn't be at all fair if you do.

I'm just hoping and praying that you'll come home instead. I'll be so happy to have you back.

Mother & all said hello.

I'll always love you only Love & Kisses Eliz

I mentioned that I would include dad's letter from February 4 that mother was just responding to in her previous letter. His letter was dated February 4, 1945, Sunday Afternoon and was postmarked February 6, Air Mail:

My Darling Little Sweet Wife,

Sweet how are you today!! Fine I hope. For myself I am doing pretty good at this time. Sweet this is another beautiful Sunday over here. I wish I could be with you today Darling, back in Hamilton are Opelika, any where back in the states – Just so I could see you and Roger. Sweet you dont know how proud I was I was to git you sweet letter Last night. I was proud you all was well, and I hope you all stay well and in good health. Sweet I dont know how long it will be before I can be up. I hope I dont haft to go back on the front. I hope this war will soon be over, but if I do I pray that God will take care of me and all the Rest of the boys. Darling I love you and you only. I pray that God will provide a way for us to be back togather Someday Real Soon. I know God was with me up on the Front. I wasent in battle long but that was longer anought. Shells was bursting all around me and bullits Flying every where, but we had a job to do, and thank God we got it done. The Germans Are back where they started what Few got back, the people back home dont know how thankful they should be they do have their homes and clothes and something to eat. those people in France and Belgium dont have anything. Sweet it's a Long Sad Story which some people will never give it a thought. I saw loots of Little boys about the size of Roger. I thought that Could be My Darling Wife and boy. I thank God that the Germans and Japs dident get that far along before they got stoped. I just hope and pray that they will soon be stoped For good if it's God will, And All the boys that's Living Can Come home to there Love Ones, thoes that gave there Lives will never be forgotten by the boys that Fought by their sides and Lived through it. No body knows what it is like to see your best budy go down in battle right by your side, all you can do is wait for your time to Come and pray that you will be Reddy to go when that time comes.

Darling take care of your self and Roger and Remember I am always thinking of you all. I will Always Love you my Darling Wife and if its Gods will I will be back some day.

Love And Sweet kisses, Yours true, James

This is probably a good place to return to some of dad's letters to mother. I will return to January 1945 and begin with a letter that dad sent to mother informing her that he had been wounded and was in the hospital in England.

The first letter is a V-Mail dated January 4, 1945 and postmarked January 13, 12 pm, 1945. So, you see the letter was delayed 9 days before it was mailed to mother:

My Darling wife,

Just a few lines to let you know I Am doing pretty good. hope you are well and feeling fine. I dont know when I can git up and start wondering around again. My ankle is my worse wound I think. dont wory Sweet I will be OK again. I hope and trust in god that I will. did you have a good New Year I hope so. I guss I had a good one I was still living that something to be thinkful for I know I was. Sweet I dont know what to write I dont git any mail to help me out. I dont know you might be sick are something I hope not when your mail do catch up with me I can take a day off and read all the news. Tell Roger all the Nurses said he sure was a cute boy. I showed them his picture you sent I lost every thing but my pictures Testament and pocket book (This may explain what happened to all the letters dad got from mother. He lost them when he was wounded.).

Sweet bee good and take care of your self and Roger. Yours love forever.

Loots of Love, James

This next correspondence from dad to mother was a letter rather than a V-Mail and was dated inside January 7, 1945, Sunday Afternoon:

My Dear Darling Sweet Wife,

This is a blue Sunday with me sweet – wish I was with you going to church and Enjoying myself, but all I can do is lay here and wish all them things and wait till the day God sees a way for me to come back, that will be a happy day when we can Come home to our love ones. I know that will be a sweet day when I can come back to my darling wife and Roger boy. I would give any thing in the world if I could see you all today. have you started to work yet. you said you wanted to when I left. is Iva still working in Bham tell her I said hello and I sorry I had to send the bad news home but it could have been worser. I was doing my best to stay out of the way but it was my turn to git it and I got it. Where is Gerry have he crossed over yet. When you write send me his and Harrison's adgress I lost Harrison. I got a letter from him but dident have time to answer it. How is Arthur making out with the Navy? I hope he is OK. did Harrison and Arthur git to come home for Christmas?

I was looking for Curtis to come down this weekin to see me I sent him word through the red cross, dont guss he have time. I dont know how far he is from here. Sweet dont worry about me I am doing alright. We have Good Doctors and Nurses and they are doing all they can for me. I will be back some day and make you another sweet and happy home if its God's will. Darling I love you with all my heart. Be sweet till we meet again.

Love and sweet Dreams – James

This V-Mail from dad to mother was written the next day and dated January 8, 1945 and postmarked January 17, 3;30 pm, 1945. As you can see with all these V-Mails, they were not mailed until a least nine days after they were written, and it probably took them that long to be delivered:

Hello Sweet heart,

Just a few lines hope you are well for myself I am doing pretty good I guss. I sure will be proud when I can hear from you all seem like two years since I got a letter I hope to git one in a couple more weeks. Sweet dont be worried about me. I am doing alright. I am proud I am still living it will be a good while before I can walk like I use to but it will take time to do anything. I think it was a blessing I got out this light. God was with me dont give up hope just keep praying God will bring me through and when this war is over I will be coming back to my sweet darling wife. I feel like this war wont last to much longer. So bee sweet and dont worry.

Love and Sweet Kisses, James

Here is a V-Mail from the very next day. It was dated January 9, 1945 and postmarked January 20, 2:30 pm, 1945, eleven days after it was written:

Dear Sweetheart,

Hows my little girl today Fine I hope. For myself I am doing pretty good. Still taking shouts (shots) which dont feel good. Sweet have you learned to drive yet (As I've mentioned before, in her 84 years mother never totally learned how to drive and never drove,)? do you git anought gas to go any where? What did you git Roger for Christmas? I bet he had a big time. I wish I could have been there with you all. My Christmas wasent so good after all, but I was doing my duty just like the rest of the boys we knowed some of us was going to git hit but we had a job to do and the boys that got through are still doing a good Job. think (thank) God, I pray for them every night and day I know what they are going through with. Sweet darling dont be worried just think (thank) God that I am still living and keep praying that we will be back togather some sweet day. Tell your mother and all the boys I said hello. darling Remember I love you And I will do Every thing in my power to come back to you my darling Little wife.

Love and Sweet Kisses, James

I will continue with dad's V-Mails to mother as there were many letters that I could not find from mother to dad. It was possible they were never delivered to dad or that he lost them when he was wounded and therefore, they were never taken back to the U.S.A. when he returned.

This V-Mail was dated January 11, 1945, with a postmark of January 19, 11 am, 1945:

Dear Sweetheart,

Hows my Darling today fine I hope for myself I havent felt to good today but I dont expect to feel good every day (Dad had pneumonia but he didn't tell mother about it early on as he didn't want to worry her.). I have some cold I guss that why I havent felt so good. I got the purple heart today. I am sending it home you can keep it for me, I sure will be proud when I git a letter from you it have been so long since I herd from you. I feel worried sometimes. tell Roger I said to be a good boy I will be back home some day to stay and not leave him any more this war will be over someday I hope. I will stop so be sweet and dont worry, Love and sweet kisses James

I won't include all the V-Mails dad wrote as he wrote them every day and they were pretty much similar in nature. This one was written around January 13, 1945. It had no date written on it and no envelope with postmark, so I am making a calculated guess about the date:

> My Darling Wife,
>
> Just a few lines hope you all are feeling fine tonight, for myself I feel pretty good at this time. I guss you went to church today I would give any thing in the world to have been with you but I just lay here and think about it, praying that God will see a way for me to come back someday where we can bee togather darling wouldent it bee sweet if this war was over and we was to gather tonight maby someday we can be back to gather, all we can do is pray. God knows best, darling dont wory some day we hope it will all be over with, and we can have a sweet home once more.
>
> I will stop now Love and Sweet Kisses Yours true, James

This next V-Mail also mentioned that dad has a bad cold which really was a serious case of pneumonia that he almost died with. As always, he did not want to worry mother, so he never told her the full nature and extent of the sufferings he was going through. The V-Mail was dated January 16, 1945:

> Hello Sweetheart,
>
> Just a few lines hoping you all are well and feeling fine, for myself I feel pretty good I guss, having some trouble with my chest I guss it is cold. I think it will be OK. how are you and Roger making out. I guss it is pretty cold in Hamilton now, how is mother and them. I havent herd from them since I came over. last letter I got from you was

wrote the 23 of Nov. I should git some mail before long,
I will stop love and sweet kisses.

PS – Send me some candy Love James

Many of the V-Mails I found had no envelopes, so I have had to
depend upon them being dated by dad at the beginning of each letter,
For the most part he did date them. He dated this one January 17, 1945:

My Dear Darling Wife,

Just a few lines hope you are well and feeling fine for
myself I am doing pretty good at this time Still taking
shoots (shots) you know I like that, but I dont mind taking
any thing that will help me. It will be a good while before
I can walk yet but Dont wory sweet I think every thing
will be all right. I think about what my testament have on
the back your mother gave me (It was her grandmother
"Mammy" that gave it to him.), May the Lord be with
you, you can tell her if the Lord hadent been with me I
woulden been here today. I woulden have been this lucky.
I think (thank) God that he brought me through this
far. I just hope and pray that this war will soon be over
where we and all the boys ca come home to our Love one.
Sweetheart dont wory just think (thank) God that I am
still living.Remember Sweet I Love you with all my heart
and if its Gods will I will be back.

Loves true Forever Love James

Dad sometimes got philosophical with his letters and commented on
the awful nature of war and how few people really realize how horrible
war really is. This V-Mail was such a letter and was dated by dad January
18, 1945:

Dear Sweet heart Darling wife,

Just a few lines hope you are well and feeling fine for myself I am doing pretty good I guss. Sweet I would do any thing if I could see you all and Roger and all the rest of the family. I git so lonesome laying here all I do is think about you all and hope and pray that this war will soon be over with where we will be back togather once more. Sweet have you heard from Mary? do you know how Tucker is Are what have happened to him. I know he was somewhere pretty close where I was, Sweet war is an awful thing no body knows what it is like but the soldiers that fights it. They go through the hardship then haft to face death. some come through and some dont. I prayed that God would be with me. Now I know he was. I know my prayers was answered. I prayed that he would keep me safe and some day bring me safe back to my darling wife and son and he have so far.

I love you always, Yours true, James

This next V-Mail gives some indication of how badly dad was doing in the hospital during his bout with pneumonia. He tried to spare mother from what he was going through as much as possible. In my previous chapter on dad's war stories, I related the story of how he almost died from pneumonia and had such a high temperature that his nurse had to pack him in ice and sit up with him all night to keep him alive. I do not believe dad ever told mother what really happened in the war or in the hospital in England as she would have worried too much about it. This V-Mail dated January 19, 1945 does expand upon the details somewhat:

My Darling wife,

Just a few lines hope you all are well and feeling Fine for myself I am doing pretty good at this time. I have been having a pretty tuff time, but I am better now I think I feel some better. I havent been up any yet, as I have had a chest cold (pneumonia) and some temperature. My ankle is still in a cast. I wont be able to walk on it for a good while yet but dont worry about me everything will be OK, it just takes time. I would give any thing to be with you sweet, maby it wont be much Longer this war will be over with I hope and maby it will be real Soon. So just Love and hope and Remember I will do every thing in my power to live through it and come back with God's help I feel like I will make it.

Love and Sweet Kisses forever true, James

This next letter was not a V-Mail but a longer letter of great interest for its content about his condition after being wounded, but also because dad stated that he was wounded three weeks previous from the date of this letter which was January 20, 1945. That would have made the date he was wounded December 30, 1944. It was ironic because Robert was killed almost 5 months to the day before that at St. Lo, France on July 31, 1944. Robert was killed when a German artillery shell exploded over his foxhole. Dad could have been killed in exactly the same manner if he had not been told to get out of his foxhole by his sergeant about 30 seconds before a German artillery round exploded over it. The sergeant had told dad to get out of the foxhole because it was full of water and he was concerned that dad would get pneumonia if he continued to stand in it. So, dad was on his way to take cover behind a hill when the shell hit, and he avoided the major force of the blast. He was severely wounded from the blast, but he recovered after spending four months in an English hospital. Dad had left his sleeping bag next to the foxhole and I remember him telling me he had been resting his head on the sleeping bag before the sergeant told him to get out. He later remembered seeing a huge hole in the sleeping bag where he had been resting his head. Had it not been for the sergeant asking him to get out, neither dad nor I would be here to tell this story. I know that I have told this story in Chapter Five, but I thought it such a meaningful story that it should be told again.

Here is dad's letter of January 20, 1945:

My Darling wife,

How are you today, Fine I hope, for myself I am doing pretty good I guss I am still living any way. Sweet I havent got any mail are the boxes you sent me yet. I would give any thing to know how you all Are. I hope you are well and Feeling Fine. I will Never forgit today three weeks ago. Saturday morning (That was December 30, 1944.) about ten o'clock I got hit. I havent felt Like the same than since. You woulden know me I have lost loots of weight. I think I would Feel loots better if I could see you sweet be with some one that I knowed Relly Cared for me. I think about you all time darling Just hoping and praying that some day the war will be over with and we can be back togather again, and have a home with some peace and happiness the Rest of our life, where we can be togather all time, and go places and do things that we Always wanted to do, but all we can do is Live in hope and pray that God will see a way For me to come back. I think About what Roger said when I left that daddy was going to kill them old Japs and Germans with that big gun. Well you can tell him that them Germans Liked to have got me for keeps with their big gun, but they was getting all they wanted and more to, and they will As Long as this War Last. Sweet I bet you havent learned how to drive the car yet have you? You better Learn how before I get back, if I keep Falling off I wont be bigger anought to drive a car. Sweet be good and take care of yourself and Roger. Dont worry about me I will be OK. Some day I am coming back to Hamilton. I feel Like I will with Gods help.

Sweet I love you with All my heart, Love James

This next letter from dad was a V-Mail dated January 20, 1945, the same date as the previous letter. Here he gives a bit more information about what happened when he was wounded by the artillery shell:

My Darling Wife.

Just a few lines hope you are well and feeling fine tonight darling. For myself I am doing pretty good at this time I wonder what you are doing tonight at the show I bet, that where we use to go nely (nearly) Every Saturday night when we was at Hamilton. What I would give to be at Hamilton with you to Night. God only knows. tomorrow is Sunday, but I cant go any place but I am looking forward to the day when I can be back with you sweetheart, then we can go places togather. I wonder how mother & Dad is making out. I know they are worrying their heads off about me. havent been Long since Robert got killed. Now me All messed up. I done my best to not git hurt, but when you cant see them are hear them you cant dodge them. All I know a Shell bustered about five feet from my hole in a tree. I think (thank) God I am still living.

Darling be sweet and Remember I Love you true, Love James

Here is a sweet letter from dad which rises to the level of poetry. He reminisces about the good old days when he and mother were dating and first married, and also makes observations about how peaceful and beautiful life seemed in England now that the war seemed close to an end. It was dated January 21, 1945 with a postmark of January 23, 1945:

My Darling Little wife,

This is another blue Sunday with me to be sucher beautiful day – the sun is shining so bright out side – the sky looks high and blue Darling what would I give to be with you. Just to look out, it dont Look Like there should be A war going own. Look Like the people should be enjoying their selves going to Church and Sunday School, where I would like very much to go with you today. Looks like some of the beautiful weekins when we use to date and have a nice time back in the good old U.S.A. where someday I hope to come back And live the rest of My Life in a peaciful world with you My Darling Wife and Son. Some of the boys Are getting to come home it makes me feel good to see the Look on their Face. I know they was happy once more to think they was going back to ther Love ones. Some was married men. I just hope and pray that the day will soon come when we all can come back knowing the war is over and we can stay in the good old U.S.A. I guss this Country is OK for the people that Live over here, but for me I will take the States any time back with you. Sweet that's what I wont. So Just Live in hopes and dont give up. Some day I will be coming back your way when this mese is over with which I hope and pray wont be very much longer, then we will be togather to stay as long as we live I hope we will never haft to be apart again, Darling I Love you with all my heart. I will always be true to my darling and that's you sweet.

Many Sweet Kisses for them I been missing Love James

Dad wrote V-Mails to mother every day and they were just short notes to let her know how he was doing. He was not getting any mail from anyone though which made communication difficult and letter writing repetitive with the same thoughts and observations repeated each day. Nonetheless, I will include as many of them as I think are needed to keep the flow going.

This V-Mail was dated January 23, 1945 and postmarked about a week later February 1, 11:30 am,1945:

My Darling Little Wife,

How are you today sweetheart! Fine I hope, for my self I am doing pretty good at this time. I havent got any mail from Anybody yet. I hope you all Are OK. I havent herd from Curtis yet. dont guss he will git to come to see me.

I wrote him a letter about two weeks ago. I should git an answer pretty soon. how is Roger doing? have he had Any Colds yet be sure to take care of him and your self. I think I will be back in pretty good shape in A couple of months if I dont have any trouble any way. If you can and wont to go down home And stay A few days, you can go some Friday and come back the next week, If you Are not working And feel like going, it might make them feel better. I know they would like to see you and Roger, but if you are working Are dont feel Like making the trip dont go. Sweet I hope some day I can be back with you and Roger. When this war is over maby we will have Peace for a while. I just hope and pray we do darling.

I Love you with All my heart Love James

In this next V-Mail dad mentions how he is progressing with his injuries and admits that he has had pneumonia for the first time. It was dated by dad January 24, 1945:

Hello Sweetheart,

How are you making it these Long Lonesome days? Fine I hope. For myself I am doing pretty good I guss. Sure would like to see you all Darling I would give any thing to be back with you. I sure do git lonesome Lying here in bed thinking about you and Roger and things back home, wondering when this war will ever be over where we all can be coming back to the good old U.S.A. they still have my leg in a caste it still hurt some, but I dont expect it to feel good. My hip is doing OK I think. My pneumonia have Just about cleared up to. I feel Loots better, but I am still pretty weak. Sweet I cant think of any thing to write. it have been so long since I got any Mail From you I dont know what to write. I try to write something Every day if it is the same thing, Sweet dont worry I will be OK again some day, bee Sweet and Remember I Love you And I will Always.

Love and Sweet Kisses James

With this next V-Mail dad mentions his ankle wound and hip injury and gives some detail about them. His recovery was slow, but he thanked God that he was alive and that his injuries were not any worse. The V-Mail was dated by dad January 26, 1945:

Dear Sweetheart,

Just a few lines hope you all are well. For myself I am doing pretty good I guss. I havent been up any yet. My ankle will be a pretty good while getting well yet. I got two holes through it, and one bone broke, so it will take a little longer than my hip to git well. It dont take long to git hurt, but it takes time to git back in good shape Like you was before you got hurt and all you can do is wait, time will tell. I sure do git Lonesome and tired Laying here but I cant do nothing about it, I am lucky to be here and in this gooder shape. I think (thank) God I am Not hurt any worser, so dont worry sweet, pray for me. God knows best for us All. I pray that he will take care of me and bring me back to my Darling wife some day. Sweet be good and take care of your self and Roger boy, tell your mother and the boys I said hello.

Your true Love One forever, Love James

Dad mentioned in this next V-Mail that was written the next day on January 27, 1945 that he had not received any mail from mother since November 23, 1944, which was more than two months. The most likely reason was that he moved around so much and had so many addresses, that his mail just had not caught up with him yet. Just like dad, mother wrote every single day, it was just that the letters were not getting to him. Here is the January 27, 1945 V-Mail:

My Darling Sweetheart,

Just a few lines hope you all Are well and feeling Fine. for myself I am doing pretty good at this time. Sweet I havent got any mail yet. My what would I give for a letter From you that was wrote this month. the Last Letter I got From you back before Christmas was wrote the 23rd of Nov, I dont know what kind of Christmas you had, are what have been happening. I guss when I do git my mail I will be stocked up for a few days. I know you have been writting but I have been moving so much and my Adgress have been changed to, so thats why I havent been getting it. Let me know if you have been getting my Mail. I have wrote every day Since I been in the Hospital. Sweet dont worry, God have been with me and always will From Now own darling I Love you with All My heart so bee sweet till we meet Again whenever it may bee.

Yours true James

This V-Mail from dad states that his pneumonia had just about cleared up and in it he asked about mother's friend Johnnie's husband who was a prisoner of war in Germany. It was dated January 29, 1945 and remarkably postmarked the same day January 29, 3 pm, 1945. Dad must have been lucky and caught the postal service just when they were sending out all the mail they had been holding back:

My Darling Sweetheart,

Just a Few Lines hope you all are well and doing Fine. For myself I am doing pretty good Now, My Pneumonia have Just about cleared up. Anyway I feel better. I know my prayers have been answered God have been with me, I sure will be proud when I can git some mail From you. I feel like you are OK, but I miss your Letters so much I sure will be proud when we wont haft to be writting Every day. We can be seeing each other every day, then we wont haft to be worrying about why we dont git any mail. do you here from Johney Now! how is Conway do she still hear From him. I sure will be proud when this war is over And we All can come home. I hope Carr (Conway) is still OK. write Johney and tell her I said hello and that I was doing all I could but I Just wasent Lucky that day. I guss I was Lucky to I am Still Living. Sweet I will stop for this time – hoping to git some mail soon.

I Love you James

Dad wrote in this next V-Mail that he was now able to get up and move around a bit. He was slowly improving but still had a long way to go to be recovered. The V-Mail was dated January 30, 1945, but not postmarked until nine days later, on February 8, 7:30 pm, 1945:

My Darling Wife,

How are you today Sweet? Fine I hope. For myself I am doing pretty good at this time. The Doctor told me that I could git up a Few minuts every day, if I felt like it. I have been up some today but I am still pretty weak. I could tell that I havent got much use of myself, it will take a while to gain my strength back, but I am improving I feel better than I have been Feeling. I sure have Lost Loots of wait I can tell that but I will gain it back when I git out of this bed. A well man will loose weight Lying in the bed all time, I think my ankle is doing pretty good I still have the caste on, it dont hurt so much now, only when I stand up are hold it off the bed, but I will be OK some day. So dont worry sweet God knows best, write me a long Sweet Letter.

Love and many sweet kisses

Love James

My dad's next V-Mail related that he thought he had been suffering from kidney stones. Dad had problems with kidney stones for most of the rest of his life and had several operations to relieve them. This would have been one of the first occurrences of them at the hospital in Bristol, England. However, the doctors later discovered that it was not kidney stones that caused the problem but the sulfur that he had been given to treat his wounds. There was no envelope with this V-Mail, but it was dated by dad February 1, 1945:

My Darling wife,

Just a Few Lines, hope you All are well and Feeling Fine. For myself I havent been Feeling so good today. My side been giving me some trouble I sure hope it gits OK And I dont haft to have an operation. The doctor said he thought it was a kidney stone. I havent had but one spell with it so Far. All I can do is pray. God knows best For me I have put all my trust in him, so what ever I haft to go through with God will be with me. I am willing to go through the hardship and pain if it takes that to git back to my Darling wife and son, if its Gods will I know some day I will be back with you all. So dont worry Sweet Just pray for me and God will make everything alright Some day.

Darling I Love you true with all my heart

Many Sweet Kisses – To my Darling Wife Love James

Curiously, there was a gap of nine days that I could find no V-Mails from dad to mother. The next one was dated February 10, 1945 and postmarked February 21, 1945. I must assume that the V-Mails that he wrote from those nine days were lost. In this V-Mail he stated that he had finally received his first letter from mother in over two months:

My Darling Little Wife,

I just recived your very Sweet Letter, proud you all are well. For myself I am doing Fine now. The Doctor said I Could git up some in A few days. Darling it is very sweet of you to want to send me some thing but I dont know of anything I need over here but you my darling. I need you every minute of my Life if I could only be home with you Sweetheart. I would be the happiest Soldier ever lived Darling. I Love you with All My Heart. I think of you day and night, God is the only one that knows how much I Really Love you, my Darling Wife. Sweet I will Just Keep Writting to Hamilton. I dont know how long you will be down home. Your mother cand send them to you. Sweet I havent got any of your old mail yet. I should git some of it any time now. I wrote my mail clerk back in my company when I first got here. I got a letter from Alma today also. Darling if I could see you I could tell you loots of things it is impossible to write in words how much I Love you sweet. I sure will be proud to get the letters from Robert and them. I havent herd from Curtis yet I think I will write him tomorrow. I guss Roger is having a big time down home with the cats and every thing else. I sure would Like to see him. Sweet I will stop now, so be sweet and take care of your self and Roger. I will always Love you sweet heart.

All my Love and Sweet kisses

Yours Love Forever my darling wife, Love James

I will continue with dad's V-Mails to mother as I do not have any letters from her until March of 1945 and really do not know what happened to all her letters. After including dad's V-Mails, I will return to the mail that he got from relatives and friends before picking back up with mother's letters to him.

This next V-Mail from dad to mother related that dad's brother, Curtis Brown, who was stationed in the Army Air Corp in England, had come to visit him in the hospital. It was written February 11, 1945:

Dear Sweet heart,

Just a Few lines hope you All Are well And Feeling Fine. For Myself I am doing pretty good at this time. Darling this have been another Long Lonesome Sunday with me been Raining Just about all day. I sure do miss going places Like I use to do. All I can do is Lay here and think about the good times we use to have. Sweet what do you think. I looked up and there stood Curtis. I never been shocked so in all my Life. I started this letter Last night so he come and I thought I would wait till this morning it will catch the mail OK Anyway. I sure was proud to see him, he said he would have done come but he dident git my letter tell Last Friday. he dident know my adgress, he got your Letter Last week I read it. I dident know they had been cutting stuff out of my letters. Sweet dont worry I will be OK. I try to write all I can but I guss I try to tell to much some times, but I havent got Any Letters back yet. Well I will stop now. Curtis is setting here he have got to go back this afternoon Monday he got a 48 hour pass. he said tell you all hello.

Love and Sweet Kisses, yours true James

Dad by this time was beginning to receive more of mother's letters to him. These were likely letters from her that were written much earlier. This

V-Mail from dad was dated February 13, 1945 and postmarked February 23, 5:30 pm, 1945:

My Darling Wife,

Darling I just got your to very sweet letters, sure was proud to git them, proud you are all well for myself I am doing OK at this time. I got a very nice Valentine from Horrice Edward (mother's youngest brother). I also got a letter from Mama and Alma. Sweet I coulden get any Valentines to send anybody, but I did send you one I hope you like it just something to let you know I am thinking of you. Sweet I think of you all time not just on Holidays. I sure would like to have been at church with you Sunday. I havent been to church in three months I sure would like to go. maby some day I will be back home where we can go togather again like we use to do. I dont enjoy going any place unless you are with me. all I can do is live right and pray that God will take care of me and some day we can be back togather. I hope this war will soon be over. Darling take care of your self and Roger. Sweet I will always love you true –

all my love and many sweet kisses to my Darling wife
Love James

This V-Mail came a bit later and in it dad mentions mother's recent letter and the fact that he has never received any of her older letters. Most likely the letters were lost and never delivered, The V-Mail was dated February 17, 1945 with a postmark of February 26, 2;30 pm, 1945:

My Darling Wife,

How are you feeling today Darling Fine I hope for myself I am doing OK at this time. Sweet I have been thinking about you a lot since I got your sweet letter last night. Darling I dont think you are not writting me. I know you are. I was worried because I dident know how you and Roger was getting along. I dident know where you was well or sick. I havent got any of you old mail yet, it probly got lost if it dident, I will git it all at once from my Company (This may explain why there was none of mother's letters written during this time to be found among all the other letters I found,). I got a letter from Mama she was telling me about you and Roger being up at Alma thin she told me she got a letter from Eloise (Robert's fiancé) and that she stayed sick all time. I thought she said she got it (Eloise's letter) from you and that you stayed sick all time I liked to have fell out of my bed. I thought something was rong – so I looked back and saw it was Eloise. What a relife of course I hated for her to be sick, You see I havent been getting all of your mail. I just hope and pray that you are OK, you havent sayed any thing about it anyway.

Darling I love you true with all my heart, Love James

Dad revealed that he was finally getting the cast off his leg in this V-Mail. He was slowly progressing although his ankle needed much more time to heal. It was dated February 18, 1945 and had a postmark of February 27, 5;30 pm, 1945:

Dear Sweetheart,

I will try and answer your sweet Letter I recived Last Night. Proud you all are well. For myself I am doing OK at this time, the doctor took my caste off yesterday (That would've been almost 60 days that the cast was on him.). My ankle havent heald much yet. it will be a good while before I can use it to walk on, Sweet I guss you are going to church this morning I wish I was there to go with you

331

but I know I Cant Now. if it is God's will I will be back some day to be with you sweetheart. I like to go places with you sweet, I always have a good time when I am with you Darling. Sweet it wont be Long before you will have a birthday which is the 24ᵗʰ are the 25ᵗʰ of March I git both of these dates in my head and I cant remember which is Right (It was March 24ᵗʰ.) I think it is the 24ᵗʰ you write me which is Right, maby by then I can go and git you something to send you. Sweet I wrote you About that allof (awful) photo. I had it made before I left Camp Thanks I know I wouldn't need the money so I had it sent to you. I havent spent two dollars since I left Sweet. take care of your self and Roger. till Roger I got his letter and the pictures, was very good of you and him ha, if you have got to be Looking that way I think I will stay over here (Dad is talking about a drawing that mother did of herself and Roger.). You better draw better the next time Darling.

I Love you true For Ever, Love James

This V-Mail from dad was dated three days later on February 21, 1945:

Dear Sweetheart,

I will try and answer your letters I recived to night. I got four I think, and one from your mother and almas. I sure did get a sweet letter from your mother. sweet I am proud you and Roger are well, for myself I am doing fine at this time I bet Roger was proud of his wristwatch. I wish I could get something to send him, tell him he had better keep been a good boy, and that I dont forgit him in my prayer every night neather. Darling God is the only one that knows how much I care for you two, tell mama that I am thinking of her and all if I dont write every day, and that I remember them in prayer every day, and to not wory about me. I am doing fine now. sweet I will write you a air mail letter tomorrow and try to answer all thim letters I got tonight. Darling I am always thinking of you, you are my only sweetheart. I love you with all my heart sweet. Love and kisses, James

There was about a three-week gap with the next group of V-Mails from dad to mother. I suppose they were lost. One would expect some to have been lost over the 75 years that they had been stored away. I did find one air mail letter from him though that was dated Saturday, March 3, 1945, in which he wrote about finding out his kidney trouble was not caused by kidney stones but by the sulfur he had been given to treat his wounds. He also mentions that he was in great pain, couldn't eat and had to be fed through his veins:

My Darling little wife,

I will try and answer your letters sure was proud to get thim, as I was feeling bad at that time, but I am feeling lots better now I am just hoping I don haft to have an operation. I dont think I will . I sure have been through some pain this week moore thin ever, got where I coulden eat any thing had to feed me through my vains. I got pretty weak, but I am doing OK at this time. the doctor said it wasent kidneys stone. It was caused from the suffer (sulfur) tablets I had to take when I got wounded. and that it would take a while to clear it up. so dont worry I will be allright in a few more days, sweet I got into that box of Candy today it sure is good I will be slipping back in it again afterwhile. I havent got my box of valentine Candy yet, I hope to get it when I git better. till Roger thinks (thanks) for the Candy he sent me in the letter. sweet it is a pretty day over here today just right for me and you to have a big time. you said you all was having some pretty weather. it would be nice if I was back and we could take a stroll some place in the sunshine I know I would feel better you probly would have me well in a few days woulden you sweet. I sure would like to see you in that new dress you got. I bet it fits just like I want thim to, sweet I dreamed the other night I was kissing you and that you were so cute lying back in my arms. My what would I give if you was lying in my arms today, woulden it be sweet darling I am praying that some day my dream will come true real soon and this war will be over. I am proud that Harrison don't haft to come over seas. I will take good old florida any day. I havent forgot what you use to say when I was at Blanding. Darling I could see you only every weekin I though that was bad, now I cant see you at all and I know this is bad. I am praying that God will provide a way for us to be back to gather some day real soon.

I sure would like to see Jim and Ella Mai, I hope he dont haft to go to the army. I am hopping this dont need any more Soldiers, but I am afriad it will take lots of thim to win this war yet.

Darling dont worry about me to much God knows best. sweetheart I love you true with all my heart.

all my love and kisses, James

This V-Mail from dad was dated Sunday night, March 4, 1945 and postmarked March 11, 11 pm, 1945:

My Darling Wife,

This have been a Long Lonesome Sunday with me. It have been pretty all day the sun have been always pretty and bright made me want to bee with you more than ever, but after all I got them sweet Letters from you tonight which made it better for me. I also got one from Mama. I sure would have liked to been with you at church did you say---------------had a baby (I couldn't decipher the name.)? I didn't know that, I know mama and Daddy will miss you and Roger at least mama said in the letter, they sure did miss you and Roger, any body would miss you two, I miss you so much I dont know what to do Darling. I pray that the day will soon come when we will be back togather to stay. I know I could make you a better and happy home when I come back. I can Realize lots of things now after I have been through what I have if its God's will I will be back some day and I will live the kind of life he would want me (My dad kept that promise to God.). Darling I love you true with all my heart

Love and kisses, James

There were many daily V-Mails from dad that were similar in nature but this next one was an unusually long letter in which he responds to mother's letters in which she enclosed the clippings about Alabama War Casualties and an article entitled "May and December" about "True Love". You will remember that I included that letter from mother previously. Dad also makes observations on the progress of U.S, troops advancing into Germany as well as many other topics.

It was an informative letter and an interesting letter and was dated March 9. 1945 with a postmark of March 11, 1945:

Dear Sweetheart.

I just recived your two sweet letters, one had the casualties list of the alabama boys, and the other was the case of true love. I hope they hold out in their true love, the girl looks to be more then thirteen years old, he dont look to be fifty. I guss he is if he have got eleven children by his other wife, no telling how many he will have by this one, if he dont have a nervous break down, he looks to be in pretty good shape though. I got a letter from your Aunt Rhoda Boyet (I included this letter earlier.) – she sent me a Valentine to,

I got a letter from Marry (I included this one earlier also from Mary, Tucker's wife.) to, she said Tucker was OK the last time she herd from him, said she was doing fine to but would like to see tucker – I know she would. I hop some day he will be back with her. She sent me his adgress. I am going to write him tonight I think – his outfit is making a big drive now I sure hope he makes it through OK and all the rest of the boys but I know some of them wont git through, thats all in it. they are doing good they crossed the Rhine about much trouble so the news said, everybody was wondering about that – that suposed to have been Hitler's main strong point. I was looking for us to loose lots of men trying to cross, but the news says they dident loose a man crossing, but I am afriad they will have some hard fighting to do before they git to Berlin. I hope and pray that they go ahead about any trouble and this war will soon be over. I dont know how long it will be before I will be able to go back to the front, not to much longer I dont guss. I hope it will be over by that time but if not all I can do is to make the best of it and pray that God will bring me through it safely.

Sweet you said you was driving pretty good now I am proud you are learning fast, and I hope you all the luck in the world because I woulden have you to have a rack and git hurt for nothing, sweet when the weather starts to git warm after yall stop having freezing weather have Herbert to drain that anti-freeze out and wash it out good, he knows how he helped me do that last year tell him to let the motor run while he is running the water in, you keep driving out in the country the next thing I know you will ne writting me that you have been to Birmingham, ha, when you do that you will be doing gooder anought, sweet after you drive a while you will git where you can back allright so dont worry about that.

You said you was working its OK with me. it will help pass the time off, you can be just as sweet working as you can any place els. I dont worry about that part any way – any body can be good that wants to, you dont haft to stay at home to be good. So remember I love you only and I will always be your true love one as long as you are mine. Darling I love you with all my heart. I think of you every day and night, and I pray that God will provide a way for us to be back togather some sweet day real soon. tell Roger I said for him to sang the next time he went to Sunday school, Darling I love you true

all my love and sweet kisses, James

I will include one more V-Mail that I found from dad to mother and then return to some of mother's letters to him. This V-Mail from dad was dated March 13, 1945:

Hello Sweetheart,

Just a few lines hope youall are well and feeling fine, for my self I am doing fine at this time. Curtis just come. he got here about six oclock, he is doing fine, havent got but a forty eight hour pass so he will haft to get back to morrow at one oclock. he said he wrote you a letter the other day so you should get in a day are two. sweet I dident get a letter from you today but I got two yesterday. Darling I have been thinking of you a lot every day. I sure would like to see you sweetheart. I know we could have a big time, and how sweet it would be to be back togather once more. Darling I love you with all my heart and I will for ever, so be sweet and good. I will always. I will stop now. Curtis said till you and Roger hello.

all my love and sweet kisses, Love, James

I did find more of mother's letters to dad written in March of 1945, I will include them now rather than continue with dad's letters to her as I believe there will be a better flow between the two of them if I place mother's letters here instead of placing them later.

This letter was dated Hamilton, Alabama, March 2, 1945:

Dearest Sweetheart,

I will now answer your very sweet letter. Sweet, I know you were very proud to get the caste off your leg, but do be careful, I wouldn't want you to have any more trouble with it.

Gee! I just wish you could come home when you are able. That would be the nicest thing I know of that could happen. Sweet I think of you so much, just wish I could be with you.

Sugar, you were asking about my birthday. It is March 24th, but don't worry about getting me anything if you aren't able to get out. You have already given me enough. I had rather have you back than anything.

Well, I don't suppose you could guess what I weigh 132 pounds even, I really don't look fat. I'm just all hard, hips, legs ha!

Everyone tells me I look good, And they also say I look so healthy. Roger looks healthy too. We are both <u>toughies</u> ha!

Yes, Sweet I got the other allotment which was $13.00. I put it in the Bank, and going to each month,

I hope you got the candy I sent you.

I got a letter from your Mama & Dad, yesterday. They really were glad that Curtis went to see you.

Did I tell you that Harrison isn't going overseas after all? He is stationed at Tampa, Florida.

Gerry is in Hawaii. He says it is like Alabama in Summer time. I think Arthur is there too. We don't hear from Arthur so much.

I haven't tried to drive the Car anymore lately as I've worked almost every day.

Oh! I must tell you that Opaleen expects to be a mother in July. I was so surprised Aren't you?

I'm just proud that it didn't happen to me and you gone. I'm glad that I have Roger though as he is so much company to me.

I'll stop now & write your mother.

Take care of yourself.

I love you only.

Love & Kisses Eliz & Roger

Roger wrote you too. He writes on his blackboard lots. He learned to make an O.

(I have included a scan of Roger's letter below.)

The next letter from mother that found was written three days later, on March 5, 1945:

Dearest Sweetheart,

I really do miss your letter today. It is the first time in over a week that I haven't had a letter from you.

I got one yesterday. I hope you are still getting mine.

I'm very happy that you are getting along fine. I do hope & pray though that you won't have to fight anymore. I feel that you have done your part, but if you do have to go back, be careful and remember we're all praying for you.

I just hope & pray that the day isn't far off when you'll be coming home.

Iva was here, yesterday. She hears from Gerry almost every day.

We haven't heard from Arthur in quite awhile. I do hope he is O.K.

Sweet, that was O.K. about the money. I had intended to get a string of pearls with it for an anniversary present from you, but I'll get them anyway and it will be the same thing.

I know you were glad to see Curtis again. I'm glad that he could go to see you.

One of his English girl-friends wrote your mother a letter while I was down there. She was a married girl, as her name was a Mrs. Something.

I suppose the girls over there are like some of the girls over here. It doesn't make any difference with them about being married.

I'm just glad I'm not that cheap.

Sweet, I want you back more than anything in the world.

Be sweet, Remember I'll always love you only. All my Love Elizabeth

I thought I'd include this V-Mail that I later found from Uncle Curtis as it relates well to mother's previous letter. Mother mentioned that one of his English girlfriends wrote Grandmother Brown and that the girl was a married woman. I think that the girl Curtis talks mentions in this letter may well have been the same girl. Curtis gives his address: A.S.N. 14183051 P.F.C. William C. Brown 1251 M.P. Co. PM NY, NY, FEB 28, 1945. It had a postmark of March 3, 1945,

Dad's address was: PVT. JAMES G. BROWN A.S,N. 84837097 DET of PAI. 4134. US. ARMY HOSPITAL PLANT APO #508:

Hello James

I will drop you a few lines to let you know that I got back OK and doing fine. I met a girl on my way back and stayed at her home in london that night and had a good time but dident git any sleep. I dont know when I can git to see you agan but will come when I can. I will stop. Wishing you good luck.

Love Curtis

This was the next letter I found from mother to dad and was dated March 7, 1945, Hamilton, Alabama:

Dearest Sweetheart,

How are you today? We are fine, and hope you are too.

Iva sent Roger a box of candy. He really was tickled too.

I really did miss your letter today. I suppose I can't expect to get one every day though. I'm always so blue when I don't hear from you.

Sweet I do hope if you have to go back on the front that you will have good luck.

I just wish this thing would be over before you have to fight anymore though.

Have you tried to walk any yet? Be careful when you do.

I suppose you have gotten the candy I sent you by now, haven't you?

It really is pretty here today. Roger is playing out for the first time in quite a while.

Sweet we don't have lights yet. Iva went to Headquarters in Birmingham and talked to them. They say they will fix it as soon as they get the material.

They are wiring all County houses now. I don't see why ours can't be fixed. Maybe it won't be long now.

Sugar, Christine has just left, she came to see me & we went to town. We also saw Hazel & Nix in town. They seem to be very happy.

I know he is happy to be back in the States after being overseas so long.

I hope the day will soon come that you will be back home with us.

Be sweet. I'll always love you only.

Love & Kisses Eliz & Roger

I believe this letter from mother to dad may have been written about the same time as the previous one, probably around March 8, 1945. There was no date, so I am guessing on that:

Hi Sugar,

I was very happy to get your letter today. I'm proud that you are still doing fine.

I got a letter from your Mother, Eloise & Johnnie.

Your mother and all are O.K. said she had gotten a letter from you.

Johnnie says she had another letter from Carr and that he is still O.K.

Eloise wants me to come and spend the weekend with her.

I may go next week and I want to go to B'ham and get Roger some things anyway. She works in Loveman's Basement now.

Hamilton really is a lonesome place now. I'll be so happy when you get back. It is lonesome everywhere without you.

Christine, Inez & I went to a show last night. It was rather cute "Riding High" was the name of it.

Roger wrote you too. He said "mother you said I could write Daddy today".

It really has been pretty here this week. I just hope it stays that way.

Take care of yourself & remember we love you.

All our Love & Kisses Eliz & Roger

Mother was indulging in her sweet memories of better times in this letter to dad. When they were first married mother and dad lived in a little house across the street from her mother and grandmother. She was longing for those good old days and wrote down some of her memories of those times for dad to read. Her letter was dated March 10, 1945, Sunday Afternoon:

Hi Sweetheart,

Well this is another very pretty Sunday.

We went to Church this morning. Roger goes to the Card Class every Sunday. He really enjoys it too. They sing songs & get cards,

I wish you could see him in his new suit. If I could get some film I would take a picture of him and send it to you.

I'm sitting here now looking at the house you & I lived in. I think of all the good times we once had there and it makes me wish you were here to go walking with like you, Johnnie, Carr & I used to do on Sunday afternoon.

The peach trees have already bloomed, it really looks like spring here now.

If only this world wasn't in such a mess. Well, maybe it will be over some day & then everyone will really appreciate a peaceful world. I know you get lonesome staying around the hospital too. I just wish you were over here, so that I could be with you.

It wouldn't do if they were to pass a bill that all girls could visit their husbands over there. I would be the first in line ha!

Be sweet and take care of yourself.

I love you only. Bye until tomorrow Eliz & Roger

I will continue with mother's letters to dad as I have most all of them that she wrote to him in March of 1945 and after. I will return to dad's letters that were written to her during this period afterward, in order to establish some semblance of communication between them.

This letter from mother to dad was dated March 13, 1945 and had a postmark of March 14, 1945, Hamilton, Alabama:

Hello Sweetheart,

I hope you are feeling better today.

I took Roger to town to get his hair cut. He still enjoys it as much as ever.

Well Mamma & I have done some cleaning today. We took down her wood stove & are using our oil stove. It is so much nicer.

She is going to buy her an oil stove from Lehman too.

Sweet, I'll be so happy when you get back here & we can have a home again. It is so lonesome for us.

Everyone is gone from H'ton now. At least there is none here except old folks.

I missed your letter today. I suppose that is why I am more lonesome than usual.

I do hope you won't feel bad anymore. I know you've had so much to go through with. I would give anything if I could be there with you.

Be sweet, I love you only – All our Love, Liz & Roger

I am happy to say that I managed to find all the letters that mother wrote to dad each day in this group of letters. They seem more precious as many of her previous letters were missing.

This was a V-Mail written March 14, 1945:

Hello Sweetheart,

Well here comes another letter. I don't know very much to say as I haven't had a letter from you in two days. I'm just hoping to get one tomorrow.

You said something about feeling bad in the last letter. I hope you are feeling better now. Roger says "hi". He is riding in his Jeep that you made for him.

(I will include scans of the toy plane that dad made for Roger. They are a bit worse for the wear from 75 years.)

He enjoys all toys that you made for him.

He likes grapefruit as much as you always did. Every time I go to town he thinks I ought to get it for him.

We really are having some nice Spring like weather now. Be sweet & take care of yourself.

All our Love Eliz & Roger

The next correspondence from mother to dad were letters and were longer with more content which will expand upon the knowledge of their lives and of the lives of their friends and relatives during this time. The first letter was dated March 15, 1945 and postmarked March 16, 1945, Hamilton. Alabama:

Hi Sweet,

I really was happy this morning when I went to the post office, as I got five letters from you.

I'm so proud that you are feeling better and can eat now.

I'm glad you got your box too. I sent that one the first week in Dec (It took three months to get to him!). It really took a long time to get to you didn't it?

I got that letter from Mrs. Frade (I will include a section in the next chapter after this chapter of that letter and other letters from mother and dad's relatives and friends.). She thinks her husband is out of the Hospital now. Is he? She says they have been married fifteen years & have three children.

I'm going to write her today. I think I'll enjoy writing to her very much.

That was a rather cute idea of yours starting the picture frame business.

I had an enlargement made from the one of you, Roger & I, for myself, your mother & Alma.

I got a letter from Alma today. She said they & your mom & Dad spent last Sunday with Mary & Griff (Mayberry).

Roger is writing you too. I have to read every one of your letters to him, so that he will know how to answer ha! He is sending it in a separate envelope, (I would include a scan of it here but was unable to find it,) He put the stamp on.

Sugar, I'll be so happy when you get home again. This is such a lonesome place without you. Be careful, Remember, we love you. Love & Kisses Eliz & Roger

This next letter was in the same envelope as the previous one from mother to dad and I assume it was written the same date of March 15, 1945. It was a letter from Cora Lee Palmer, mother's mother and my grandmother.

I am including scans of photos of Cora Lee
Palmer. The second one includes Roger, age 3.

Dear James,

I received another nice letter from you today and thanks a lots.

I hope this will find you still improving. I would have written to you sooner but I have had the flue again and haven't felt like writting, I didn't have to go to bed this time but sure did feel like it. I am O.K. now. We are having some spring weather now everything is green and the peach trees in bloom the ground its wet most of the time.

You said you didn't have to worry about Elisabeth. No James you wont have to worry about her because she loves you and will always be true to you.

A man or a woman that loves each other will always be true because they always want to do the right thing.

I dont see how the girls could go out with other men when their Husbands or over there fighting for them but there are some here in town is guilty of such things. I am thankful I taught my girls the right way.

I dont believe Eliz or Iva either one will ever be guilty of such things – sometimes I think mothers are to blame about their girls. I may be wrong but I think if my girls was doing wrong I would give them a good talking and let them see where they were wrong but I believe my girls will always be true to their Husbands because they believe like their mother – one man only.

Yes I was glad when Eliz and Roger came back for I dont get lonesome now. I had a letter from Arthur today he wanted to know how you were. I sure am worried about Arthur. I dont know where he is he cant tell us. I'll stop now, write when you feel like it.

love and prayers Mother

The next several letters from mother to dad were V-Mails and, of course, much less lengthy. This one was dated March 16, 1945 and postmarked March 16, 1945, 9:00 am, Hamilton, Alabama:

Dear James,

I hope you are still feeling better. We are all O.K. I got a letter from your mother today. She said Curtis wrote her to send me the money, so your Dad put it in the Bank for us. I'll write a check and get something for our Anniversary present as I planned, I think I'll get some pearls as I've wanted some so long.

I'm going to see Eloise tomorrow. I think I'll have some pictures made while I'm there and send you one.

Mamma said tell you hello she will write you later. (That probably was the previous letter,)

Roger is fine. He is reading his book. Be careful. All my love Elizabeth

There were daily V-Mails to dad from mother, mostly all short and sweet. I will move on to some longer letters though, that were all put into the same Air Mail envelope that was postmarked March 21, 1945. Here is the first letter dated Hamilton, Alabama, March 19. 1945:

Dear Sweetheart,

How are you today? We are fine.

I hope you haven't been feeling bad anymore.

I really enjoyed the week-end with Eloise. It is nice to get away from Hamilton occasionally.

Sweet, I got the pearls I wanted. They are very pretty. I'm going to have some pictures made for you.

(I have a picture of mother with the pearls
on. I will include a scan of it here.)

I got Roger some new clothes. He is really proud of them.
He waited up for me until my bus came last nite.

I got a very pretty blue blouse with black ribbon insertion.
I also got two slips ha!

They are very pretty. Just wish you could see them.

I hope to get some mail from you tomorrow as I haven't
had any in two days now.

Are you still getting my letters?

Everything really is pretty and green now & all the fruit
trees are in bloom.

But that still doesn't keep things from being lonesome
for me. If you were here everything would be just perfect.

Iva says Gerry is on the ship again. She is worried about
him. Of course she doesn't know where he is going.

(I will include a scan of a photo of Mother and Iva here.)

Gee! if this awful mess would ever end. Maybe it will someday.

Well be sweet & write often.

All my Love Always – Elizabeth & Roger

I am not sure why there were several letters included in one envelope but here is the second one dated March 20, 1945:

Dearest Sweetheart

I'll write you again Although I don't know very much to write.

I haven't had a letter from you in three days now, and I'm just hoping to get one tomorrow. I hope you are still feeling O.K.

We are all fine. Roger is out playing with some little boy.

I got a letter from Mary the other day. She says Tucker is still O.K. but that his hair is all grown out long.

I imagine he is really in some tough fighting right now.

I also got a letter from Ella Mai. Jim isn't in Service yet. But McKinley is. You know Katie's husband. They were the ones who lived in the Government houses in Childersburg.

Mr. & Mrs. Carell have them a car now. I bet they are proud of it.

Sweet, I'm sending you another newspaper clipping. I thought it was rather cute, What do you think of it? I'm just sorry for the mother who has all those kids to put up with ha!

Sugar, Iva wants me to move to Birmingham the Both of us to get an apartment together. She doesn't like where she is. Neither do I like here, as I can't use my Refrigerator, Iron or radio. I can't get a house here either.

Of course I wouldn't work. I would just keep house & she will work. I think it would be better for Roger too. He gets lonesome here.

Of course I'll leave the car here in the Car house & we can come home and drive it enough to keep the battery from going dead.

We've already had it greased & when the weather gets warm we'll remove the antifreeze.

I'm not sure about moving yet though..

I wish you were here & we could move someplace. I would like that much better. I would give the world to have you back again.

It is lonesome everywhere without you.

Be sweet & take care of yourself.

All my Love Elizabeth & Roger

The third letter that was enclosed in the envelope finds mother finally having received four letters at once from dad. It was dated March 21, 1945:

My Dearest,

I was so happy to get your four letters today. I'm glad you are doing fine. We are O.K. It really is Cold as blizzard here today.

I'm glad you went to Church. I didn't go Sunday as I was in Birmingham. Roger went with Mammy though.

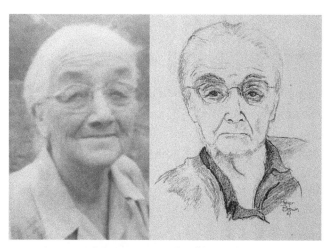

(I am enclosing a scan of a photo of Mammy
and a drawing of her that Roger did.)

She said everyone complimented him on behaving so nice. He really does enjoy going in the class. I'm very proud of Roger as he minds me good.

I got a card from Alma today. She says she had two letters from you last week.

I'm glad you enjoyed your box. Hope you get the others I sent too.

Sweet, it will be the happiest day of my life when you get home. We just miss you so much.

Roger is always telling me what we will do when you get home.

Be sweet & take care of yourself. I love you only, Eliz & Roger

I'm going to include a couple more of mother's letters to dad and then return to his letters to her written from about the same time period. I will return to mother's letters to him later. This letter from mother was dated from Hamilton, Alabama, March 23, 1945:

Dearest Sweetheart,

I got another letter from you today. Glad that Curtis came back to see you again.

I suppose I'll get his letter in a few days.

I also got a letter from Arthur today. He seems to be doing O.K. He doesn't tell me where he is.

Well. sugar the men have finally gone to work on wiring our house. They are here now putting up the post, so it won't be long now. I am so glad we can use our things now.

I think Roger is just about as thrilled over it as the rest.

Sweet, I don't ever know much to write as there is never very much news here. Same old H'ton ha! Gee! if you were just back it would be the best news I could ever hear.

I do wish this war would end. I think maybe it will. The news sounds good now.

Roger is really getting a kick out of watching the men climb the light pole.

Sweet, I wish you were here. I would make you some "icy ice cream" ha! That is if the Refrigerator is still O.K. I hope it is.

Be sweet and don't try to walk too soon. I don't want you to have to go back to the front.

All my Love Always Elizabeth

Here is one more letter from mother to dad before I return to his letters to her written before or during the same time period,
This letter was from March 24, 1945:

Hi Sugar,

Well, how are you today? We are fine, except a little tired.

We went to Winfield today to get some pictures made, but made a complete flop of it, as we couldn't get any except at a little 3 for 15 cent place. I'll try to get some good ones made someday anyway. You can see how my pearls look, or at least get an idea. You can see how Roger looks in his suit. He took so much interest in having them made for you. You can also see the coat I got some time ago. You can't tell very much about it though.

Sweet, I didn't get a letter from you today. I hope to tomorrow though. I'm always so lonesome when I don't hear from you.

Sugar, I'll be so happy when you get back. We'll have lots of fun for all the time we have missed since you have been away.

Be sweet and take care of yourself.

We love you, Eliz & Roger

These next letters are from dad to mother, and I am picking up from where I left off before. This letter from dad was dated March 18, 1945 and was postmarked March 24, 4 pm, 1945:

Dear Sweetheart,

Just a few lines hope you are well and feeling fine at this time for myself I am doing OK but I cant get those bananas off my mind (Dad is referring to the bananas a store owner accused him of not paying for that mother wrote about in a letter I have previously included,), I wish I had some of them to eat proble thats why my stomach have been hurting me, he have been worried so much about it, I sure will have a good one to tell on him, I am going to put this in the papper. Well sweet you can tell him I am sorry about it, and I hope we can win this war soon where he will have a free and peaciful country to spend his money in. Darling if its God's will for me to live and get back, I don't think you will live around there so dont worry. I know the people around there dont like me any to much, because I always tryed to make something of myself with God's help I have done pretty good and the best Darling wife that ever lived. Sweetheart I love you true with all my heart. Darling I would give any thing to be with you tonight. I will always be true and thinking of little you my Darling wife.

So good night and sweet dreams, Love James

In his next letter, dad is still upset about the local merchant in Hamilton, Alabama who had accused him of taking bananas and not paying for them. As you've probably noticed, this topic has been mentioned more than once in their letters. This letter was written the same day on March 18, 1945:

My Darling wife,

I wonder what you have been doing today Darling having a nice time I hope for myself I havent been doing anything but lying around. I did go to Church I enjoyed it very much wish you could have been with me but back in the states. Darling I think about the day when I can come home what a sweet day that will be, if its God's will for me to come back to you. I feel like I will some day, any way I live in hopes and pray that I do. Sweet I dont rember getting any bananas from anu one and not paying for them, any way why did he wait so long to say any thing about it, seem like I have more trouble with things like that then any body – if he had to sleep in a foxhole and dodge shells he woulden have time to think about what some Soldier owed him for a few bananas. I dont care for paying for the bananas, it is the principle of the thing, me over here fighting and sheding my blood for some many (money) glut like that so that is what kind of people we have back in america - I wouldent thought. be sure and pay him he might be in bad need of it. be sure and let him read this.

all my Love James

This V-Mail from dad to mother was dated March 20, 1945, I believe. It, like many of his letters, even though it may have been short, it was sweet and a very endearing love letter. The date was hard to read but it was postmarked March 29, 12:30 am, 1945:

My Darling Wife,

Darling how are you feeling? Fine I hope For myself I am doing fine at this time. Sweet I havent got any mail for the last three days, but I hope to git a bunch of letters tomorrow night seem like I git my mail all in a bunch here lately but that's OK I git it. Sweet you said you wasent driving much now you had better keep driving some every day. I want you to Learn to drive good by the time I get back do Roger still like to ride in the car Like he used to do? I wish I was back where I could take him for a Log (Long) Ride. Sweet heart I miss you and Roger so much, I would give any thing to be back with you all. Darling if it's God's will, I will be back some day and we can have some more good times like we used to. Darling I love you true with all my heart. I will Never Love anyone but you Darling so dont worry about what other people does. I dont go for things Like that, you know Like Curtis is and some others are doing. I have a Darling wife waiting for me and I am waiting for the day when I can come home to you my sweet heart. I will always be true to you my Darling wife.

All my love and Sweet kisses to you my Darling wife – Love James

In this next V-Mail dad indicates that he has walked for the first time since he had been put in the hospital. It was dated March 22, 1945 and postmarked April 1, 1;22 am, 1945:

Hello Sweetheart,

How are you and Roger today? Fine I hope for myself I am doing OK at this time. I walked some yesterday but coulden do much good. my ankle is pretty stiff and sore yet. you said Roger had been pretty sick with a cold, be sure and take good care of him. I keep a cold just about all time myself you know I had a head cold just about all time when I was at home Well I still have trouble with it, Sweet you said Olan Shorts was fixing to be called to the Army. Well I hope all the boys the best of luck. tell Olan I said hello and to be careful when he started picking them Germans and Japs off because they can shoot straight to. I found out that the germans could the first thing. I dont want to find out any more about them neather. Darling be sweet and good. I love you true always.

All my love and sweet kisses Love James

The next group are letters from dad to mother, rather than V-Mails, and are much longer in content. The first one is a long letter and was dated March 21, 1945 and postmarked March 23, 1945:

My Darling wife,

I will try and answer your four sweet letter I recived to night, sure was proud to get them, as I havent got any in several days, proud you all are well and doing fine, for myself I am OK at this time, but sure would like to see you sweetheart. I git so lonesome around here I dont know what to do, but some day I hope to be happy again, that will be when I can be back with you Darling. the day I can hold you in my arms will be the day I will be happy again. Darling you dont know how much I miss being with you. I think of you all time sweetheart. I think of all the sweet times we have had togather how sweet you have been to me Darling I will never forgit. Sweetheart I know you git lonesome for me, any one do that cares for their loved one. Darling I hope to be back some day if its God's will for me to, I feel like I will. I live in hopes and pray ever day that some day I can be back with you and make you happy sweetheart because I love you with all my heart. I have always been true to you and will forever Sweetheart. Darling I tryed in ever way to make you happy when I was back home with you. I hope you feel that I did. Darling if I live to git back I know I can make you happy. I will never forgit the months and days and minuts I have been away from you. the minuts seem like months and months like years. Darling my love for you is something words can never tell.

Sweet my hair have grown back out like it used to be now so I can comb it just like you always wanted me to. I dont think I will git any more G.I. haircuts – they like to have ruined my hair, but I can do OK with it now, Sweet the boy that I wrote you that his wife was going to write you, have gone back to the front – he left last week. I sure do miss him as he always came around and talked to me a lot. Sweet you said you went to a show with Christine. Where is her husband? in the army I guss where all the rest is. I saw a good show last night best one I have saw since I have been over here. The name of it was foller the stars.

Sweet I wanted to git you something for your birthday and you and Roger a easter present, but I dont guss I can. So I will send you my love sealed with a kiss and let you know how much you all are being missed. Darling I miss you and Roger more than words can ever till,

Sweet I dont want you to be worrying about me doing things like Curtis, and lots of others. God knows I love you only and will forever. I am living a Christian life sweet read proverbs fifth chapter and verses 18 & 19 is what I mean, always with her love, with me it's always your love my Darling wife. (Proverbs 5:18, 19: 18 Let thy fountain be blessed and rejoice with the wife of thy youth, 19 Let her be as the loving hind and pleasant roe; let her breasts satisfy thee at all times, and be thou ravished always with her love.)

Sweet you said you was going to B'ham for the weekin. I wish I was there to go with you sweet, but dont worry Darling just keep praying and some day God will make every thing sweet for us if it's his will, so good night sweet.

all my love & kisses, James

Dad wrote several long letters like the one I just included. They were often love letters and were full of emotion and often very insightful and poetic. They offer much detail about what was going on in his life, mother's life, and the lives of their friends.

There were two long letters from dad written on March 23, 1945, the day before my mother's twenty third birthday, The first one was postmarked March 27, 1945:

Dear Sweetheart,

I will try and answer some more of your letters I recived last night. I got a very nice letter from your Grand mother (Mammy) wishing me all the luck, and a real soon return home. I hope you are well and feeling fine sweet, for myself I am doing fine at this time, my ankle is doing OK I guss. yes sweet I think I would git well lots sooner if you was with me becaus I worry a lot when I am away from you. If I was back in the states where you could be with me I know I would be lots better, sweet, the candy I got was the one that you sent me before Christmas. I also got the valentine heart you sent me, the candy was very good in both boxes. tell Roger his candy was very good he sent me and thinks (thanks) a lot. sweet I would like to see Roger in his new suit I bet he looks good. I would like very much if you would have some pictures mad of you and Roger and send them to me.

Darling I would give any thing to be there and we could take a walk like me and you Johny and Carr use to do. I think about that a lot. I sure hope Carr gits out of Germany OK they are relly bombing that place now. I sure will be proud when this war is over, and we all can come home to our love ones. Sweet you said it, when you said this world was in a mess but you dont know half of it. You should see this place over here – it's awful the way people does. look like they would try to do better, maby this war would git over with sooner at least I know it would. Sweet I dont know where I will haft to go back to the front are not, but if I do I will do my best to take care of myself – that's one thing you never know you might go all the way through and not git a scratch. they throw shells every where up there I havent saw that safe place yet that they told me all about when I was taking my training – of course you can git in a hole and be lots safer than you would if you wasent, but you cant stay in a hole and wind a war – you would be fighting the rest of your life.

So all you cand do is to dive in to it and if you are lucky, that is fine, but if not that is to bad. when they say go that's what they mean but most of the time you dont git very far. war is a awful thing, just look around and see your best buddy dying are shot up so bad he cant go – and you looking for your time to come any minute. I found everything lots difference thin I thought it was. I am just hoping and praying that it will soon be over, where we all can live in some peace the rest of our life if it's Gods will.

Sweet I miss your letters to when I cant git any it makes me feel blue to not git one, but I know it's not your folt. Sweet I write you every day and sometimes twice.

Darling I love you true with all my heart,

all my love and sweet kisses, Love James

Here is the second long letter that dad wrote to mother that was dated March 23, 1945. This one was postmarked March 27, 1945, as well:

My Darling little wife,

I just recived to letters from you sweet, one was wrote Jan. 14, which was very sweet, and I also got a picture in it which I am very proud of. I gave Curtis the one I had like that, that was the only one I could give him with Roger picture on it, unless I gave him two are three and I dident want to do that, sweet, I feel fine today as it have be a beautiful day. the sun shined so pretty all day. the first day of spring, and what a beautiful day it would be to, if I could have been with you my Darling. I sit outside some to day. I though of you ever minute I was out there sweetheart. how sweet it would be if I was at home, and could walk around with you. I would be one of the happiest Soldiers in the U.S. Army. You said in one of you letters that the peach tree was blooming. I bet every thing do look good around there, if I was only there with you Darling every thing would be OK and the war was over, if I Could be there to night and look you in thoes sweet eyes, and kiss the smile on your face, my last prayer would be answered through God's will. as I was reading your letter sweetheart tears come in my eyes. thoes few lines that said I pray that God is taking care of you and will continue to wherever you go and what ever you do. I am proud I have a sweet wife. I pray that God will keep you well and safe, for me. sweet when I say you I mean Roger boy to. I am always thinking of him, I guss he will forgit me this time good. whin I came on my tin day pass he dident know me so good, sweet you said you dreamed about me nely (nearly) ever nigh. you said you dreamed that I was fighting the germans and you was with me. well I would like for you to be with me but not bad anought for you to be up thire. I would like for you to be here at the Hospital with me, but I know you cant, you said you wish they would pass a bill to let the women come over here to see their Husband. I bet you would be the first one in line, well you let me know when some thing like that happens, and I will be there to meet you when the boat lands. sweet are you still working? you havent said any thing about it for the last few times you wrote me. I hope you are still liking the work and can git along OK with ever one there. I know you can if they don't bother you, so be careful. sweet are you still driving the Car. I want you to learn to drive good by the time I come home. I guss by that time you will be done learned to fly a plane. I hope not though because I would like to come home some day. sweet I took my first plane ride whin I come from france to the Hospital here in England. I liked it fine, but not the way I had to take it. (This is a different story from what he told me. He told me the plane lost altitude twice going across the channel and he thought he was going to die. He swore he would never fly again after that. I guess he told another gentler version for mother.) I wish I could come back to the states in one when that time comes for me to come back home, if it's the lords will for me to come back. I feel like some day I will be coming back to you Darling. I hope and pray I do any way. Darling I love you only, and will always, there is no one that can take your place sweetheart never. So dont wory Darling my love is all for you, I know I will be true to you and I feel that you will allways be a true and sweet darling wife to me.

All my Love and sweet kisses, Love, James

This next letter is another long, insightful letter from dad and again very loving and observant about the awful nature of war and the toll it took on humanity. It was written the next day on March 24, 1945 and postmarked March 27, 1945:

My Darling little wife,

Hi Sweetheart, how are you and Roger making it now? Fine I hope for myself I am doing fine I guss at this time, Sweet I have been thinking of you and Roger a lot today – been lonesome around here with me nothing going on in here but the same old thing every day listening at some are suffering. if some people would go through the Hospitals over here and see some of the boys, they would start thinking about this war and the way they are living more. most of the people back in the states dont know what war is like and I hope they never find out – if they could see how the people are living over here special in france they woulden never say any thing about what they have to eat and the clothes they have to wear. God have relly blest our nation by keeping the war off our home land so far, the news was very good today. they crossed the rhine in several more places. I sure hope they can keep going after they have started and dont have to much trouble. I know they are going to have some trouble but I am praying that it wont last to much longer. Darling this the 24, and I hope it have been a happy day for you. I hope and pray that you will have many more birthdays to come and that I can be with you to make you happy. I know we both would be very happy if we was togather now, what a birthday it would be if I could walk up now and be with you. Darling I would give any thing in the world if I could be with you but I know I wont be with you, but Darling remember I love you, and will forever no matter where I

367

am are what I am doing, I will be thinking of you ever day and night I am away from you sweetheart.

Sweet you said you havent got any power yet. I hope you will soon git it as it would be lots of help to you and the Referator will soon be ruined if not already if you dont have some way to run it. you need the Referator any way it will soon be getting hot weather. I sure hope the power man will try and git it fixed before hot weather any way? Have you had any punctures? I hope not. (I am not sure what he meant by that.)

Sweet you was telling me about you and Iva taking a walk down to the School. I bet it did make you feel blue to think that's the place where me and you use to have lots of fun. I will never forget thoes good old days – if it's God's will, we will have some more days like that Darling – So be sweet and keep praying I will.

Sweetheart I hope you a real happy Birthday. All my Love and kisses, James

I didn't find another letter from dad to mother until the one that was dated March 27, 1945, a few days later than the previous one. It was postmarked March 30, 1945:

My Darling little wife,

Just a few lines tonight sweetheart hoping you are feeling good and in the best of health for myself I am doing fine at this time Darling. I dident git any mail tonight So I dont know much to write about. Sweet I saw a good show last night, they showed it again so I went back to see it again. the name of it was a home in Indena (Indiana), it Sure was good lots of loving – just like you and me always liked. I thought of you a lot wishing I was back home where we could be togather. Sweet I am always blue when I dont git any mail to. I am always looking for a letter from you. I sure was worried when I went two months about getting any mail from you. I was praying that you was OK. so everything was when I herd from you. sweet I think about you so much I sure will be happy when I can be back with you. no body knows how much you mean to me Darling but God. I pray that he will provide a way for us to be back to gather some sweet day. I know you git lonesome staying around home and no one to have fun with like we always did, you are so sweet and loving. I would give any thing for a sweet kiss from you Darling. I miss all you loving and good times we use to have. no mater what time I come in from work you would always meet me with a smile and a kiss. do you remember at Childersburg when I would come in off the grave yard. I told you I coulden go to sleep unless you went to bed with me. well any way it woulden be long before you would have me asleep and what a sweet way you had doing it. it would be cold in the bed, but when you git in there, it woulden be long you would have me warm and sweet your little arms around me and a sweet kiss, some one that relly loved me and wanted to keep me for ever. I hope you do in your little heart Darling till I git back if it's God's will for me to git back. if I git back I am going to show you the best time of your life darling. Sweet heart go any place you want to and pass the time off and buy any thing you want.

Darling I love you true for ever,

all my love and kisses, James

I really have enjoyed these longer letters from dad as they told me so much about him and his personality that I had no idea existed before. My parents were both young when they wrote these letters, and by the time they had me, they had matured and become much more reserved in their behavior. So, I never experienced the younger, freer and more exuberant personalities that they had in those war days. Reading and writing about these letters has been very enlightening and has made me love and understand both my parents in ways I never did before.

This next letter from dad to mother was another long and heartfelt letter that had two letters inside the envelope addressed to Roger as well. Roger was always tickled, as mother would say, when his daddy would write him his very own personal letters.

The letter was dated March 28, 1945 and the two to Roger were dated March 26 and March 28, 1945. It was postmarked March 30, 1945:

My Darling wife,

I will try and answer your two letters, sure was proud to git them, as I dident git one last night. I am feeling pretty good, hope you and Roger are OK. I am proud you had a nice time with Eloise and Iva in Birmingham. I will be looking for that picture you said you was going to send me with the pearls on I got a letter from your mother to night. She said she had been sick with the flue, I sure hope she dont git down like she did last year. I also got a letter from mother and them they was OK at that time. I hope they stay well and able to go around some. you said you got a letter from arthur but he coulden tell where he was he dont haft to tell, you know where he is dont you, they have been giving the Japs all they wanted for the last week I sure hope he will be lucky and can be back home some day when this war is over and I hope that will be real soon. Sweet I know you have a lot to wory about but dont worry to much sweet. I think Arthur will be OK, and I feel like I will be coming back some day. I know you worry a lot about arthur you all ways seem like you thought a lot of each other more so then the rest of the boys. I think a lot of arthur to and all the rest of the family but arthur is having a bad time now. I know how he feels, no one haves

370

that feeling but the one that is doing the job, so all we can do is pray, and if it's God's will he will take care of you.

How are you and Herbert making out with the car? have you learned to drive good yet I hope so. But do be careful sweet I dont want anything to happen to you Darling you know I love you to much. I would never git over it if something happen to you sweetheart (Mother passed away in 2006, two years before dad, and he never got over it.).

I wish I could see you dressed in all thoes new things you have got since I left. have you stopped gaining weight yet. I dont want you to git to big sweet. when I come home I dont want you to be so big I cant carry you around like I used to.

Sweet if you need any money I want you to git it out of the bank and cash your war bonds, You can have the war bonds do any thing you want to with them – buy all the clothes you want are any thing else. I want you to sweet. I have never give you half as much as I wanted to. I will never give up though. I have give you all my love Darling. I love you more than any one in this whole wide world. I will always be true to you my Darling little wife.

all my love and Sweet kisses,

Love James

There were two letters included inside this envelope that dad wrote to Roger. The first one was dated March 26, 1945:

Hello Roger boy,

I was proud to git your letter and hear that you are well and being a good boy for mother. my ankle is doing OK now.

some day I will come home and show you where those old Germans shot me. mother said you liked grapefruit like I use to. well I still like it to, you make mother git you all you want. You keep being a good boy and take care of mother for me and write me some more.

Love to Roger from Dady

Here is the second letter from dad to Roger dated March 28, 1945:

Hello Roger Boy,

How are you feeling today? fine I hope for myself I am doing fine. mother said she got you some things in B'hm. I bet you was proud of them. I have made you an airplane but I dont know where they will let me send it to you are not. I will if I can. I will let you know if I can send it. it is a small plane something you keep for a souvenir. (I still have the larger plane dad made for Roger. I have included scans of it earlier.) be good and take care of mother for me. Love Daddy

The next letters are all V-Mails from dad to mother, so they were much shorter in length but still rich in detail. I will include them in chronological order. The first V-Mail was dated March 28, 1945 and postmarked April 1, 1945:

My Darling wife,

Just a few Lines hope you all are feeling good today for myself I am doing fine at will it this time. this is another pretty Day the sun is shining pretty and bright and the sky is pretty and blue the trees is buding out and the grass is getting green and I am thinking of my Darling wife is far away. what a lovely time we could have on a day like this, if we was only togather. sweet you said arthur was in California at that time. I bet he did have a time with all the girls, he is a good sport any way, but I guss he is sailing the deep blue sea some where now. I know how he feels. I sure hope he have good luck, and some day he can be back home. this war sure have messed every thing up, but God knows best for us all, so all we can do is hope and pray for a better and peaciful world some day – if it's God's will it will be over soon. I am praying that it will any way. tell your mother and all I said hello. you said Herbert had washed and shined the car. I sure would like to be there and take you for a ride maby some day I can, Darling take care of your self and Roger. I love you true with all my heart.

all my love and sweet kisses, James

The next V-Mails from dad to mother were dated March 30, 1945, April 1, 1945, and April 2, 1945. They were all enclosed in an envelope that was postmarked April 8, 1 pm,1945. Here is the first one dated March 30, 1945:

My Darling Wife,

Just a few lines hope you all are well and feeling fine for myself I am doing pretty good at this time. Darling I would give any thing to be back with you tonight. I am sitting here by my self and do I feel blue and lonesome for you my Darling. I dident git a letter from you tonight. I sure hope to git one tomorrow night. Frade came by to see me this afternoon he was on his way to france. he was pretty lucky they put him driving a truck. Sweet I dont know any thing to write so I will stop now. So be good and sweet Darling. I love you with all my heart.

all my love and sweet kisses – Love James

The next V-Mail included in the envelope was dated April 1, 1945:

My Darling Wife,

Hello sweetheart how are you today fine I hope for myself
I am OK at this time. my ankle is giving me some trouble.
sweet be seeing you before long, the Doctor told me I
might be seeing you before long. I sure hope so any way
if it's God's will. this is Easter and what would I give to
be with you my sweetheart. it have been raining here all
day dont seem much like Easter. I went to church this
morning. I enjoyed it very much sure did have some pretty
flowers there. Sweet I got that picture of all them kids. I
dont know what to say about that sweet. I wonder what
will happen next. Somebody will try to beat him I guss.
but I dont think any body can (This must have been from
a newspaper clipping that mother sent dad about a man
that had a large number of children. I was unable to find
that clipping.). I will stop for this time.

all my love and kisses – Love James

The third V-Mail enclosed in the envelope was dated April 2. 1945:

Dear sweetheart

I will answer your two sweet letters I recived tonight.
Sure was proud to git them. Glad you and Roger are well
and doing fine. for myself I am doing pretty good at this
time. I went to a good show tonight sweet, have you been
any lately? I would give any thing to be there where we
could go togather Sweetheart like we used to do. Curtis
havent been to see me in good while now I am looking for
him any day now. I sure hope he can come pretty soon,
as I am looking to leave this Hospital any time now. I
bet your mother's bed room suit is pretty. I hope to git to
see it pretty soon if it's God's will. Darling woulden it be
sweet if I could come home how I would like to hold you

374

in my arms one more time. Darling be sweet and keep praying for me.

I love you true with all my heart, Love and Kisses, James

The next correspondence from dad was a long letter rather than a V-Mail and he was responding to mother's earlier letter about her moving to Birmingham to live with her sister Iva. The date was unclear but was probably written around April 1 or April 2, 1945 as the postmark was April 3, 1945:

My Darling little wife,

I just recived three sweet letters from you, and was I proud to git them, proud you are well and doing good for myself I am doing pretty good. my ankle is still giving me some trouble yet, but I hope it will be OK someday. God knows best.

Tomorrow is Easter, and would I like to be with you Darling, but I know I cant. I will be thinking about you sweetheart. tell Roger to save me an Easter egg.

Sweet you was saying some thing about moving to B'ham and staying with Iva. sure its OK with me sweet, but I want you to wait a while before you do. I cant tell you why I want you to wait. I dont want you to move in, and then maby haft to move out and leave Iva by herself. I might send for you to come and stay with me. I am praying that its God's will for this war to be over soon so we all can come back to the states. Sweet if you havent already moved when you git this letter wait till you hear From me again but if you have already made plaines to move and have the apartment go ahead and move because it would it would mess things up anyway with you all if you dident go ahead, but be sure and take care of yourself and Roger boy for me and be a sweet little girl. Sweet I know you git lonesome staying in Hamilton but it is like you said, it is lonesome everywhere when we are not togather, but I am praying that it wont be to much longer before we can be togather again.

Darling you said Mr. Carell had bought them a car. I woulden never thought it I thought they loved money to much to buy a car. but I guss they got so much of it they had to do something with it.

Yes sweet I knew McKinley. I sure hope him good luck he was the one that liked you so well ha do you remember sweet? I liked Jim and him they was very nice I thought. I would like to see them tell them I said hello when you write again. I will stop and go to bed now. So be sweet Darling. I love you only for ever.

all my love and kisses, James

Here is another letter from dad in which he had acknowledged receipt of the photos mother had made of herself in her new pearls and of Roger in his new suit. It was written April 4, 1945 and postmarked April 13, 1945:

My Darling little wife,

I just recived three sweet letters from you and was I proud to git them, proud you are well and doing good for myself I am doing pretty good at this time. I sure was proud of the sweet pictures of you and Roger. they are very good. Sweet you said the reason you coulden make a good picture was because you wasent good looking. you cant say that and make me believe it. I know you are good looking. I wish I was with you right now sweetheart, everybody says Roger was a cute boy and that you are good looking. I like Roger's suit and your coat and pearls. I hope to come home some day soon where I can see you and Roger and all – Darling be sweet.

I love you sweet for ever all my love and kisses, Love James

The next letters that dad wrote to mother were V-Mails and I will include two of them here, then I will return to mother's letters that she wrote to dad during the same time period. Of special note here is that dad had been receiving at least three letters a day now, so the mail is finally beginning to catch up with him.

This V-Mail from dad was dated April 5, 1945. It was postmarked April 13, 11;30 pm, 1945:

My Darling wife,

Darling how are you tonight? fine I hope for my self I am doing pretty good at this time I got a letter from you last night and one from Mama. Sweet I sure would like to see you, you looked so good in the picture. you have fleshened up in the face some havent you? I woulden take anything for the pictures. Roger sure do look good and healthy, I hope he stays that way. Sweet I weigh 160# now everybody sayes I dont look to be over twenty years old (He was 24). they dont believe I have a boy three years old. I would give anything to see you and Roger tonight. Darling be good and take care of your self and Roger. I love you true with all my heart. I will always be true, Love & Kisses, James

Here is another of dad's V-Mails to mother. After including this one, I will return to mother's letters to him. It seemed that his mail delivery was sporadic at best as he relates in this V-Mail he has not gotten a letter in two days. This V-Mail was written the next day on April 6, 1945 and postmarked April 13, 11:30 pm, 1945:

My Darling wife,

How are you tonight sweetheart? Fine I hope. for my self I am doing pretty good I guss. Sweet I havent got any mail in two days. I hope to git some tomorrow I guss they have got the house wired by now. I hope so. Sweet are you still working you dont say any thing about it lately. Darling I sure would like to be back with you. We always had a good time togather. I miss you so much sweet I hope it wont be long before we can be back togather if its God's will.

I love you true with all my heart —

all my love and sweet kisses Love James

The last letter I included from mother to dad was the one she wrote March 24, 1945 which was her twenty third birthday. I will pick back up with a letter she wrote the day before on March 23, 1945:

Dearest Sweetheart,

I received your two very sweet letters today. I'm very happy that you can get around some now, only don't try to put your weight on your ankle if it hurts you.

I'm glad you like the Valentine candy. I thought it was rather pretty.

You will still get another one yet. I sent it about three weeks ago.

Write and let me know if you want anything else as I can't send anything without a request.

I'm glad Curtis can go to see you. Hope he can go back before long. Next time you see him tell him I'm still looking for that letter he owes me.

Sweet, I hope you get the picture I sent yesterday. I think the one of Roger was cute, but mine are horrible as usual. I never take a good picture though. I really don't look that "Droopy" ha!

Iva has gone back to Birmingham. Gerry is in the "Marrannas" Now.

Well it is raining Cats and dogs here as usual.

Sugar I saw Mr. Brassfield yesterday (you know the Lehman Furniture Co Man). He was asking about you and was surprised to hear of you being wounded.

Mamma bought her a new bedroom suite. It is very pretty. Light Color and large round mirror.

Roger is asleep now. He still hates to go to bed as bad as he ever did.

He really is a prissy little fellow.

Last Sunday he was dressed to go to church, so he sat down in a chair in front of the mirror and discovered he could see himself in it so he said "Ah! My collar is all messed up". so he began to straighten it. He is just like you.

Sweet, I suppose this is all for now. I could tell you more if I could be with you.

So bye until tomorrow.

All My Love, Elizabeth

The next letter I have from mother to dad was dated Hamilton, Alabama, March 26, 1945:

Hello Sugar,

I was happy to get your letter this morning.

Sweet, I'm sorry I said anything about the money. I wished after I had written you about it that I hadn't even mentioned it. I get mad too easy I know. I got the money anyhow, so forget it please, hear?

Sweet you know I trust you. I never think of you doing me wrong, and don't ever worry about me, as you know I won't ever do a thing like that.

Sweet, I think I've lost a couple or three pounds to my joy. I don't want to be so fat.

You asked for some pictures of us. I sent you some a few days ago. They aren't very good but it was the best I could do as I can't get any film now.

I'm going to have some better ones made of myself sometime.

They haven't finished wiring the house yet, don't know what they are waiting on. I get disgusted sometimes. Maybe they will be back soon though as they have already put two posts up.

Roger is out playing with some boys. He still enjoys cooking cakes etc.

Christine is going back tomorrow. I hate to see her go too as I will have no one to talk to when she leaves.

You know I never knew what a dump Hamilton really was until I got away from it and came back.

When you used to talk about it and say you didn't like it I just thought it was the grandest place on earth.

Now I think it is the rottenest place on earth (I never thought I would ever hear mother say that about her beloved Hamilton,).

We got another letter from Arthur. He is still O.K. Said he had received letters from almost everyone.

Be sweet and remember we love you. All My Love, Elizabeth

With this letter the saga of the stolen bananas continues as mother tries to placate dad's anger about the whole thing. It was written the next day on March 27, 1945:

Hi Sweetheart,

I hope you are feeling good today. We are fine. Have just finished washing. It really has been a very pretty spring day.

Christine went back to Mass. today. I am really going to miss her too.

I got three letters from you today Gee! I'm always glad to get several at a time as I can have plenty to read.

Sweet, you're wrong about the people here not liking you. Everyone seems to think lots of you. Someone is always asking me about you.

About Mr. Sullins and the bananas, just forget it, as I've already paid it long ago. Sweet don't worry about it. Mr.

Sullins' mind isn't right anyway and he just got kinda mixed up I think.

It just made me kinda mad because he brought something up like that.

I shouldn't have written you about it but you know how I am. I always have to tell everything ha!

So don't think anything about it. He is just a curious kind of fella anyway.

I got a letter from Mary today. She said Tucker is still in Germany.

She sent me a picture of herself too. She still looks the same I suppose.

I really would like to see her. She is such a sweet kid.

We all had such a good time in Fla, didn't we? Gee! What I would give if you were back there and I was with you. It would suit me much better though if this war would end and you could get out of the army. Then we could go where we wanted to.

Sweet, I'm glad you liked the candy. Write me if you want me to send you anymore or anything that you want.

I wish I could come over there and talk to you. Gee! that would be so nice & lots of fun wouldn't it?

Sweet, I was telling you that we might move to B'ham. I don't suppose I will if they come back and hook the electricity on. I just don't want the refrigerator to ruin.

Iva just wanted me to come and live with her, as she gets so lonesome there by herself.

Be sweet & take care of yourself. I love you,

Love & Kisses, Eliz & Roger

With this next group of letters I found, there were letters written each day from mother to dad. As the content retains much similarity from day to day, I will not include them all but will try to maintain a reasonable flow. As you will see from the next letter of mother's, even she remarks how she had to keep writing the same thing over and over. It was written the next day and dated Hamilton, Alabama, March 28. 1945:

Dear Sweetheart,

Well, here I am with another letter. I don't know very much to write. I just have to write the same thing over and over. Anyway we all are fine and hope you are still feeling better.

We got another letter from Arthur today. He said he had just got his box of shaving lotion & cream that Mamma sent him.

He is still at the same place and says he keeps rather busy.

I also had letters from Iva and Eloise. They both had just come in from work.

Eloise may come with Iva some week-end. I hope she will.

I didn't get a letter from you today. I usually get several one day and not any the next. I suppose you get yours the same way. Anyway, I'm always glad to get several at once.

Sweet, I think I told you about Harold Ballard being seriously wounded. He wrote his mother that he would soon be sent back to the states, just as soon as he is able.

She really is proud that he is going to get to come back.

Gee! I would give anything if you were coming home of course I wouldn't want you to be hurt seriously to get to come back. But I don't think it is fair for you to have to go back and fight again, after being wounded.

Sugar, I'm glad you can go to church now. Roger and I go every Sunday. He really enjoys his class. It will be nice when you can be back and we three can go together.

I'm always looking forward to that day.

Be good and of course I'm never no other way.

I love you only, Elizabeth

Here is a nice longer letter from mother to dad that was written at Easter time and was dated March 31, 1945:

Hi Sweetheart,

I was so glad to get your letter today. I am happy that you are still doing fine. We are too. Mamma got a letter from Gerry. He says he is in a rather safe place he thinks. Says there aren't any Japs around the place, and I can imagine he hopes there won't be. He is doing the same kind of work.

I hope you have gotten some more of my letters. I suppose they are boring sometimes as I write the same things over and over.

Tomorrow is Easter and Roger is planning a big time with his basket full of boiled eggs.

The town is full of people today as it is Saturday and such folks! You know, some with high heels, ankle socks and others with clothes hanging. You know how it is here on Saturday – cheese eaters ha! That reminds me though I wouldn't mind having some cheese right now. That is something you can hardly get now. Do you ever have any? I hope you are getting plenty to eat.

It seems that I am as I'm getting so Fat. I think I'll stop eating so much & see if I can lose some weight. I'm not too bad yet though if I don't gain anymore. If I keep getting fat you won't want me when you get back ha! Anyway I'm not going to get that fat if I can help myself. I still weigh 132 pounds.

Roger is fat as a pig too. He says he doesn't want a fat mother he wants a big and tall one.

Sweet, I'm gonna drive some more. I just have to wait until the notion strikes me ha! I guess I've never been very interested in trying to drive. I think it is much more fun to sit on the other side of the driver anyway.

Be sweet. Remember I love you.

Love & Kisses Elizabeth & Roger

As I have related before, during these times there were letters from mother to dad every day. I have them all and am including most of them. Here is another that was dated April 2, 1945:

Dear Sweetheart

Hope you are feeling fine, We are. We have just gotten back from Winfield. Got Roger a cute pair of white oxfords. Also had some more pictures made.

When the lady finished the pictures Roger asked "Did I smile?" So I am sending you one of the best ones in which he was smiling as he wants you to have it.

(I have included the photo of Roger smiling spoken of here earlier.)

Mine aren't much as usual, but of course it isn't possible for me to make a pretty picture.

I haven't had a letter from you in two days, sugar and I am really missing them too.

I'll be so happy when we can be together again then we won't have to be waiting for letters from each other. I miss you so much, and sweet I don't worry about you doing me wrong, for I know that you aren't that kind and you also know that I love you only and wouldn't think of doing you wrong.

All I worry about is if you are doing O.K. and hoping and praying that you will soon be back with us.

Sweet, you know May Bravin the blonde haired freckled face – fat girl who stayed at Mrs. Norris when I was in Starke. Her husband was wounded in Germany the fourth of March. He was slightly wounded. Mary wrote me about it. They were from Maryland. Mary said Tucker is still in Germany. She said she got a letter from you too.

Be sweet and take care of yourself.

All my Love Always Eliz

I am including one more letter of mother's before returning to the ones dad wrote to her. Amazingly, in this letter, mother states that she has gotten nine of dad's letters at once. The letter was dated April 3, 1945:

Hi Sugar.

I've just finished reading your sweet letters I received today. I got nine. I think that is the most I have gotten at one time.

I really enjoyed reading them a lot.

Sweet, I'm glad that you can get outside some. I know it is so much relief to get outside the Hospital awhile.

I'm glad that you are getting all my letters too. I write you every day and sometimes more.

Mamma got her bedroom suite today. It really is a pretty one.

I suppose you have gotten the pictures of Roger and I.

Sweet, I know it hurts you worse about Robert now that you have been through what he has. But try not to worry so much about it. You know Robert wouldn't want you to.

I wish you could come home. I would be the happiest person on earth if you could.

Roger was tickled when he heard that you had gotten his letter. He is writing you again.

Sweet you said that he would forget you sure enough this time.

I don't think he will as he is older now and he talks about you lots. He knows all your pictures even the ones taken before you & I were married.

He might be a little shy the first time he sees you, but if you bring him chewing gum and candy he will be all over in a little while ha!

He'll never forget when you were home on furlough, about you getting him chewing gum & candy out of the bag.

He very often says that he will be glad when his daddy comes home and we can move back to our Childersburg house.

Yes, sweet I still work occasionally for Mr. Carpenter. He doesn't have very much work.

Sugar, I love you. Be Sweet.

All my Love & Kisses Elizabeth

The next three letters are from dad to mother written about the same time period and they were not V-Mails, but longer letters dated April 7th, 8th and 9th of 1945. Here is the first letter dated April 7. 1945 and postmarked April 10, 1945:

My Darling wife,

I just recived three sweet letters from you. glad you are all well for my self I am doing pretty good at this time. I got the box of candy to day it sure was good thinks (thanks) a lot. Darling I have never been so blue in all my life as I am tonight. I think of you all time sweet heart. I would give any thing to be with you to night sweetheart, it will be a happy day when this war is over and we all can come home. I got a letter from tucker to night, he said he was OK at this time, said he sure had been lucky. I sure hope his luck holds out to and some day he will be going back home. you said Harold Ballard was coming home when he got able. I sure hope he can. My Doctor told me I might be coming home are back to the states before long. I sure hope so all I can do is to wait and see, if it's God's will I will come back dont look for me till you see me coming. tell the boys and all I said hello. I guss I had better stop and go to bed now. good night Darling.

I love you only – Love and Kisses James

The second letter from dad to mother was written the next day on April 8. 1945 and postmarked April 12, 1945:

My Darling wife,

Dear sweetheart jusy a few lines hope you are well and feeling fine today – for my self I am doing pretty good only I would like to be with you Darling. this is a beautiful day in England, the sun is shining so pretty and bright and the grass is pretty and green. I have been out some today. went to church and around. I would have given any thing if we could have been togather. Darling I miss you so much. I get so down and out sometimes I dont know what to do. I hope and pray that some day we can be back togather.

I got a box of candy and sweets from Harrison today that he sent me for Christmas (over three months late) sure was nice. I have been looking for Curtis this weekin but he havent come dont guss he could git a pass. I guss you and Roger went to church today. I wish I was back home where we could go to gather. Roger sure does look big and healthy in his picture I would give any thing to see you and him. I dream about you nely (nearly) every night sweet. I sure will be proud when this war is over where I can come back and never haft to leave you again Darling.

sweet I love you true with all my heart.

all my Love and sweet kisses Love James

Here is the third long letter from dad to mother that was dated April 9, 1945 and postmarked April 12, 1945:

My Darling wife,

I will try and answer your four sweet letters I got this afternoon. Darling I am doing pretty good now glad you and Roger are well and doing fine. I got the pictures to, they are very good I like them. sweet you look good and dont say you dont any more are I will give you a spaking (spanking) when I come home. ha, if you keep getting big and fat I dont know where I can or not. Sweet you said I woulden like you when I come back. Darling I will always Love you no mater how fat you git. I like big legs any way and a few other things I like big to ha, you dont way to much anyway 132 pounds are just right for me. I always did want you to be just a little larger anyway, you know big hips and legs and so forth. I am proud you are getting fat the way you are and not the way I thought you was a month are two ago. When I got your name and Eloise mixed up. I am proud you are OK sweet heart. I would have been worried so much. I would have went crazy if I coulden have come back and stayed with you. I am so proud you are allright becaus it is bad anought as it is. sweet you said you had been working in the garden. I bet you done a lot of work. I bet I will never git the laziness out of you when I git back, ha. I bet one thing I will git plenty of loving that what counts anyway isent it sweet? I think of you all time sweet heart wishing I was back with you where we could love all time like we use to do. I am hoping it wont be long till we will be back togather. Sweet I have already made me a picture frame for my pictures. Darling I love you only for ever. So be sweet I will always. I am sending my love sealed with a kiss. I love with all my heart –

Love and Kisses, James

P.S. I just thought of some thing tucker told me to tell you hello for him – drop him a few lines sometimes, it will make him feel better, mary writes me so it will be OK. I want you to write him this is his adgress in case you dont know it.

P.F.C. Wilmark Tucker 34837096
Co, H. 137 INF. H.P.C. 35
%P.M.N.Y.N.Y.

As I've mentioned before, dad wrote mother every day and most letters were short repetitive V-Mails just to let her know he was OK and to keep in touch. I will include one V-Mail here and after will include a much longer letter from him which was likely the last one he wrote to her before being shipped back to the states.

This V-Mail from dad was dated April 11, 1945 and postmarked April 17. 10 pm, 1945:

My Darling Wife

Just a few lines hope you are all well and feeling fine tonight. for my self I am doing pretty good at this time. I dont know much to write. I havent got any mail from you in the last two days. I git my mail like you do all in one bunch ever two are three days. Darling I sure would like to see you and Roger and all the rest. I sure hope it wont be as long as it have been before I will be seeing you all. you was telling me about all the people in Hamilton last Sat. I bet it was a sight. I wish I could have been with you we would have had a big time watching them marching around ha. I know you had some fun out of it. Darling be good.

I love you only – Love & kisses, James

This next letter from dad to mother was a long one and in it he made observations about how the death of his brother affected him. He also reflected on the negative impact that war had on humanity and he also mentioned the sad passing of Franklin D. Roosevelt. It was a deep and meaningful letter and I believe the last one he wrote before being shipped back to the states. It was dated April 13, 1945 and postmarked April 15, 11:30 pm, 1945:

Dear Darling Wife,

I recived you very sweet letter tonight sure was proud to hear from you as I havent got a letter in the last few days. proud you all are well and doing fine for my self I am doing pretty good at this time, all except my ankle. I have lots of pain with it yet special when I walk on it a lot. All the swelling havent gone out of it yet. I am hoping some day it will be OK, but I am afraid I will always have some trouble with it. I sure hope my kidneys and back git OK. I am taking a treatment for that every day now and also my ankle.

I got two letters from Alma and one from mama they was all doing OK. mama said they spent last sunday with Alma, and went to a sanging sunday afternoon. I will never forgit all the sangings they had around Hamilton when the CC Camp was there. I wish I was back in the camp and it was still there. We had lots of fun back in thoes good old days dident we sweet? do you remember all that good ham I use to fix for you when you was sick? I wish I had some ham like that now dont you and you could fix it for me, Darling. I would give anything to be at home with you and Roger. we are just the right age to enjoy life now, still young and full of fun. Sweet dont think because I have got all bumbed up that I just want to lay around, not me sweet. I might not be able to git around as good as I use to, but I can still show you a good time. I still have the spirit, you know you use to tell me to snap out of it and have some life about me. Sweet you said for me not to worry to much about Robert and things. I try not to but I cant help it sometimes, the way he had to go, and all he had to go through with before he got killed. War is something History cant explain, things that happen in battle you coulden never make people belive. It sure was bad about our President but when your time comes it dont mater who you are you are going, the Lord knows best, no one knows how they will die or when.

Sweet I guess I had better stop and go to bed. Darling I love you true with all my heart, tell Roger to be a good boy and I will bring him some thing when I come home. good night Darling – all my Love and sweet kisses, James

The previous letter of dad to mother dated Friday, April 13, 1945, was the last letter that I found from him until May 3, 1945. Dad was being shipped back to the states and obviously did not arrive until that date. He was transferred to Foster General Hospital in Jackson, Mississippi and did not get to see mother until much later. If he wrote letters to mother while on the ship coming back to the states, I do not have them. Many of mother's letters to him during that period were postmarked Returned, so I assume if he wrote letters to her that they were never delivered.

Dad mentioned in his letters to mother while he was in the hospital in Bristol, England that he received many letters from her that I do not have either and I do not know what happened to them. He may have lost or misplaced them during the confusion of being shipped back. (Note: I later found these letters and included them in Chapter Eight.)

I do have letters that mother wrote to dad beginning on April 7 1945 and ending on April 29, 1945. I will include them here before moving on to the next chapter on Foster General Hospital. I found two letters from mother that had no envelopes that were dated April 4 and April 5, 1945. I will include them beginning with the one from April 4:

Dear Sweetheart,

I hope you are feeling fine today. We are.

Mamma & I washed today. Well it seems that we may have lights eventually.

They have started it at least, step by step.

They have finally hooked the wire to the house and all we like now is for Mr. Mowyer to turn on the electricity. I suppose he will be down soon.

I kept pestering them until they had to do something.

Lorenzie Nickels put the switch box and meter up for me.

Roger is helping Herbert and Horrice put up a chicken house.

(I have included scans of photos of my Uncle Horrice Edward Palmer, my mother's youngest brother on the previous page, from about the period that this letter was written in 1945,)

Iva Lodens daddy's house burned down last night at 12:30. I really am sorry for them, as they didn't save a thing.

Harold Ballard is back in N.Y. now. You know I told you that he had been seriously wounded. His dad is going to see him.

I know he is so glad to be back in the States.

I'll be so happy when all of you boys are back in the States and this war is over.

I didn't get a letter from you today, but got one yesterday.

Take care of yourself sweet. I love you.

Love & Kisses Elizabeth

Here is the other letter from April 5, 1945:

Hi Sweet,

Well, we're all feeling fine and in good spirits today, as the power has been turned on and everything works fine.

Your wiring was just right. The radio, refrigerator & Iron works fine, as I have tryed them all today.

I'm so glad. I just wish you were here to enjoy it too.

Sweet, you remember tieing the light Cord around the bulb in the living room. I untied it for the first time today. I suppose you made a wish on it didn't you?

I got two letters from you today and enjoyed them so much. Roger was very proud of his letters too. He said he hoped you can hurry and send the airplane to him.

I got another letter from Mrs. Frode Jenson today. She says her husband is back on the front.

He sent me a picture of herself, husband and three children (I could not find this picture.). I enjoy writing her very much.

Sugar I saw that show "Home in Indiana" too, and enjoyed it immensely. It also reminded me of you and I back in the good old Courting days. We always had such a good time.

You said something about working Graveyard shift in Childersburg. Gee! I wish you were back, of course I hope you won't ever have to work graveyard any more as it is so hard on you, although we had a good time then didn't we?

Be sweet and be careful.

I love you only, Elizabeth

This letter from mother was dated April 7, 1945 and postmarked April 8, 9:30 am, 1945:

Dear Sweetheart,

How are you? We are all fine.

Today is Saturday, and there really was a crowd in town.

I saw Hershel King. He is home on furlough. He is in Field Artillery.

You know who I'm talking about. He is the fella who runs Kings Store here.

He was asking about you. Said to tell you Hello and he hopes you will soon be O.K. and back home again.

I also saw Leona and Ray Irvin. They are the same ole kids.

Roger went with me. Everyone says he is so cute. Of course we knew that didn't we sweet?

They say he is just another Little James Brown.

Boy! it's nice to hear the Refrigerator hum again. It works fine. I'm so happy that it isn't ruined.

The car still shines like always. Everyone wants to buy it. But of course I'll never sell it, ha! I want it to be here for you when you're home again. I don't know but I suppose I'm kinda funny about selling things. If I had sold the Refrigerator we would need it now. The same about the radio and iron.

I like to wait as long as I can before I sell. That's me O.K., isn't it? ha!

Be real sweet and I am always,

All my Love "Liz"

This next group of letters from mother are the last ones she wrote to dad while he was in the hospital in England. In fact, the last few were marked Returned as dad had been released and shipped back to the states. I will include all the ones that I deem pertinent to the communication between them. This letter was dated April 8, 1945:

Hello Sweetheart,

I was so happy when I got your two letters today.

I also noticed that you are a pfc. Doing pretty good eh! You didn't tell me in your letter but I saw it on your address.

Sweet, I didn't quite understand what you said about "you might send for me to come stay with you.".

I hope it is what I think it might be that you are coming back to the States Gee! would I be happy if that were only true.

No, sweet I'll not move to B'ham or anywhere.

I'll be right here waiting for you to come home.

I just meant that I would move to B'ham if they didn't hook the electricity on, but now that our things are all hooked up again, I'm staying here until you come home of course, and then I'll go wherever you do.

Roger and I went to church today. It has been a very nice day.

Sweet be careful with that ankle. You said it was giving you trouble.

The war news sounds good now. I hope it will soon be over. Surely it won't last very much longer.

Our Little Radio is still the best one out ha! You know I always wanted to keep it instead of getting another one ha!

Be good. All my Love & Kisses Always – Elizabeth

P.S. Anytime you get ready to send for me, I'll be ready to come.

It is easy to follow these letters from mother as they usually follow those that she had received from dad and were her responses to his letters. I have tried to include those letters from dad before these from her so that a communication may be established between them.

This letter from mother was written the next day and was dated April 9, 1945 with a postmark of April 10, 9:30 am, 1945:

Hi Sweet,

Hope you are feeling good – we are fine.

I worked today. Had a rather busy day as it is court week.

Roger is fine. He asked this morning when he awoke "Is Daddy In there>" He must have dreamed you were home. He looked disappointed when he found you weren't here.

I hope you will soon be home.

Harold Ballard is back in Atlanta Hospital.

Emma & Shelby are going to see him. I know he really is happy to be back in the states.

I hope I get some more mail from you tomorrow. I didn't get any today.

The days are so long when I don't hear from you.

Gee! If I just had you back here. I would be the happiest person on earth.

Sweet, I'm going to Illinois with Iva next week. She gets a vacation from the Bank and wants me to go meet her parents-in-law. I think I would enjoy the trip lots as I've always wanted to see Chicago.

We won't be gone over a week. So Momma will forward all my letters & I'll write you every day.

Momma will keep Roger.

I love you Love & Kisses Elizabeth

This next letter from mother to dad was written April 11, 1945 and postmarked April 12. 9:30 am, 1945:

Hi Sweet,

I hope you are still feeling O.K. I haven't heard from you in three days. Just hope I'll get some mail from you tomorrow.

I worked some in the garden today, not enough to hurt me though as I don't like garden work ha!

I got a letter from Ella Mae today, Jim's defferment is up she said. She is worrying that he may have to go into the Army.

Herbert drained the anti freeze from the car yesterday. It is warm here now.

I think I am going to the show tonight the name of it is "Laura".

Sweet, I hope you will be coming home soon. I would give anything if you could come back to the States, then I could go stay with you.

Roger is fine, He has been helping plant the garden.

I got a letter from your Mom today. She said Eloise was down there last weekend.

Take care of your self. I love you.

All my Love, Always Elizabeth

This letter from mother finds her relieved to have gotten letters from dad indicating that she might be seeing him soon. It was dated April 12, 1945 and postmarked April 13, 9:30 am, 1945:

Dear Sweetheart,

Gee, I was so happy when I got your letters today telling me that you may see me before long.

I'll go to see you just as soon as you're back in the States. I hope that won't be very long.

That is just the news that I've been waiting to hear so long.

I told Roger about it and he is so thrilled.

I got a letter from Mary today. She says she hears from Tucker often. He is a P.F.C. too.

Sweet, I'll stop now. I'll be looking forward to seeing you soon.

All my Love always, Elizabeth

This letter was from mother to dad was dated April 13, 1945 and marked Returned. So, dad never got this letter. He probably had left the hospital and was on his way back to the states:

Dearest Sweetheart,

How are you? We are O.K. I didn't get a letter from you today.

Gee! I'm just happy that you will soon be back home. You said in a letter yesterday that you would probably be leaving the hospital any time.

I'll be ready to come and see you just as soon as you get back to the States. I'm hoping that won't be very long.

I'll be happy to see you.

Roger says he wants you to fix his toys up when you get back, as he has just about torn them up.

I hope I get some mail from you tomorrow.

Be Careful – I love you, Elizabeth

This letter finds mother in Birmingham where she is about to leave for a trip to Illinois with her sister Iva. It was dated B-ham, Ala 4-14-45 and postmarked April 15, 9 pm, 1945:

Dear Sweetheart,

I'm here with Iva. We went to the show and are just back. It was very good. We are planning to leave Monday morning on our trip to Gerry's mother & Dads.

Sweet, I hope it won't be long now until you're back here in the states and I can be going to see you.

I'll be so happy to see you, in fact I can hardly wait.

I left Roger & all fine.

Mamma will forward all my mail to me.

Continue writing me to Hamilton as I'll only be gone a week or so.

Be sweet and take care of yourself. I'll be looking forward to seeing you real soon.

All my Love Always Elizabeth

The following letter was a V-Mail from mother dated 4-16-45 and postmarked April 23, 1945 and was marked Returned. Again, I am assuming this was because dad had left the English hospital and was on his way back to the states:

My Dearest,

Iva and I are now here in the train station. We'll be leaving for Ill in a half hour or so.

I hope you are O.K. and will soon be back home.

Mamma will send my letters from you to me. I'll write you every day. Will be back in Hamilton soon, and will be ready to go stay with you as soon as you're back.

I left Roger fine. Hope you have gotten the pictures I sent.

All my Love – Eliz

The next V-Mail finds mother and Iva on the train headed to Illinois. Her V-Mail to dad was dated the same day as the previous one, 4-16-45 and was postmarked April 24, 1945, and marked Returned:

Hi Sweetheart.

I'm on the train somewhere in Kentucky. I have enjoyed the trip very much.

I hope you can read this. I can't write very well while riding. It won't be very long until we'll be to Gerry's mother & Dads.

You said you would be leaving the Hospital any time. I hope you'll be back soon.

Bye now all my Love, Elizabeth

The next letter from mother to dad finds her having arrived at Gerry's parents in Illinois. This letter was dated April 17, 1945 and postmarked April 18, 3 pm, 1945 and marked Returned. The letter was written on stationery from the Harrison Hotel which advertised itself as Chicago's newest hotel. Mother and Aunt Iva spent the night there as they were not able to get a train out the day they arrived in Chicago:

Hello Dear,

Well, we are here now with Gerry's Mom & Dad.

We are having a nice time. His parents are very nice.

This is a picture of the Hotel where we stayed last night. We couldn't get a train out, so we had to stay over until the morning.

We had a nice trip up. Came on the streamliner "The City of Miami".

I hope to get a letter from you tomorrow certainly are missing them very much.

Hope you'll be back in the states by the time I get back. I will be happy to see you. I'll be able to see you just as soon as you get to the Hospital in which you will stay.

Sugar, be sweet – I love you only.

All my Love, Elizabeth

Mother's letters about her trip to Illinois are of importance I think because they expand upon the knowledge of what was occurring in her life and in the lives of those around her. Therefore, I will include these letters in the order that she wrote them. She was visiting her sister Iva's in laws in Alpha, Illinois. The first letter was dated April 18, 1945 and was postmarked Alpha, Illinois, April 19, 3 pm, 1945. As was the case with most of her previous letters to dad this one was also marked Returned:

Hi Sweetheart,

How are you? We are fine – Are having a nice time.

Iva & I enjoyed being in Chicago. We didn't get lost ha! Everything is so much different from the South.

The land is so level. They live on a very beautiful farm.

We went to town today, It is just about the size of H'ton, but different of course.

Gee! I'm hoping to go see you when I get home.

I just hope you'll be back in the States by then.

It really is Cold here. It was so hot when we left home & when we got out in Chicago we almost froze. There was ice last night.

I hope it will soon be warmer as it is kinda tough when you're accustomed to hot weather.

Be Careful. I love you All my Love, Elizabeth

This letter from mother was also written from Alpha, Illinois and was dated 4 – 20 – 45 and postmarked Alpha, Illinois, April 21, 3 pm, 1945. It was not marked Returned but had to be as mother had it with all the rest of the returned letters:

My Dearest,

I was so thrilled this morning when I got your six letters.

I'm so happy that you are doing fine and gaining weight. I know you look good would give anything if I could see you.

I am glad you liked the pictures. Sweet I'm not so fat I have lost two pounds and only weigh 130 lbs now, just about the same I weighed when you were home.

I'm glad you got your candy, also what Harry & Margaret sent you.

We went to town today and got some ice cream ha!

We also went to a women's Club meeting with Mrs. Gamel, they served Jello, cookies etc. We enjoyed it lots.

The weather is some what warmer now. I hope it will stay that way.

I really do like that picture of Roger too, he is such a cute thing in his little suit.

I miss him lots but wanted to make this trip in order to see different states. We came through five, I think, Ala, Miss, Tenn, Kentucky & Ill. We also saw Iowa. So that adds a few more to my list, as I had only been in Ala, Miss, & Fla.

Be sweet & write me. I love you Always, Elizabeth. P.S. I'll write Tucker

Here is another letter written to dad from mother on the same day from Alpha, Illinois. It was dated 4 – 20 – 45. I can only assume it was also returned:

Hello Dear,

We're still here in Ill. Are having a nice time. We went to the show last night in Moline, Ill. We were almost in the state of Iowa too. It was just across the river from where we were. Well, at least I can say I saw Iowa.

We have met several of Gerry's Aunts. They are all very friendly.

I really hope to get some mail from you today, as I'm anxious to know if you have left the Hospital yet.

I hope you'll be back in the states by the time I get home & I can go to see you.

If you're coming back soon, you may not get all my letters (That is why many of these letters were stamped Returned.) but I'm writing you every day anyway.

It really is cold here. We brought our winter clothes along and it is a good thing too, I suppose.

It was Summer back home when we left.

I'll be glad to get back home to see Roger as I miss him so much.

I love you only Love & Kisses Elizabeth

Another letter from Alpha, Illinois was Returned on April 23, 3 pm, 1945. Mother dated the letter 4 – 22 – 45:

My Dearest,

I hope you are feeling fine today. We are fine. I suppose you went to church too.

We went to the Presbyterian Church today, it was quite a bit different from other churches.

We also took some pictures today, I hope they will be good.

It is still rather cool here.

We'll be going back home Saturday.

Have enjoyed being here a lot, just wish you could have been with us.

I suppose Roger is waiting to see me. I really will be glad to see him too.

I'm still hoping that you will come back to the states. I was so happy after you wrote me that you would probably be home soon.

I really do hope you will get to come. I would be the happiest person on earth.

I think maybe this old war will be over before long.

What do you think of our new president Truman? I think he is going to be O.K.

It really was a bad time for Roosevelt to die. I was sorry to hear about it.

We haven't heard from Arthur in quite a while. I hope he is O.K.

Iva still hears from Gerry often.

I hope to get some more mail from you tomorrow.

Sugar, I'm sending you some lilac flowers that I've been wearing in my hair, but suppose they will be dead when you get them.

I Love you always Love & kisses Elizabeth

Here is a V-Mail from mother to dad dated April 24. 1945. It was postmarked April 30, 1945. I suppose it was Returned like the others. At this point mother is still getting letters from dad as she states she had gotten four from him in this V-Mail:

My Dearest,

I was happy to get your four letters yesterday. Sorry that your ankle keeps giving you pain. Sweet, you said that you supposed you would always have trouble with it, don't worry about that, for I think it is going to be O.K. when you get home, especially, then I can take care of you. I'll be so happy when you do get home, only hope it will be soon.

Glad you liked the pictures. Would love to see your frame.

We ate supper at one of Gerry's Aunts last night. She really served a nice meal. Will write more this afternoon.

All my Love, Elizabeth

This letter from mother to dad came two days later and was dated April 26, 1945. I could not read the postmark, but ii was marked Returned to Fletcher General Hospital. That was the hospital in Jackson, Mississippi that dad was transferred to in the states. Dad left England April 13, 1945 so it must have taken about two weeks to cross over:

Hi Sweetheart,

We have just gotten back from visiting another one of Gerry's aunts. Had a nice time, and a swell dinner.

We saw a cute show last night. "Love in a Harem" with Bud Abbott and Lou Costello.

It is still very cold here. It will be quite a change, I suppose, when we get back in Alabama Sunday, as it is so hot there.

I hope you are still doing O.K. Would give anything to see you.

Hope you will be coming home soon.

I haven't had any mail from you in two days. I'll probably have several waiting for me when I get home

I'll stop as I don't know very much to write.

Be careful. I love you.

Love & Kisses Elizabeth

This next letter from mother to dad was dated April 28, 1945. It was postmarked April 30, 2 pm, 1945 and marked Returned to Fletcher General Hospital as the previous one was:

Hello Dear,

We are on our way back home now, only our train is late and we're having to wait for it. We'll spend the night in Chicago and leave in the morning at 8:00 for B'ham.

We are now here in the Hospital with Mrs, Gamel. Her daddy is being operated on.

I'll be glad to get started as we have a long way to go.

We'll get home Sunday night. Have had a very nice trip.

I hope I have some letters from you when I get home.

It is still cold and looks as if it might rain too.

I hope that you are feeling O.K. and that your ankle isn't still bothering you. I'm hoping that you will be back soon.

All my Love, Always Liz

This letter from mother to dad brings the welcome and long-awaited news that the war with Germany has ended. It was dated April 28, 1945 and postmarked April 30, 2 pm, 1945. It was marked Returned to Fletcher General Hospital in Jackson, Mississippi:

Hi Sweetheart,

Well, we're back again in our Hotel room. We'll leave for Birmingham tomorrow at 8:00 am.

The headline of the Chicago Sun Times said "Germany Quits" (Mother saved that newspaper and I will include a scan of that newspaper headline at the end of this letter.) I really hope it is true but of course I can hardly believe it.

I've really had a nice vacation – just wish you could have been with us. Maybe it won't be long now until you will be home. I hope it won't.

I'll stop now and go to bed. Good night Dear. All my Love Elizabeth

This next letter from mother states that the headline "Germany Quits" was just a rumor. Germany surrendered unconditionally to the Allies in Reims, France ending World War II in Europe on May 7, 1945. Mother was on her way back to Alabama on the train as she wrote this letter the next day on April 29, 1945. It was postmarked April 29, 1945 and Returned to Fletcher General Hospital:

Hello Dear,

We are about eight hours from home now I suppose.

We are still in Ill. I think. It is beginning to get hilly again so I think we are nearing Kentucky.

I'll be glad to get home to see Roger.

I bought him a commando cap & Iva bought him a dump truck. I know he will be happy to get them.

It is a rather pretty day out but I suppose it is cold.

We are on the Streamliner train "City of Miami" is the name. It is really much more comfortable than riding on the bus.

I saw the paper again today and that was a rumor about Germany surrendering. I was afraid that it would be that way. I sure hope they will surrender sometime soon though.

I hope you can read this. I don't think I can. I never could write very well & especially while riding.

There is a baby sitting behind me & it is yelling.

I hope I'll have some mail from you when I get home. I haven't had a letter from you in several days (Because he is at sea on the way back to the states.).

Hope you are still doing O.K.

I'll stop & write you more later.

All my Love, Elizabeth

There was about a month-long period that I had no letters from dad or mother from late April to mid May 1945. I believe this was the time that dad left the hospital in Bristol, England and was shipped back to the states to a hospital in Jackson, Mississippi. I will pick back up with their letters in Chapter Nine, entitled "Letters Written after Dad's Return to the States". Before I return to their letters though, I want to include several letters that were written to both mother and dad from relatives and friends during the time dad was in training and later when he was overseas and in the hospital in Bristol, England. I will Include these in Chapter Seven, "Letters of Relatives and Friends Received Before and During Overseas Duty".

$$Chapter\ Seven$$

Letters from Relatives and Friends Received before and During Overseas Duty

Dad received many letters from relatives and friends as did mother during the time that he was in the service. I have already included a number of these in previous chapters but the ones to be included now are those written later just before and during the time he was shipped overseas and was in an English hospital for four months,

The first letters to be included were from my Uncle Gerry Gamel who was my Aunt Iva Palmer Gamel's husband. This first V-Mail from Uncle Gerry was dated Sunday, December 3, 1944:

Dear James,

I received a letter from Eliz and Roger yesterday containing your address. I see you didn't stay at Fort Meade long. Anyway, I believe you are lucky in getting a New York APO number as I think the European War will be over long before the Pacific War is. Eliz is fine and so is Roger (who wrote me a letter of his own!!) I hear from Iva every day, and she is getting along fine in the apartment with Polly.

I got here the 19th of Nov. and would have shipped out by now with my Will Rogers Field buddies, but I was in the hospital with a bad cold when the shipment came up. Then after I got out, the dentist pulled 4 teeth, and I'm being held up now because of that. Right now I'm not even in a casual squadron because the dentist won't release me. But as soon as I'm fixed up, I believe I'll be on my way too within a few days.

This place is high and mountainous & cold. I don't like it a bit here & will be glad to ship out. I'll send you my APO number as soon as I know it through Elizabeth. Hope you are doing alright at your new station. Write me soon & best of luck.

Sincerely, Gerry

This is a second V-Mail from Uncle Gerry dated January 5, 1945:

Dear James

Got a letter from Eliz yesterday saying you had landed in southern France near Marseilles. That was good news, as I was wondering if you had landed in Belgium during the big German push up there just before Christmas (That was exactly where dad wound up after General Patton's 3rd Army marched across France in the bitter cold and arrived there just after Christmas in 1944,).Now that you have landed and know a little bit more about the setup you will be better prepared towards taking care of yourself (Nothing could have been further from the truth as dad was wounded and almost killed just a few days before Uncle Gerry's letter was written.).

Eliz and Roger are fine and so are the rest of the folks in Hamilton. I called Iva the other day and talked to her. Harry and Margaret were there when I called. He is in Texas, but I doubt that he will be there very long as that field is the shipping and receiving center for his AAG Group.

I am still awaiting my orders. Have no idea when they will come, although I did get a readiness order about two weeks ago. Right now I have been put on a typewriter because I can ride one of those things pretty well. It is a lot better working inside where it is warm than the cold outdoors. The permanent party men are all being shipped out one by one to the Infantry or MP's, So they are temporarily replacing them with us arrivals. And I might add that shift hasn't hurt this place a bit.

The weather has turned warm for once today. It's been snow and cold since Christmas. Been to Salt Lake City only a few times. It's a dull town and not much doing for a married man. About the only items of sight seeing interest are the statehouse and the Mormon Temple. The Salt Lake is some 16 miles from town. It looks right next to it on the map. Seems like its drying up at the rate of a mile a year. And the salt mines are on the other side. The only beautiful sights are the Rockies which rise up on both sides of the valley. Well that's about all I have room for right now, Write when you have time,

Sincerely, Gerry

This third correspondence from Uncle Gerry came much later, well after dad has returned from overseas and had been discharged, I chose to include it here as it mentions the war finally being over. It was a letter written on the back of a card addressed to Master Roger Brown and was dated Friday, August 24, 1945:

Dear Eliz & James,

I received your letter with the pix a few days ago. Sure was glad to get them. James sure looks good & Roger is cute as the dickens. Yes, I'm in Okinawa, but it is a lot better than Guam because the climate is a lot better with a cool breeze – No palm trees or tropical vegetation at all.

Sure is good about the war being over! They put up quite a display when the Japs asked to surrender.

Don't know when we'll start back – or if we will. One thing sure, they haven't a hold on us very long with the war over. I'd give anything to get back to Iva now. Hear from her every day, but you know how it is. Will write soon again & you do the same.

Gerry

The previous letter from Uncle Gerry was on the back of a card that he sent to Roger which was dated August 24, 1945. The following is the note written on the card to Roger:

Dear Roger,

I received your letter with the swell pictures of you and your daddy. Thank you for sending them. You must have grown a lot since I've seen you. I hope I'll see you again soon now that the Japs are finished, I'll bring your Aunt with me when I visit you. Love from your Uncle Gerry

The following letters are from relatives writing to dad or to mother. They are not necessarily in chronological order. The first letter is from "Mammy", Mary Dizenia Palmer, my great grandmother, and my mother's grandmother. It was written to my mother January 29, 1945. Mammy has just found out that my dad had been wounded.

Dear Sis and Roger

I was glad to hear from you. Yes I heard about James Was awfaly sorry to hear it I was thankful to that it wasent no wore (worse) I hope they will send him back on this side Kate Greens man is back on this side going in a rolling chair, he hasent got to com home yet thanks (thinks) he will soon tell Roger I tryed to com home before he left thoe I missed the Buss and couldent get hear lets all pray the lord will take care of James and all the other Boys.

Love Dizenia

Sis I am sending you a coppy of the letter my sister got from the man that was with Wallace when he died. Roberts mother might like to read it – you can send it back to me or bring it when you come I got a Girl to tike (type) it off for me.

There was another letter I found from Mammy or Dizenia Palmer written to dad which was dated about a month and a half later, on March 11, 1945, Hamilton, Alabama and postmarked March 12, 9:30 am, 1945:

Dear James

I shure was glad to get a letter from you and heare you was feeling so well. Wee ar all well except colds. James you must take good care of your self and not walk too soon it might ruin your ankle for ever maby you will be sent back to the States Some of the Boys has bin sent back that had ben wounded I hope and pray tha will send you home Roger has just gone out he came and ate Some Jelly he sed he would be back in a minit he comes every little while he hasent for got you yet. I told him I got a letter from you and he sed let me See it mamy can I open it he wanted it in his hands. Wee hear from Hairrson and Gerry often but dont hear much from Arthur and he cant hear from home poor child I hope and pray that god will take care off all you Boys and you all get home Soon I wish I could do something for you all thr is nothing that I can do but pray to the lord to bring you all home safe and for this war to be over Well James I cant write vear well maby you can read or guess at it and write me agane and be shure

419

to take good care of that ankle and stay off it until it is well hope you get to come home soon is my prayer Write Soon love Dizenia

(Here is another scan of Mammy's photo.)

This next letter is from my Uncle Harrison Palmer, my mother's oldest brother who was in the Army Air Corp during World War Two. I have included a photo of him while he was stationed at Scott Field in Montgomery, Alabama in 1941.

The letter was dated January 25, 1945 and postmarked January 26, 1 pm, 1945. He had just learned that dad had been wounded:

Dear Liz & Roger,

We were very happy to hear from you but were terribly sorry to learn that James has been injured. I had just written to him the day before I received your letter – but wrote again as soon as I got the new address in your letter.

It is bad to think of his being wounded but we have one thing to be thankful for and that is that we know he is living and is getting the best medical attention possible. The army has some very good hospitals and the best of doctors. Then too, as long as he is there in the hospital we at least have the satisfaction of knowing that he isn't out on the battlefront. Yes, let us be thankful that he is no worse than he is.

And Liz, don't worry about him now, because I know he is being given the best treatment that medical science can give him. It is very comforting indeed to know this. What they are doing for him there in the hospital is worth far more to him now than all the worrying you or I can do. I'm sure he is going to be all right now. I worried about him before I heard he was in the hospital – but now I don't worry. I am just thankful to the Good Lord that he is where he is instead of out there on the frozen battlefront. I'm sure in a few weeks he'll be a new man again and as good as ever. Those army doctors are the best and have performed many miracles of medicine.

How are you and little Roger? Be sure to write us all about yourselves. Tell Roger his uncle "Harry" says "hello" to him.

Margaret and I are enjoying Texas quite a lot and will probably be here another month before I leave.

Write soon and Remember us to all our friends.

Best of Luck and Lots of Love, Harry

The next group of letters was from my Uncle Joseph Arthur Palmer, my mother's second oldest brother, who was in the Navy during World War Two. I have included them in chronological sequence and the first one was dated April 18, 1945, U.S.S. Randolph:

My Dearest Sister,

I received your letter and was indeed very happy to hear from you, and to hear all family is ok.

Its nice that you can hear from James every day and I know he must have been very much happy to be able to meet with his brother Curtis. I surely wish I could meet up with him.

Yes I'm glad that the men have finally decided to wire the house. I know you will be happy that now you can use your things again, and now we can have a big party when we come home again, I mean James and the rest of us. I guess it will be quite some time before I will be able to come home.

I have already saw both those movies before you (I'm not sure which movies he was talking about.).

That sure was a nice present James sent you and I just bet those pearls are lovely.

Yes, I want you to send me some of those pictures when you get them. You see I have a picture album and I want my family to help me fill it. I would like to have some pictures of all of you.

Iva tells me you are going to spend her vacation with her in Ill – guess you will enjoy yourself. After all it is nice to get out and stir around not just stay pin in all the time.

Well Eliz this is all for now, but don't do like me, ans soon. Your Brother Joe.

P.S. Tell Mom hello and to write – Joe Joseph A. Palmer – S/2 division

The second letter from Uncle Arthur was dated Somewhere at Sea, 28 May 1945 and postmarked May 31, 1945, Randolph:

My Dearest Sister & Roger

It was really swell hearing from you again. Just keep up the good work and I shall write often likewise.

I know you and Iva must have had a wonderful time in Ill. As you say Mrs. Gamel was so nice to you. it must have been a pleasure trip as well as a venture as it was your first long trip.

It was nice meeting Gatman Green in Chicago as he was someone you know. Did you ride the same train to Birmingham with him.

Say, what has my two sisters doing now, flirting with the Sailors I hear. You had better watch out all Sailors are Wolfs. Laying all jokes aside it was nice of them that they should offer you the seats and that they behaved so nicely.

Yes, I received the pictures of you and Roger and thanks a million, how about sending me some more as I am still working on my picture album "thanks"

Thanks a lot for the birthday card it was really nice and as for the news which was wrote on the back I just hope I am one of the lucky Seniors that received their diplomas.

It was certainly good news to hear that James is getting to come home. I know you are one of the happiest women on earth now that you will be able to go see him again.

Well Eliz answer real soon and give my love to the rest of the family. Tell James I said hello and get well soon. I am going to write him again when he sends me his address.

Love Arthur

Here is a third letter from Uncle Arthur to mother. It was dated Somewhere on the lonely Sea 5 June 1945 Randolph:

My Darling Sister,

I was so very happy to have received your wonderful letter. The only trouble with your letters are I don't receive enough of them.

I also received a letter from Iva with a picture of you and her taken while in Ill, they surely were nice. you will split your sides when you hear what one of my pals had to say about yours. I was sitting here looking at them, getting ready to write you, when he comes walking in and takes a look at your picture, he says, boy I could go for that baby, boy is she a nice kid how old is she 17. I laughed and show him the picture of Roger, told him you were 23 he blushed and said he could not believe it he said you looked so young and said your husband surly must feel proud to have such a lovely girl for his wife. I told him if he only knew. They really were nice pictures.

I am trying to get mom to have a nice picture made for me. (I included that photo of her earlier.) I also would like some more from you As I am still working on my picture album.

It was swell news to hear that James is getting to come home for a while, I would surly like to be there to see him when he arrives. maybe I'll get to come home someday, just when I don't know.

Well sis I will write more when I have time – We just had mail call today and I have quite a few letters to answer.

Ans soon my love always Arthur

This next letter from Uncle Arthur came three months later. There may have been others, but I could not locate any. This one was dated 21 September 1945:

My Darling Sister,

Thanks for the Marion County paper. I surly did enjoy reading it. I will write this although I haven't heard from you in quite some time.

Well I guess by now you have already heard the good news about my being in Pearl Harbor. Yes, I am now in hopes to be in route to the states. Don't get your hopes all up because anything can happen in the Navy. As far as we know now we are suppose to be in the states for Navy Day. Lets all keep our fingers crossed and maybe it will come to pass.

I bet you are really happy now that you can spend as much time with James, I'm glad for you because he need you to help him out in different ways. I guess that Roger misses you. (Mother was in Miami Beach, Florida with dad at this time on a vacation that the Army provided for the troops and their wives.). The boys will keep him so busy that he will forget for awhile.

(I have a photo of mother and dad at Miami
Beach that I will include here,)

Tell James hello for me and that I would like to hear from
him some time. I wrote him some time ago and the other
day I got the letter back. It was sent to the wrong address.

I guess this is all that I can think of to write as I have some
time to spend on writing some other letters. I hope you
want mind me making this a short letter.

Thanks I know you wouldn't. All my love to a wonderful
sister, Arthur

(Here is a scan of Uncle Arthur in the early 1940's.)

I will continue with including letters from other relatives that were written to my dad while he was in the hospital in Bristol, England. This was a letter from Aunt Rhoda Boyett who was Cora Lee Palmer's (my mother's mother) sister. She wrote this letter to dad on January 30, 1945 and included a get-well card with it:

Dear James,

how are you by now I hope you are doing fine sure sorry to hear you was wounded but glad it wasn't any worse. I just hope and pray the Lord will bring you through safe. I have a boy some where not so far from you. I haven't heard from him in over 2 weeks. Surely hope he is O.K. I am just praying this war will soon be over and you all can come home. I had a letter from Harland he was O.K. but awful homesick. it will be 4 year in July since he left home and just been home once since.

I will send you Stanley's address

Pvt. Stanley Boyett 34809633 314th Inf.
Co. E A.P,O. 79 % Post Master New York N.Y.

I hope you see him I know he would be glad. You may know Calvin Abercrumbee he was buried today Also Talmage Reel. Just thought would write a few lines to let you know I thought of you Boys over there and praying for your return. Carmel would write but he is at the saw mill hope I haven't worried you with this May the Lord watch over you and all the other boys over there is my prayer.

Your friend

Rhoda Boyett

Dad was always close to mother's mother, Cora Lee Palmer. This letter from her to him was dated Friday night with a postmark of February 3, 9:30 am. 1945, Hamilton, Alabama:

Dear James,

I received your letter and was proud to get a letter from you.

I have already written you twice since you got hurt but don't guess you have received them yet.

I am so lonesome tonite sitting here by myself. Elizabeth and Roger is still in Opelika she is with your mother and Dad.

I hope you or lots better now. yes James, the lord was with you and I am so thankful he spared your life the lord takes care of his people. he can help you in your sufferings and troubles. you are so far away we cant be with you – but put your trust in the lord and he will always be with you. I pray you soon get well and get to come back home.

Arthur and Gerry is gone over seas. I am so worried about them. Harry is still in Texas.

We sure are having some cold weather now but I stay out of it. I havent been sick any this winter. I am afraid you want know me when you get back. I am getting so fat I cant wear hardly any of my clothes.

Herbert Horrice Edward and I all went to the show last nite. I didn't like it much just went to keep from staying by myself.

Remember James you are in our thoughts ever day. And I'm praying if it's the lords will to bring you back to your love ones.

I'll stop now. good night love mother write when you feel like it.

The next letter is a very colorful one with dad's uncle including humorous details about a fishing trip they once went on together. It was from dad's Uncle Arthur Owsley, his mother's brother. The letter was dated February 4, 1945, Opelika, Alabama:

P.V.T. James G. Brown Dear Neph-

will answer you welcom letter we got Saturday P.M. Sure was glad to heire from you. But sorry to heire that you was in hospitel. But take it Easy Boy Dont worry you will soone Be ok Agin. Thin nurses over theair Can't Kill A good man Just put your Fatin (Faith) in good (God) he is your Best Friend. This War Cant last always you no. Herman is over theair in it sum where May god Be with him. All that is in it Be Brought to a Speedy Victory so we All can Be Back home togher (together) Agin listen As you Siad In your letter about that Fishing Trip We Taken last Sumer – Well we will take it Agin Where we can catch Sunething Besige (besides) Cold an Muskiters Bites Ho Ho I injoryed (enjoyed) Every minute Except the Time I was fighting gallnipers (gall mites, 4 legged mites) an Scratching Red Bugs Ho Ho. Will Boy that time will come Agin Soon. So we all will be Reddy when you come home. Tell Curtis to write to me I would like to heire from I hope he can Be with us. listen Gordon and Bettie (dad's dad and mother) is Doining Fine. We told Alma About getting a letter from you. So I will halft To Close As newes is shorte But love an Menery (memory) is long.

So Take Care of your self an Dont worry about eanny thing. Just By good Answer soon to your uncle Arthur Owsley

By By with love & Best Wishes.

Although I could not decipher all of this next letter, I will include it also. It was from Uncle R.L. Owsley, another of dad's mother's brothers. I could not find a date on it, but it was probably written around February of 1945 as well:

Nefue how are you today. I am not feeling so good. Wife and kids spent last Sunday with Betie an Gordon Saw you wife in town Saturday all is well. Write us let me know how you are getting on tell Curtis to write me dont no his address, so soon to – you'll (I could not decipher the rest of this letter.)

Uncle R.L. Owsley

This is yet another letter to dad from a third Owsley brother, his uncle, Tom Owsley, which was dated February 5, 1945:

Mr. James C. (should be G,) Brown Opelika, Ala.

My Dere Nefew I will try to ancer you most welcome letter I recived I was more then Glade to here from you this Lines (Finds) us all sick with Bad coldes But I sure Hope that you are Better now I sure woulde Love to see you today You mother and dad ar doing all wright at present. My prays and hope you and the rest of the boys over their an I hope that By Allmighte Power of God an his will that the war will soon Be over nor their wont Be Any more war. (I think he means: My prayers and hopes are with you and the rest of the boys over there and I hope by the Almighty Power of God and his will that the war will soon be over and that there won't be any more war.) we ar having a Hard time over here we ar working Every day an evening Every Thing on the Home front that we can to Help you Boys and hope that God will Give you all Health an streanks (strength) to win the war.

My prays will Be for you Every day of my life.

I will close Anser real soon an a sweet Letter you deare Uncle Tom Owsley

Opelika, Ala Pepperell Branch, Box 1238 Tom Owsley

There were numerous V-Mails written to dad from his family members including his mother and dad, his sister and also relatives from my mother's side of the family.

This first V-Mail was from dad's mother and dad and addressed Mr. Gordon Brown Route #4 Opelika, Ala. It was dated January 8, 1945. At this point my grandmother had not yet found out that dad had been wounded:

Dear James,

Will try & write you a few lines to let you heare from us
we are doing veary well I guess. I dont never feel well,
hope this letter finde you well & doing alright hoping &
praying you wont have no bad luck & can soon come back
home. I got a letter from Elizabeth today she said you was
cooking – I hope you can keep that job, I dont guess is
anny good one over there. Pearl is here she come yesterday
(Pearl Owsley was my grandmother Betty Owsley Brown's
sister,) Elizabeth said her & Roger was coming in two
weeks. I sure will be glad when they come I know Roger
will have a lots to tell us when he comes. Alma & them
doing alright. I will close wishing you the best of luck
write soon. lots of love Mother & Dad

These next four V-Mails from Grandmother Brown to dad were
written a couple of months later. This one was dated March 9, 1945, Mrs.
Gordon Brown, Opelika, Alabama, Route #4:

Dear James,

Will answer your letter I received was glad to heare from
you glad you can walk sum I know you are glad to be able
to get up I sure and I know you do get tird & worried
dont worrie just trust in god he knows best for us all. he
will take care of you I think this war will soon be over. I
just hope & pray it will & you can come home soon for us
we are doing verry well I have got a cold hope this letter
finds you feeling fine, harry (Alma's son) is here to night
he come from school he will stay till Sunday I got a letter
from Curtis he said he had bin back to see you I sure am
glad he can go to see you just only wish I could go to see
you. hope it wont be long till you will be back with us all.
I got a letter from Eliz every two or three days they doing

all right. I will close for this time wishing you the best of luck write soon.

lots of love to you Mother & Dad

Here is the second V-Mail from Grandmother Brown to dad dated Mrs. G Brown Opelika Ala Route 4 March 12, 1945:

Dear James,

Just a few lines to let you heare from us we are doing alright I guess hope you are feeling fine & still improving, I havent got a letter from you in a week I got one from Eliz today she said she had got sum letters & you was doing fine. I hope you will get along alright & soon be well. I got a letter from Curtis he said he had bin back to see you & got sum money from you & for me to send Elizabeth 40.00 Your daddy put it in the bank for her. Jeff & Alma said tell you they said hello hope you would soon be well but hope you wont have to go back to the front any more.

I went to Preachin Sunday with Alma & Jeff we went home with Mary & Griff (Mayberry) for dinner. first time I bin up there sents you was here. I will stop & write to Curtis & Elizabeth. Write me soon.

With Lots of Love & best wishes Mother & Dad.

Here is Grandmother Brown's third V-Mail to dad in which she mentions she has finally gotten his letters and is responding to them. As usual she begins with Mrs. Gordon Brown Opelika Ala Route 4 March 18, 1945:

Dear James,

Will try & answer your letters sure was proud to heare
from you, but sorry to learn you was having trouble with
your side agin hope you are feeling fine now & will soon
be well as for us we are doing verry well I guess for my self
I dont never feel good. Alma & them was here today Alma
said she had got two letters from you last week. I got one
from Curtis he was OK. he said he was going back to see
you when he got his pass. I hope he did get to go. I hope
you wont have anny more trouble with your side. We are
having pretty weather now for fairm (farming) work your
daddy hadent done anny yet. I just hope & pray this war
willsoon be over now so you can come home. Maby they
will let you come home on furlough when you get better
I hope so anny.

I stop with lots of love Mother & dad.
Here is the fourth V-Mail from Grandmother Brown and after this
one there was one longer letter that I found from about three weeks later.
As before the fourth V-Mail was addressed Mrs. Gordon Brown Opelika,
Ala Route 4 March 25, 1945:

Dear James,

Will answer your letter sure was glad to heare from you
glad you can hop around hope you can soon walk for us
your daddy doing alright. I have got a cold & head ake
hope this letter finds you feeling fine. I sure will be glad
when I can see you back home where I wont have to write
& look for letters if it be the lords will, hope it wont be
long now till you all can come back. I know you was glad
to get all them letters. I dident get but one from you last
week & onefrom Curtis two from Eliz I guess Curtis has
bin back to see you by now I wish Eliz was down here with
the Car I would ride with her I hope she wont have no rack
& get heart (hurt). I dont guess she drives much hope you

will soon be back to drive. I know I will ride then, harry bin here 4 days he comes from school every week he just left to go home he was sick about all the time he was here. Alma still works.

I will stop write soon with love & best wishes Mother & dad.

The next letter from Grandmother Brown was not a V-Mail but a longer letter addressed Betty Brown Opelika Ala Rt 4 April 2, 1945:

Dear James,

Will answer your letter sure was proud to heare from you. glad you was better & could walk a little hope you will get along alright now & can soon come home to stay. for us we are doing very well I guess I got a letter from Curtis last week he said he had a bad cold. I hope he is well by now. I got one from Eliz Saturday said they was doing fine, I sure did want to send you a box of candy & cake for Easter I hope you had Plenty anny. We went up to Alma Sunday Jeff come after us Alma had a good dinner We went to the singing after dinner at union grove they live abough a mile from the church.

They had all days singing & Eloise is coming Saturday night & spend Sunday with us she is going to Alma Saturday night & come here Sunday.

I sure will be glad when Elizabeth & Roger comes back to stay with us a while I have got my garden planted your daddy havent got his crop fixt for planting he havent planted anything yet, we bin having pretty weather for the last month, your grandpa havent come back yet. I guess him & Pal will stay up there I hope so anny way I got a letter from Ola She said he was doing fine (Ola Piper was

435

Fate Brown's daughter, So grandpa Fate and Pal or Palmer Brown, his son, were staying at Ola's place.). I will stop & write to Curtis & Eliz Write soon with lots of love & best wishes Mother & dad.

Here is a scan of a photo taken of my Grandmother, Betty Brown, bottom left, her sister Pearl Owsley, bottom right, Lee Owsley, her older brother, top left and Frank Owsley, another brother, top right.

I will continue with letters written to dad from other relatives. The next letter was a V-Mail that I missed earlier from dad's brother, Curtis Brown. He addressed it as PFC William Brown (His middle name was Curtis.) and it was dated March 14, 1945 with a post mark of March 20, 1945. He gave the address information for himself as A.S.N. 14183091 1251 MP Co AUN APO 597 % PM NY NY and gave dad's address as PVT James G. Brown ASN 34837007 DET OF PAT 4134 U.S. ARMY HOSP PLANT A.P.D., #508:

Dear James,

I will drop you a few lines to let you know that I got back O.K.(He had just returned from a visit to dad at the Hospital in Bristol, England,). I'm doing fine but have a bad cold that had me feeling bad a few days but it better now. I got a letter from home sat day. Moma said she got Robert pin pocket book (I have Robert's wallet and bracelet saved at my house today. I will include a photo of it here, and bracelet from the war D,P,)

I will stop write soon – love Curtis

These next letters are letters from dad's and mother's friends from the time they were at camp Blanding, Florida when he was in training and there are also letters from others that dad was friends with after he went overseas and met while in the hospital in England.

The first letter is from PFC Frode P. Jenson Gr. Force Rep/Pas/A.P.O. B74 37589707 % U.S. Army. It was postmarked March 26, 1945 and was dated on the letter England March 24, 1945. Dad met Frode at the hospital in Bristol, England and became very good friends with him, They were both patients there:

Pal James –

I better write you a few lines as I am not busy. I have been just moving from here to there since I left the hospital. I got limited service so do not know where I am going as yet. I suppose I will land in France some day. I feel pretty good only my stomach pains once in a while. We can only get 6 hr pass so I can't go see my girl friend (Frode was evidently cheating on his wife.). I am in hopes she may come up here as I can see her for a few hrs.

I hope you are getting alone fine and will soon be going home. Hoping to see you in the States someday in the near future.

Don't do much here but detail work. Had K.P. the first day I was here and suppose I will so be due again.

Today is my wife birthday and I'm sure lonesome for her (Just don't let her find out about your girlfriend,) Next Thursday will be my birthday and I wonder where I will be by then. I hope I am able to get a pass on that day.

Hopping this fines you as it leave me – Your Pal Frode.

In God we trust and in him shall we stand,

Frode asked his wife to write to my mother and gave her address to her. My mother was glad to get her letters and wrote her back several times. I have the letters that Mrs. Frode Jenson or Irma wrote to mother, and I will include them here. The first letter from Irma Jenson to mother was dated Tyler, Minnesota, March 11, 1945 and postmarked March 12, 3;30 pm, Tyler, Minnesota:

Dear Mrs. Brown:

I got your address from my husband and he asked me to write to you. Your husband is such a blessing to him, he mentions him in nearly every letter I get. I suppose that my husband is out of the hospital as I write this. I haven't gotten any new address, but he expected to be out Mar 3 or 4. Was it "trench foot" your husband has? (No, dad was severely wounded in the ankle and hip by shrapnel from a German artillery round.)

Would enjoy hearing from you. We have three children. The oldest a girl, Mary Lou is 14. Next a boy 12, his name is Wayne, the youngest a girl, Joan she is 8. They are all in school so I work in a dry goods store, clerking to fill my days. I really have plenty to do if I didn't work, but I just can't be alone. I miss my husband so much and much work helps a lot to spend the time. It will be a year Mar 21, since my husband went into the service. Seems much longer. We have been married fifteen years, so I really feel lost. Anyway it was after my husband went into the service about 2 weeks, that he was saved. I had been a Christian for 4 years. I'm so thankful for that and I know the Lord had a hand in it all.

Remember us in your prayers, the children miss their daddy so much and are at an age when they need him. Write some time tell me about yourself & family – God Bless you may He soon end this war. In his Service Mrs. Frode Jenson (Irma)

Here is the second letter from Irma, Mrs. Frode Jenson dated Tyler, Minnesota, April 1, 1945 and postmarked Apr 2, 3;30 pm, 1945, Tyler, Minnesota:

Dear Mrs. Brown:

It's been quite a while since I read your nice letter – will
answer this evening. Just finished writing my husband.
What do you hear from your husband? How is he? Frode
is in a replacement camp in Eng. Now. I had hoped
he wouldn't have to go back to the front, but I believe
anywhere in God's will he will be safest. Praise him,
we can be assured of his care over his children. Frode is
awfully lonesome, but he doesn't get any mail so long after
he moves it's no wonder. I hope it will soon end. It was
Frode's birthday last Friday and I wonder what sort of one
he had (You don't really want to know Irma!). He was 36
yrs. And I bet he feels 63 most of the time.

We had a real windy Easter Sunday today. It has gotten
quite cold now. Surely hope we don't get more snow. This
past week the farmers have been busy putting in their
crops. It is so much earlier this year than last year. Nearly
a month earlier I believe. This past week the children had
Easter vacations, so I just worked half days. I don't like
vacation days, my attention is so divided I'm afraid I'm a
failing all around.

One of my brothers, who is at Ft, Benning Ga Is home on
a furlough now. Don't spose he will come down to see me
and it is quite an extra trip. Guess they don't look forward
to the bus rides. Can't blame them either. My husband
wrote that my other brother, who is in France, came to the
hospital to see him so I spose your husband met him too.

Did you have nice Easter weather? My little girl has
measles, so I didn't go to church this morning. Went
tonite tho. We have a nice little church and we think a lot
of our pastor. He is a very fine person.

Will send you a picture of my husband and I & children taken when he was home on furlough before going across. (I could not locate this photo.) It isn't a good picture but will give you an idea who your writing too – Am looking forward to getting one of you & family, at your convenience.

Write when you can and may God Bless and Watch over you and your loved ones.

Lovingly Your friend Mrs. Frode Jenson

This next letter was the third letter from Mrs. Frode Jenson and, as far as I know, the last one. It was dated Tyler, Minnesota, June 8, 1945 and postmarked June 8, 8:30 pm, 1945, Tyler, Minnesota:

Dear Mrs. Brown

I haven't written for some time now. I hope by now you have news of your husband that is good. Will he be home or possibly he is home I hope so. I'm still waiting to hear that Frode will be coming home. He hasn't enuf points and his age don't yet either, so if he comes it will be by the hand of God. Frode is on guard duty near Paris. He writes that he'd like to have a few days leave and go to Denmark. He has relatives there – if they are still alive. Would be nice if he could.

Thanks for the pictures. Can't see very much how your little boy & husband look. You are nice looking. Are you short. I would imagine so. I am 5 ft. 6 not short that's sure (Mother was 5 ft. 5.). My daughter is the same size, Her Daddy will be surprised to see how she has grown.

Spose you have returned from Chicago. Did you enjoy your trip? What did you think of the Northern States? I've never been south either.

I am a member of the Missionary Alliance Church. Guess the two churches are much the same.

My! We are having nasty weather. It is foggy & rainy most of the time. The sun hasn't shone for many weeks now, It is hard on crops too. The corn is so yellow,

Frode borrowed $10 from your husband and he asked me to send it to you. I will enclose it this letter. Hope it reaches you safetely.

This is my last week to work the rest of the summer. I will get my house cleaning done now. The children are finishing Bible School this week.

It is too hard to work, when the children aren't in school. It makes me so nervous – then if by fall, when school starts again & Frode isn't home, I will work again. Write to me and tell me all about your trip north and if your husband will be coming home.

Are you working now? I plan to see if I can paint the outside of the house this summer. It needs it so badly. You can't get anyone to do it for you except some old drunkard or the like & they want no less than $1 an hour.

I surely miss my hubby. I get so lonesome times, but I'm sure it is worse for them over there.

Write when you can – A friend Irma

The next letter was from dad's best friend while he was in training at Camp Blanding, Florida. It was a V-Mail addressed from PFC Wilmark

Tucker 54837096 Co. H 138 Inf F.A.P.O. 35 % P.M. N.Y., N.Y. It was postmarked March 26, 1945:

Tucker begins his letter with: Somewhere in Germany March 19, 1945.

Dear James

I just got your letter a few minutes ago and was so glad to hear from you. Mary keeps me up with you as your wife writes her and she tells me about you. I sure hated to hear you had been hit and got pneumonia too. I hope you are better now and maybe they won't send you up to the front next time. I sure hope not for your sake.

As for me I've been pretty lucky so far. I just hope my luck doesn't run out on me before this thing ends and maybe that won't be too far off. I hope not anyway.

I'd sure like to see you as I miss you lots. Sure wish they would have put us in the same company but things just didn't work out that way. If there is ever anything I can do for you don't hesitate to let me know as I feel by you as I would a brother of mine. Let me hear from you and take care of yourself. Tell Liz I said hello will you. Your Pal Tucker

Here is a second letter from dad and mother's friend Wilmark Tucker. It was a V-Mail written to mother and dated May 2, 1945:

Hello Liz,

Got your letter yesterday and was glad to hear from you, I also heard from James several days ago and I've lost the letter so I don't know his address. If you write again I'd like to know his address or maybe you can tell him why I didn't answer.

I'm sure glad James is getting along so good now. He had a tough break getting hit so quick but was lucky for it could have been far worse. We were in the same division but I never saw him after we'd been in France awhile.

You said you thought James may get to come home soon. I sure hope he does as that's what we are all looking toward.

Drop a line as I sure like to get letters. Sincerely, Tucker

Here is a letter to mother from Tucker's wife Mary which was written about five days after the previous V-Mail to mother from Tucker. It was addressed inside from Phenix City, Alabama, May 7, 1945 and postmarked May 8, 5;30 pm, 1945. Phenix City, Alabama:

Dearest Liz,

Will now try & answer your very sweet letter I got the other day & was more than glad to hear from you.

I think its wonderful that James is coming home & I know you are crazy with joy. Do you know where he is in the states? I know you are planning on going to him soon as you can. I'm so happy for both of you Liz. Give him my best regards when you see him. Gee, I wish Tucker was coming home too & from the war news he'll be here pretty soon unless they send him right on to the Pacific & I do hope he'll get a 30 day furlough between. if he does its going to be as hard to say good bye again. I hope this will soon end so all the boys can come home to stay.

I got a letter from him written April 20 & he said he was leaving the hospital that day. I haven't heard since from him. I got a package of German souvenirs & he sent the cutest little watch, ring, German helmet, wooden shoes, money, camera and all kind of pins.

This is some weather we are having lately. Imagine having fires & wearing heavy coats here in May. It all beats me ha,

I got a letter from Mae today saying Wanita Burreck's husband (Bernard) was killed in action April 13. I am so sorry & words can't express my grief for her. I hope Wanita will find comfort some where, though I know her heart is breaking.

I'm so glad you wrote Tucker honey cause I know how much mail means to them over their. I know he'll be more \than glad to hear from you. I wrote him James was coming back to the states & I know he is happy for him.

I got a new dress today but don't like it so much but you can't find any thing here much so I took what I could ha ha.

Well honey, be sweet & do let me hear from you all along. I hope you'll be with James real soon.

I'll close for now & go to bed. Be sure & write me now – Goodnite

Love ever Mary

I'm including a couple of letters here from my Aunt Iva Gamel, mother's sister, and Gertrude Gamel, Aunt Iva's mother-in-law. They both had written about the trip mother and Aunt Iva took to Illinois, which I think makes each of them well placed here. In addition, Gertrude Gamel made a lot of keen observations about Germany's surrender.

This first letter was from Aunt Iva dated 4-9-45 and was written to dad addressing him as Dear Brother:

Dear Brother,

I was so glad to get your letter a few days ago. I do hope you are feeling fine now.

I'm sure Eliz- has written to you about her plans & going north with me to visit Gerry's folks. I asked her to go with me because I want some of my folks to meet his & get acquainted. She will like them very much & really enjoy the trip. Mrs. Gamel wanted me to bring Roger but the trip will be too hard on him. Mama won't hear to it. I wish you & Gerry were here to go with us.

We cannot really enjoy anything without our husbands and how we'd all love that hotel in Chicago!! We have a room reserved so we can get some rest before going on west to see the folks. We will write you all about it.

Harrison came through the other day & I got to see him. Gerry is in the Maraines Is. I don't like that at all but I guess it could be even worse. I got a Cablegram from him last week. The electricity is working at home now. you did a swell job on it and it will really be nice now.

Do write to me soon, with love, Iva

The next letter included is one from Gertrude Gamel, Aunt Iva's mother-in-law, written to mother a few weeks after she and Iva went to visit in Illinois. The letter was dated Alpha (Il) Sat May 5, 1945:

Dear Elizabeth

We read your letter yesterday with the good news that James was coming home, so I think I must write & tell you how glad we are for you & him that he gets to come back to the U.S.

We hope he will be able to stay here now too.

Wasn't that awful about the hotel making such a fuss over room. It just seemed everything had to go wrong for you.

I'll bet Roger was glad to see you & I'd love to see him in his little hat. He sure would look cute.

We didn't hear the rumor of surrender on the Radio & by the time we did hear it the news had cooled off some what but I didn't expect it & will have a hard ntime believing it when it is true. Tho of course there isn't such bad fighting now, even if bad in spots – so it is a good thing just to have it slow down. But still I don't see how we can take care of those prisoners. I think we will be loaded with the job of feeding all of Germany because if they don't surrender & make peace terms we'll have to go on feeding them – so who wins out in that kind of a deal! Looks like we are the goats again.

We are glad if you enjoyed your visit Elizabeth. You can be sure we were happy to have you & happy to get to know you and think you and Iva are wonderfully nice girls. It is so nice to see two sisters get along so grand.

Iva had two letters come on Monday after you left here.

We heard from James this week. The letter was written Apr 20 from the hospital. He was OK & said he should be leaving there at once – But didn't know where to. But I don't suppose he'll be put on the front now, since there is less fighting – He is worrying a lot about having to go to Japan – and so am I.

Well, we hope you get a telegram soon from James & he will soon be home to see you. But if he is discharged it will take quite a while, so don't get too anxious. You are lucky

447

he can get started home again. It is good sign he is on his way if you don't get any more letters (This likely explains why there were no letters from dad during this period.).

Most Sincerely, Wm. & Gertrude Gamel

P.S. Almost forgot to write how my Dad was. He is getting along allright only slowly & he is quite a care. He has been so miserable & had so much medicine & treatment he is hard to take care of.

We have been there every hour. He got out of head at first so we take turns staying – But now is not delirious but the nedicine keeps him sort of bewildered & he can't hear so well. He misunderstands the nurses which makes them mad. They think he is just acting "onery" – of course he does get mad when the poke so much medicine & enemas, as such – I don't blame him. Dr thinks he may go home this next Tues. We all hope so for running down there is terrible.

This next letter was written to mother from Johnnie Conway. Mother's best friend that she grew up with in Hamilton, Alabama. Mother and Johnnie wrote each other at least three times a week for all their lives. This letter was written about the time of mother and Iva's trip to Illinois, so it is well placed here, I think. It was dated Ft. D (Deposit) 4 -24-45 and postmarked April 23, Fort Deposit, Alabama 1945, 1 pm:

Dearest Eliz and Roger,

I thought I'd wait and write in time for you to get it about the time you get home off your trip. I surely was glad to get your letter with all the good news. I'm so happy for you Eliz that James is coming back to you. You are so good and sweet and I love you a lot. You're the closest thing to a sister I've ever known.

I hope you had a wonderful trip but I fear you were anxious to get back afraid James might come while you were away. I don't believe he did or will as it'll probably take a good while to get back from England.

Do you suppose that James will be given a discharge? He'll probably get a furlough. I wish you could come to see us. Please do if you possibly can.

I think the little picture of Roger is so cute. Thanks a lot for it.

I've been making pajamas lately made 3 prs and one to go before I'm finished. Big Mama and I set out Tomato and collard plants in the garden this P.M. We have still got some cabbage to put out. I think it's a good idea to raise what you can especially if you like vegetables like we do. I suppose your mama has a pretty garden.

Last week I got a letter from the government giving me Carr's new address in Germany. It is at Moosburg about 30-40 miles from Munich, I think (Carr was in a German prisoner of war camp.). So you can listen to the radio as it seems the 7th Army is mighty close to him. I hope and pray he is O.K. and will soon be back. I haven't had any news from him later than a Dec 13 (Big Mama had a Dec 17) card except for a letter from an exchanged P.O.W. who knew him and saw him last Jan 6, I think it was. The navigator's (He was a P.O.W. too.) mother got a card from him written Feb 27 after they had moved so maybe I'll get one too from Carr. Maybe it won't be long now with Germany. One of Carr's first cousins (a bomber pilot I think) was reported "missing in action". He was from the Italian Theatre of Operations.

Where is Iva's better half now? Be sure and tell me about your trip when you write. Did you get any new things to wear? Did I tell you I got a blue "Dutchie" hat from Sears. Also a pr. of multi – colored play shoes $3.39 (with a bow on them) I like them a lot. I hate to wear dress shoes foe casual wear.

Jr. hasn't been so well lately. His bowels were kinda loose. I think it's his teeth. I got him some medicine Sat havt had to give it to him yet. I hope I don't.

I'll stop this rattling for now. Have Fun Write soon.

Lots of love Johnnie Conway Jr, C (Carr Jr,)

Here is a card from Johnnie Conway saying that her husband Carr is now home from a P.O.W, Camp in Germany! It was dated 6-7-45 and postmarked June 8, 8 am, 1945, Fort Deposit, Alabama:

Dearest Eliz & James & Roger

Just a card to tell you Carr is at <u>HOME</u>. It is simply wonderful. He has 60 days leave then Miami. We have been under such excitement until I can't think straight. We're so very happy and thankful. I hope you're having a good time too.

P.S. Excuse this hurry Love Johnnie & Carr & Jr.

I will continue now with more letters from friends of mother and dad that they knew before dad was drafted and from those made while dad was in the service. These letters will span a period of time from late December 1944 to September of 1945 and later. These letters will provide further information about my parents' lives and the times that they lived in as seen through the eyes of various friends that were dear to them.

The first set of letters was from Mrs. Ted Carell of Childersburg, Alabama whose husband worked at the Dupont ammunition factory in Childersburg where dad worked before being drafted into the Army.

The first correspondence was a post card dated Thursday morning and postmarked December 21, 1944, 3 pm, Childersburg, Alabama:

Dear Friends

Just a few lines to let you know that I havent forgotten you all – I have been so busy I havent had much time for anything. I got a Xmas card from Mrs, Sanders (Alma, dad's sister) yesterday. I dident mail her one because I dident know her address. So now I do and mabey I will write her a letter soon. Well we are going home for Xmas. Ted is back on straight days I am sure glad of it for we sure have been having some cold weather down here. We are going home Saturday and back Monday, not long to be with Mother & Dad but glad to be with them for a little while. I will write more next time.

Write Soon

Here is a second letter from Mrs. Ted Carell dated March 18, 1945 Childersburg, Alabama. It was postmarked March 19, 2 pm, 1945, Childersburg, Alabama:

Dear Mrs. Brown & Roger

I will try to answer your letter received a few days ago.

We are still about the same and are still here in Childersburg. We are sure having plenty of rain down here and I guess it is like this all over Alabama,

We were sure glad to hear of James improvement But we wishing like you that he wont have to fight any more.

Well we have us a car. It isn't a pretty one like yours. But it is a pretty good old car. We are not much better off than we were though. We just have an A gasoline Book and unless we can Buy some Coupons from somebody we won't get to go mutch in it. But, we will get to go home in it when we get our vacation if no more. I did hope to get to go home on Mother's day But unless we find a couple of coupons some place I just dont guess we can drive it then (Wow! She wouldn't be fishing for mother to give her some coupons, would she?).

I am planning to go home for Easter. But of course I will ride the Buss.

Well, Mrs. Burleson caught her husband with that bed girl the other day. I don't know what she is going to do about. They are on their vacation now. I sure feel sorry for her for she seems to be a good woman.

Garland White will have to soon go to the Army. He has to go the 20 for Exzam so I am sure it wont be long with him now.

I guess he will think about how he has treated his wife when he caint be with her any more. Well I have just about said all there is to say (You sure have given your share of the local gossip, that's for sure!) so I will close and write Moma a letter. You all come to see us and write when you can,

As Ever, Flossie & Ted

This third correspondence from Flossie, Mrs. Ted Carell, was a postcard which was postmarked June 9, 1945, Blountsville, Alabama. She dated it Friday Night on the card. The postmark indicated that they had moved from Childersburg to Blountsville:

Dear Mr. & Mrs. Brown and Son

Just a few lines. We moved Sunday Eve! they come a day
a head of time. But we have sure been Busy all this week.
I wish you all could visit us now since we have the house
about in order. We are sure proud to be at home We dont
have mutch passing by here But I am not lonesome for it
is home to me here. I will write you a letter next time (If
she did, I never found the letter,) You write us soon. We
hope James will get his discharge

By as ever, The Carells The following are letters from
two of mother's friends. They were written from April
to September of 1945, generally the same time period as
the previous letters. The first letter is from Chris (Mrs.
C. Rae Bassett Jr.) dated Sunday Night and postmarked
April 12, 9 pm, 1945:

Dear Liz,

Was glad to get your letter. Seems good to hear from some
one around Hamilton.

Gee it is Cold here tonight. The paper said the temperature
would be freezing tonight. I wore a big coat today & it
felt good.

I guess you are on your trip now, It's fun to travel when
you don't have any children. Gee it's tough with a baby.

I bet your dress is pretty. I like the material & the pattern.
I haven't had a chance to look for any material since I've
been here.

I am making a cover for my couch and that will keep me
busy for some time.

I have never made one before so I am hoping I have good luck.

Baby is fine only mean. Gee I'm all faged out by the time I get him ready for bed & in. He is so stought I have to hold on for dear life.

I guess Roger is worried about the president dieing. think he cant eat any more I guess – poor kid.

I wrote Rene when I wrote you but I haven't heard from her. She hasn't written me since she married. She doesn't seem to want to have any thing to do with anyone. Tho, I guess it hasn't been so easy with her. I know how she feels about having a baby the first thing.

I wish you & Iva could come up to see me while you are on your trip, but I know its too far. I was planning on moving down there before next winter but Rae has his heart set on staying here so I guess I'll mope around with a lost look on my face & bear it!

I'll stop now. I've got to see about the furnace the house is getting too hot for a change.

Write soon & tell me all the news, Love Chris

The second letter that I found to mother from Chris came several months later and was dated September 17, 1945. It was postmarked September 22, 11 am, 1945, Attleboro, Massachusetts. Mother and dad were in Miami Beach, Florida at this time and were caught in the middle of the Miami Hurricane of 1945.

Dear Liz

I meant to answer your card long ago but you know how it is. I've been in bed with a cold & Lee's (Lee was the baby.) had one. They last forever.

Are you in Fla now? If so, I guess you got the hurricane (Mother and dad did get trapped inside their hotel during the Miami hurricane of 1945.). We will get it late this afternoon & tonight & tomorrow. I don't like them myself.

How is every thing? I never get much news from H'ton (Hamilton, Alabama). Mother writes what goes on around the house but not much more.

I got a letter from Johnnie C. (Conway) today. The first time I've heard from her since Carr came home (from the German P/O/W. Camp).

Gee its cold as heck here. I wore my winter coat last night. We started the furnace. I am still wishing we could get back down there for the winter. Sure do hate to spend another one here. It gets so cold having to stay in week at a time.

James will get a discharge soon won't he? Where do you plan to live? Gee I hope we can get to Memphis Hamilton realy is growing – No?

Did Katherine Cooper have a boy or girl? I've heard both.

How is Roger? Still fat?

Lee is growing so fast & getting fat as a pig. Walks all the time. He stays out most of the time & he isn't half as much trouble.

Do you have any new fall clothes? I haven't – only some sweater & a skirt. I want to get a black dress next week or the next. We are going to Boston. We were in Boston two weeks ago. They realy had some nice things I wish I was rich for a day or two.

Don't wait so long to write as I did, and tell me all the news. Love Christine

(As far as I know this letter was the last letter mother got from Christine.)

This concludes the letters that I was able to find from relatives and friends to my parents during the later part of World War Two. My next chapters will resume with letters that mother and dad wrote after his return to the states.

I was elated to find a missing packet of letters and V-Mails that I had filed away over 13 years ago after moving furniture and other belongings out my parents' house. What this discovery came to be was the missing letters that I have been pondering about throughout the book so far. I found that most of the letters that I thought were lost or missing were not lost or missing after all. My dad had kept them with him probably in his pack and brought them back with him when he was shipped back to the states from England on April 13, 1945. He had tied the letters together with a boot lace that had two fabric prints of Our Lady of Mt. Carmel and St. Simon attached to it. He had also folded over a thick stack of V-Mails that he had received from mother and other relatives and friends. There were also over a dozen copies of "Good Tidings", a religious periodical, included in the treasure trove,

So, I had to decide about what to do with all these missing letters. Should I go back and place them in the chapters they belonged in and basically do a re-write or should I put them into a separate chapter in date sequence. I decided to do both. Some of the letters I went back and placed where there had been gaps, but I decided to put the greater part into a new chapter called "The Missing Letters".

And so, my friends, the next chapter will be just that, "The Missing Letters".

Chapter Eight

The Missing Letters

These next letters came as a complete surprise to me as I had filed them away thirteen years ago with some family documents and papers and forgotten about them. I had put dad's Purple Heart and Discharge papers away in this file but I had also put away some packets and stacks of letters that were not located with all the other letters that mother saved. In short what I discovered were most of the letters that I thought were missing.

There was a thick stack of V-Mails that dad had folded together and a packet of letters that dad had tied together with a boot lace tied into a bow with pictures of Our Lady of Mt. Carmel "pray for me" and St. Simon "pray for me" attached.

(See my photo at the beginning of this chapter and the closeups included here.)

I have decided to add these V-Mails and letters to this chapter. They are from family members and friends, and many are from my mother and grandmother that I had previously thought were missing. I will begin with the V-Mails and try to place them in reasonable order. The first one is from mother and was the first letter in which she acknowledges that she has been notified about dad's being wounded. So, it took over three weeks for her to find out about it. It was dated 1 – 17 – 1945:

> Hello Sweetheart,
>
> I was so sorry to hear the bad news about your being wounded. I didn't know about it until I got down to your mothers this morning. I hope and pray that you aren't seriously wounded, and that you will soon be O.K, I just hope that they won't put you back into battle again and

that you can come home. I wish I could be there with you. I am so proud that you are having good care. I hope Curtis will get to see you. I'm so thankful that you weren't killed and hope and pray that the Lord will take care of you and send you back to us soon. I'm going to send you something when I go to town, I'm always thinking of you. All our love, Eliz and Roger

The next V-Mail is from Aunt Iva, mother's sister. She was with mother in Opelika at dad's parents when they found out about the news that dad had been wounded. This V-Mail was dated the next day on 1 – 18 – 1945:

Dear James,

I suppose that you will be surprised when you hear that I am in Opelika. Eliz, went to Johnnie's and then came on to Opelika last night. I came down from B'ham and met her last night. We stayed with Alma and went to your mother's today. James I do hope you are alright. We didn't know you had been wounded until we got to your mother's. Eliz. had failed to get your mail and there was a letter which Mama had sent on to Opelika. She didn't know about it. I'm praying that you will be alright. Gerry is going across in a few days. I'm worried about him.

James I will write you more when I get to Birmingham. I am wishing you the best of luck.

Your sister, Iva

Dad received many letters from his family wishing him well and expressing hopes that his wounds were not life threatening and that he would soon recover. This V-Mail was from my Aunt Alma Sanders, my dad's sister, and was dated January 21, 1945:

My Dear Brother,

I recived your letter yesterday was sorry to hear that you were in the Hospital. But I thank God that you are able to write & hope & pray that you soon be O.K. for us we all well except bad colds. James have Curtis got to come to see you yet I sure hope he have I know you would be proude to see him. you said you havent got no letter from me yet I have been writing you I dont know why you not getting them I rote you since we moved on the old columbus road to farm. James I have been down to mothers and daddy today Eliz & Roger was down there they was well. James I am praying that this war soon be over so you boys can come home to your loved ones. James you have got a sweet wife and little boy I pray that you can soon be at home with them. The kids are going to school at Beauregard now. James take care of yourself and just keep praying & you soon be back home. Write us when you can,

Lots of love and best wishes, your sister

The next V-Mail was from my Uncle Harrison Palmer. My mother's oldest brother who was stationed at Sheppard Field, Texas at the time. He was a second lieutenant in the Army Air Corp. It was dated January 23. 1945:

Dear James,

We just received word from Liz that you are in England. We are awfully sorry to learn that you have been injured and we hope that by now you are feeling better. We feel sure that you will have excellent attention in the hospital there in England.

Margaret says she has a friend who is a nurse there in England whose name is Miss Lillian Kumli. If you should happen to come in contact with her be sure to tell her who you are. She will remember Margaret as Margaret Witty of Birmingham.

I wrote all the latest gossip to you last night to your old address. Perhaps you will receive that letter soon. We just got your new address today. Be sure to write us when you feel like it. We shall be looking forward to hearing from you soon and hoping you a rapid recovery. Love Harry & Margaret

There were several V-Mails from mother and there were also letters. I think she chose to write both, as the V-Mail was better for shorter correspondence and the letters could be written much longer when needed, This V-Mail was dated January 25, 1945:

Dearest James,

I was very happy to get your two sweet letters today, I'm so glad that you are still feeling O.K. You said that you would feel better if I could be there with you. I only wish that I could be there.

Your mother said to tell you that she was glad to hear to hear that you are getting along O.K. She got a letter from Curtis written the 15th but he undoubtedly hadn't heard about your being wounded as he didn't write anything about.

I had a letter from mother, she said that she Horrice & Herbert have written you. I hope you are getting my letters now,

We went to town today. I looked for something to send you but, couldn't find what I wanted. I want a nice box of chocolate. Maybe I can get it later. I don't think I can send anything without a request though. I just wish you could get the boxes I sent you before Christmas. Sweet I hope and pray that you will get along fine & can soon be home again.

Love Always, Elizabeth & Roger

Here is another V-Mail from Alma Sanders, dad's sister. As you can see, she wrote often. This V-Mail was dated January 26, 1945:

My Dearest Brother, I recived a letter from you yesterday and was I glad to hear that you doing pretty good just thanking God that you seem to be OK again and can come home has Curtis got to come and see you yet I hope he has I know it lonesome for you to be there in that hospital but just keep trusting in God and you soon be back at home with your love ones. Eliz & Roger are at Mama they all are doing very well. Little roger thought when he got to Grandmother Brown his Daddy coming. He tole Marvin & Harry he wanted to see his Daddy Maby by God help it wont be long till he can see you. Aunt Perl is here for four days she siad hello and hopes it soon be where you can be back home. James if is any thing you want me to send you write & tell me candy cakes any thing that you think you able I know you have a plenty But you like something from home, So write. Jeff & I sill working in the mills You wanted to know if we was moved yet (They were moving to the country to farm I believe.) we bought Marvin & Harry a mule to plow. Going to try to make something to eat. I will stop now take care of yourself and write me times you can.

Lots of love, your sister

This next V-Mail from mother finds her visiting Aunt Alma in Opelika, Alabama. It was dated 1 – 28 – 1945:

Dearest Sweetheart,

Well, here I am at Alma's again. I hope you are feeling better today. We are all doing fine. We went to Church today. Roger went in the Card Class today. He was so proud of his cards. I have finally gotten him to bed. He wanted to play at first, but I soon changed his mind for him ha! He told you good night.

I 'll probably be here four or five days. I don't know when I'll go back to Hamilton in about two more weeks here, I suppose.

Mamma forwards my letters from you every day. Just continue to write me to Hamilton.

It is still raining here as usual but we have had several pretty days.

Sweet, I hope you will soon be well again. Take care of yourself.

All our love, Elizabeth & Roger

I will include another V-Mail from mother and then include several of dad's mother's V-Mails. She did not date some of them so I will sequence them as best I can. Here is the V-Mail from mother dated 1 – 31 – 1945:

Dear Sweetheart.

I was very happy to get your letter today, but sorry you have flue. Just hope you will soon be feeling good again. You said that you haven't sat up yet any. I hope it won't be long until you can, for I know you get awfully tired of lying in bed. I'm so happy that you are able to write me and let me know how you are. I'm hoping and praying that you will soon be back home with us.

I got a letter from Harrison today. He, Margaret & Coralie are still in Texas. He was sorry to hear of your being wounded, said he has written you. I'm sure you are getting our letters now, aren't you?

Momma said that she got your Purple Heart yesterday.

All my Love, Elizabeth & Roger

This first V-Mail from Mrs. Gordon Brown or Betty Brown, dad's mother was dated January 16, 1945, as near as I could tell. As with all the family this was the first she had heard of dad being wounded in in the hospital in England:

> Dear James I will answer your letter I recieved to day sure was sory to heare you had got wounded & in the hospital hope you will soon be well wish I come & stay with you till you get better but I cant I know god will be with you he can take care of you I am just hopeing and praying he will take care of you & you will soon be well & this war will soon be over so you can come home the lord is the best friend we got just trust in him every thing works for the best for them that loves the lord he knows best for us all he will take care of you. I hope Curtis can go to see you I know he will if he can, write often and let us heare from you I will cose (close) wishing you the best of luck we all praying for you god be with you
>
> Mother & dad

This second V-Mail from Grandmother Brown was dated three days later on January 19, 1945. Mother and Roger were staying with her and Gordon, my grandfather and grandmother had just informed mother of dad's being wounded that very day:

Dear James will write you a few lines hope you are feeling fine & will soon be all right. I sure am proud & thankful the lord spard your life & know it could have bin worse if you just Can Come back home I will be thankful I hope & Pray that the lord will take Care of you & you will soon be back home with us. Elizabeth & Roger is here thay come today I sure was glad to see them Elizabeth hadent got your letter dident know you were wounded till she got here I sure do hope you will get our letters hope Curtis has bin to see you by now, I got your letters tuesday dont you worry abought us we will be alright write let us heare from you every time you can we all are praying for you I will stop now,

Lots of love Mother & all

This V-Mail from Grandmother was dated also and was written almost two weeks later on January 31, 1945:

Dear James Will answer your letters I recevied this week sure was proud to heare from you glad you are able to write hope you will soon be able to walk & can soon come home if you want any thing we can send you write & tell us we will send anny you want that can be sent Elizabeth & Roger is up at Alma this week she wants to send you sum thing dont know what to send. I hope you are getting our letters by now hope your cold is better & you are feeling better I bin writting you ever sents you both gone over seas I hope & pray this war will soon be over now guess you have heard from Curtis by now, hope he will get to go see you you write every day if you can & let us heare from you We are having cold weather now I sure do miss Roger this week I got a letter from Eloise today she stays sick most of the time I will stop. wishing you the best of luck

Lots of love Mother & Dad

This V-Mail from Grandmother Brown to dad was not dated but it must have come a week or so after the previous one I included, so that would have made it around the first or second week of February 1945. After this one I will return to the V-Mails sent by mother and other family members. There were more V-Mails from Grandmother Brown, but I will include them with all the others in chronological order as much as is possible:

Dear James will answer your letters sure was proud to heare from you glad you are improving hope you will soon be well, for us we are doing very well I guess sure am glad you are getting sum of our letters I know you was glad to get them. I havent heard from Curtis this week hope he alright and have bin to see you. I got a letter from Eliz – today thay got home OK I sure do miss them wish they could have stade with us Roger said he come back this summer I will be glad when summer comes maby we will have sum good weather Alma has bin writing you all the time. I hope you wont have anny more troble with your side & will get along fine & can soon come home Ihope this war will soon be over now so all the boys can come back home that is living it will be a happy day when this war stops I will stop for this time god be with you all is my prayer

Lots of love mother & dad

I will return now to another V-Mail from Alma Sanders. There were several letters from her and this V-Mail was dated February 1, 1945:

My Dearest Brother

I will try & answer your letter I recived yesterday sure was proude to here from you But know you havent been feeling good hope & pray that you are feeling good now

for us we all well Eliz & Roger are here with me this week
I sure am proude for them to be here hope & pray it wont
be long till you can be back with us all again I had a letter
from Curtis yesterday he is well and in the best of health
it was rote Jan the 18 he hadent herd about you getting
wounded then I guess he have by now sure hope he gets
to come to see you James Mama & daddy is doing pretty
well at this time, Jeff & I are still working in the mills The
kids said Hello Roger & Marie sure have a time playing
& fighting ha. I will close for this time hoping to here
from you soon

Love & best wishes your sister

This next V-Mail was from Mrs. J.M. Mayberry, dad's Aunt Willie. It
was dated February 2, 1945:

Dear James – I hope this finds you feeling good. I recieved
a letter from you last week written (Jan. 22nd) this leaves
everyone well at present we have been having some real bad
weather back here but the Sun is shining this afternoon. I
had a letter from Roy and Preston last week I sure was glad
to hear from them and you too. Was glad to know you
were able to write remember behind the clouds is the sun
still shining this war can't last always. Virgil is stationed
at Riley Kansas he entered the Army Jan, 4th. Roy is still
in Australia and Preston is in Belgium. Thomas Walter
and Wilmer are going to farm again I guess Walter may
have to go to the army before the year is out. I'm glad to
hear you say you have found Jesus for we all need to know
him. We will pray for you and the other boys too hoping
the war will soon be over.

Love from all the family "Aunt" Willie

Here are two V-Mails from February 4 and February 5, 1945. The first is from mother to dad and the other from his mother, Mrs. Gordon Brown. Mother's V-Mail was dated February 4 and appropriately mentions Valentine's Day chocolates that she had sent to dad. Also, this is the first time that mother acknowledged that dad had pneumonia:

Hi Sweetheart,

I was very happy to get your letter, but sorry to hear that you have pneumonia. I'm so thankful that you are getting along O.K. now. Be careful sweet. I was afraid that was what was wrong with you when you said you were having trouble with your chest.

Roger is fine. He said that he dreamed that you came home and brought him a sack of candy. He talks about you lots.

I'm sending you a box of valentine chocolates. I do hope you get it O.K. Have you gotten any more letters from me? I hope you have as I know how it is to miss getting letters. Take care of yourself and write when you can.

All my love Eliz

This V-Mail from Grandmother Brown written February 5, 1945, echoes the information given by dad's Aunt Willie in her letter to him that I previously included:

Dear James will answer your letter I received to day sure was proud to heare you was better for us we are doing very well I guess, your aunt willie was here sunday she said Roy & Preston was OK the last letter they got she said they had wrote to you Arthur & Lee Tom (Her three brothers) got a letter from you I guess they have answer by now, they

468

all doing alright, I got a letter from Elizabeth to day they was doing fine

I hope Curtis will get to go back to see you hope you can soon walk if you could walk around you would feel better I know you do get home sick I be glad when you get well but hope the war will soon be over so you can come home & all the boys if it be god will. I hope they wont be another war. I am sending you Eloise address here it is Eloise Greene 813 No, 50th street Birmingham (6) ala, I will close hope this letter finds you feeling fine write soon

Lots of love Mother & Dad

Mother wrote every day and I have most all her letters and V-Mails, especially after my having rediscovered the missing ones. This V-Mail from her to dad was dated 2 – 6 – 1945:

Dearest James,

I didn't get a letter from you today, but I read the one to your mother. I bet you enjoyed that snow cream. It isn't quite that cold here, but almost. We've had three light snows in Hamilton. I told Roger about your having snow cream. He said he wished he had some too,

Arthur and Gerry have already sailed for the Pacific I think. You were asking about Conway (Carr Conway, Johnnie Conway's husband). The last time I had a letter from Johnnie she was hearing from him regularly.

I hope you are still feeling better. Take care of yourself and write when you can.

I love you Elizabeth

Here is a V-Mail from mother dated two days later on February 8, 1945:

Hello Sweetheart,

I was very happy to hear that you are still improving and
hope that your leg will soon be well. I will be so happy
too, when you can come to the U.S.A. Maybe it won't be
so long now.

Sugar you said you hadn't pulled your ring off yet, I
haven't either.

It really is cold here today.

Roger is fine, he is still dirty as usual. It is a problem to
keep him clean though.

I don't know very much to write, so I'll stop now.

Be careful. I love you, Elizabeth

Alma Sanders, dad's sister, wrote him often and here is another V-Mail
from her dated February 9, 1945:

My Dearest Brother

I will try and write you a few lines this cold morning, hope
you are feeling fine, for us we all well. I havent got a letter
from you this week & I am worried I am going down to
mother & see if she has got one. I was getting two or three
a week. I may get one today. I hope I will. I wish this offel
war would end.

I havent herd from Curtis this week either. I hope he is
O.K. this last letter he was sick with a cold. hope he has
got to come to see you by now. Arthur and them havent
herd from Herman in two months they are worried about
him. Well maby some day we all can live in peace again.

James Eliz & Roger are with mother you sure got a sweet
girl for a wife. I am proude she loves mother & Daddy and
all of us if she dident she woulden come and stay with us
like she does Well I hope & pray that you soon be O.K.&
be back at Home with your Love one.

Lots of love & best wishes, your sister

I am including these V-Mails according to the dates given on them and
not necessarily in the order that dad received them. I debated on whether
to include them in the order that dad folded them or by date order. Like
all the letters I have included thus far, I put them in date order to insure
a better flow from one to the next. This next V-Mail is another one from
dad's mother dated February 12, 1945:

Dear James just a few lines to let you heare from us we
are doing pretty good I guess, hope you are feeling fine &
will soon be well, & have got sum of our letters by now
have you heard from Curtis I hope so anyway Elizabeth &
Roger went home to day I hope thay get home OK I sure
do miss them they stade with us three weeks Eliz. worries
about you not geting her letters she writes every day we
sure did miss you not being here with us we dident get to
go anny whire much dident have no way to go, I hope you
will soon be back with us all agin & this war will be over.
Roger said he would be back sum day to see me agin. Your
grandpa havent come back yet I got a letter from Ola last
week she said thay was all well I guess he will stay up thire
with them. I will close write soon let us heare from you

with lots of love mother & Dad

The next V-Mail that I found from mother was dated February 15,
1945, but keep in mind she was writing letters as well so some of the gaps
may have already been filled by letters from her that I included before.
Also, I have a packet of letters that I have not included yet that may contain

471

her letters from the missing days. Here is her V-Mail from February 15, 1945:

Hi Sweetheart,

How are you today? We are fine. Today is a beautiful day. It is just like Summer.

I hope you have received more of my letters. I got one from you today that was written Jan. 21 and one yesterday that was written Feb. 3. I am so happy that you are improving and hope that you continue to do so.

I've been trying to drive the car some today. Herbert said I did fine. I'm going to try every day until I learn to drive by myself.

I don't think Harrison is going overseas for awhile longer.

All my love

Elizabeth & Roger

Here is a V-Mail from two days later That mother dated 2 – 17 – 1945:

Hi Sweetheart,

I was very happy to get your letter today and hear that your side hasn't given you any more trouble. Maybe it won't be long now before you can be up again. I just wish that you could come home when you're able.

I do hope your friends wife will write me (Mrs. Frode Jenson). I enjoy reading letters. I'll write her too. I don't know what I'd if I couldn't get letters from you and my friends too.

I had a letter from Mary today. She says she hasn't had a letter from Tucker in over a week. Maybe she has heard from him now. I know how she feels. It had been over a week that I didn't hear from you when I heard you were wounded.

All my love Eliz

Here is another V-Mail from Alma Sanders, dad's sister. Her writing is hard to read, and she made a lot of spelling and grammatical errors but with patience I have managed to record them reasonably well. This V-Mail was also dated February 17, 1945:

Hello James

Just wonder how you are feeling to night fine I hope for us we all doing very well sure cold to night James I havent got no letters from you this week but hope to get some soon Mamma siad she got two letters from you siad you got mail from all but me I dont know why you dont get my mail I write you two & three letters a week I got a letter from Eliz the other day she siad she got home O.K. James I sure had a house full to day Jane Mary & Griff all they kids & mother & dad wish you could had been here then. I could have enjoy them better. I hope & pray to the Lord it won't be long till you can be back with us all. Jeff & the kids went to church today siad they sure had a good meeting. Well James take care of your seffe and write me ever time you can.

lots of love your sister

I am back on track with mother's V-Mails to dad now. This one was dated the next day on February 18, 1945:

Hi Sugar,

Well, I suppose this will be news for you (It is certainly news for me, mother!). I drove the Car to Church today. I think I did O.K. Maybe it won't be long now before I can drive good. I'll keep driving occasionally.

Iva came home this week-end but has gone back. Opaleen is back in H'ton for two weeks while her husband is on Bivovac. She came over today.

I got a letter from you today that was written Jan. 29. I hope you are getting a letter from me every day. You should as I write you that often. I get one from you almost every day.

Roger is asleep now. He tells you goodnight every night. I'll stop now and go to bed. I'll always love you.

Good night Elizabeth

We are on a roll now! I have V-Mails from mother to dad from every day starting with those of February 17 and 18 that I have already included. This one was dated February 19, 1945:

Dear Sweetheart,

Well here comes another letter. I don't have very much to say though as I didn't get a letter from you today.

Christine Walker Bassett is here visiting her mother. She came by and stayed with me awhile today. And oh! I must tell you Hazel Ballard finally got married to Olin Nix. He had been overseas for three years or more and is now back in the States. He was in Camp with you. I suppose you remember him don't you?

Roger is fine. He is standing here begging me to read his mouse book to him.

How are you getting along now? I do hope you are still improving. I'll be so happy when you can come home.

Love & Kisses Elizabeth

In this next V-Mail, mother was explaining to dad that she had been sending her letters by Air Mail. She found out it was faster to just send them by V-Mail though. That explains why there were gaps and why dad wasn't getting her mail every day. I have included previously those letters and there are others that I will include after this grouping of V-Mails. This V-Mail from mother was dated February 20. 1945:

Hi Sweetheart,

I was so very happy to recieve your three letters today. I'm glad that your side is better. Just hope you won't have any more trouble with it.

I hope you have gotten some more mail from me again. I have been writing airmail letters to you every day, until I found out that V-Mails were so much faster. That is why you haven't been getting them very often, I suppose. They will get to you eventually though, I hope.

I'm glad Mary wrote you. I asked her to. I thought she could tell you where Tucker was.

Well, it is still raining here as usual. I had a letter from your mother yesterday. They are fine.

Roger is coloring his color book. He enjoys writing on his blackboard too. James take care of yourself for we want you back home real soon.

Yours forever Elizabeth & Roger

Mother was telling dad about all the company Alma had in this V-Mail. I included Alma's V-Mail about that earlier, so I know I am ordering these pretty well. This V-Mail was written the following day on February 21, 1945:

Hi Sugar,

I hope you are feeling good today. We are all O.K. It is still raining as usual. I worked again today.

We got letters from Iva & Alma today. Iva says she has had six letters from Gerry. He is in Hiwaii. Alma said she had <u>Company</u> Sunday. Griff, Mary and Their crew. Also part of Wash and Irma's your mother and Dad and all the neighbor folks. I don't see how she ever lived through all the excitement ha!

Roger is playing with his toys. He is so mad because he can't get outside.

Sweet I'll be so happy when the day comes for you to come home. I only hope it will be real soon.

I think I told you about getting the extra allotment you made out, which was thirteen dollars. I put it in the bank and will every month, I've had several people down wanting to buy the car I'm not selling it though. I'm learning to drive.

All my Love and Kisses Elizabeth

In this V-Mail dated February 22, 1945, mother mentioned her friend Mrs. Carell from Childersburg where dad had worked at Dupont before being drafted into the service. Mrs. Carell told mother that she and her husband would be moving into a new home in the town they lived in before moving to Childersburg:

Dearest Sweetheart,

I hope you are feeling good today. We are fine. It has finally stopped raining and has turned cold.

I think I'm going to a show tonight. I haven't been to one for some time. I only wish you were here to go with me. Roger enjoys shows so much.

I got a letter from Mrs. Carell today. She says their new house, where she live before they moved to Childersburg, is about completed. She really wants to get back to it to. She also told me to tell you that they think of you lots, and hope that you will soon be well again.

I hope and pray that it won't be long until you can come home to stay. Take care of yourself and remember we're always thinking of you. All my love Eliz

Mother was happy to learn that Curtis, dad's brother, had come to see dad and mentioned it in this V-Mail dated February 23, 1945:

Dearest James,

I was so happy to hear that Curtis came to see you. I know you both were so glad to see each other. I hope he can go back to see you again soon.

I wish that I could see you too, but I know that is impossible now. I hope it won't be long before I see you, home.

Roger was so tickled when I read your letter to him, about your calling him a man. He thinks he is one too. He says he wants to grow big and tall, but not fat. This morning when he awoke, he told me that he dreamed you came home. He said "be sure to write daddy about that'.

I drove the car again yesterday. I've learned everything now except backing, and that is quite a lot of trouble to me.

I saw a cute show last night. The name of it was "Man from France". I'll stop as I don't have anymore news. All my Love, Elizabeth

I will backtrack a little now and include a V-Mail from dad's mother that was dated a couple of days earlier on February 22, 1945:

Dear James just a few lines to let you heare from us, this few lines leves us doing very well I guess, hope thay find you doing fine. I havent heard from you this week hope to soon hope you are getting along fine I guess Eliz has heard from you I havent got a letter from her this week yet hope to get one I havent got a letter from Curtis in two weeks I hope he is OK I wish he would write let me heare from him, You will have to write to me now I cant read Elizabeth letter she is gone home I sure do miss them. I hope you will soon be well & can come back home & this war will be over. the weather is bad here about all the time it bin raining all this week havent bin anny farm work don yet. Alma and them is doing alright I will stop just hoping and praying you will soon be back home with us

all our love Mother & Dad

Continuing with mother's V-Mails to dad, this one was written the next day on February 24, 1945:

Hi Sugar,

I have just finished reading your two sweet letters. I'm always so glad to get them and hear that you are getting along O.K. I was really very happy to hear that Curtis has been to see you. I bet you were kinda shocked to see him standing there. It was nice seeing him again after almost two years I know.

I hope he will write me too. I think he owes me two letters.

I know that your mother & Dad will be happy to hear that Curtis went to see you. I wrote them about it, but I suppose you wrote them too.

Well you know I have to have a request to send anything overseas. So you said all that you needed over there was me, so I ought to take that to the post office, and I could go myself ha! I got a letter from Johnnie today. She says that she has had another letter from Carr written Dec. 9.

Take care of yourself. I'll always love you, Elizabeth

This V-Mail from mother was written on their 4th Anniversary, February 25, 1945:

Dearest Sweetheart,

I will remember tonight four years ago, don't you sugar? It doesn't seem that we have been married that long does it?

I want to tell you how much I thank you for the very nice valentine. It was so very sweet of you to draw it for me. Where did you get the cute idea?

I got a letter from Mary today. She said that she has had several letters from Tucker. She also said that she got a letter from you, and enjoyed reading it very much.

Sweet, I'm so happy that you are doing O.K. I hope that it won't be long before you are home again.

We got a letter from Arthur today, He can't tell us where he is though. Be sweet and take care of yourself, All my Love, Eliz

Here is another V-Mail from Alma Sanders in which she mentions that Curtis Brown has written her and told her that he had been to see dad in the hospital. The V-Mail was dated February 26, 1945:

Hello James,

I will ansur your letter & was I happy to git it. I hadent gotten one in Just about two weeks sure am happy you are doing O.K. for us we all O.K. I had a letter from Curtis yesterday He siad he had been to see you I sure am proude he got to come to see you. I know you was more than proude. Just hope & pray it wont be long till you both can be back at home to live in peace once more. I dont think this war can last much longer with the Germans the way the news is Just keep praying that you can be back home to your loved ones. I was at home Sunday mother & Dad and all of us went to church.

I will stop write often Love your sister

This V-Mail from Grandmother Brown also mentions that Uncle Curtis had been to see dad in the hospital. It also was dated February 26, 1945:

Dear James will answer your letter I recevied to day sure was proud to heare from you glad to know you was better hope you will soon be well for us we are well as common, I know you was glad to see Curtis I sure am glad he got to go to see you wish I could come to see you I am proud Curtis is doing alright I got a letter from him to day for the first time in 3 weeks I was glad to get it to he said he had bin to see you and was going back to see you if he could I sure do hope he can he said you would be OK when you got well I hope you will & can soon come home & this war will be over, if it is the lords will. I got a letter from Eliz- to day thay was well she write me when she get a letter from you I dident get one from you last week but she did I sure do miss her & Roger you might get a letter from her every day she write every day you write to me every time you can let me heare from you I know you was glad to get to set up I just hope & pray you will get along alright now. Love Mama & Dad

This V-Mail from mother to dad finds her discussing some details about the job she had doing secretarial work in town. She dated this V-Mail February 27, !945:

Hi Sweetheart,

I've just gotten in from work. I really put the day in too as I cut several stencils and ran them off. I like the work though as it is something to do, and I don't have to work regular either.

I was very happy to get your four letters today. Horrice got your letter too. Sweet, I'll send you some candy tomorrow. I hope I can find some that is good.

Roger is fine, He is reading the funnies now. I'm always happy to hear that you are getting on O.K. I just hope that you will soon be well and back home with us. Sweet, I know it is lonesome for you to have to be there. Maybe it won't be too much longer though. Just wish I could be with you then neither of us would be lonesome, I'm just thankful that you are doing as well as you are.

Be good & take care of yourself, All my Love & Kisses, Eliz

I feel fortunate that I have found almost all the V-Mail from the time that dad was in the hospital in England, because before I thought they were missing or had been lost. Having them gives me an insight into what was happening in my parents' lives during that time. This V-Mail from my mother was written the next day on February 28, 1945:

Hello Sweetheart,

I was very glad to get your three letters and hear that your pneumonia and kidney trouble has cleared up. I just hope that you will continue to improve. I also got a card from the War Dept. saying that you were making normal improvement the 18th.

Sweet, you said it would be quite awhile before you can walk. Don't try too soon. Mamma said to tell you to take your time about trying to walk because we want you to take care of yourself so that you can come back home to us someday soon.

I'm sorry that you thought I was sick instead of Eloise. No sugar I haven't been sick any. Roger and I both are doing fine.

I got a letter from Alma today. They are all O.K. I got one from Mary too. She says she has had three or four letters from Tucker and he was O.K. Sweet, I'm sending you some candy. I hope you get it. Bye for now.

All my love, Elizabeth

The next V-Mail was from dad's mother and was dated March 1, 1945:

Dear James will answer your letter I recevied to day, sure was proud to heare from you glad to heare you was better, as for my self I dont feel good I have got a cold. hope this letter finds you feeling better. I know it is bad to have to stay in the bead I be glad when you can get up & walk you will feel better I know you will be glad. I havent got Eliz- & Roger wish thay was here I sure would be proud to keep you & them & hope it wont be long now till you can be home with us I got a letter from Curtis this week he said he was home sick I know he is. just trust & pray that you all will soon be home you grandpa havent come back yet I guess he like up thire he was doing fine the last time I heard from him, we are having sum pretty weather now if it will stay pretty. havent bin anny farm work done yet I will stop for this time

Write soon

Lots of love mother dad

The next V-Mail from mother has her reminiscing about the good times she and dad had before he was drafted into the service. Dad had asked her in his letter to her if she remembered going to the Fair with him and of course she did, and it warmed her heart to reflect upon those memories. I know that dad won prizes at those carnivals and fairs, and I am going to include scans of two of them that I still have in my possession today. One is a chalk figure of Charlie McCarthy, and the other is a chalk figure of a Scotty dog. Mother cherished and saved these all her life and I am cherishing and saving them now. Her V-Mail was dated March 1, 1945.

I am including the scan of the Charlie McCarthy chalk figure on the left and the Scotty Dog chalk figure on the right and the V-Mail from mother to dad from March 1, 1945, will follow:

Dearest James.

I've just gotten home from the Show, I enjoyed it very much. The name of it was "Madame Curie". I went with Opaleen.

Sweet, you said that you were sending me some money for an Anniversary present. It is very sweet of you. I'll buy something with it that I can keep for you to see when you get home.

Yes, I very well remember the Night at the fair in Opelika. I really enjoyed that night very much. I just hope it won't be long before you will be back and we can go places together again. It is so much nicer to have you to go places with.

Roger is asleep. It is getting late so I had better stop and go to bed too.

Good – Night Sweetheart

All my Love Eliz

This V-Mail from mother skipped a day and was dated March 3, 1945. It could be she wrote a letter instead on March 2 or it could be the March 2 V-Mail was misplaced. Mother mentioned dad's Purple Heart that had been sent to them in this V-Mail:

Hi Sweet,

I've just recieved another letter from you. Glad to hear that you are doing fine. It has begun to rain for another week, I suppose. It rains just about all the time here.

Sweet, you said something about your mail will be messed up when you leave there. Do you think you will leave very soon? I do hope and pray that you won't have to go back to the front again.

Roger keeps telling me he wants to see your Purple Heart. He likes to look at it. Several people have come to see it.

I'm glad you are getting my letters every day. I get one or more from you every day too. Take care of yourself. We love you. Love & Kisses, Eliz & Roger

Here is another V-Mail from Aunt Alma that was written the same day on March 3, 1945:

Hello James

I will answer your letter I have just gotten was Happy to get it. happy that you are doing O.K. for us we are all well at this writing We sure have had two pretty days look like it rain now tho, Jeff got the car tore down and is working on it. I sure be proude when he gets it fixed. I want to go to town but I guess he needs more work time to get it fixed, Griff Mayberry came after us to take us to work. I got a letter from Eliz yesterday siad she was working just about

485

ever day. James I sure wish this war would hurry up & end so you boys can come home. I think of you boys over there all time. Jeff may haft to go be for it over. I hope not. They tole him at the board to stick to his job at the mills. I will stop so you write me ever time you can. Marvin will write you tomorrow.

Love & best wishes to you your sister

This next V-Mail from mother was from the following day but there was a gap after that in her V-Mails. I may find that she had sent letters instead when I continue with transcribing the packet of letters I discovered. This V-Mail was dated March 4, 1945:

Dearest James,

Mother & I got your letters today. Glad you are doing fine. Hope you won't have to go to the front anymore. Iva was here today. We went to Church.

Yes, you should write Mammy. I think she asks about you every day.

Well sweet I had planned to get a string of pearls with the money you were going to send me, but now that you gave it to Curtis, I'll just buy some with my money, and I can still count it as an anniversary present. If Curtis ever sends the money I'll get something else with it. I suppose he is still having fun with the girls in England ha!

You were right when you said we don't want a shack on some red hill, Jeff's & Alma's was enough for me ha! All my love, Elizabeth

This concludes the V-Mails that dad had folded together and had kept together along with a packet of letters that he had tied together with the boot lace that I mentioned before. I am now going to undo the boot lace and open the letters enclosed inside the packet. All these letters were placed inside an envelope that had Cora Lee Palmer's

address on it. I am including a scan of it here.

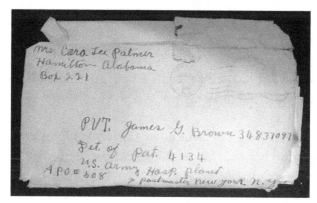

This was the letter from my grandmother, Cora Lee Palmer, that was enclosed in the envelope I have scanned. It was not dated but for having "monday nite" at the top.

The envelope was postmarked January 23, 1945:

Dear James

I hope you are feeling good by the time you get this letter. was so sorry to hear of your getting wounded. but we are all so thankful to hear you are still living we miss you so much and hope it wont be long till you will be back with us again. I am lonesome tonite Elizabeth and Roger is down at Opelika with your mother & Dad. She was down there when the telegram come saying you were wounded she looks lonesome without you. she thought it would help pass the time away to go and stay with your mother some. Iva went down there and stayed a day or two.

We went to church Sunday and heard a good Sermon preached and they sung one of the sweetest songs the name of it was (Im praying for you,) I had heard the song before but never had it sounded so good before we had got the news about you being wounded and of course everything was sad to us.

Just remember you have a lots of good friends and love ones praying for you trust in the lord and he will take care of you.

For the lord takes care of his people any where. he has been my friend in all my troubles and hardships

Arthur didn't get to come home Christmas he got a seven day leave but couldnt get home and back he was at San Fransico Cal. And it was to far.

he is on a ship now going over seas. says he wont be back in 18 months that sure is a long time a lot can happen in 18 months I hope and pray that nothing bad happens to him

he said he had a nice time on his leave he went to new york and Holly wood seen a few actress and actors and Stars.

he said the Hotel palace give the Boys of the USS Randolph a farewell dance before they left. the ship he is on is the USS Randolph Gerry is still in utah him and Harrison has been lucky so far. Harrison is in Texas Im expecting Gerry and Harrison to go over seas any time now.

I sure will be proud when Elizabeth and Roger comes back up here I get so lonesome without them Roger is so much company and gets prettier every day.

have you got many of Elizabeths letters she writes you every day if you havent you sure will have a lots to read when you do get them(I think anyone that reads all the letters in this book will attest to that!) did you get any of your Christmas Boxes I hope you get them. say you like

Sausage now. well we have a lots canned and plenty of fresh ham and we are getting lots of eggs now sure wish you were here to help us eat .

I found a can of eat well Sardines so we had them for dinner. I thought of you when you and Elizabeth lived over here I hope it want be long till you and Elizabeth and Roger can come to see us togeather I'll cook some more good old Alabama Chicken.

Well I guess this long letter is getting you tirred. I'll stop now wishing you good luck. write me if you feel like it.

Love and prayers Mother

This was the first letter from mother to dad that I found in the packet and this letter was the first one in which she had heard of dad's being wounded. It was dated Opelika, Alabama, January 20, 1945:

Dearest Sweetheart,

I wonder how you are feeling now. I hope you are doing O.K. I just wish I could be there and take care of you. I'm sure it would make you feel better wouldn't it sweet? And I know I would feel much better if I could see you and know how badly you were hurt.

I'm sorry that it had to happen to you, but I'm so thankful that you are still living and will be back with us someday.

I got the first letter that you wrote me after you were wounded, today. I got some yesterday that were written after it.

Sweet, I didn't even know it until I got here (Opelika at dad's parents). I can't tell you how I felt when they started telling me about it.

I don't know why I didn't get your letters sooner.

I haven't gotten the telegram yet. I'm so proud I got your letters first, because it was bad enough to hear it from you. I do hope & pray that you will get along fine and will soon be well. I only hope you will get to come home. I hope this war will soon be over. The news seems better now.

I heard Roosevelt's fourth term inauguration this morning. He also spoke too.

I haven't heard from Mary in over a week. The last time she wrote me, she said that Tucker was fighting. He ia in the 35th Div. of the 3rd Army.

Here is Harrison's address. I wrote him about you.

Lt. H.R. Palmer 0588021
78th A.A.F. Base Unit
A.A.C.S and R. Center
Shepperd Field, Texas

This is Arthur's
Joseph A. Palmer SIC
Div. S-2 (CV-15)
U.S.S. Randolph % Fleet P.O.
San Francisco, California

I don't have Gerry's with me now. He says that he will write you.

I write you every night. I don't know why you can't get them. I wish you could get your packages I sent you.

I'm going to send you something else when I get a chance to go to town. Write and tell me if there is anything you want.

Have you gotten the pictures yet? I sent them so long ago. I just wondered.

Your mother & Dad are O.K. Pearl is still here.

Roger and Harry are playing.

Sweet, I wish you could be here and we could go to Almas. She lives in the Same red mud that Jeff has wanted to live so long ha! You know it is this side of where she lived on that red hill. I don't like that place at all (My mother always had a horror of red mud and despised it all of her life,). But you know Jeff is actually satisfied with that place.

Your Dad has some false teeth, but he took them back to the Dentist to have them made over. He says that they don't feel right in his mouth.

Sweet write me as often as you feel like it as I'm anxious to hear how you get along.

I'll always love you only. Take care of yourself.

Love & Kisses Elizabeth & Roger

P.S. Mamma wrote me that two power men came from B'ham & were going to fix the lights right away. I wrote to Headquarters about how Mr. Manyer was doing & they came to fix them as soon as they get to it.

Here is the second letter from mother that I found in the packet. As I mentioned before, mother wrote both V-Mails and letters to dad so that accounts for what may seem like gaps in her daily letter writing.

This letter was dated Opelika, Alabama, January 22, 1945:

Dear Sweetheart.

I was so happy to get your three letters today. Two were written since you have been in the hospital & the other was written while you were in France.

I'm so glad that you got the pictures and liked them. I'm also glad that you still have them and your testament (It was amazing that dad managed to hold onto them after being wounded.).

Roger was tickled when I told him that the nurse thought he was a cute boy.

He is writing you too. He kept on until I had to draw his & my pictures. So don't get too amused at them ha! (I am inclosing a scan of the mother's drawing here.)

I got something about another allotment this morning. I think it said there would be $13.00 come after the 15th of February.

Sweet, if there is anything that you want, write and let me know. The postman said I couldn't send you anything unless you ask for it.

I'm so happy that you are getting along O.K. Maybe it won't be long before your leg will be O.K. and you can walk again. I only hope that you can come home.

I got a letter from Ella Mai today. She said that they were shocked to hear that you were overseas so soon. I think just about everyone was.

No, sweet I haven't been sick. You just haven't been getting my mail. I write you every day, so you'll have plenty to read when you do get them.

Your mother got a letter and greeting card from a girl who Curtis has been writing in England. Did he get to go see you? I hope he did.

We are still having rainy weather here.

Take care of yourself. I love you only, Love & Kisses, Elizabeth

These are the letters from mother that I had been wondering about and they were written daily as you will see from the dates. This one was dated Opelika, Alabama, January 23, 1945. Many of these will have Opelika, Alabama on them as mother was visiting dad's mother and dad at that time:

Dearest Sweetheart,

I was so glad to get your letters today, and hear that you are doing fine. I do hope that you will continue to feel good. I hope your cold is much better.

Take care of yourself and try not to get any more cold than you have,

I got a letter from Mamma today. She really did hate to hear about you, but happy that you weren't hurt any worse.

She forwarded the telegram to me.

It said that you were slightly wounded in Belgium 30th of Dec.

I hope you are getting my letters now, I write you every day and wish that you could get them every day.

Your mother & Dad are O.K. Roger & I will probably be here a few weeks, but you can continue to address them to Hamilton so that when we do go back we can continue to get your letters O.K.

Gerry sent Roger a toy wrist watch today. It really is a cute thing. Roger was so proud of it. Gerry thinks he'll be leaving there in a few days.

Roger still says "bless Daddy" every night before he finishes his prayer. He also tells you good – night every night. He says he hopes you can come home when your leg gets well.

I'll take care of your Purple Heart for you when it comes.

Your mother and Dad got Roberts the other day. It is nice, but too it is sad to get them.

I hope & pray that yours will never mean the same that Roberts did.

I would give the world if you could be home now so that I could take care of you. Maybe you can someday soon though.

Be sweet and Remember I'll always love you Love & Kisses Elizabeth & Roger

With the following day came another letter from mother to dad. It, like the others, was written from Opelika, Alabama. It was dated January 24, 1945:

Dear Sweetheart,

I hope you are feeling good today. We are O.K. and are always wondering how you are. I just hope and pray that you will get along fine and can soon come home.

I dreamed last night that I was sitting on Mamma's porch and looked out the road. And there you were coming. You can imagine how happy I would be if that were only true. I thought you looked so nice, just like you did when you were on furlough.

Sweet, I know you must feel bad because you can't get any of my letters. Don't think that I haven't been writing you, for that is one thing that I do every day, whether I do anything else or not.

I've written you every day, and sometimes twice since I heard you were wounded.

Maybe you will get them sometime.

I recieved several nice letters from friends today one from Johnnie, Mrs. Conway. Mary Tucker, and Mrs. Carell, they all said to send you their best regards for a speedy recovery.

Mary is worried about Tucker, she hasn't heard from him in over a week.

It really has been cold here for the last few days.

Sweet, I told you about getting the car house built & the car in it, in some other letters but I'll tell you again, as you might not get the other letters for awhile.

It is a very nice one. I'm so proud of it, so that the car won't be out in bad weather.

I do hope it won't be long before you can come back and drive the car.

I'll stop, so be sweet & take care of yourself.

I'm always thinking of you, all my Love,

Elizabeth & Roger

This letter was dated Opelika, Alabama. January 26, 1945 and as far as I know there was not a letter on January 25, or at least I could not find it:

Hello Sugar,

I hope you are still feeling better today. We are all fine.

Your mother & I have been doing some cleaning today as we are expecting Mattie Lou & her family Sunday. They said they might come, and I suppose we'll go to church too.

I mopped & dusted, seemed like old times for me to be doing that huh?

I'll be so happy when I can clean house for you, Roger and myself again.

I didn't get a letter from you today. I hope you have gotten some from me by now.

I've been writing you every day, but have been sending them to your other address before I heard you were in the Hospital so I suppose they will go to Belgium then back to England before you get them. So it will be quite awhile before you get all of them. Maybe you'll get the later ones right away though.

Roger is O.K. He has been eating walnuts and playing guns. He says he is shooting Japs. He says tell you "hello".

He is a very sweet boy. Minds me <u>almost</u> every time ha!

Your mother said to tell you to write her often, that I write for her too.

Sweet, just continue to write me to Hamilton. That way Mamma can forward them to me & my mail won't get messed up when I go back.

I wish you could be back here with us, so that we could take care of you. I do hope you will soon be O.K. Maybe this war will be over and you can come back home.

Mary said that Tucker is in Co. H 137 Inf. APO #35. She says he is in the 35 div of the third Army under Gen Patton.

I suppose you know where he is by that.

She hasn't heard from him in over 4 weeks & is worried about him.

I think Arthur is out to sea again. He will be gone 18 months.

Well, sweet be careful, remember we love you and want you back real soon.

Love always Elizabeth & Roger

Here is the next letter from mother that came the following day on January 27, 1945, also written from Opelika, Alabama:

Hello Sweetheart,

I was so happy to get your two sweet letters today.

I know you don't feel good. I wish there was something I could do to help you, but I know there isn't, except to write you every day, and I do that.

I do hope & pray that your leg will soon be well and you can get up. I know it is hard having to stay in one place so long, but it could be worse if you were still out in battle.

I'm proud that you are still able to write me, just hope & pray that you will be back with us soon.

The war news seems good now. I just hope it will continue to be.

Tomorrow is Sunday, I suppose I'll go to Church, just wish you were here to go with us.

I got a letter from Mamma today, She says Arthur has gone out to Sea for 18 month. I hope nothing will happen to him.

It really has been a pretty sunny day today. Roger really has been enjoying it outside.

I think I've already told you about having two of his jaw teeth filled before leaving H'ton.

He really was a sweet boy too. Said it didn't hurt, The Dentist said that he was a regular little man not to cry. He told him to write you about it.

He had been crying with his teeth so I decided to have them fixed. The dentist wouldn't pull them and they were supposed to stay in until he is twelve years of age.

Roger really is a talker now. He never meets a stranger, talks to everyone just like he was as big as they were.

I'm proud he is that way though. I don't want him to be bashful.

He can't wait to read your letters every day. He always wants to know how your leg is.

I wish you could be here with us. We really would have a good time. I remember the last time I was here you were here with me.

Maybe it won't be long before we can be together again.

I bought me an orange – red coat for spring. I think I have already told you about it though. I wish you could see it. I think it is very pretty. I know you will too when you see it.

Sweet, I'll stop now, hoping that you will soon be feeling good.

All my Love, Eliz. and Roger

Here is a letter from Grandmother Brown dated Monday, February 5, 1945:

Dear James will answer your letters sure was proud to heare your cold was better hope your leg will soon be all right and you can walk soon I know you are tird laying down all the time it could have bin worse I am proud & thakfull your are living I can have hope of you coming back I hope that wont be long it bad to be sick when you cant be at home I wish you could be here all we can do is hope & pray that you will soon be well & can soone come home if it be the lord will for us all we are very well excep bad colds Roger is just as sweet as ever I sure will miss him & Elizabeth when thay go home I hope you have got sum of our letters by now I got a letter from Curtis to day he said he had a cold he said he hadent heard from you in a good while but hoped you was OK he hadent heard abought you being wounded when he wrote I guess he has by now I sure do hope this war will soon be over now so you all can come home I will stop for this time hope you will be feeling lots better when you get this letter

Mother

The next letter I found from mother to dad was written on February 5, 1945, as well. She mentions that dad had told her about being wounded and that he had given her some details about what happened, but she does not reveal much about it other than to say he was lucky to have not been more seriously injured

Hi Sugar,

I was so very glad to get your four letters today, and hear that you are better of your pneumonia. I've been so worried since you told me you were having troubles with your chest.

I do hope you will get along fine now. Take care of yourself & maybe you'll soon be up again.

I only hope you will get to come back to the States and never have to go back into battle again.

Shelby Ballard, you know the night watchman in Hamilton got a telegram that Harold, his oldest son, was seriously wounded.

Lots of people over here are having things like that or even worse.

I do hope that this war will soon end so that everyone can come back home.

I'm so thankful that you are feeling better & just hope you will continue to do so.

The last I heard from Mary, Tucker was still in Belgium. I don't think she hears from him very often.

I'm glad you could tell me how you were wounded. I don't see how you came out as light as you did & you so near the tree where the shell busted. It was just luck, I suppose.

I'll be so happy when you can come back home to stay. Then we can go places together & have fun. I never go anywhere now, except to Church.

We spent last week with Alma. Roger looked up at the walls & ceiling of their house & said "Uncle Jeff, this is a country house".

That is just like me isn't it? ha! It certainly did tickle Jeff,

He says he likes country houses but he likes town houses better.

It is still raining here as usual.

Well, be sweet & remember I love you.

All our Love, Eliz & Roger

With this letter dated February 9, 1945, mother has had letters from Mary Tucker and Johnnie Conway her closest friends and has found out more information about their husbands. Tucker was still in battle in Belgium but had been sent back to a rest camp in France and Carr Conway was still a P.O.W in Germany but had written eleven letters to Johnnie:

Hi Sugar,

How are you today? I hope you are still improving. I'm sorry you had to have pneumonia too. Just hope you are well of it now. Be careful and maybe you'll be back with us sometime real soon. I pray that that day will be soon. I miss you so much every day. I remember all the good times we once had together.

We'll have some more good times when you get back too.

Your Mother, Dad, Roger and I are all fine. If you could only be here with us things would be complete.

I had a letter from Mary today. She had a letter from Tucker, which was written Jan. 21st. She said he had gone back to a rest camp in France then, but might be back in Belgium now. He said it was nice getting to bathe without anyone around shooting at you. Also hadn't had his clothes off in six weeks.

Roger just has poured the ink out. I had to stop writing and clean the mess up.

I also had letters from Johnnie & Ella Mai.

Johnnie says she has had eleven letters from Carr in the last two weeks. The last was written the 24th of Nov. He must be doing O.K.

Ella Mai says she is afraid that Jim may have to go to the Army soon. Jim said he really would like to see you. They all said to tell you that they hoped you would soon be well & back in the states.

Sweet, I had an article put in the Opelika paper about your being wounded & recieving the Purple Heart. I also had it put in the "Marion County News" at Hamilton.

So many people that don't know how you were wounded can see it in the paper.

I'm going back to Hamilton Tuesday. I've been here almost four weeks.

Sugar, take care of yourself and remember I'll always love you.

Be sweet & write often

All our Love,

Elizabeth & Roger

As dad had not been getting many letters from mother those first weeks that he was in the English hospital, mother often found it necessary to catch him up on the news from back home. With this letter she is catching him up on what they all did at Christmas time, although she had already sent him letters about that earlier that he had not yet received. This letter was dated February 10, 1945, and there was a notation encircled at the top that read "Candy from Roger". Evidently, Roger had enclosed some candy for his daddy:

Dearest Sweetheart,

I was so happy to get your two letters today. I'm so sorry that you haven't been getting my letters Sweet, I have written you every day. Maybe you will get them some day.

I told you all about our Christmas in the other letters.

Harry, Margaret & Coralie were with us. Roger and Coralie really had fun Christmas morning unpacking their stockings. Roger got a blackboard from you & I. He really enjoys marking and drawing things on it. Iva gave him a pair of house slippers, Harry, Margaret & Coralie gave him a toy car & a bar of fish soap.

Alma & Jeff & kids, gave him a color Book & paint brush outfit.

Alma gave me a gown. Iva gave me some sachet bath powder & a tube of very nice lipstick. Harry & Margaret gave me three towels & a very pretty pair of panties with lace on them ha! and I was so proud of the Bracelet & musical powder box you gave me. They are the nicest things you could have gotten for me, sugar.

I only wish that you could have gotten your boxes I sent you for Christmas. I'll get you something real nice though when you come home.

I hope you get your Valentine & box of Valentine Chocolate candy that I sent you.

It was the prettiest box of candy that I could find, I do hope it will be good.

Sweet, it is such a pretty day today, I'd give the world if you could be here & we could walk around and enjoy this weather etc. Maybe it won't be long before you will be with us.

Sugar, I'm sorry your ankle is in such a bad condition. It'll take time for it to heal, I'm sure, but just be careful & it will be well before you know it. I'm so thankful you are still living. I do hope & pray that you won't have to suffer any more.

I think of you in every thing I do. Roger asks about you lots. He says he'll get those mean Germans.

He tickles me sometimes. He Calls Wash's store the "little town" & Opelika the "Big town". Yesterday he said, "mother lets go to the little town and get some candy.".

I went to town today. I got me a new blue crepe dress with rose embroidery on it for Spring.

I know you'll like it when you see it sugar. It is one that fits tight in all the places that you like for it too ha remember don't you?

Sweet, I got that $13.00 check that you had made out. I put it in the Bank, am going to put all of them in.

Your mother got two letters from you too. I know they are going to be lonesome when Roger and I go home. We're going Monday, Feb. 12, if nothing happens.

Well, I've just about written out so take care of yourself & be sweet. I will too. I love you with all my heart. Love always, Elizabeth & Roger

This next letter from mother finds her having returned to Hamilton after about a four week stay in Opelika, Alabama with dad's parents and his sister Alma. This was the last letter from her that I found in the packet and it was good to find all of these letters and V-Mails as it has filled a lot of the gaps that I was experiencing with my parent's letters. This letter was dated Hamilton, Alabama, February 12, 1945:

There was a note added at the top of this letter from mother which read: "Mamma said she had a very nice Banana pudding and thought of you when she was eating it."

Dearest Sweetheart,

Well. here I am back in Hamilton again. And to my joy I had four of your letters here waiting for me when I got here.

It is late in the night, but I will write you so that you will hear from me every day.

Sweet, you said something about losing so much weight. Don't worry about that sugar, you'll start gaining it back just as soon as you are up again.

Sweet, don't try to get up too early. I know it is hard to have to lie around, but it will be so much better for you in every way if you stay off your leg for awhile yet.

I'm so happy that you are getting along so well, I pray that you won't ever go into battle again. I just hope you will be back with Roger & I soon.

Sweet, I haven't driven the car any yet but I'm going to soon. It still looks nice. I have a real nice car house for it.

I'll keep your Purple heart for you sugar. It is very nice.

I'll stop & go to bed. Remember I'm always thinking of you and love you only.

Your wife & son

Eliz. & Roger

I will end this chapter with a V-Mail that I discovered that was written to my great grandmother, Mary Dizenia Palmer or Mammy as all her grandchildren and great grandchildren called her, from my dad while he was in the hospital in England. The V-Mail was dated April 5, 1945:

Hello Mrs. Palmer,

I will try and answer your letter. proud you are well and doing good, for my self I am doing pretty good at this time. I think I will always limp some, my ankle is stiff. I sure hope someday it will be OK. I am gaining my weight back now, I was in pretty bad shape at one time, but I am happy and think (thank) God I am still living. I just hope and pray that some day real soon I can be back with my wife and boy, and youall. Eliz. sure did send me a sweet picture of her and Roger the other day. Harrison sure was lucky wasent he? I hope he never haft to come over seas, I will stop as news is short.

wishing you the best of luck Love James

Chapter Nine

Letters Written after Dad's Return to the States

Dad had returned to the States and had been admitted to a hospital in Jackson, Mississippi. Mother had received a notice that he had returned to the states and I am including it here:

11 May, 1945
Mrs. Mary E. Brown
Hamilton, Ala.

Dear Mrs. Brown

This is to inform you that pfc. James G, Brown was admitted this hospital 10 May 1945 for further observation and treatment.

You are welcome to visit him at any time. Visiting hours are from 6:00 pm to 9:00 pm daily and 2:00 to 9:00 pm on Sundays.

His mailing address until further notice will be: Foster General Hospital. Jackson. Mississippi

Sincerely yours.

David B. Plasman

1st Lt., MAC

Register

Here is dad's first letter to mother from Foster General Hospital in Jackson, Mississippi. It was dated May 10, 1945:

Hello Sweet

Well here I am at the Hospital got here this morning at six o'clock. The Captain said we would get a thirty day leave in three are ten days after we are here. I might get one in the next few days being not much rong with me. So I might be there most any time now. I sure did want to git off in B'ham last night. We came through about seven o'clock. I wish I could be home for Mothers day but I dont think I will make it that quick. If I knew I would be here 10 days I would have you to come and stay with me, but I dont know, I might not be here but three are four days! I hope not any way (I think he means he hopes he won't be there 10 days.). I guss you got my letter I wrote in B'ham last night and card.

Darling I cant wait to see you. I wont write much. I want to wait and hold you in my arms and tell you lots of things. So be sweet I hope to see you and Roger soon. I could keep writing lot I will wait till I see you.

All my love and kisses James

This letter from mother to dad was dated Hamilton, Alabama, May 3, 1945. This was the first letter in which mother knew about dad's being shipped back to the States from England as she had been sent a notification of evacuation from the War Department:

Hello Sweetheart,

Well, I'm home again. Had a nice vacation. I liked Illinois fine. I'm glad to be home again.

I got a card from the War Dept. saying that you were evacuated to the United States April 17. I didn't know whether to write you anymore until you land or not. I do hope I'll soon hear you are somewhere near here, or at least somewhere in the States so that I can see you.

Gee! I was so happy to get the card saying that you were coming back. I've been looking forward to hearing that so long.

Roger was so glad when I told him you were coming home.

I got a letter from Arthur a few days ago. He still seems to be rather busy. Says he doesn't know very much to write.

I'll stop now hoping to see you soon.

All my Love Always, Elizabeth

This letter from mother to dad was her written on 5-12-45 and postmarked May 13, 9"30 am, 1945:

Hello Sweetheart,

You can't imagine how happy & surprised I was to hear that you were in B'ham and on your way to Jackson, Miss.

I got a card from the Hospital in N.Y. saying that you were there.

Sweet I'm so happy that you're back in the States. I'll just be so glad when you get here.

I hope you'll be home in a few days. I was hoping you would be here tomorrow too, but of course I know you can't come until they tell you.

Today is Saturday. It would be nice if you were here and we could walk around the court Square like we used to and see all the folks ha!

Roger said "I am so tickled". I asked him why and he said "because my Daddy is Coming home".

I would give anything to see you right now. It seems years since we were together.

I wrote your mom that you're coming soon. I suppose you wrote her too.

Well, I'll stop, hoping to see you real soon.

All My Love, Always Elizabeth

If you don't get your leave soon, let me know & I'll come to see you.

I suppose it put them both in quite a quandary trying to decide whether mother should come to see dad immediately. The Army wouldn't let dad know when he would get his 30-day leave, in three days or ten, so it made it impossible to make plans to travel to Jackson, Mississippi for mother. Her next letter to dad was dated 5-14-45:

My Dearest,

I was so happy to hear that you are so near home now, of course I wish you were with us now, but maybe it won't be long now.

I look for you every day I'll be so glad to see you.

Herbert and I talked about driving down there to see you yesterday but we were told that it was 300 or 350 miles

& I know we couldn't get that much gas & if you were coming right away, I would keep the gas for you.

I would come to see you if I knew you would be there several more days. Let me know. I hope you'll be home now soon.

Roger begged and begged to go see you.

I don't know who looked for you the most yesterday, Roger or me.

bye for now, sugar

All our love Always Eliz & Roger

The next letter I found from mother to dad was dated May 18, 1945 and postmarked May 18, 1945. At this point dad was probably near to getting his thirty-day leave:

Hello Sweetheart,

I was so glad to get your letter this morning. I'm sorry though that you can't come home this week-end, if you're not here by Sunday, I'm coming to see you.

I was just hoping so much that you would be here this week-end, but I'm thankful though that you are as near home as you are.

I'll be so happy when I can see you – Gee! We're both fatties eh! You weighing 170 & me 131.

Roger is still fat too. He had two more teeth filled yesterday and acted like a perfect Gentleman. The Dentist just thought he was a perfect child to be so good. I had my last wisdom tooth pulled & it hasn't bothered me any thus far. I'm certainly glad to have it out as it was the one that was so hard to come through the gum.

Roger came running to my bed this morning when he got up and asked "Did Daddy Come"? He looks for you every day.

If you don't think you can come this week-end, send me a tele gram & I'll be there right away.

I want to see you so bad, but I didn't know whether to come or not as you said you might come any time.

Thanks so much for the picture, sugar, It is good of you. I'm so proud of it. We got a letter from Arthur. He is O.K. I got a letter from Tucker yesterday. He was wounded April 13 or did you know? He is in Germany now though.

All my Love, Eliz

Mother wrote dad this letter the following day on May 19, 1945 and by this time she knew that dad may probably have already been on his way home on his leave:

My Dearest,

I got your letter last night saying that you would probably be home today or tomorrow.

I thought I would write you anyway and tell you that I won't come if you don't get in this week-end, that is if you think you'll be home by next week.

I surely want to see you, but like you said if I was on my way down there & you on your way here, that would never do, would it sugar? I'm just hoping that you'll get home today.

Everyone around H'ton asks when you're coming. Marvin Knight came here to see you & Olan & Reese Shotts said they sure wanted to see you.

Johnnie got a telegram from the War Dept. saying that Carr has been freed from the prison camp & he'll be home soon. I'm sure glad for them.

All my Love, Eliz

There was a letter from Alma, dad's sister, that I will include here as it was relevant to dad's coming back home and everyone's anticipation about when he would get his leave. Her letter was dated 5-14-45:

Dear James

I got your letter just now & was happy to get it. So happy you back in the states - how I thank God for – you to get back. I can't hardly wait to see you & sure hope you get to come home this week. I got a card from Eliz. Sat – siad she got a letter from you & you thought you see us all in a few days.

I just hope & pray that Curtis can come home now We havent herd from him in about three week I just hope he on his way home. James we all well & still working in the mills the Kids in shool this is the last week I be proude in a way it out they had a play Fri night & they was in it they did good. Betty Jane & Harry sure did do there part good. Marvin was a little shame. We all went to the church yesterday had a all day sanging Mama & I taken dinner head (had) a plenty dinner & sure did have a good singing. I give mama a dress for mother day. She got a present from Eliz & Eloise to. Well I guess I better close for this time hope to see you real soon.

Your sister as ever

Now I will return to dad's letters to mother beginning with May 15, 1945. His last letter from England was written April 13, 1945. I am assuming he must have been on board ship on his way home during that month long period. This letter from dad to mother was dated May 15, 1945 and postmarked May 16, 12:30 pm, 1945. I found it interesting as he expanded upon the details of his ankle injury and commented on the seriousness of that injury. He wasn't sure at the time if he would ever recover from that injury and the pneumonia he contracted while at the English hospital. He had also mentioned that he would send a photo of himself at that hospital which I still have today. I've been told that photos like that were rare because the Army would not allow soldiers to send them home for security reasons. He was writing from Foster General Hospital in Jackson, Mississippi:

My Dearest Darling Wife,

I just recived your two very sweet letters was I proud to hear from you all. I also got one from Alma to they was all well said they had a sanging in the church Sunday and dinner. I bet they had a nice time said her and mama carried dinner. I wish me and you and Roger could have been down there to help them eat all that stuff dont you sweet. Where did you go sunday. I bet I know – you stayed at home looking for me Darling. I would have give the world to have been there where we could have gone some place together. They take there own time here at this place, but they have so many to send on furlough and do everything else to. I might not git home this weekin. I was talking to the Doctor today he said we all would be on furlough by next week. I dont know what to do if I had known I was going to be here this long I would have had you come and stayed and we could have went back togather, but as it is, I dont know when I will be leaving. I do know if they dont make up there minds I am going to make it up for them, Sweet you said you and Herbert started to come down I wish you had come if you could get enough gas. Always same thing. I cant get a leave and you coulden get any gas, but God knows best we will be to gather when the time comes for us to – so I am praying for the best and try to stay here for a few more days as bad as I hate to Darling. I want to see you so bad and love you I know we could have more fun to gather now thin we ever did. We know what it means to be away from each other. I have prayed and sheded lots of tears to get this clost back to you. I woulden never thought I could have stood what I have and bee in good condition like I am now. I am 170 pounds and feel good all except my ankle pains me some I got it pretty bad in the ankle in the joint. I have a picture I will send you was taken in England at the Hospital few days after I got up with the pneumonia.

Darling be sweet and take care of yourself and Roger.

It looks like we might have some bad weather tonight bad cloud coming up and lighting.

Sweet stay good and strong I might come in most any time now and I might be hard to handle.

by for now, and good night to you and Roger boy.

P.S. Sweet I dont know where to tell you to come are not. I might come most any time now. I will send you a telegram if I haft to stay over this weekin and you can come notice my adgress have changed some ward 96, and pvt. Since I got back, I hope I will be a civilian next.

Love James

Dad continues to be in a quandary with this letter with this letter to mother in that he still doesn't know when he will get his furlough to come home, This letter was dated May 16, 1945 and postmarked May 17, 12:30 pm, 1945 from Foster General Hospital, Jackson, Mississippi:

My Darling Wife,

How are you today sweet? fine I hope for me I am OK – only want to see you all. Darling one day seem like a week around this place. They are still checking on me the Doctor said I would be getting my furlough Sat are sunday. so you can see they keep me thinking I am leaving, so I dont know what to tell you to do, Darling dont think I dont want you to come you know I do but I dont want to be on my way home, and you on your way down here. I dont know where you could get a place to stay are not if you do come, but I am pretty sure I will leave by the first of next week anyway I hope So pull fore me hope I do you know how the army is.

I love you true Love James

I am assuming dad got his thirty day leave about this time of May 16, 1945 or so because there were no letters from him until June 11, 1945 when he had returned from his leave and was now back in the hospital. He was thanking mother for loving him and was so appreciative of how she would do anything for him. He was so proud to be loved by such a pure and sweet girl who was loyal to him while he had been away. This letter from him to mother was from Foster General Hospital and dated Tuesday night, June 11, 1945:

Hello Sweetheart,

I hope you are feeling fine tonight sweetheart, I know you wasent feeling good when I left you Monday morning,

I could tell you was trying to make your self feel good. you sure was sweet all the time I was there I feel so good about you I was wanting to come back before I got here last night. I thought of you all the way back sweetheart. Darling I would give any thing to get out of this place and come home to stay with you always. I have never saw any one change so much you proved that you loved me and wanted to be with me, by not going ahead working and doing things you would lay around with me and do anything I wanted to do. you dont know how proud I am of you to have some one that loves me only and was a true little girl while I was gone. I love you more thin any thing on earth sweet.

Sweet I am proud every thing was OK after our P.X. Rubber dident stand up ha. I know you are to, you sweetheart, sweet I hope I can soon be back to stay. we can have so much fun to gather of corse we lost lots of sleep while I was there and we dident feel so peppy at times but when I come to stay we will have plenty time to catch up on our sleep when we loose some and wont haft to be worrying about when my furlough will be up wont that be a happy day? Then we can do what we planed and I can be with you ever night and what a good time we can have. Darling I wish I had you here tonight are I was there. You are my true and Sweet Darling wife. I love you with all my heart. all my Love James

Here is a letter in response to dad's previous letter from mother acknowledging that he had returned to the hospital from his furlough. It was dated Hamilton, Alabama, June 15. 1945 and postmarked June 15, 4 pm, 1945:

My dearest,

I was so glad to hear that you got to the Hospital O.K. Am sorry you had so much trouble though.

I suppose you were worn out and ready to sleep some weren't you?

I hated for you to go back and miss you more than ever before. I'm still hoping that you will get that discharge.

Roger said that he didn't want you to go back.

Harrison, Margaret & Coralie came the next day after you left. He was so disappointed because he missed seeing you.

He looks nice in his civilian clothes (Harrison had diabetes and received a medical discharge.) He has a job in the Airplane factory in Birmingham making $375.00 per month, He goes to work Monday.

Iva is here too. She is getting along fine now, Can eat almost anything.

Sweet, I do hope you won't be sent very far. I'll be so happy when you're home to stay.

We had such a wonderful time together the three weeks you were here (So, he didn't get a 30 day leave but only a three week one.).

The weather is really scorching here now.

Well, be sweet, I love you only Eliz & Roger

I have a bundle of letters that were sent back (This explains what happened to so many of mother's letters, but the ones she was talking about here were not included with the ones I found.) The ones I wrote you before Christmas. I'll keep them.

This next letter from mother to dad was incorrectly dated 7-16-45. It should have been 6-16-45 as it was postmarked June 16, 4:30 pm, 1945:

My Dearest,

I've just received your three very sweet letters. Roger was so proud of his chewing gum & I was too ha!

That was so sweet of you to tie the letter up with a ribbon. It was so cute I'm keeping it for my scrap book too.

Sugar I had a wonderful time while you were here with me. That is the way I like it too, just you and me. We always have such a good time. I hope you will be out of the army so that we can be together always.

I really miss you sleeping with me too. I hated to wake up the next morning after you were gone and see that you weren't in the bed with me.

Harry & Margaret went back yesterday.

I got the recapped tire yesterday & it looks O.K. it was $8.50.

We got the rest of your furlough gas too.

We've had several rains here too and the weather is scorching hot here now.

Be good. you know I am always.

All my Love Always, Liz

I am returning to dad's letters to mother now so that communication may be kept flowing consecutively between them. This letter from dad was dated Wed, 13 -1945 and postmarked June 13, 6:30 pm, 1945:

Dear Sweetheart,

Just a few lines hope you all are well for me I am doing OK I guss – only I would like to be with you sweet. I miss you more thin ever now after having such a good time. now all I can do is to lay around and think about you. I went to the show last night sure was good dime a dance was the name of it. I hope you get to see it some time I know you would like it, lots of loving and so own. how is Roger's sores better I hope if not you had better cary him to the Doctor, sweet they havent done any thing yet, lots of the boys are leaving that came back from furlough last week. So I guss I will get a thirty day furlough when I get to the other Hospital at least the other boys are but dont build up your hopes to much sweet. I guss Iva is there by now till her I said hello and I hope she will soon be O.K.

Well sweetheart I dont know much to write.

Darling you know I love you more thin any one on earth, so always be as sweet as you was while I was there. all my Love and kisses James

Dad wrote several letters postmarked the next day on June 14. I will include two of them. The first one was postmarked June 14, 3 pm, 1945 from Foster General Hospital, Jackson, Mississippi:

My Darling Wife,

Well it have rained here all day have you all had any rain since I left? I hope so, your mother said she needed some on her garden tell her if she had part of this she wouldn't need any more for a long time. sweet I sent you a little package today I hope you get it OK and like it they quit letting the boys have any------?(couldn't decipher) and things like that, cant no body get them but the nurses. Sweet I am proud I brought my picture I can sit here and see where I have kissed you if I cant now, I hope it wont be long before I can kiss you and love you again, sweet I miss you so much. I feel like I could love you more thin ever now since you was so sweet while I was there. you sure wasent joking when you said you was going to show me a good time when I got back. I can say I relly enjoyed thoes 21 days. you know it is nice to have a sweet little wife to come home to some one you know relly loves you, and want to be with you and no one else. Sweet I am so proud of you I dont know how to explain my self all I can say I am all yours Darling. sweet I coulden get started telling you all I wanted to while I was there. I was proud to be back with you and find you looking so good, and ready to have a sweet time, you know it is good to have a sweet wife to huddle up with at night some one that never forgits you when you are away are at home and she huddles with no one but you. I have a wife I am proud of Darling I love you true with all my heart.

Love James

lllll xxxx

This was another letter from dad dated Thursday, 14 (June 14, 1945) and postmarked June 14, 1945, Jackson, Mississippi. Dad gets very romantic in this letter and very descriptive of the parts of mother's body and how he enjoyed them, so be prepared:

My Darling Sweetheart

How are you today sweetheart! fine I hope, for myself I am ok to be at this place. I wont never be perfect till I get back home with you to stay sweet, I am hoping that will be soon dont you? I went to two good shows last night, wish you could have been here and went with me, they would have been lots better every thing are better when I am with you sweet, best time I ever have is when me and you are laying around loving. I know you are the sweetest and lovsings (loveliest) girl in the world. I guss you will get tired reading the same old thing all time, you should like the same old thing, I still love you I want yours to be that always sweet, I want you to love no one but me my sweetheart. I know I love you and no one else. I cant hardly stay in this place now after being with you. Sweet I want you to stay big like you are now you are just right I think you have pretty legs just the way I always wanted them to be, that's the only place you have gained any I think and I woulden take anything for that. you know what I like better than any thing is to lay on you and love and kiss, just like laying on a feather pillow so soft and smooth, and what a sweet girl. do I like that little squise you have. when I get out of this Army I am going to give you a good working over. I bet I can stay with you, we wont mind thin if something does happen. I wont haft to be so careful about leaving any thing in you will I sweet? as often as me and you do it when we are together, three and a half years are pretty good for a couple that relly likes to love and have a big time like me and you do dont you think so. Darling you can belive with all your heart that I love you true and no one else can never take your place, because Darling I loved you at the start and I will love you forever more, not but one thing that would relly brake my heart in Love would be for you to say you dident Love me any more, I hope we will never say that sweetheart dont you? Sweet they havent told me any thing about when I would leave yet. I will stop writting but I wont stop love you, so be sweet till we meet again, soon I hope.

all my Love James

xxxx

This next letter from dad to mother was the last one I found during the time he was in Jackson, Mississippi. For about two weeks there were no letters so I am assuming that he must have gone on leave and returned to mother and Roger before being reassigned to a new hospital. This letter was dated Friday morning and postmarked June 15, 2 pm, 1945:

Hello Darling,

sweet how are you feeling? fine I hope Darling – for myself I am OK only I would like to be with you sweet. I know I could have a big time. I feel just like having some fun. I bet you do to by now. Darling I have never felt so in love with you. I want to be with you ever minute something you done to me while I was there that makes me love you more than ever, I belive you can love a man more in a minute thin any other girl could the rest of her life. you are the sweetest girl that ever lived Darling, you mean all the world to me sweet. I wish I could spend the rest of my life with you and could be like thoes 21 days was. I had lots of fun with you sweet. I sure will be happy if I ever get a discharge where I can come home to stay with you not 21 days but always sweetheart. I hope to get a letter from you today. I would like to hear from you, you wasent feeling good when I left. I hope you are feeling fine now sweet, well they havent told me when I would leave yet some of the boys from Ala left for florida last night. I sure hope I can go some place where I can get a place for you to stay. I want you to be with me all you can. they are sending

524

some of the boys to Georgia. I hope to be one of the boys that goes there. I won't be so far from home thin.

Sweet when you get tired of this stuff let me know. I know you get tired reading the same old thing ever day. I love you always sweetheart, All my Love and Sweet Kisses
James

llll lllll lllll lll xxxxx xxxxx

There was a two-week gap with the letter writing from dad to mother because dad had finally gotten a leave and was home with mother and Roger. The next letter from dad had no date written inside but was postmarked July 1, 4 pm, 1945. This letter had Saturday afternoon written at the beginning so that would probably have been June 30, 1945. Evidently dad had gone on leave as he indicated in this letter he had just returned from one:

Hello Sweetheart,

Just a few lines hope you all are feeling better by now. for myself I am doing OK I guss I got here this morning about eight o clock. I mean I was out and sleepy to. it have been raining down here this afternoon and called everything off, maby I can sleep good tonight I hope so. I sure will miss going out to see you now, but it looks like ever thing happens rong for us but maby some day we can have some more fun like we use to. tell your mother I said I hope she will soon be well. I will stop. tell Roger hello for me. Love James

The next letter from dad to mother was written two days later on Monday, July 2 1945 and was postmarked July 2, 1:30 pm, 1945, Jackson, Mississippi:

(There was no salutation on this letter which was unusual.)

I just got your letter sure was proud to hear from you all. glad your mother is better hope she will soon be well – about that Discharge I am afraid I wont get it. I think I will git limited duty. I dont know yet, I will let you know just as soon as they let me know.

I hope you dont get sick from that washing dont be doing to much. I sent you thoes letters (He may be referring to the ones mother was sent back that were written by her around Christmas of 1944.). Alma said she might come. I wrote her that you was back home so she might come up there, I was hoping to get a three day pass for the fourth but they wont give me one. I dont know when I will be seeing you again soon I hope.

all my Love and kisses James

This next letter was the first letter I found from mother in response to dad's letters that he wrote to her after returning from his leave. This letter was dated Hamilton, Alabama, July 6, 1945, so dad must have gotten a three pass after all for The Fourth of July:

Hello Dear,

I hope you got in fine without any trouble we're O.K. except a little tired. Lina & I canned the beans today. We got 24 quarts. I'm really glad it is over.

I'm not going to do anything tomorrow though. I'm resting until Monday & then start canning peaches. Gee! As you know it is really a busy time here.

I hope you know something about what they are going to do with you now.

I hope you will be back on a pass soon, or I had rather it would be a discharge.

I really miss you so much. I know I worried you out by working so much, but I promise you I won't be working when you come again.

Roger is fine. He is still playing with his canning. I can't get him to play like a boy.

bye for now all my love, Liz

There was also a letter to dad from his mother, Betty Brown, included in the same envelope as the previous letter. It was addressed Opelika, Alabama, Rt #4, July 5, 1945:

Dear James,

was glad to get your letter today. glad you was doing fine. for us we are doing very well I guess for this hot weather. I got a letter from Elizabeth this week proud Roger was doing fine hope Mrs. Palmer will soon be OK.

I got a letter from Curtis tuesday he was still in England said he was proud you got back OK said he hadent got a letter from you sents you left england said he thought he would be home by now but hope he would be soon, I sure do hope you will get a discharge so you can come home looks like they would give you a discharge. It sure is raining here now, Arthuers (Arthur Owsley was her brother.) boy is here they come yesterday they going home tomorrow they work all the time your Daddy find sumthing for them to do all the time well I will stop write me soon, love mama dad

Also included in this same envelope was a letter from Alma Sanders, dad's sister. It was dated Friday morning, July 6, 1945:

Dear James,

I will answer your letter I got yesterday was proude to here from you glad that you was well. for us we all well. James I could not get off work this week. I sure did want

527

to. Jeff is drinking and I coulden leave the boy with him you understand how it is with me. did you get to go home for the forth I hope so. I will stop for this time write soon.

Love Alma Betty Jane & Marie said Hello

The next letters are from dad to mother. I will include mother's letters to him during this time period after his letters to her. The content of this first letter seems to indicate that dad had just returned from another leave, so he must have gotten The Fourth of July off. It was dated July 6, 1945 from Foster General Hospital, Jackson, Mississippi:

Hi Sweetheart

I got hear this morning about nine oclock made in OK only got pretty sleepy. I hope you are feeling OK. Well tomorrow is the day I go before the board I hope I make out OK, out of the Army dont you Sweet? two boys in my ward went before the board while I was gone they are going to fort McPherson Ga to be discharged I think that is a Separation center, but where I go I dont know, if I get a discharge I am going to buy me a new suit to wear home. I saw a good show tonight at least this afternoon, did you go last night after I left?

Well so long sweet and keep pulling for me to get that discharge. I Love you only forever, tell Roger I said hello.

all my Love James

Dad had finally learned about where the Army would be sending him with this next letter dated Saturday afternoon, July 7, 1945, and postmarked July 8, 1:00 pm, 1945:

Dear Sweetheart

just a few lines to let you know how I come out. they are sending me to fort mackperson (Fort McPherson) Ga. I dont know where I will go back to duty or not. I guss I will I havent anought points to get out. I will leave sometime next week about monday I guss. I dont know where I will get to come home. I dont know where I will get a furlough from there or not, this sure is a lonesome place here today no where to go and nothing to do. if I had the car down here I would come by when I left here.

did Alma Come, I havent herd from any of them this week How are your mother better I hope tell her to hurry up and get well.

I will stop for this time, by Darling and be sweet, till Roger I said hello

all my Love and Sweet Kisses James

Dad wrote another letter to mother the next day on Sunday, July 8, 1945 from Foster General Hospital. It was postmarked July 9, 2:30 pm, 1945, Jackson, Mississippi:

Hello Sweetheart,

Well this is old blue sunday still nothing to do. I guss you are at church I should go but havent got courage anought to do anything. my Lt. told me this morning I would go back to General duty in three months, they are sending me to limited duty now – they havent saw any one buck yet. I have made up my mind plenty boys getting out and not half as much mater with them as there is with me, so I will haft to get my discharge the hard way, the way I get ever thing – but I wont worry about that you cant be honest and get by in this man's Army.

I know I am not able to go back to duty if I was they would discharge, CDD. that's about all I know right now. I will get that Discharge yet.

So be sweet I love you only Darling
Dad mentioned having received two letters from mother in this last letter from Foster General Hospital in Jackson, Mississippi. It was dated Tuesday, July 10, 1945 and postmarked July 10, 7:30 pm. 1945:P

My Dearest Sweetheart,

I just got your two letters – proud to hear from you, but sorry to hear all the bad news – sure hate that about Miss Britton – I know the little boy took it hard, he was just about bigger anought to relize what it mint. I sure hope your mother will soon get well I know she will worry more now thin she have sweet I am leaving from here tonight to mcperson Ga for limited duty. I dont know where I will go from there, home I hope. so dont write me any more down here. I will send you my adgress when I get there. if you need me for anything before I send you my adgress, the Red Cross can get me quicker than any one.

I will stop for this time I love you with all my heart Darling. I sent you some Clinex (Kleenix tissues) I hope you get it. Till Roger I said hello and to be a good boy. Till your mother I said take care of herself and not be trying to work.

Darling I Love you sweetheart so by now Love and Kisses
James xxx

xx

Here are some letters that I found from mother to dad during this time period. The first one was dated July 9, 1945, It was postmarked July

10, 1945 and stamped Returned as were others written after this. Dad had already left Foster General Hospital in Jackson, Mississippi and was on his way to Fort McPherson, Georgia:

> Hello Dear,
>
> I was glad to get your letter & hear that you got back O.K.
>
> Well, I suppose you've been before the board and I do hope you're going to get that discharge.
>
> Gee! I would really Be thrilled if I saw you walking home with a new Civilian suit on.
>
> Yes, I went to the show the night you left. I saw "There Comes the Waves". I've been so busy since though that I couldn't think of a show.
>
> I washed today and canned 14 qts. of peaches, the ones on the tree above the house. They really do look pretty and I'm glad it's done.
>
> I'm trying to get up with the work so that I won't have anything to do when you come.
>
> Mamma's arms don't seem to get any better. She still can't do anything.
>
> Well be sweet, I love you Liz

The second letter from mother was dated July 10, 1945 and postmarked July 11, 9:30 am, 1945. I am not sure but this letter must have been returned also but it was not stamped "Returned":

Hi Sugar,

I surely did hate to hear that you aren't getting your discharge. My hopes were high until I got your letter today.

I suppose you have already left Jackson if you left Monday. I hope you won't ever go back overseas. I don't think you will. I wish you could come by here on your way to Ga, Mamma's arm got worse & she went back to (Dr,) Stone. He lance it and I think it is going to be better now. He said she had 12 absesses. He said to tell you Hello. I finished the ironing today and am resting at present. Roger is fine.

Herbert came back today. He didn't get a job as usual. I'll stop now, so be sweet & take care of yourself.

All my love, Always Liz

This letter from mother to dad was never opened until I opened it seventy-five years later. It was postmarked July 12, 1945 and stamped "Returned" from Jackson Mississippi. The letter was dated July 11, 1945"

My Dearest,

I know it is very disgusting that they are going to keep you in the Army. I suppose there isn't anything we can do about it though.

I really don't see why you couldn't get a discharge if the rest can. I think the best thing to do is play off on them as much as you can. That is how just about all of them get out.

I know your ankle will bother you if you have to be on it very much anyway. I don't think they will send you back to duty, surely as many strong healthy men as there is still in the states, but of course they're the ones who get the discharges.

I do hope that when you're stationed some place that Roger & I can be with you. If we can find him a place too, then I can stay as long as you're there.

Mamma's better. Herbert & I cut & dried 2 bushels of apples today. We'll keep working for the discharge.

All my Love Liz

This was another letter from mother to dad that he never received and was never opened except by me seventy-five years later. It was dated 7-16-45, Hamilton, Alabama:

Hello Sweet,

I've received two more letters from you since I wrote yesterday. They were very sweet.

I'm so glad that you enjoyed being with me the three weeks. I wanted you to & tryed to do everything to make you enjoy your furlough, I had such a beautiful time too.

I'm just hoping you'll be home soon to stay.

I also saw a good show last night –"Winged Victory". I enjoy shows most though when you're with me.

Roger's sores are just about well. He doesn't ever say anymore about them hurting. I hope he won't get anymore.

I surely hope you will get your 30 day furlough or even more, a discharge would be better. Harrison said to tell you "hello" for him. They are going back to Birmingham today.

I sent your Dad two nice pairs of socks for "Fathers Day" also a pretty card. The socks were blue and brown rayon I didn't know anything else to get.

Well, sugar I did something you will be proud of. I cut and hemmed my red checked & white dresses. They look so much nicer now, that they are shorter.

Be good and get out of the army if you can. I love you only, Elizabeth & Roger

With this last letter from dad I will close this chapter of the letters written while dad was at Foster General Hospital in Jackson, Mississippi. With this letter he was on his way to Fort McPherson, Georgia and was on a layover in Birmingham, Alabama. It was dated Wednesday afternoon, Birmingham, 2:00 pm, July 11, 1945 and postmarked July 11, 9 pm, 1945:

Hello Sweet,

Just a few lines hope you are feeling fine now. for myself I am not doing so good I left Jackson last night at 9:00 pm got to B'ham at 1:00 am. I have a four hour layover here I leave at 3:15 pm (Did he mean am?) for McPerson. I am about dead for Sleep. They are sending me back to duty my racards say. I have them with me. I dont know where I will be limited duty or not. I was hoping to get a discharge where we could start having some fun again but it looks like my fun is over for a while. I will stop for now.

All my love and sweet kisses James

Chapter Ten

Letters Written While at Camp Gordon Johnston, Florida

There were no letters written from July 11, 1945 to around September 19. 1945. I know that dad was on a furlough during this period, so that explains why. Mother and dad were also given a trip by the Army to Miami Beach, Florida during this time that would have made for the nice honeymoon that they never got to have. They stayed at the St. Moritz hotel in Miami Beach. Unfortunately for them, this was the time of the 1945 Miami Hurricane and they were trapped inside their 6th floor room a good part of the time. I remember my mother telling me that they had to save water in the bath tub in order to have drinking water.

This letter from Cora Lee Palmer, mother's mother, places mother and dad at the St. Moritz Hotel, Miami Beach, Florida on September 17, 1945. It was dated Sunday Nite (September 16) 1945:

Dear Elizabeth and James,

We were proud you got there OK. I began to think you wasn't going to write. I have been worried about you and James. I've been hearing about the bad Hurricane in Mamami Florida, I hope you all dident get hurt in the storm.

Roger is OK and being a sweet Boy. I carried him to town the Saturday you all left. We went around all day he enjoyed it. he also went to church today with Grany (Mammy). I had company and couldn't go. Mrs. Fowler from Florida was here last Sunday.

I sure have had a time trying to make jelley and can Muskidimes. Ola and Lina her kids here. Horrice got eleven gallons of muskidimes – sounds like lots dont it they sure are plentiful this time. I didnt have sugar to make much jelley so I caned most of mine. We gave Grany some sent Iva a box and he sold some he wants to get some when you all come home to eat. Well I have good news. I had two letters from Arthur he is OK I was so proud and excited when Horrice brought the letters to me I let some of my jelly burn how good I felt just to know my boy was still living. he wrote me he would be in the states in a few months but didnt know where he would get a leave or not as they didnt seem to like to give him a leave. but I believe they will if he gets back to the states. he sent Harrison one of his ships paper and Herbert spent the weekend with Harrison so Harrison sent me the paper to read it is like a book with the picture of the U.S.S. Randolph on the back it tells every thing about where Arthurs been and what they have been doing – so he has been through plenty and is still living. his ship was hit twice but the paper said the Randolph was the only ship that didn't have to come back to be repaired. Arthur will have something to tell if he ever does get back. he said in my letter if he ever got back to the States or land anywhere the first thing he wanted to do was get a pail of dirt and eat it of course he was kidding. he had seen water water till he wanted it mixed with something else.

Well I must stop and get some sleep the boys is turned out from school for two weeks so I'll have to get them up early to go to work.

Roger says good nite Daddy and Mother every nite

by now love Mother

Dad had finally found out where his new assigned location was with this next letter to mother, and he was not at all pleased. This letter was the first one from Camp Gordon Johnston, Florida and was dated September 19, 1945:

Hello Sweet,

I got here OK this is one more place. I woulden make my old suck egg dog stay in a place like this. I never saw a place over seas that would come up with this. tallasas (Tallahassee) was the last I saw till I got here. I sure hope you made it OK. I know you was worried out and sleepy. they havent told me what they was going to do with me. I dont know where I will stay here or go some place els. I sure hope I dont haft to stay at this place. sweet I dont know much to write about just be sweet till I see you again. I hope that will be real soon. tell Roger I said hello and to be a good boy,

all my Love, James

This letter from dad to mother seems to have been written about the same time as the previous one judging from its content but it was dated Monday with no calendar date. It was postmarked September 25, 10:00 am. 1945:

Dear Sweet,

I got hear this morning about six oclock in time for breakfast. Was I tired and worried out. havent done any thing this morning but lay around and sleep. I had company all the way down here. I sure will be proud when I make that last trip to the army. I hate this place more every day I stay here. I would be willing to take any kind of discharge to get out from here. Sweet I dont know much to write. I got my birthday card today was very nice. Sweet when I find out where I am going to be stationed I will

try and see if I can find you and Roger a place to stay. I
will stop for now.

I Love you only Darling

Love James

The next letter from dad was dated the next day on Tuesday, and also
postmarked September 25, 10:30 am, 1945:

Dear Sweet,

How are you? fine I hope for me I am doing OK in this
fox din. I am still alive any way I am going on sick call
this morning, at least they told me to come down I guss
they want to tell me I am in good shape for the Inf. I cant
make them like you do. you said I wasent any good but I
cant make them belive that. I think I will be station here
till I git out maby driving a truck are doing something like
that, but I will haft to do something till I get out.

I havent wrote mama are Alma any yet I guss they think I
have forgot them I havent felt like writing any body much,
sweet dont forget I love you and remember I will always
be true where ever I go.

all my Love and kisses, James

I am now going to include some of mother's letters to dad so as to
continue some sense of communication between the two of them. These
letters from mother were written to dad's new post at Camp Gordon
Johnston, Florida, where he was sent after their vacation in Miami Beach,
Florida. This first letter from mother was incorrectly dated September 19,
1941 and was of course supposed to be dated 1945. It was postmarked
September 19, 4:30 pm, 1945, Hamilton, Alabama:

Hello Dear,

Well, I'm home and didn't have too much trouble getting here. We had a flat tire outside of Tallahassee and had to get on another bus. We had to change busses in Marriana but didn't change anymore until I got to B'ham. We got there at 1:30 and didn't leave until 6:00 this morning so I got here at 9:30 this morning.

Roger was really glad to see me.

Gee! I surely miss you sugar. It just doesn't seem right for you to be away as we have been together for quite awhile (This explains the 2 month gap in letter writing as dad was on furlough from mid July to mid September, 1945 it appears.).

How do you like the camp? I just hope it isn't bad.

If you're gonna be stationed there try to find a place for us.

I hope you can get a pass before long.

I'll stop as I'm so sleepy that I can't hold my eyes open.

Take care of yourself I love you, write us soon, Liz & Roger

Roger said to bring him some more coconuts (These were the coconuts that dad brought from the Miami Hurricane. They are over 75 years old.)

The next letter from mother to dad was written the very next day and was dated September 20, 1945, and postmarked September 21, 4:30 pm, 1945, Hamilton, Alabama:

Hello Dear,

I suppose you have gotten settled down to your camp now. I hope it isn't too bad.

I feel better now that I got a good nights sleep last night.

I started minustrating yesterday. I really was early caused from riding so far.

I surely do miss you. Roger asked the first thing why you didn't come back.

I saw Maxine Sims & her husband in town today. You know he was the Sergeant in the C.C.C.

I got a letter from Johnnie & Carr. They are in Texas.

I also got a letter from Arthur. He sent a paper which was printed on his ship. It told everywhere he had been & how many times his ship was hit, three times I think, and he has really been places.

I hope you can get from down there. Do you think you will get a pass anytime soon I hope so.

I'll stop now, so be careful write me.

I love you Liz & Roger

I sent you the birthday card as I already had it and didn't have it with me on your birthday (September 11).

Mother's next letter was written the following day on September 21, 1945 and was postmarked September 22, 9:30 am, 1945, Hamilton, Alabama:

Hi Sweet,

Got your letter this morning. I'm sorry that you have to be in such a bad place. I know it is terrible being so far from nowhere. Maybe you won't stay there long. I surely hope not.

I miss you so terribly much. It doesn't seem right for you to be gone now.

I've kinda gotten over my sleepy spell & have all my clothes clean and hung up.

Do you think there is any chance of your getting a pass? What are you doing now?

If it is that far from town I don't suppose you could even find a room for Roger & I, but if you stay there we want (not ?) to be with you (I don't understand why she said not to be with you.).

If you can find any Ipana toothpaste send me some please. Well I'll stop be sweet & write me. I love you, Liz

Here are two more letters from mother that were included in the same envelope postmarked September 26, 9:30 am, 1945, Hamilton, Alabama. The first one was dated September 24, 1945:

Hello Dear,

I hope you got back to camp O.K. and didn't have any car trouble (Evidently dad was able to get a weekend pass and went to Hamilton to see mother. He was able to drive his car back to camp.). I've been afraid that you might go to sleep while driving. I know you are so sleepy and worn out that you feel terrible. I surely wish that you could have stayed with us. Sweet I want you to keep going on sick calls every day. I believe then they will give you a discharge. Oh! here I go again talking about you getting out and you said you didn't want to hear that anymore!

I do hope if you have to stay there that Roger and I can stay with you.

I hope you can come home again this weekend. Well write me soon and be sweet.

I love you only Liz

The second letter enclosed in the envelope was dated September 25, 1945:

Hi Sweet,

I don't know very much to write as H'ton is still the same dull "No News" place.

We got good news from Arthur though. He tells us that he is in Pearl Harbor and is on his way home. He expects to be home before long. Hope you can be home when he comes.

Have they told you anything yet? I wish you could get out.

I miss you so much. I guess you are still plenty sleepy. I'm going to the show tonight.

Well bye for now all my Love Liz

Here are more of dad's letters to mother written around the same time as those written by mother that I included. This one was dated Wednesday 26 (September 26, 1945) from Fort Gordon Johnston, Florida and postmarked September 26, 4:30 pm, 1945:

Dear Sweetheart,

just a few lines hope you all are well and feeling fine for myself I am doing OK. I am in the Hospital again I sure hope they do something this time. I dont know what they will do yet all I can do is wait and see, you know how the army is they never tell you any thing just let you wait and find out for your self. I hope this time I will get what I want. I dont guss I will get to come home this weekin. I hope I will be coming with a discharge pretty soon, but I wont feel good tell I git it, and on my way home thin I will know I got what I have been wanting dont build up your hopes I might not git one this time. I dont know how long I will be here in this Hospital. I will let you know how I come out.

I have the car down here with me – this Hospital is just a little ways down the road from where I was. be sweet and take care of your self I love you only –

all my love & kisses, James

Dad was constantly in hopes of getting at least a weekend pass, but it just didn't seem to be in the cards. I believe he did eventually get one but not until about two weeks of waiting. He wrote mother every day though and this letter was written the next day and dated 27 September, 1945. It was postmarked September 28, 10:30 am, 1945, Camp Gordon Johnston, Florida:

Hello Sweetheart,

How are you today fine I hope for myself I am doing fine at this time they gave me to blood test today, you know how I like them – everything working my way now if they dont stop it on the way some where they sure are discharging lots of boys from here. I wont say I am going to get one yet that all depends on the board. I sure hope my luck is with me this time.

How is Roger and his Cold making out? I hope he is OK. I wrote mama and alma yesterday I guss they had give up hope.

What have you been doing sweet? working with your buddy – for me I am lying around waiting for some good news I hope. You never know what they are going to do till they do it, so be pulling for me. I might need a little help! Sweet I havent got a letter since I come back. I hope you still love me like you said you did.

Darling I love you with all my heart so be sweet and keep your chin up and dont forgit to smile, all my Love and kisses, James

The letters were redundant but sometimes they were written just to let one another know that they were thinking of each other. There were no emails, Facebook, Twitter or any social media in those days, just the U.S. Mail and Western Union so one did what one could. I will include just a few more of dad's letters to get the gist and then return to more of mother's letters.

Here is another of dad's dated 28 September. 1945 and postmarked September 28, 2:30 pm, 1945, Camp Gordon Johnston, Florida:

Dear Sweetheart.

just a few lines hope you are feeling fine for me I am doing OK. I havent got any mail yet. I guss they are holding it up at the reciving center where I left, but they know where I am. I sure would like to hear from you sweet. I Love you ever minut of my life, if you do say I dont act like I do sometime. Sweet I havent herd any thing new yet. I dont know how long I will be here in the Hospital it might be a month are long are it might not be that long, then I might go back to duty you never can tell, so I am not going to build up my hopes till I know.

Sweet, I dont know much to write, only I sure would like to be with you this weekin if you do think it is to far fore me to come. I havent never been to far but one time to come to see you sweet, so be sweet till I can see you again which I hope will be real soon.

all my Love and kisses, James

Dad had finally gotten two of mother's letters that he responded to in this letter dated Saturday afternoon (September 29, 1945).

Dear Sweetheart,

I got two letters from you yesterday, proud you all are well, for me I am doing fine at this time. sure proud to hear the news about Arthur, I hope he will soon be home. Well I havent herd anything new yet – if I do get out it will take at least three weeks for them to discharge me. Sure is a lonesome place here cant get out and go any place – we have classes to go to every day escept Sat & Sunday something like we had at Mimia (Miami). The Red Cross gave all the boys a party last night that had birthdays in Sept. also give us a birthday present we played games and had ice cream and cake. Wasent any girls so you dont have to be thinking any thing – you dont never haft to worry about that sweet you should know by now I love you and no one els. I wanted to come home this weekin but I dont want to be running around to much they might think I am in good shape for duty again – they might think that any way – but I want to git out if I pospil can, thin I can stay with you all time sweet. you be a sweet little girl – if I do get out we can have plenty fun like we plained to do.

Darling I Love you with all my heart – Love & kisses,
James

I'll include one more letter from dad to mother then return to some of mother's letters to him. This one was dated Sunday afternoon (September 30, 1945) and postmarked Camp Gordon Johnston, Florida, October 1, 10:30 am, 1945:
(Dad decorated the letter with floral vines that he drew around the borders of each of the pages.)

My Darling Wife,

How are you sweet? Fine I hope For my Self I am doing Fine At this time. I went to Church this morning. Very good preaching. Did you go to church? Not a bad thing to do, should go some time. ha you know I nock you out of going to Church ever Sunday I Am at home, dont I sweet? How is Roger doing? Fine I hope – tell him I said for him to write me sometime and to be a good boy Sweet all I know I am waiting to see what they are planing to do with me. I hope they do what I wont them to do.

Darling I Love you with all my heart – Love & Kisses, James

The following letters are some of the letters in which mother responded to the letters that I previously included that dad wrote to her. This first one was dated September 27, 1945 and postmarked September 28, 9:30 am, 1945, Hamilton, Alabama:

Hello Dear.

I'm writing you a few words tonight. I don't know whether you will get it or not, that is if you come home this weekend I know you won't until you go back to camp. I do hope you can come. I miss you so much, I would be so happy if you could come home to stay.

I was so glad to get your two letters today. Sweet I know that place must be terrible, but if you have to stay maybe Roger & I can be with you. That would make it better wouldn't it? I know it would for me.

Sweet, I'm sorry I said that about you not being any good. I really didn't mean it. I was only joking and you know that. I love you and you know that too.

I got letters from your mother & Alma too. They say Eloise came down Wed. & will stay until Sunday.

Alma said Mrs. Sanders moved in the house with them.

I saw a good show tonight also Tuesday night the name of it was "The Very Thought of You".

I don't think of anything else to write so be sweet and remember I love you only.

All my love Always Liz

Mother's next letter was dated September 28, 1945 and postmarked September 29, 9:30 am, 1945, Hamilton, Alabama:

Hi Sweet,

I was quite surprised to hear that you are in the hospital again.

I hope that you are O.K. I surely hope that you will get your discharge this time.

Maybe you will. I'll miss you so this weekend if you don't come home, but if staying in the hospital will get your discharge it will be fine and then you can be with us every day.

I've been working for Mr. Carpenter a few days this week. He paid me 50 cents an hour so I've made about $9.00 I think ha! that is pretty good don't you think?

I sent $40.00 of your money to the Bank. I mean the money that you were paid in Miami Beach.

Take Care of yourself Sweet

I love you Liz

Here is one more letter from mother before I return to dad's letters to mother. I will include two more letters from his mother Betty Brown as well.

This letter from mother was dated September 30. 1945 and postmarked October 1, 1945, Hamilton, Alabama:

Hi Sweetheart,

Roger and I have just gotten back from church. I received your two letters today and was glad to hear that you have hope of a discharge. I hope you won't have to stay in the hospital long and also I hope you won't have to take too many shots and blood tests.

I'd be so happy if you could get a discharge. I miss you so much sweet.

Sugar I've been writing you every day I don't know why you don't get my letters, I surely hope you are getting them now.

Sweet, you know I'll be pulling for that discharge too. I've surely missed you this week-end. Hope you can come next week-end as I would give anything to see you.

All my love always Liz

P.S. Roger is fine. His cold is well. Nora Ann is out here with him.

At this point I will include two more letters from my grandmother, Mrs. Gordon Brown (Betty) written from the same period of time. The first one was dated September 30, 1945 and postmarked October 1, 1945, Opelika, Alabama:

Dear James

sure was proud to get your letter Saturday glad you was doing very well I guess, you said you was back in the hospital are you having troble with your foot and leg I hope they give you a discharg so you can come back home I have had three letters from Elizabeth she dident say you was in the hospital she said you had been home & you dident like whire you was. I hope you wont have to stay thire long I had a letter from Curtis last week he said he was doing fine at this time but dident know when he would be home. I sure do hope he will soon be home. Eloise come last wensday & stad till saturday we was all proud to see her she spent one night with Alma. Alma has quit work Pearl gone back to Arthurs harry not doing so well he stays sick most of the time. I have got your puppy he sure is pretty he thinks he is all the dog the (there) is I am afrad he will get killed. Roy Piper and Ola & your grandpa come down here about to weeks ago they come one day & went back the next they doing fine you wanted to know how tom killed his self he shot his self in the head with a rifle, they say preston is one (on) his way home he may be like Curtis he bin going to come for two month he havent got here yet I hope he soon will we sent him sum money last week well I will close for this time write us soon let us heare from you with love & best wishes Mother & Dad

The second letter from Grandmother Brown was dated October 15. 1945 and postmarked October 16, 1945, Opelika. Alabama:

Dear James,

Will now answer your letter I received today was proud two heare you was doing fine hope this letter finds you feeling fine, for myself I dont feel good it sure has bin a bad day up here to day it bin cold raining all day.

I dont know just when we will move soon as we can I will be glad when it is over with, your daddy is through pulling corn. I dont know when he will get the syrup made. I havent a letter from Curtis in three weeks I hope he alright & will soon be home he may be on his way if he is it sure do take him a long time to get home Preston come home last night I havent see him yet I sure do hope you get a discharge & can come home Alam & Jeff was here Sunday we went to preaching.

Joe brought his wife down here Sunday was a week ago & all her folks come with them thay dident stay just a little while I dont like joes wife much. they going to build a new church at Providence they going two start one (on) it rite a way. I got a letter from Eliz & Roger Saturday. I wrote her today she said Roger dident want us to move he wants to come see us I hope you all can soon come well I will stop for this time write soon

lots of love to you mother & Dad

I will return now to my mother's letters written to dad and to those written by dad in response to her. I will begin with this one from mother dated October 1. 1945, Hamilton, Alabama:

Hello Dear,

I didn't get a letter today. I surely hope I will tomorrow. I wonder how you are getting along.

I suppose you have gotten some of my letters now haven't you?

I got a letter from Mary the other day. She says Tucker is leaving the 5th. He will go to some camp in Kentucky. She says he won't have to go overseas anymore.

I surely hope you will be home soon sweet. I miss you so much. I surely get lonesome staying around here.

I went over to see Opaleen yesterday. Her baby really has grown.

Well sweet as you can see I don't know much to write. I'll just write you a few lines to let you know I love you.

All my love Always

Liz & Roger

I will continue with mother's letters to dad then pick back up with some of dad's to her that were written about the same time period. This one from mother was written the next day on October 2, 1945 and postmarked October 3, 1945, Hamilton, Alabama:

Hello Dear,

I was happy to hear from you today. I know you get tired of that place but if you can get a discharge that way O.K. I surely hope you will. I surely miss you though. I'll be so happy when you get home, only I hope you can stay this time.

It was very nice of the Red Cross to give you boys the birthday party. I'm glad you had a good time. Say! It was a good thing that you told me there wasn't any girls present for I might have wondered about it ha!

I got a letter from Mrs. Carell and she said that they had $72.61 picking cotton this fall pretty good eh. They would do anything for money.

Well, sweet I hope it won't be long before you will be home.

All my Love Always Eliz & Roger

I will include all of the next letters from mother, even if they are redundant at times. This first one was written the following day on October 3, 1945 and postmarked October 4. 1945, Hamilton, Alabama:

Hi Sweetheart,

Well we put in the day today. Washed this morning & moved the furniture around in the front. It is so cool here that we have to put up the heater soon. Herbert is painting the floor too.

I bet it is still hot there isn't it? Everyone here have been wearing coats for the last few days.

I finally got some black material to go with my red for my dress. I'm getting Mammy to make it right away.

Sweet, I enjoyed your letters I got today very much. I surely hope you will be home soon. Sure we'll have lots of fun we always do. I still love you "bushels" and always will.

Well, get that Discharge! hear!

I love you only Liz

P.S. Roger is fine. He & I went to the show last night. He enjoyed it very much as there was a grand comedy on You Know Rabbits etc.

Mother wrote again the next day on October 4, 1945 with a letter postmarked October 5, 1945, Hamilton, Alabama:

Hello Dear,

I was happy to get your letter and hear that you are still in good hopes of the discharge. I'm still pulling for you too. Honest I hope you will get out. I think it would just about be too good to be true.

Your mother wrote me that Tom Mayberry shot himself with a rifle. That is how I thought it happened.

Alma writes that the doctor had her stop work. Mrs. Sanders has moved in with them. I don't see how they manage.

Arthur says he will be in the States on Navy Day which will be on the 28th of this month. His address is N.Y. N.Y. now. I hope you can be home when he is.

Harrison is in Washington now. I don't know whether he has found a job or not.

Well, sugar take care of yourself & write me the latest news.

I love you only Liz & Roger

In this next letter written by mother on October 5, 1945, she mentions that dad had been home with her just about all summer, so this explains why there was a two-month gap in their letter writing. The letter was postmarked October 6, 1945, Hamilton, Alabama:

Hi Sweetheart,

I'm hoping that you are going to be home before long with that <u>Discharge</u>. I wish you could be home this week-end. You said you missed me. I can't get used to being gone either as you were with me just about all Summer.

You asked about your mother and Alma. They're all O.K. except Alma & the Doctor made her stop working. Said she needed a rest.

Roger is fine. I bought him some new overalls and he had to go to town today so that he could wear them.

I got a letter from Johnnie today. Carr has been transferred to another camp in Texas. She and Jr. are staying on with him.

Well, bye sweet, I love you only Liz

There were two letters from mother in an envelope postmarked October 8, 1945, Hamilton, Alabama. The first one was dated October 5, 1945:

Hi Sweetheart,

I can hardly wait for you to get home with that Discharge. I surely hope it won't be long. Of course I wish you could come home this week-end but if staying in the Hospital will get you out of the army for good, then O.K.

We're looking for Arthur about the last of the month. I hope you will be here too.

Roger, Mama & I are going to "The Western Show" tonight. Wish you were here to go with us. I always enjoy shows more when I have you with me.

I haven't worked anymore for my "buddy" as you call him, sweet, I only work for him because I can get that experience in typing & also I can make more money at that than anything else – and it is easy. I just like to work occasionally for part-time.

Sweet, I love you & no one else and I know you love me too. I just like to kid you some times.

I hope you'll be home soon.

All my Love always Liz

P.S. Thanks for the gum.

The second letter from mother that was inside that envelope was short but sweet. It was dated the next day on October 6, 1945:

Hi Sweetheart,

I was so happy to get your letter and I'm so happy that you are about to get a discharge. I surely hope it works this time.

Roger & I went to church today. We also spent the day with Opaleen. Roger really enjoyed playing with Annette.

I'll really be glad when you get home. It seems ages since I've seen you. I'll just be the happiest girl on earth if you do get out of the army.

Sweet, I love you, be sweet and write me every day.

All my Love & Kisses Liz

The process dad went through to get his discharge seemed to have gone on endlessly and there were many more days of frustrations and waiting to be endured before his discharge was finally granted. These next letters from dad to mother are a few of the many that he wrote to her every day. He was afraid that if he left the hospital to go on weekend passes to see mother that they would believe him fit for service and not grant him a discharge. So, mother and dad thought that enduring the separation from each other was a necessary sacrifice that must be made in order to achieve their goal of getting dad discharged from the army. The whole experience must have been excruciating and must have tested their patience to the maximum.

So, I will continue with dad's letters to mother. This letter was dated Monday night (October 1, 1945) and postmarked October 2, 10:30 am, 1945:

Dear Sweet,

How are you tonight sweetheart? fine I hope for myself I am doing fine. I went to the reciving area today and checked all my clothing in. I dont know what they are going to do. if I do get out – I will be here at least two more weeks. I havent went before the board yet. I should go this week sometime. Well take care of your self and dont work to hard and make to much money. I love you only my Darling, Love and sweet dreams

Yours true forever James

The next letter from dad to mother was a bit longer and dated Wednesday afternoon (October 3, 1945) and postmarked October 4, 4:30 pm, 1945, Camp Gordon Johnston, Florida

Hello Sweetheart,

How are you fine I hope for my self I am doing fine far as I know. I got a letter from mama this morning to she told me how Tom (Mayberry) killed him self like you said, he shoot him self through the head with a rifle, she said alma had quit work some thing she should never started.

that man she has are able to make a living for two familys
if he was any good.

Well all I know about that discharge is that I am waiting.
The Doctor examed me from head to toe yesterday. he
told me I would get a CDD when I come in the H.C.
but I wont belive it till they give it to me. So dont get to
feeling good over that yet you know how the army work
things. I am pretty sure I wont git to come home this week
in but I am trying to do the best thing and git out of this
place so try and be patient with me, it is hard for me to
stay down here knowing I could be with you sweet but
whin I come this next time, I want to be where I can stat
always Darling. You know I love you and no other. You
got ever thing it takes to make a man love you sweetheart.
So dont worry about me not loving you Darling, I am
crazy about you.

The car is OK out in front of the ward, but this hot sun is
not doing it any good, but I cant help that. have you herd
any more from Arthur I sure hope he gets to come home
and I can see him. I sure would like to see the old boy. I
know he will be happy to get to come home. I know how
he feels on that old ship headed for the states instead to
Japan. I am proud for him.

I guess you are still working for your buddy. I want you
to stay in good shape I might let you go to work for me,
what I mean me stay with Roger and you work what about
that? no sweet I woulden do that to you. I love you more
than that Darling. So be sweet. I will be seeing you soon
I hope. All my Love and kisses James

The next day brought another letter from dad dated Thursday morning
(October 4. 1945) and postmarked October 4, 4:30 pm, 1945, Camp
Gordon Johnston, Florida:

Dear Darling,

Just a few lines hope you are all well and feeling fine. for myself I am doing fine at this time. Well every thing still working fine so far, if it dont back fire on me if nothing happen now I think I will be out in two are three weeks. I sure hope so any way. Sweet I sure do miss you. I would give any thing to see you and have you down here with me all that sweet loving are going to waist I hope – being I am not there. it seem like a real long time since I saw you sweet heart. I will be so happy when I do get a discharge and can come home to stay. I have been pushed around so much in this army. I am fed up with it. I wont to get out and live like somebody with the sweetest girl in the world my sweet little wife. Darling I love you more than any thing on earth. I will always be true and I want you to. I know you will. I dont worry about that you sweet little Darling. I hope to be with you soon. So stay sweet, every thing looks good now. I think I will make it.

So be sweet till I see you – all my Love and kisses James

xxxxxx xxxxxx

I continue to include dad's letters with this one dated the next day on October 5, 1945 and postmarked October 6, 1945:

Dear Sweetheart,

I just got through reading your letter. I am doing all right I guss I hope you all are well. yes sweet it is still plenty hot down here during the day, but pretty cool at night. you said you had been working hard. You shoulden do that sweet I dont want you to be working to much, next thing your back will be hurting again.

I have been taking ex rays for the last two or three days. I sure will be proud when I get out of this place – they sure do worry you this and that all time, hurry up and wait. wont have any thing to do Sat, and Sunday but lay around. maby I will get out sometime pretty soon. I guss they are working fast as they can. they have so many to take care of.

I sure would like to see you this weekin but I dont guss I can make it. I cant get a pass they have me down a bed patient, but I dont stay in bed much well be careful and take care of your sweet self, I love you only always – Love James

These letters do get repetitive, so I will just include a few more of the longer letters from dad to mother, This letter was written Sunday afternoon 1945 and postmarked October 8, 10:30 am, 1945:

Hello Sweet,

How are you Darling? fine I hope, for my self I am doing fine. this sure have been a long lonesome day for me. nothing to do but lay around. I went to church this morning – did you and Roger go? you said Arthur would be home the last of this month you thought. I sure hope he does. I think I will be home by thin to if nothing happens. I dreamed Arthur came home the other night I hope it comes true. Well I havent give up hopes getting my discharge yet. I still think I will get it, it looks better ever day for me so far so good. I dont have any complants this far. sure do have a good Doctor he wont let me do anything, not even the exercises. I hope you and Roger and all are well. tell the boys and your mother I said hello. I hope to be Home soon.

Darling I love you for ever with all my heart.

Love and Sweet Dreams, James

lll

Dad gets very romantic in this next letter as he many times did. It was a longer letter that was dated October 10, and postmarked October 11, 10:30 am, 1945, Station Hospital, Camp Gordon Johnston, Florida, Ward # 10:

Dear Sweetheart,

I got your letter, glad you all are well and doing fine. you said you was very lonesome sweet. Darling I know how you feel, I am the same way. I want to see you the worst kind Darling I miss you so much after having such a sweet time with you at home and at Miami Beach. I enjoyed it very much all except I couldn't go back home with you. I sure hated to see you go back on that bus from tallassa (Tallahassee), and me not going with you sweet heart. I love you Darling more thin any one on earth. I want you to belive that sweet in the bottom of your heart. Sweet I could never tell you how much I loved in words are in this letter if I could hold you in my arms right now, the way I feel, I dont think you would wory about me not loving you because no man could love you the way I feel like loving you, and not love you Darling. loving one girl may get old to some men, but the more I love you the more I want to. you know ever angle and move to loving sweet heart. I ment ever thing I have ever told you about the way you could do things and love, you are tops in ever thing to me Darling.

Tell Roger I am not saying much this time, but for him to be a good boy and I hope to see him real soon. I think I will get that discharge but I dont know how long it will take, days seem like weeks, when I am away from you sweetheart.

so keep pulling for me, I want to be home with you to stay when I come the next time.

you have all my Love and kisses for ever Darling –

Love James

This next letter from dad to mother was much longer than his usual "Drop a Line" letter he wrote every day. It was dated October 11, 1945 and postmarked October 12, 10:30 am, 1945. You probably have noticed that dad put marks like "X's" at the end of some of his letters. For example this one had six rows of "X's" starting with a row of six then consecutively proceeding down 6,5,4,3,2,1 at bottom as xxxxxx

xxxxx

xxxx

xxx

xx

x

Dear Sweetheart

I recived your letter this afternoon, Thurs Oct 11, glad you all are well, for my self I am not feeling so good. I just took a doss of Caster oil, you know how well I like that stuff. they are getting me ready for that exray tomorrow. I cant eat any thing before tomorrow night, I sure will be proud when they get through with me.

you said it was getting pretty cold in ala. It has been cold down here to. I been sleeping under a blanket and could have used another one. I wish I was in ala with you sweet. I belive I could keep you warm in a way that you would like very much Darling, maby I will get to come home before it gets to cold, boy wont it be lots of fun if we do get to sleep together this winter. I dident get to see you any last winter, you know we can huddle up together I like that more thin any thing – to have you by my side. I can sleep better and feel better you are the sweetest wife ever lived Darling. I cant keep from telling you when I write. Sweet I sure would like to be with you now and forever more a free man from the army.

I bet that dress you are having made will be pretty – have it ready to wear when I get home. I want you to look your best when I come with that Discharge. I feel like loving you like old times sweet so you know what that means dont you sweet heart.

I saw a good show tonight. Shirley Temple played in it. kiss and teel (tell) was the name of it. if you can ever get to see it dont miss. that was the best one I have saw in ages – lots of love and some marrying – I really liked it. Well sweet I dont know any thing else to write.

so be sweet and remember I Love you only Darling.

all my Love and kisses James

xxxxxx

xxxxx

xxxx

xxx

xx

x

I will again return to mother's letters written to dad during this time period. I believe that you will see that there was good communication and response from mother to the letters that dad had written to her. This letter was dated October 8, 1945 and postmarked October 9, 1945, Hamilton, Alabama:

Hi Sweetheart,

Received your letter today. I hope to hear in every one you are getting your discharge right away.

I know you must get tired of lying around down there in the Hospital. I get awfully lonesome too, but if you can get a discharge that way, then it is worth it.

I do mis you so much though sugar. I'll be so glad when you can come home.

When I got your letter this morning and opened it, Roger asked "Well Mother what does he say?"

Mammy is making my wool dress today. I got some black for it & I think it will be quite pretty.

Sweet, I don't work very much, not enough to hurt me anyway. Well be sweet & take care of yourself.

All my Love Always Liz

Many times, as with these next two letters, mother just wrote a few lines to let dad know she loved him and was always thinking of him. They both wrote each other every day even if it was just a few lines or so. This letter was dated October 9, 1945 and postmarked October 10, 1945, Hamilton, Alabama:

Hello Dear,

We have just come in from the Show. It was a very good one, but we almost froze to death. It really has been winter time here for the last few days.

Well sweet I suppose you have been before the board by now. I surely hope you will get that discharge, sugar I want to see you so much. I know you want to come home too. It will really be wonderful when you can be back with us to stay.

I'll stop now & roll my hair. I'll be thinking of you.

All my Love Always, Liz

This was another letter I found, that was just a bit longer, from mother. It had no envelope but was dated October 10, 1945:

Hello Sweetheart,

I'm surely anxious to hear how you will come out about the Discharge. I just can't wait to hear. I'm just keeping my fingers crossed & hoping that you will soon be out of the army & back with us to stay.

We're still looking for Arthur right away we'll really be glad to see him.

Momma said to tell you that we are planning for your discharge as we've boiled out your white shirts.

Thanks for the gum. Roger said Daddy sends us gum every time.

Sweet, it seems months since I've seen you. I'll be so glad when you get home. I'll be so glad when you get home.

I love you only

All my Love & kisses Liz

The next letters from mother are somewhat longer with more detail and information. She tried to give dad as much news as possible, but as she mentioned many times, Hamilton was a pretty boring place to be. This letter does have a bit more news though and was dated October 11, 1945 with a postmark of October 11, 1945, Hamilton, Alabama:

Hello Sweetheart,

I received your letter today. You said you were getting letters from me every day now. I write every day, although I never know very much to write about.

I hope by now that you know whether you will get the Discharge or not. I surely hope you will and write me as soon as you do hear.

Stanely and Roberta are here now. He has a discharge and he said to tell you "hello".

Oh! yes! And Laura Gene Burleson also told me to tell you hello. She is the girl that works in the Ration board.

These girls are always asking me about you. I think there is something fishy about it ha! Oh No, I'm just kidding.

Well, guess who I saw today in town. "Connie Lundy" I was so surprised to see her. I didn't know her at first. She has gained weight like the rest of us have.

I wish you could see my new dress that Mammy made. I think it is very pretty.

Well Be careful and I hope to see you soon.

All my Love & kisses Liz

The next letter from mother was written the next day on October 12, 1945 from Hamilton, Alabama. There was no envelope that I could find:

Hi Sweetheart,

Sweet I hope they aren't going to keep you in the hospital so much longer. I'm so hoping that you will get home before long.

We got the candy and chewing gum and thanks a million for it. It was very sweet of you. You always think of the candy when I am wanting it. And that is the kind I like so well. Roger was tickled over it too. Of course I didn't let him see it all as he would eat too much.

No, sugar I don't believe you know the boy who died. He was a brother to Fay Millican the boy who was in the C.C.C. with you. He died with a hemmorage of the brain. It was a mistake about the Airplane Crash.

I'm sending you a picture of myself the one that you said you would like to have it enlarged. I hope that it won't be in the way I mean too large for you to keep.

Well, sweet I surely hope you won't have to stay there too long. Of course it will be better for them to keep you there until your back & kidneys are well. I really hope they won't find anything more wrong with them though as I want you to come home before long.

Be careful and write me.

All my Love Always Eliz

I'll include one more letter from mother to dad before returning to his letters to her. This letter also had no envelope and was dated October 14, 1945, Hamilton, Alabama:

Hi Sweetheart,

Sorry you aren't feeling well. I know that castor oil was bad.

Have they taken the Ex-Ray yet? I surely hope they won't keep you in the Hospital long.

Roger & I went to church today. He is a very (good) boy in church. He is learning several new songs in his class. I can't get him to sing very much though.

I got a letter from your mother a few days ago. They haven't moved yet. She said she was really dreading to move. I haven't heard from Alma in several days. I suppose she stays plenty busy now that Mr. & Mrs. Sanders are living with them.

Sweet, I hope you will be home this winter too. It really will be nice having you to sleep with these cold nights.

I'll have my new dress ready to wear when you come. I know you will like it as I think it is very pretty.

Sugar, I'm really enjoying the candy you sent. I suppose I'll put on a few extra pounds too from eating so much of it ha! You know me though, as long as there's candy I eat.

I really would like to see you sweet. I know we could have a wonderful time.

Be sweet & write me. All my Love, Always Liz

I am returning once again to dad's letters to mother from this same time period. You will be able to see that dad is responding to and answering her letters to him. This one was dated 12 October 1945 and postmarked October 13. 1945, 10:30 am, Camp Gordon Johnston, Florida:

Dear Sweetheart,

Just a few lines hope you all are well and feeling fine for myself I am doing OK, I took my exrays this afternoon. I hope they came out OK and I can soon get out of this place. sweet you dont know how much I hate this place. I have never been in a place like this since I have been in the army.

I havent been before the board yet, they haft to get my record all fixed up first. I should go sometime next week. I dont know yet.

tell your mother I hope to wear those white shirts pretty soon. you can have my pants cleaned to if you dont mind sweet. I might not need them any time soon but in case I do they will be clean.

I dont know where I will git to come by the time Arthur gets there or not, if I don't get a discharge by then, I will try to get a weekin pass and bring the car home, where he can go around some. I am hoping to be out by thin but you cant never tell what they are going to do. they may take that peace of still (steel from the German shrapnel) out of my behind before it is all over with – but if nothing else dont hold me up, I think I should be out of here in a couple of weeks. Maby less than that I cant tell my self for sure I am just hoping I will get out sometime soon.

Darling I love you with all my heart Love James

The next letter from dad came the next day on Saturday, October 13, 1945 and was postmarked October 14, 1945, Camp Gordon Johnston, Florida. With this letter dad is getting upset with mother for saying their was something fishy about the Hamilton girls asking about him all the time, He gives her a good talking to about it too:

Dear Sweetheart,

How are you? fine I hope for my self I am doing fine. I dont know when I will get out. they havent told me any thing yet. the Doctors are looking my exrays over now. They will let me know in a few days what they are going to do. I might haft to go to another Hospital if they find anything in me that they think needs cutting out - the army keeps you gussing. if this havent come up, I would have been out by next week it all depends on how my exrays come out. If they think I will be OK I will get home quicker, so you know just about when I will git out as I do, dont worry everything will work out for the best I hope.

Sweet why did you say something was fishy about me and the ration board girl. You havent ever saw me out with her have you? I know you havent because I havent never been out with any girl. Sweet you know I love you and no other girl can never come between us, so get that in your little heart and keep it there sweet but if you belive fishy things are going on between me and her tell me so in the next letter. I have tryed to be good to you and do ever thing I could to prove that I love you, but it havent worked you still dont trust me do you? well sweet I thought when I come in here I would be home by now, but you cant tell what will happen can you sweet? somebody picking on you and the army trying to keep me. I sure would like to be with you all this weekin I get so lonesome hanging around this place, and nothing to do to pass off the time.

I bet that dress is pretty. I would like to see it. sweet keep your chin up and dont belive ever thing you hear, you might loose a good husband that way. I sure dont want that to happen.

So be sweet and dont let any thing worry you, special those girls. You have forgot more thin they will ever know about loving and looks and every thing els.

Darling I love you and you only so be sweet.

All my Love and kisses, yours true for ever, James

Dad wrote a couple of letters the following day on Sunday, October 14, 1945. The first one was dated Sunday morning, October 14, 1945 and was postmarked October 14, 1945, 10:30 am. Camp Gordon Johnston, Florida:

Dear Sweetheart,

I got your letter this morning, proud you all are well for me I am OK – lying around taking it easy hoping I will soon git out with a discharge where I can come home and stay with my sweet little wife. Sweet you said you wanted me to come home this weekin, not no more thin I wanted to come sweet Darling. I would like to see you very much but I coulden make it this weekin. I am hoping to make it for good some day real soon if every thing work out right for me. I am proud you will go places when I am away. like to the show and anyplace you wont to. I havent saw any shows since I have been down here. I saw one but it was so sorry I dident count that a show.

Sweet I know you dident mean I wasent any good. I know I am not any to good but I will let you by this time any way. I will try to be better next time. I can say one thing you are plenty good Sweet. When I get my discharge we will see if we can do what we have planed to do. I know you havent forgot what it was Sweet. I havent much to wtite about so I will stop.

all my Love and kisses – always James

Dad's second letter that Sunday was dated Sunday afternoon, October 14, 1945 and postmarked October 15, 10:30 am, 1945. Dad has just about reached wit's end with all the uncertainty and waiting to see whether or not he was get his discharge and he compared the hospital to being just like being in a prison:

Hello Darling

How are you today? fine I hope, for my self, I am doing fine at this time. it sure have been lonesome around here today. I would give any thing to be with you sweet. I miss you so much Darling. you dont relize how it is here, just like being in prison, but I will haft to try to tuff it out some way. I sure hope they start doing something this week and get me out of this place, and I hope with a Discharge.

I went to church this morning have a good chaplin. I like his preaching very much. young man about twenty eight. I guss you and Roger went to church.

Sweet tell Stanley I said hello and that I am proud he got out OK and that I am still sweating it out.

Sweet you said Arthur adgress was ny,ny. I saw in the paper this morning where lots of the Hotels in new york was turning down civilian they had to have room for a bunch of navy boys from the fifteen of Oct to the sixth of Nov. maby Arthue is in that bunch. I hope he will soon be home. I sure hope I get to see him. I feel like I will be out by then I sure hope so,

Sweet I love you true forever All my Love and kisses James

xxx

xx

x

The next letter from dad was a fairly long one where dad was reminiscing about the good times he and mother had on his last long furlough at home and in Miami Beach, Florida. It was written the next day on October 15, 1945 and postmarked October 16, 10:30 am, 1945, Camp Gordon Johnston, Florida:

Dear Sweetheart,

I got your letter and picture today thinks a million for the picture it is very good, The glass was broke but I can fix that. sweet you know your picture are not in my way I woulden take any thing for it. I always have room for your picture. I was thinking about that picture the other day wishing I had one – you will never make one any better it is just like you. I git home sick ever time I look at it thinking about the good time we had at mimma (Miami) and home to. I always have fun with you no matter where we are all I want is to be with you for good once moore. Darling thin we can have our fun and not be worrying all time. I wont to Be home with you more thin any thing I know sweetheart. do you get cold at night? I bet you do. I wish I was there to keep you warm. it sure have been cold down here for the last few days. I been sleeping under two blankets and I still needed you and if I had all the blankets I would still need you sweet, you mean ever thing to me Darling – all the boys said you sure was good looking they dont haft to tell me that – I have two good eyes, all the boys think you are cuit (cute) ever where I go sweet. I cant blame them for that – one said you sure did have pretty teeth just like a movie star – said they liked to kiss girls with pretty teeth like yours what about that. dont let this give you the big head now and dont forgit I like to kiss you not other girls, you are tops sweet. I love you with all my heart forever.

Keep your chin up and keep smiling, I hope to be home sometime soon so dont be worrying .

I Love you only Darling all my Love and Kisses, James

xxxxx

xxxxxx

We are drawing close to the end of my parents' letters to each other. Dad's discharge was finally going to happen, and he would at last be able to return to his beloved wife and son. I will include a few more of mother's letters to dad from this time period and you will see that they are responses to the letters I have included that he wrote to her. There would only be eleven more days to wait, although they didn't know that at the time. Dad was honorably discharged on October 25, 1945. According to his discharge papers he had served from June 23, 1944. He had received two bronze stars, a good conduct medal and the Purple Heart for wounds received at Bastogne, Belgium on December 30, 1944.

This letter from mother was dated October 14, 1945 but I could not locate an envelope for it:

Hello Dear,

I was so happy to get your sweet letter today. I enjoyed reading it very much. In fact I've read it three times already.

Sweet I know you love me, and I love you too. I wish you were here and I would show you. It really would be nice if you were here to go to the show with me tonight. We always have such a grand time together don't we?

Sugar, I wish you could see me in my new dress. It really fits too. All the curves as if I had any ha! No kidding! I think it is the prettiest one I have ever had.

I do hope it won't be long before you are out of the army. Keep trying for that Discharge as I'm betting on your getting it.

You said it when you said that days seemed like weeks! They surely do but if it will get you a discharge, then O.K.

Sweet I love you only

All my kisses Liz

This letter from mother was from the next day and dated October 15, 1945, Hamilton, Alabama. There was no envelope:

Hello Dear,

We are fine, except Roger has a cold, as usual. Of course it isn't bad though.

I hope you are fine and that you will soon be coming home.

I put your pants in the cleaners today and have ironed one of your white shirts. The others are clean. I surely hope it won't be long until you will be wearing them.

Arthur's ship is to arrive in Baltimore, Maryland in a few days.

Harrison is working in Washington, (I should explain here that Uncle Harrison had received a medical discharge from the Army Air Corps when it was discovered that he had a severe case of diabetes.) He got a job in Radio like he wanted. Maybe he can meet Arthur in Md, as it isn't far from Washington.

Iva is going to try to meet him in Chicago. I surely hope they will get to see him and of course I'm hoping that you are going to be home then.

Mary wrote that Tucker got a 15 day extension and will be home until the 20th then he goes to Kentucky.

I got a letter from Iva. She thinks Gerry may be sent back to Miami.

I know he is hoping he will be sent there as he will be so much closer to home.

Be sweet and take care of yourself.

I love you only Liz

Sweet, be careful about picking up Hitch-Hikers as you never know what they might do. There was a man here got his car stolen that way and the fella knocked him out too, a few days ago. He is in the Hospital now.

This next letter from mother was in response to dad's letter in which he got so upset about her joking with him about the ration board girl. It was dated October 16, 1945 but had no envelope:

Hello Dear,

Sweet, I'm so sorry that you misunderstood what I said about Laura Gene, the girl who works in the Ration Board. I was only kidding you & meant for you to take it that way. I didn't one time think of you that way. I didn't one time think of you getting the wrong impression about it.

I know you don't go out with anyone and I never dreamed of such a thing when I wrote you that.

I'll tell you how it all came about. One morning Laura Gene was asking us about our husbands just to be nice, I suppose. She just told us to tell our husbands "hello". I just wrote you about it to be doing and thought nothing more about it.

Laura Gene is a very good (girl) and I know she wouldn't go out with anyone.

I merely meant the whole thing as a joke, sugar and I'm sorry you think I don't trust you. I do though. I never think of you going with anyone else.

Sweet I know you love me and I love you too.

So please don't be mad at me sweet for I didn't mean it in the way you thought I did.

Sugar, I surely hope you won't have to go to another Hospital. I would like to see you so much.

I had your pants cleaned for you. They look very nice.

Arthur wrote that he has been rated to Yoeman Petty Officer. He has passed through the Panama Canal and expects to be in Maryland soon.

I love you only, all my kisses Liz

This letter from mother to dad had no envelope either and was written the following day on October 17, 1945 according to mother's date on the letter:

Hello Dear,

I hope you are feeling good. We are fine except lonesome of course.

Today is a very beautiful day, The sun is shining bright and it is really warm for a change.

Opaleen & I went to a rather good show last night. "Tonight and Every Night" was the name of it. Wish you were here to go with me. I always enjoy going places more if you are with me.

Sweet, I know that you are tired of that place. I know it is tough to have to stay in so long. Maybe though you will get a discharge soon and it will be worth it. I will be so happy when you can be home with us to stay. We miss you so much.

I'm glad you can go to church. Roger and I go every Sunday.

I got letters from your mother & Alma. They all seemed to be doing O.K. Alma said the kids were all in school.

Your mother said Preston Mayberry is home. I know they were all glad to see him.

Roger is fine. He is enjoying playing out in the warm sunshine.

Well, sweet I hope you won't be too lonesome down there. I wish I could be down there with you and I know you would feel O.K. then. I would too.

All my Love & kisses Always Liz

The next letter from mother to dad was written about a week before he got his discharge and was dated October 18, 1945 with a post mark of October 19, 1945, Hamilton, Alabama:

Hi Sweetheart,

How are you tonight? We are fine, I suppose. I do hope you will soon be home with us. I miss you so much. I would give anything if you were here tonight.

I'm glad you liked the picture, but am sorry the glass was broken. I should have written "glass" on the package, but it is too late to think of that now. OK! Well you can fix it up.

You said it was cold there at night & you had to sleep under blankets. You said it when you said you needed me to sleep with. I need you too.

Well, we've finished painting the floors. Herbert did it. Momma got a new rug for the front room.

Good night Dear All my Love & Kisses, Always Liz

I will return now to including some of dad's letters which will serve as a communication between the two of them. Dad's letter was a bit risqué so be prepared. He was really missing mother and describing just what it was that he was missing most. It was dated Tuesday, October 16, 1945 and postmarked October 17, 10:30 am, 1945, Camp Gordon Johnston, Florida:

Hi Sweetheart,

I got your two sweet letters this afternoon glad you are well and feeling fine. for my self I am doing fine at this time. Darling I wish I was there where you could show me how much you loved me. When I do come, I am going to look for that loving you are talking about, when I come sweet you had better be ready – when I git home if I ever get out of this place we are going to have some fun. I love you sweetheart you know I do dont you Darling? I know I would go crazy if any thing ever happen to you sweet. I know I am crazy about you. Darling I wish you could feel one time how much I care for you, you was saying we always have a good time togather – you can say that again. I always have a lovely time with you sweetheart. I always like to play with your big pretty white legs and ever thing els about you it's lots of fun dont you think sweet? you said your dress fit the curves what few you had. I bet it had a time trying to get around all thoes curves. you relly have the curves sweet. I would like to fit in one of thim my self right now sweetheart. I dont know where that Ford will run fast anought are not when I leave from here sweet. I hate to say it but I hate this place. All the boys call it over seas here and it is just about that bad to. only I could come home from here if they would let me. Sweet my ex rays came out OK I think. I hope to go before the board this week. I am gussing I dont know. sweet be patient with me, you know I want to get out just as bad as you want me to. this is the only chance I have getting out. you can say I was lucky if I do get out to. I am doing all I can to make it but you can never tell any thing can happen now. you know how the army is.

I am proud you like the candy sweet – I hope I can come and bring you some before long. Darling I love you only always.

All my Love and sweet kisses, Your true James

Dad felt he was getting close to getting his discharge at this point and although he didn't know then, he was little more than a week away from achieving his dream of a discharge. This letter was written the next day on Wednesday, October 17, 1945. The letter was postmarked October 18, 10:30 am, 1945, Camp Gordon Johnston, Florida:

Dear Sweetheart,

I got your letter, sorry Roger has a cold, hope he will soon be well of it. I am doing fine at this time glad Harrison got him a job like he wanted, have margret gone to him yet? Are did she go to start with. I hope I dont have any trouble finding me a job like I want when I get out.

I am proud to hear the good news about Arthur. I know he will be a happy boy and your mother to. I am proud he made it so far. poor boy has been through plenty. he desirves the best of ever thing. I sure hope he gets home OK and dont have any trouble. I sure hope I can be there with him some. I think maybe I will.

Sweet you keep your fingers crossed. I think I am squeezing through. I am not going to tell you I am getting out something might happen.

I got a pass this morning from 11:00 am to 5 pm and drove the car around some. still run good. I never went far, had the tires checked and some water and oil put in, ever thing OK only I would like to be coming home in it now. Sweet I dont think I will pick up any one when I come I might get a not on my head. Darling I sure would like to be there to sleep with you tonight. I git so lonesome staying around here no one to have fun with.

Sweet I love you true always.

Take care of your self Love James

The next letter I have of dad's was written a couple of days later on Saturday night, October 20. 1945. The letters from Thursday, October 18, and Friday, October 19 were missing. This letter was postmarked October 21, 12:00 pm, 1945:

Hello Sweetheart,

How are you tonight? fine I hope, for my self I am doing fine at this time, only I still have a pretty bad cold.

I never got a letter from you today first time I have missed in a long time, maby I will git two tomorrow I hope.

I bet you are at the show tonight, wish I was with you sweet, are you still working for your buddy? Well sweet I guss I will be home by next Thursday week (That would have been November 1, but he was discharged October 25, a week earlier than that,) if nothing happens. I think maby I passed the board yesterday. it takes from ten to fifteen days to git out after you go before the board. Sweet I wish I was with you now. I am so lonesome and blue lying around here. I sure will be happy when I get in the car and head for home for good. I sure will be proud to get out of this place. I am going nuts here. I dont know where I can drive in town any more are not. I havent saw a town in so long. Well sweet it is bed time. I will stop and go to bed so be sweet.

All my Love and kisses James

We are now coming close to the last letters written by mother and dad to each other, The time for dad's discharge was fast approaching and there were only a few of mother's letters left and only one of dad's. I will return to mother's last letters first and then end with dad's final letter before he was finally discharged on Thursday, October 25, 1945. I must admit that I am saddened that there will be no more letters but I am happy that I was able to travel back in time with my parents by reading their letters and discovering what they were like when they were young in 1944 and 1945, just three years before I was born on August 9, 1948. It has been a remarkable journey for me and I hope it will be so for you as well.

This letter from mother to dad had no envelope and was dated October 19, 1945:

Hi Sweetheart,

I don't know very much to write, except I would like very much to see you. I'm glad your ex rays came out O.K. Will be happier though when you can come home. I know it takes time though to get out. I do like to look forward to your getting out though.

I know that place is lonesome for you, but as you say that is the only chance of your getting out and I hope it works.

Sweet if you can find any clenix (Kleenix tissues) send me some as I'm about out (I remember that my mother could clean my entire body with one Kleenix!). I finally got some Ipana tooth paste by ordering, and you know I just couldn't do without it ha!

I love you with all my heart – bye until tomorrow, Liz

The next letter from mother came the next day on October 20, 1945 and was postmarked October 20, 4:30 pm, 1945, Hamilton, Alabama:

Hello Dear,

I was very glad to get your letter today. It is Saturday here in H'ton today and Roger and I have just come back from town. We made it without being knocked down ha! The town us really crowded as usual and preaching & shouting on every corner. They also have a "Holiness" meeting running here every night. They have a tent stretched & they have been running it for three weeks and say they are going to continue until Xmas and everyone is saved. I'm afraid they will have to run it a long time if they are waiting for everyone to be saved.

Sweet, I know you were glad to get the pass and get away from the Hospital for awhile. I'll be so glad when you can get away from there for good. I wish you were here this week-end.

We got a letter & picture from Gerry today. He looks good but he wants to get back to Iva so bad. I surely hope he will get back soon.

Take care of yourself. I'm hoping to see you soon.

All my Love, Always Liz

This is the next to last letter that mother wrote dad while he was in the Army. It was dated October 21, 1945 and postmarked October 22, 9:30 am, 1945, Hamilton, Alabama:

Hi Sweetheart,

Was glad to get your letter today. Roger is well of his Cold now. It wasn't very bad this time. I gave him Castoria to start with.

We have just gotten back from Church. Today was preaching and there was a rather large crowd there. A lot of the boys who used to go to Church there are back now with their discharges, The Lindseys & Clacks – Woodrow Lindsey was baptized today. He is Louise Clacks husband you remember him don't you?

We haven't heard anymore from Arthur. I suppose he is in the States though as he is to be in for Navy Day Celebration next week. He will be home for 30 days. Says he will be here for Thanksgiving.

I hope you will be home when he comes.

I got a letter from Iva today. She is worried about Gerry as they had a terrible typhoon in Okinawa. She hasn't heard from him since it happened.

Margaret is still in B'ham. I don't know when she will go to Harrison.

Sweet, I am sorry about the glass getting broke on the picture. I'm glad you got it fixed up. I bet it looks better in the new frame though as that frame was rather large & heavy for the picture.

I'll be glad when you get home sweet, these week ends and every day are lonesome without you.

Well be sweet & get that discharge.

All my Love, Always Liz

This letter is mother's final letter to dad while he was at Station Hospital, Ward 10, Camp Gordon Johnston, Florida. The letter was returned to Hamilton. Alabama apparently because dad had been finally discharged and was on his way home. Mother states in the letter that he would be coming home the next week, but he was discharged earlier than expected on October 25, 1945. This letter was dated Hamilton, Alabama, October 24, 1945 and postmarked October 25, 9:30 am, 1945, the day dad was discharged:

Hi Sweetheart,

I'm sorry you have such a cold. I do hope it is better now. Be careful with it and take everything you can so it won't delay you in coming home next week.

I'll be so glad to see you, and with a Discharge too. It seems almost too good to be true.

I've just finished a big washing. I'm trying to get everything clean so that I won't have anything to do when you come home,

Opaleen & I went to a show last night. It was rather good, nothing to brag about though.

Sweet, did you know that we have to have our new car tag by the 15th of next month? Do you want me to go ahead & get it now, or wait until you come?

I don't suppose Arthur will be home until sometime next week, as he is to be in New York Saturday for the celebration.

Maybe you & him will get home about the same time.

I got a letter from Alma & your mother. Alma said that Preston has a discharge. They heard from Curtis. He is trying to get out through the Red Cross. I don't see why he can't get out, as he has been over so long.

Your mother said they are moving this week. I know they will be glad to get it over & everything straightened out.

Well, be good & I'll be looking for you home soon.

All My Love & Kisses Liz

As I said, the letter I just included was the last letter from mother and dad was probably on his way home when she mailed it. This letter from dad may have been the last one he wrote but it was dated October 21, 1945, four days before he was discharged. If there were other letters, I could not find them. It was postmarked October 22, 10:30 am, 1945, Camp Gordon Johnston, Florida:

Dear Sweetheart,

How are you? fine I hope, for my self I am doing fine except I have a bad cold – dont look like I can git rid of it, (It looks as if mother received this letter from dad before she wrote her last one as she mentioned dad's cold in that letter.) been taking ever thing maby it will git better before I come home. I hope so. I sure dont want any one to catch this, worst one I have ever had.

I went to Church today, they are going to have meeting four days this week at the chapel night and morning, so I will have some place to go this next week maby the time will pass off faster.

I dont guss Arthur have come in yet have he? he should be on his way by now I hope he is and will be soon be home he should have anought points to get out if he wants out, and I am sure he does. he has a pretty good ratting now that wont make any difference with him getting out though.

I guss Herbert had a pretty hard job painting the floor. I bet you was the first one to step in it before it got dry. you are always messing your shoes up with something. sweet I dont know much to write. I am still planing on getting out some time pretty soon. I guss you get tired of me telling you that but I dont know any more about it thin you do — all I can do is to wait.

Darling I Love you true always all my love and kisses,
James

This concludes my mother and father's Letters of Love and War. I have thoroughly enjoyed the journey that their letters have taken me on, and I hope everyone who shares their story in these letters will enjoy it too. As I stated at the beginning, I had some hesitancy to share these letters as they were private and never intended to be read by anyone but my parents. I decided that they needed to be shared so that our generation and the ones that follow will know what the average families went through during war time and understand the many sacrifices that they made every day to fight for their country, their loved ones and their way of life. The fact that my mother saved all of them all these years seemed another reason to preserve them for posterity. My dad may not be pleased that I have let others read his intimate thoughts, but I think in the end he would be proud to know his son tried to preserve his generations' history. I can only hope he would understand and be proud. He always supported me in all my efforts, and he always was proud of me and loved me more than life itself.

My mother and father were true sweethearts for all of their lives. They always loved and cherished each other and their two boys for all of their lives. They were married for 67 years. My mother passed away first at age 84 in 2006, It was hard on my dad to live without her as they had been inseparable. Dad passed away almost 2 years later at age 87 in 2008. I discovered their letters shortly after my dad's passing when I was managing their estate. Mother had hidden them away carefully in her desk drawers, cabinets and closet shelves and they were all still intact after all those years. I read them over the following weeks and decided to keep them safely stored away in boxes. I kept them for about ten years until I finally began organizing them and putting them in chronological order. I knew that their letters were intimate and compelling and that they would make for an interesting story of the times they lived in. I was not sure how to approach a book on it though. Should I try to build a story from the letters or should I let the letters be the story. I decided to let the letters be the story and I have brought them to you exactly as they were written. Time will tell whether I was correct in my choice.

CPSIA information can be obtained
at www.ICGtesting.com
Printed in the USA
BVHW092208201221
624506BV00014B/1339